Jews in a
Graeco-Roman
World

Jews in a Graeco-Roman World

Edited by
Martin Goodman

CLARENDON PRESS · OXFORD
1998

Oxford University Press, Great Clarendon Street, Oxford OX2 6DP
Oxford New York
Athens Auckland Bangkok Bogotá Buenos Aires Calcutta
Cape Town Chennai Dar es Salaam Delhi Florence Hong Kong Istanbul
Karachi Kuala Lumpur Madrid Melbourne Mexico City Mumbai
Nairobi Paris São Paolo Singapore Taipei Tokyo Toronto Warsaw
and associated companies in
Berlin Ibadan

Oxford is a registered trade mark of Oxford University Press

Published in the United States
by Oxford University Press Inc., New York

© Oxford University Press 1998

The moral rights of the author have been asserted

British Library Cataloguing in Publication Data
Data available

Library of Congress Cataloging in Publication Data
Jews in a Graeco-Roman world / edited by Martin Goodman.
Includes bibliographical references and index.
1. Jews—Rome—Civilization. 2. Jews—Civilization—To 70 A.D.
3. Hellenism. 4. Judaism—History—Post-exilic period, 586 B.C.–210
A.D. I. Goodman, Martin, 1953–   .
DS122.J53   1998   938'.004924–dc21   98–24838
ISBN 0–19–815078–4

1 3 5 7 9 10 8 6 4 2

Typeset by Joshua Associates Ltd., Oxford
Printed in Great Britain on acid-free paper by
Bookcraft (Bath) Ltd., Midsomer Norton

Contents

Abbreviations

Abbreviations of the tractates by which the Mishnah, Tosefta, and Talmuds are cited follow H. Danby, *The Mishnah translated from the Hebrew* (Oxford, 1933).

AE	*Année Épigraphique*
AJA	*American Journal of Archaeology*
AJPh	*American Journal of Philology*
ANRW	H. Temporini *et al.* (eds.), *Aufsteig und Niedergang der römischen Welt* (Berlin, 1972–)
b.	Babylonian Talmud
BAG	W. Bauer, W. Arndt, and F. W. Gingrich, *A Greek Lexicon of the New Testament*, 2nd edn. (1979)
BASOR	*Bulletin of the American Schools of Oriental Research*
Ber. R.	Bereshit Rabbah
BGU	Aegyptische Urkunden aus den Staatlichen Museen zu Berlin, Griechische Urkunden
Cant. R.	Canticles Rabbah
CIJ	J.-B. Frey (ed.), *Corpus Inscriptionum Iudaicarum* (vol. i, rev. B. Lifshitz (New York, 1975); vol. ii (Rome, 1936))
CIL	*Corpus Inscriptionum Latinarum*
CP	*Classical Philology*
CPJ	V. Tcherikover, A. Fuks, M. Stern (eds.), *Corpus Papyrorum Judaicarum*, 3 vols. (Cambridge, Mass., 1957–64)
CQ	*Classical Quarterly*
DJD	D. Barthélemy *et al.*, *Discoveries in the Judaean Desert*, i– (Oxford, 1956–)
Eccles. R.	Ecclesiastes Rabbah
Enc. Jud.	C. Roth (ed.), *Encyclopaedia Judaica*, 16 vols. (Jerusalem, 1971)
ERE	J. Hastings (ed.), *Encyclopaedia of Religion and Ethics*, 13 vols (Edinburgh, 1908–26)
ET	English translation

Exod. R.	Exodus Rabbah
GLAJJ	M. Stern, *Greek and Latin Authors on Jews and Judaism*, 3 vols. (Jerusalem, 1974–84)
HTR	*Harvard Theological Review*
HUCA	*Hebrew Union College Annual*
IEJ	*Israel Exploration Journal*
JAOS	*Journal of the American Oriental Society*
JAC	*Jahrbuch für Antike und Christentum*
JBL	*Journal of Biblical Literature*
JEA	*Journal of Egyptian Archaeology*
JIGRE	W. Horbury and D. Noy, *Jewish Inscriptions of Graeco-Roman Egypt* (Cambridge, 1992)
JIWE	D. Noy, *Jewish Inscriptions of Western Europe*, 2 vols. (Cambridge, 1993–5)
JJP	*Journal of Juristic Papyrology*
JJS	*Journal of Jewish Studies*
JQR	*Jewish Quarterly Review*
JRS	*Journal of Roman Studies*
JSJ	*Journal for the Study of Judaism in the Persian, Hellenistic, and Roman Period*
JTS	*Journal of Theological Studies*
Lam. R.	Lamentations Rabbah
Lev. R.	Leviticus Rabbah
LSJ	H. G. Liddell and R. Scott (eds.), *A Greek–English Lexicon*, ed. H. S. Jones (Oxford, 1940)
LXX	Septuagint
m.	Mishnah
MEFRA	*Mélanges de l'École Française de Rome*
MT	Masoretic text
NEAEHL	E. Stern (ed.), *New Encyclopaedia of Archaeological Excavations in the Holy Land*, 4 vols. (Jerusalem, 1993)
NS	*Notizie degli Scavi*
NTS	*New Testament Studies*
OGIS	W. Dittenberger, *Orientis Graeci Inscriptiones Selectae*, 2 vols. (Leipzig, 1903–5)
PBSR	*Papers of the British School at Rome*
PCPS	*Proceedings of the Cambridge Philological Society*
PEFQSt	*Palestine Exploration Fund Quarterly Statement*
Pes. R. K.	Pesikta de Rab Kahana

PWRE	Pauly-Wissowa, *Realencyclopädie der classischen Alter-tumswissenschaft* (Stuttgart, 1893–)
R.	rabbi
RAC	*Reallexikon für Antike und Christentum* (Stuttgart, 1941–)
REJ	*Revue des Études Juives*
RivAC	*Rivista di archeologia cristiana*
SCI	*Scripta Classica Israelica*
SEG	*Supplementum Epigraphicum Graecum* (Leiden, 1923–)
SIG	W. Dittenberger, *Sylloge Inscriptionum Graecarum*, 3rd edn., 4 vols. (Leipzig, 1915–24)
Str.–B.	H. L. Strack and P. Billerbeck, *Kommentar zum Neuen Testament aus Talmud und Midrasch*, 4 vols. (Munich, 1922–8)
t.	Tosefta
TAPA	*Transactions of the American Philological Association*
TDNT	*Theological Dictionary to the New Testament*
TIR	*Tabula Imperii Romani*
TZ	*Theologische Zeitschrift*
USQR	*Union Seminary Quarterly Review*
VT	*Vetus Testamentum*
XHev/Ṣe	P. Se'elim papyri, published in *DJD* xxvii
y.	Jerusalem (or Palestinian) Talmud
ZDPV	*Zeitschrift der Deutschen Palästina-Vereins*
ZPE	*Zeitschrift für Papyrologie und Epigraphik*

Contributors

ALBERT I. BAUMGARTEN is Associate Professor of Jewish History and Director of the Jacob Taubes Minerva Center for Religious Anthropology at Bar Ilan University.

HANNAH M. COTTON is Professor of Classics and Ancient History at the Hebrew University of Jerusalem.

MARTIN GOODMAN is Professor of Jewish Studies at Oxford University. He is a Fellow of Wolfson College Oxford, and a Fellow of the Oxford Centre for Hebrew and Jewish Studies.

ERICH GRUEN is Gladys Rehard Wood Professor of History and Classics at the University of California, Berkeley.

WILLIAM HORBURY is Reader in Jewish and Early Christian Studies at Cambridge University and a Fellow of Corpus Christi College, Cambridge.

BENJAMIN ISAAC is Fred and Helen Lessing Professor of Ancient History at Tel Aviv University.

LEE I. LEVINE is Professor of Jewish History and Archaeology at the Hebrew University of Jerusalem.

DAVID NOY is Lecturer in Classics at the University of Wales, Lampeter.

AHARON OPPENHEIMER is Sir Isaac Wolfson Professor of Jewish Studies at Tel Aviv University.

TESSA RAJAK is Reader in Classics at the University of Reading.

MICHAEL SATLOW is Assistant Professor in the Department of Religious Studies at the University of Virginia.

DANIEL SCHWARTZ is Professor of Jewish History at the Hebrew University of Jerusalem.

JOSHUA SCHWARTZ is Professor of Historical Geography of Ancient Israel and Joint Director of the Ingeborg Rennert Center for Jerusalem Studies and the C. G. Foundation Jerusalem Project at Bar-Ilan University.

SETH SCHWARTZ is Associate Professor of History at the Jewish Theological Seminary of America.

SACHA STERN is Acting Principal of Jews' College, London.

MARGARET WILLIAMS is Research Associate in Classical Studies at the Open University.

PART I

The Hellenistic and Roman World:
Jewish Perspectives

I

Jews, Greeks, and Romans

MARTIN GOODMAN

How different from other people in the Graeco-Roman world were the Jews? The question is easily posed even if any answer must be cautious and nuanced. Jews in many ways shared in the surrounding political, social, and religious culture of the Hellenistic period and the early Roman empire, but in some crucial respects they were radically different. Difficulties in formulating a clear response should not prevent the question being tackled, for the consequences of even a cautious answer are considerable. If Jews lived lives much like others in their world, it would be appropriate to use the plentiful surviving evidence about Jews to help understand wider Greek and Roman culture to an extent rarely attempted by classicists; from the opposing perspective, it would be more or less impossible to study properly the history of the Jews in this period without constant recourse to non-Jewish evidence. By contrast, if Jews lived in a world politically, mentally, socially, and culturally distinct from other cultures and peoples in the Mediterranean world, it would be entirely reasonable to study the Jewish tradition more or less in isolation from other ancient evidence.[1]

That Jews differed from non-Jews in some ways is obvious, since something about them made them a distinct and recognizable group. Jews had a special religion and odd customs. They rebelled in highly publicized fashion both against Hellenistic and against Roman rule. More detailed differences are pinpointed in some of the studies in this volume. According to Albert Baumgarten, the distinctive parties within Judaism which emerged in the Hellenistic age were for some reason more all-embracing than equivalent non-Jewish groups: they were greedy institutions which engaged much of the identity and efforts of their members, unlike equivalent

---

[1] For general studies of Jewish history in this period, see Schürer (1973–87); Cohen (1987a); Schiffman (1991).

philosophical schools or clubs, which involved only a part of their members' lives. Similarly Margaret Williams argues that Jewish synagogues should not be identified with the *collegia* in the city of Rome, claiming that Jewish communal organization had a uniquely centralized character different from that of other ethnic and religious groups. This view is reinforced by the claim by Lee Levine that it is misleading to seek to understand synagogue leaders simply from parallels with the Graeco-Roman world because there is so much rabbinic evidence about such leaders that it is impossible to reconcile with the evidence about non-Jewish officials.

But similarities also abound, and that again is unsurprising. Jews in the eastern Mediterranean world were affected by the same momentous political, economic, cultural, and social changes which occurred in this period as were their non-Jewish neighbours. It would be strange indeed if Jewish reactions to the rise of Roman power, to the emergence of massive inter-regional trade, to the spread of Greek culture, and to the increase in urbanism did not parallel in some way those of other peoples.[2] But some of the studies in this volume go further, suggesting similarities in customs and ideas in areas of life not obviously under pressure from such outside influences.

Michael Satlow shows how the assumptions of Palestinian rabbis about the social significance of particular homosexual acts were closer to those of their gentile neighbours than of their brethren in Mesopotamia, and Joshua Schwartz points to parallel practices in gambling and other leisure activities (although he claims that Jews did such things with greater moderation).

It might seem difficult to go further than a nuanced statement that the Jews were like others in some ways and not in other ways, and that in all cases there is insufficient evidence for certainty. Difficult but not impossible. By a systematic check of a plausible hypothesis it may be possible to tilt the scales towards an assumption that the Jews were similar to their non-Jewish contemporaries until proved otherwise.

The hypothesis I propose is that the oddities of the Jews in the Graeco-Roman world were no greater than that of the many other distinctive ethnic groups, such as Idumaeans, Celts, or Numidians, who between them created the varied tapestry of society in this

---

[2] For general trends in Roman history in the early empire, see Goodman (1997).

region and period. The history of the Jews may only appear more peculiar to modern historians because the Jews are so much better known than these other groups, and that fact in turn may not be accidental. The preponderance of evidence about Jews in the Graeco-Roman world is a straightforward consequence of the transmission of evidence about them for religious reasons by two religious traditions with a continuous history to modern times: rabbinic Judaism and Christianity.

I suggest a test of this hypothesis by considering how evidence about Jews and Judaism would be interpreted if we did not have such material preserved for these special religious reasons. What would be known of the Jews in this period if there were no rabbinic or patristic texts, no biblical writings, no works by Josephus, Philo, or other Jewish authors preserved by Christians for religious edification, and nothing about Jews from the Roman world from the period after Constantine had placed a Christian filter over so many of the actions of the Roman state? This would be a history of the Jews based only on the references in the non-Jewish and non-Christian Greek and Latin sources before Constantine—that is, on much of the contents of Stern's *Greek and Latin Authors on Jews and Judaism* (1974–84), but without Stern's explanatory footnotes which point out where pagan authors failed to portray the Jews correctly (i.e. as the Jews saw themselves), and on the much less extensive corpus of pre-Constantinian laws in Linder's *The Jews in Roman Imperial Legislation*.[3] To this could be added the epigraphic evidence preserved in Frey's *Corpus Inscriptionum Judaicarum*, updated and augmented by the new corpora published by Horbury, Noy, and others, and by continuous new finds of fragmentary material,[4] and the papyri and parchment documents mostly collected (for Egypt) in the *Corpus Papyrorum Judaicarum*[5] and (for the Dead Sea region) in the rapidly increasing series of *Discoveries in the Judaean Desert* as well as in numerous individual publications which have been produced over the last few years.[6] Finally the picture of Jews and Judaism would have to take into account the evidence of coins minted both in Judaea and in Rome with reference

---

[3] Linder (1987) cites only six laws referring to Jews from before the time of Constantine.

[4] See *CIJ*; *JIGRE*; *JIWE*; Lüderitz (1983).

[5] *CPJ*.

[6] *DJD*. See the recent list of documentary papyri from the Near East in Cotton, Cockle, and Millar (1995).

to Jews,[7] and the results of extensive excavations in Israel and its
environs, and of the buildings and artefacts claimed by archaeologists as the products of diaspora Jews.[8] In other words, Jews would
be studied with the same tools as other peoples and other religions
in the Graeco-Roman world, on a par with Gauls or Spaniards, or
the worshippers of Isis or Mithras.

A reconstruction of this type is easier to propose than to
complete. It is extremely difficult in practice for a modern scholar
to rid his or her mind of assumptions about Jewish history,
institutions, and religion based on the images in the Bible (Jewish
or Christian) or in rabbinic tradition. The narrative framework into
which all evidence about this period is automatically slotted is that
of Josephus, and it is hard (but salutary) to imagine the fog of
uncertainty about the political history of the Jews before 70 CE
which would be almost impossible to break through if his works
had not survived. Even more difficult to deal with is the way that
even the evidence I have proposed using on the grounds that it was
not preserved because of later Jewish and Christian traditions has
none the less been shaped by those traditions. Thus some of the
pagan texts included in *Greek and Latin Authors on Jews and
Judaism* survive only because they were quoted by Josephus, who
selected them for his own apologetic purposes (and hence sometimes may have included Jewish forgeries).[9] The six surviving pre-
Constantinian laws of the Roman state to do with Jews were
similarly almost all cited in compilations made by later Christians.[10]
Nor are inscriptions, papyri, or other archaeological finds any less
prone to misinterpretation in the light of the special Jewish literary
tradition. After all, many 'Jewish' inscriptions are assumed to be
Jewish only because they include names which occur in Jewish
literature, and archaeological sites are ascribed to Jews because their
iconography can be understood in terms of the traditions enshrined
in that literature; in other words, the corpus of Jewish epigraphic

---

[7] See in general Meshorer (1982).

[8] On excavations in Israel, see *NEAEHL*. On the diaspora, see e.g. Kraabel
(1982).

[9] Most such texts (e.g. those of Apollonius Molon, Apion, and Chaeremon) were
cited by Josephus in *Contra Apionem*. *C. Apion.* 1. 183–204, which purports to cite
Hecataeus of Abdera, may have been a Jewish forgery in whole or in part.

[10] Linder (1987) nos. 1, 2, and 4 are excerpts from the *Digest* of Justinian, nos. 3
and 5 from the Justinianic Code. Both compilations date to the mid-6th cent. Only
Linder no. 6, which lays out the prohibition of gentile circumcision, survives in a 3rd-
cent. source (the *Sententiae* attributed to the jurist Paul).

and archaeological material would actually appear much smaller if the continuous literary tradition did not prevail in the interpretation of finds.

But even allowing for necessary imperfections, it is worth asking what elements of Jewish history that in fact are known from sources surviving through the Jewish and Christian traditions would be missing from a reconstruction that did not use such sources.

The political history of the Jews in their homeland would be known in outline from Strabo, Pompeius Trogus, and others,[11] but it would lack the detail about the Hasmonaean and Herodian dynasts found only in Josephus. On the other hand much could still be written about the revolt of 66–70 CE, based on the account in Tacitus, *Hist.* 5. 1–13, but bolstered by the evidence of other writers (such as Suetonius and Cassius Dio), of coins proclaiming *Judaea Capta*, of inscriptions such as those on the arch of Titus in Rome, and so on, although the propaganda value of much of this material for the Flavian dynasty seeking to establish itself in control of the empire is so patent that revisionist Roman historians might well by now have interpreted this conflict, like that between Rome and Parthia, as a product of Roman internal discourse rather than a serious confrontation between the empire and a genuine threat to its security.[12] As for the Bar Kokhba revolt, it would hardly be noticed: in contrast to the First Revolt, the suppression of the Jews by Hadrian was sufficiently inglorious, and sufficiently out of tune with the spirit of Hadrian's reign, to serve no useful propaganda purpose, and it is thus much less emphasised in surviving imperial imagery.[13] (Hence the claim, which to my mind confuses depiction with actuality, that the revolt was not in fact serious at all for the Roman state;[14] it should not surprise that inglorious wars receive little attention in Roman sources except when a thriving literature in opposition to a particular emperor happens to survive.)

Perhaps the most important element lacking from a political history based on the purely classical sources about the Jews would

---

[11] See texts and discussion in *GLAJJ*; but it is worth noting that most of the historical information from Strabo survives only through citation by Josephus in his *Antiquities of the Jews*.

[12] See Suet. *Vesp.* 4. 5–6, 5. 6; *Tit.* 4. 3, 5. 2; Cassius Dio 66. 4–7. For the propaganda value of the victory, see Goodman (1987), 235–6.

[13] On the Bar Kokhba revolt, see Schäfer (1981).

[14] Bowersock (1980).

be anything about Jewish messianic eschatology.[15] The classical narratives based on Flavian propaganda depict the Jews as religious fanatics and their cult as superstition, and they report a prophecy that a king would come forth from Judaea (which they interpret as a reference to Vespasian), but they singularly fail to pick up on any Jewish hopes of eventual domination over the world.[16] The attribution to a Jew by the pagan philosopher Celsus (*ap*. Origen, *C. Celsum* 2. 29) of the statement that 'The prophets say that the one who will come will be a great prince, lord of the whole earth and of all nations and armies' is the exception which proves the rule, since Celsus picked up this statement from the polemic between Jews and Christians. Messianic ideas can of course be found in some of the scrolls from the Dead Sea region,[17] but it would be an exceptionally rash ancient historian who, without the benefit of the Hebrew bible to indicate the origin of these ideas, would deduce from the Qumran documents anything about the mentality of Jews in general. (Not that such rash historians are wholly unimaginable: if the Dead Sea Scrolls were the only surviving documents from antiquity written by Jews, they might well be taken by some as evidence of the mainstream, as in the case, for instance, of so-called Orphic texts or the gnostic writings from Nag Hammadi).

What would be the picture of Jewish society and culture based on this deliberately limited set of evidence? In other words, what would be known about Jews in their homeland if, like most of the other ethnic groups in the Roman Near East, they were known only from the occasional comments of classical authors and the evidence of inscriptions and other archaeological remains?[18] The comments of outsiders would certainly encourage the historian to look for signs of a distinctive culture but I am not sure that all the extant remains, deprived of the Jewish and Christian evidence which in practice can illuminate them, would be very helpful. Enough Hebrew inscriptions survive from this period to suggest the existence of a distinctively Jewish language and culture in the region of Judaea,[19] and the discovery of bilingual and trilingual caches of documents in the Judaean Desert would alert historians to the possibility that

[15] On the varied Jewish messianic beliefs attested in this period, see Neusner, Frerichs, and Green (1987).

[16] For the prophecy, see Suet. *Vesp.* 4. 5; Tac. *Hist.* 5. 13. 2.

[17] For example in the Messianic Rule (IQSa). See Vermes (1997), 157–60.

[18] See Millar (1993).

[19] For semitic inscriptions, see Naveh (1992).

some of the Greek and Aramaic documents from the region might also have been produced by people who subscribed to that culture,[20] but it is unlikely that anyone would guess (for instance) the existence of a Jewish culture in the region that was partially expressed in Greek.[21] Nor is it probable that the architecture of the region would be seen as distinctively Jewish in any aspect except for the internal iconography of synagogues of the late Roman period: in all other respects, Jewish buildings either followed the vernacular styles also found in surrounding areas or adopted motifs from the wider Graeco-Roman world.[22]

It is dubious whether many signs taken as diagnostic of Jewish settlement by contemporary archaeologists would be so interpreted without the benefit of Jewish literary texts. Thus Jewish coins might be spread widely beyond areas where Jews lived simply as a means of exchange (and in the case of some of the coins minted during the revolt, because of their exceptionally pure precious metal content).[23] The distinctive bathing pools (*mikvaoth*) generally taken as evidence of religiously inclined Jews concerned to rid themselves of ritual pollution might be interpreted quite differently, perhaps as simply bathing installations characteristic of a region in which water supply in many settlements depends on the preservation and use of limited rainwater.[24] In my view such an interpretation might well in any case be correct. The *mikveh*-type pool discovered in the excavation of the Hellenistic period in Marisa in Idumaea, a city which (so far as is known) contained no Jews at that time, is unlikely to have fulfilled any Jewish ritual purpose.[25] It is more plausible that rabbinic stipulations about the design of a valid *mikveh* simply laid down regulations about the minimum requirements (for ritual purposes) for pools already in use by Jews and non-Jews alike. Such creation of rules by regulation of existing practices rather than by decree *ex nihilo* or by biblical interpretation is characteristic of other areas also in the development of rabbinic law where such law is not based directly on a biblical injunction.[26]

---

[20] On the Babatha archive, see Lewis (1989).
[21] On Hellenistic Jewish culture, see Hengel (1974); Wacholder (1974); Schürer (1973–87), 3. 470–704. [22] See Foerster (1976).
[23] On the coins minted during the revolt, see Kadman (1960).
[24] On the use of *mikvaoth* as evidence for Jewish settlement, see e.g. Netzer and Weiss (1994), 21–3, 60, 62.
[25] On the pools in Marisa, see Kloner (1996), 17.
[26] See in general Goodman (1983).

What information then would be left for the student of Judaean society? He or she would know about the size and centrality of Jerusalem and its Temple[27] and might reasonably guess, from its prosperity in comparison to the poor surrounding countryside, that their prosperity was based on pilgrimage income. But about the social and economic tensions revealed in the pages of Josephus there would be nothing. On the other hand the existence and size of the Mediterranean Diaspora would be quite well attested both through the spread of Jewish inscriptions from the middle and later imperial period, and from papyri (including the letter of the emperor Claudius to the Jews of Alexandria)[28] and the brief report of the diaspora revolt of 115–117 CE preserved by Cassius Dio.[29] There would be plenty of evidence about the separate lives lived by diaspora Jews within their host communities (although there would be little on how a Jew's status as a Jew might be recognized in the street).[30]

Jerusalem and the Temple would dominate the picture of Jewish religion. Gentile authors wrote much about the role there of the priestly caste and the high priests as leaders of the people.[31] There would be much less certainty about the divinity worshipped. Pagan writers mostly agreed that Jewish cult was aniconic,[32] but they differed widely in their views on the deity understood by Jews as the recipient of their offerings. Was it Jupiter, as Varro thought, or Dionysus, as Plutarch suggested? Other suggestions included Iao, the sky, or the god 'of uncertain name'.[33] The archaeologists who linked to the Jewish deity the huge basilica found in the centre of Sardis because of the similarities between the iconography there and that of synagogues (identified as such by inscriptions) else-where might have been led by the Sardis dedications to *Pronoia* ('forethought') to follow Varro in identifying Jupiter/Zeus as the object of Jewish worship, since Pronoia was identified with Zeus by the Stoics;[34] it is only by looking at the Jewish texts which survive

---

[27] See e.g. Polybius, *Hist.* 16. 39. 1, 3, 4 (in *GLAJJ* i. 113).

[28] *CPJ* ii. 153, dated to 41 CE.

[29] Casius Dio 68. 32. 1–3 (in *GLAJJ* ii. 385–6).

[30] See Cohen (1993).

[31] See, among others, the early testimony of Hecataeus of Abdera (*c.*300 BCE) cited by Diodorus Siculus, *Bibliotheca Historica* 40. 3 (in *GLAJJ* i. 26–9).

[32] e.g. Strabo, *Geog.* 16. 2. 35 (in *GLAJJ* i. 294).

[33] Varro *ap.* August. *De Consensu Evangelistarum* 1. 22. 30 (in *GLAJJ* i. 209); Plut. *Quaest. Conviv.* 4. 6 (in *GLAJJ* i. 553–4); Diod. Sic. 1. 94. 2; Juv. *Sat.* 14. 97; Lucan, *Pharsalia* 2. 593.   [34] Kraabel (1996), 80–2.

through the Jewish and Christian traditions, as Tessa Rajak does in her study of these inscriptions, and by adopting assumptions about Jewish monotheism, that a historian can in fact suggest that Pronoia was not (as one might have expected from the dedications) herself the object of worship in the Sardis building.

About the religious authorities among the Jews scholars might again be rather confused. The literary texts refer to priests, but the inscriptions refer also to fathers of the synagogue, rulers of the synagogue, elders, even occasionally rabbis, and other categories.[35] It is intriguing to imagine the interpretation of such titles if they were understood on the analogy of Mithraic grades, in which the initiate progressed from one title to the next in increasing holiness. As to the significance of Jewish iconography, confusion would reign, as is shown by the imaginative and ingenious studies by Goodenough, who derived the meaning of symbols from all sorts of sources, not always entirely plausibly.[36] But this study would differ from Goodenough's in that the distinction between liturgically important motifs and decoration would not be apparent from the literary texts. Would anyone know that the candelabra, incense shovels, shofar, and lulav in a mosaic on a standard floor in a late Roman synagogue were depicted because they referred to aspects of cult, but that the lions, birds, and peacocks were represented simply because they looked nice? The strip-cartoons on the walls of the Dura-Europus synagogue, and the depiction of the near-slaying of Isaac in the Beth Alpha mosaic, clearly tell narratives about something of religious significance, but if the only Jewish texts that scholars had available to aid in their interpretation were the Dead Sea Scrolls would they know what the stories were about?[37]

Judaism as known from these limited sources would appear as an esoteric cult with strange dietary customs, a peculiarly strict attitude to sacred time (the sabbath), the odd practice of circumcising boys, a peculiar avoidance of images, an objectionable refusal to worship the gods of others, and a great leader of the distant past who had been called Moses.[38] It is hard to know how seriously we would take the 'slanders' that Jews had an unpleasant smell, worshipped an ass,

[35] See in general Schürer (1973–87), 3. 87–107; on rabbis, see Cohen (1981–2).
[36] Goodenough (1953–68).
[37] Kraeling (1956).
[38] On pagan attitudes to Moses, see Gager (1972).

and had a religious duty to kill Greeks.[39] It would be known that Judaism was the religion of a particular nation, but also that it was possible for outsiders to become full members of the Jewish religion in the same way that they could embrace a philosophy.

What would be missing from the reconstruction is any notion of the centrality of the Bible as a sacred text, both in the sense that its words carry specially sanctified authority and in the sense that a scroll of scripture is a sacred object,[40] although the large number of copies of biblical fragments among the Dead Sea Scrolls, and the finds of Septuagint papyri and codex fragments in Egypt, might perhaps alert scholars to the significance of these writings,[41] and an even more acute scholar might pick up something from the description of Torah shrines on gold glasses found in Rome and identified as Jewish by the rest of their iconography.[42] Nor, surprisingly, would it be obvious that synagogue ritual was unusual in that its central rite consisted in a reading from a text rather than a sacrifice or libation, although something on these lines might be proposed on the basis of the communal lifestyle prescribed at Qumran.[43] Unless historians were prepared to generalize further from the writings of the obviously strange Jews who produced the sectarian texts found by the Dead Sea, they would be wholly unaware of the centrality of the covenant between God and Israel[44] or the importance of eschatological speculation in Judaism of this period. Nor would historians be able to guess at the variety which consisted within Second Temple Judaism. Outsiders showed no awareness that Jews differed among themselves both in theology and in practice.[45] Thus Pliny referred to Essenes but without describing them as subscribers to a type of Judaism,[46] and it is a

[39] On ass worship, see Apion *ap.* Joseph. *C. Apion.* 2. 80 (in *GLAJJ* i. 409); on the killing of Greeks, Apion *ap.* Joseph. *C. Apion.* 2. 91–6 (in *GLAJJ* i. 411).

[40] Goodman (1990) argues that Jewish taboos were a reaction to pagan perceptions of the treatment of scrolls, but there is no independent pagan evidence for such a perception.

[41] On biblical scrolls at Qumran, see Vermes (1977); on early fragments of the Septuagint, see Schürer (1973–87), 3. 4877–8.

[42] On the gold glasses, see Rutgers (1995), 81–5.

[43] On pagan comments on synagogues, see Cohen (1987*b*).

[44] On the centrality of 'covenantal nomism' in common Judaism, see Sanders (1992), 262–78.

[45] The classic expression of the variety which coexisted within late Second Temple Judaism is Joseph. *War* 2. 119–61, on the Pharisees, the Sadducees, the Essenes, and the Fourth Philosophy.

[46] Plin, *HN* 5. 17, 4 (73).

curious fact that although Jesus was known to have come from Judaea (cf. Tac. *Ann.* 15. 44. 3), Christianity was treated as a separate religion rather than a branch of Judaism. (Again, the polemic of Celsus against the Christians, in which he borrowed polemic from Jewish sources, is the exception which proves the rule.)[47]

In other words, if knowledge of Judaism was not greatly augmented by the survival of much internal literature preserved for special reasons by later Jews and Christians, historians would still be aware of Jews as a distinct ethnic and religious group, but Jews would not seem anything like as marginal in the Graeco-Roman world as they do when their own, often jaundiced, views of the outside provide the basis for understanding them. Jews lived alongside non-Jews even in many parts of their homeland to a much greater degree than scholars tend to allow, as Benjamin Isaac shows in this book. As David Noy points out in his chapter, there is good reason to suppose that in such areas they were generally buried alongside non-Jews except where there is specific evidence for exclusively Jewish catacombs. In many aspects of life many Jews may have behaved like gentiles even in those matters which other Jews, including rabbis at the time, believed should be performed according to distinctively Jewish rules, as Hannah Cotton suggests in her study of the Jewish marriage documents found in the Judaean Desert.

The corollary of this attempt to understand Jews without using special Jewish evidence is that, if it shows that Jews were after all not so different from other people, then the Jewish evidence itself can and should be used to illuminate wider Graeco-Roman history. There will of course, be a limit to such use. Daniel Schwartz shows succinctly in his essay on the political history of the early second century BCE how the tendency of classical historians to dismiss the evidence of one Jewish author, Josephus, about Hellenistic politics is unwarranted, but not all Jewish texts are equally valuable in this regard: reflections of political history in rabbinic texts are only comprehensible as such because that history is already known from other sources. It is hard to think of any aspects of wider political history that could ever be firmly asserted on the basis of rabbinic evidence alone. More might be culled from Jewish sources about the general history of ancient religion, not just because, as William Horbury shows in his paper, some very basic notions found among

---

[47] On Celsus, see Chadwick (1953).

Jews were also shared by pagan Romans, but primarily because so much more is known of the workings of Judaism than of any other cult.

Thus the important question of the relation between public cult and domestic rituals or private emotions in ancient paganism might reasonably take the relation in Judaism of attitudes to the Temple and to personal religion as its starting point; in fact the extensive Jewish evidence will confirm more than anything else the complexity of the relationship.

Thus the main use of Jewish evidence may be not so much as an instance from which generalizations can always be made but more as a means to check or stimulate models for understanding how ancient society worked. So Seth Schwartz suggests in his contribution to this volume that the experience of the Jews in the Hellenistic period provides a model of the process of Hellenization which can be applied elsewhere, and it is worth enquiring how many other (less well-documented) peoples in the Roman empire opposed the might of the state and yet, like the Jews, somehow flourished culturally, economically, and socially without ever identifying themselves with Roman society. The ability of the state to turn a blind eye to Jewish penal jurisdiction, as documented by Aharon Oppenheimer in his chapter, is highly significant for the general history of the operation of Roman government in less prominent provinces.

The contributors to this volume have approached their discussions of the relationship of the Jews to the rest of the Graeco-Roman world from diverse perspectives and with the benefit of a variety of techniques and types of evidence. It is a prime aim of the book to familiarize readers from different backgrounds with all such approaches and to persuade them that this material can be made mutually comprehensible both to classicists and to those primarily concerned with Jewish history. Obscurantist specialists in both fields have too often in the past used their expertise as a means to prevent others from trespassing on 'their' history. Such attitudes are now generally changing, and our intention in this collection is to help to open up and encourage research across the boundaries between these disciplines, to the benefit of both.[48]

[48] See for instance Lieu, North, and Rajak (1992).

2

Jews, Greeks, and Romans in the Third Sibylline Oracle

ERICH S. GRUEN

Jewish appropriation of pagan traditions took a multitude of forms. The Sibylline Oracles constitute an instance of the first order. No more dramatic example of the practice exists than the adaptation and recreation of those texts. Collections of the Sibyl's pronouncements, duly edited, expanded, or invented, had wide circulation in the Graeco-Roman world—long before Jewish writers exploited them for their own purposes. But circumstances of transmission, as so often, produce peculiar ironies. The pagan originals that served as models have largely been lost, surviving only in fragments or reconstructions. The extant corpus of Sibylline Books, drawing upon but refashioning those models, derives from Jewish and Christian compilers who had their own agenda to promote. The role of Hellenized Jews in this development is pivotal. Rehabilitation of the originals may no longer be possible, but assessment of the means and motives for the transformation raises even more significant issues of Jewish self-image.

In this quest, the Third Sibylline Oracle possesses special importance. It contains the earliest material in the collection and its composition is predominantly Jewish. That much can confidently be stated. Beyond it lies controversy, dispute, and division. A large and burgeoning scholarly literature daunts the researcher, with innumerable disagreements in detail. And irony enters here as well. A few issues do command a broad consensus, issues of centrality and importance, thus affording an ostensible reassurance. Yet the very ground on which that consensus rests is shaky, and may well have clouded rather than clarified understanding. The areas of agreement touch on fundamental matters that have not been subjected to adequate scrutiny. The time is overdue for a closer look.

First, the matter of unity or diversity of composition. Opinions vary widely on specifics. But a heavy majority of scholars have always discerned a main corpus or a principal core produced or redacted at a particular historical time. Earlier material might have been incorporated and accretions subsequently added, but the body of the work, so most have claimed, can be tied to identifiable historical circumstances that called it forth. The favoured times, each boasting notable champions, are the mid-second century BCE, the early first century BCE, and the later first century BCE.[1] Second, and in close conjunction with the first, various pointers in the text to what appear to be historical episodes have regularly been taken as disclosing the Sitz-im-Leben of the text—a sign of the author's attitude to contemporary leaders, nations, or events. The most common referents identified by interpreters are Antiochus Epiphanes, the Maccabees, Ptolemy VI or VIII, Mithridates, the triumvirs, and Cleopatra.[2] And third, a firm unanimity among

---

[1] In the first edition of real importance and influence, Alexandre (1841–56) assigned well over half of the text to a Jewish redactor of c.168 BCE. The notion of a principal author dating to the mid-2nd cent. prevailed until the sustained assault by Geffcken (1902b), 1–17, which has had wide impact in the scholarship. Geffcken, as a committed pluralist, dissected the Third Book with scrupulous care but excessive confidence, labelling various segments as products of the Babylonian Sibyl, the Persian Sibyl, the Erythraean Sibyl, or the Jewish Sibyl. Even his atomistic structure, however, includes a Jewish composer from the Maccabaean period for nearly a quarter of the lines and a Jewish revision of the Erythraean Sibyl, constituting more than a third of the whole, in the early 1st cent. BCE. Bousset (1906), 270–1, detected divisions in places other than those noted by Geffcken, but ascribed more than half the text to an author living in the early 1st cent. Schürer (1886), 794–9, believed that almost all came from the pen of a Jewish writer in the mid-2nd cent. Similar judgements were expressed by H. Lanchester, in Charles (1913), 371–2, and Rzach (1923), 2127–8. Peretti (1943), 96–9, 143–7, 317–40, 350–1, 397–9, 459–68, holds that the core of the text was composed in the early 1st cent., and certainly prior to 63 BCE, the taking of Jerusalem by Pompey, and then subject to subsequent accretions. The strongest argument for unity came from Nikiprowetzky (1970), 195–225, who set almost the entire work in the time of the later 1st cent., the period of Cleopatra VII and the triumvirate. That verdict has not found favour among more recent commentators. The current consensus inclines to the composite interpretation of Geffcken, but discerns a main corpus, encompassing more than two-thirds of the whole, as a product of the mid-2nd cent. That is the conclusion of Collins who has written extensively on the subject (Collins (1974a), 21–33, id. in Charlesworth (1983), 354–5; id. in Stone (1984), 365–71; id. (1987), 430–6). Similarly, Fraser (1972), I. 709, 711. The position has been endorsed in recent works; e.g. Newsome (1992), 93–7; Feldman (1993), 294; cf. M. Delcor, in Davies and Finkelstein (1989), 487–9. A more pluralistic interpretation by M. Goodman, in Schürer (1986), 632–8. Arguments about the Sibylline Oracles generally began already among Renaissance humanists; see Grafton (1991), 172–7.

[2] No need to rehearse the bibliography here. Specifics will emerge in subsequent discussions.

scholars holds that the bulk of Book III derives from the Jewish community in Egypt, whether in Alexandria or Leontopolis. The Egyptian provenance, so it is asserted or assumed, accounts for the attitudes expressed and the general thrust of, at least, the main corpus of the work.[3]

The modern literature, in short, has sought to locate the Third Sibyl in time and place. The aim is logical and laudable enough. Yet the search for historical specificity may miss the essence of the Sibyl's message, its apocalyptic character, and its significance for the interaction of Judaism and Hellenism. A reconsideration of the three propositions outlined above is in order.

Is there, in fact, a 'main corpus' in Book III, in which earlier oracles were incorporated and later material tacked on? The idea runs into trouble from the start. Chronological indicators are few, scattered, and usually ambiguous. The problem can be readily illustrated. Verse 46 speaks of a time when Rome ruled Egypt, a passage that can hardly be earlier than the battle of Actium.[4] A mention of Beliar who comes from the Sebastenoi occurs in verse 63. The Sebastenoi very likely signify the line of Roman emperors or Augusti, and the arrogant Beliar who comes to a bad end probably denotes Nero. Hence, this passage evidently post-dates 68 CE.[5] The sequence of kingdoms given in lines 156–61 places Rome after Egypt, again implying a date after 30 BCE, the fall of Egypt into Roman hands.[6] By contrast, the following oracle, offering yet another series of kingdoms that will rise and fall, sets the Romans after the Macedonians, gives Macedon as their prime victim, and, in describing them as 'white, many-headed, from the western sea', obviously alludes to the Republic and, presumably, to the defeat of Macedon in 168 or 148.[7] The fierce hostility and rage directed against Rome and the vengeance promised from Asia in

---

[3] See e.g. Collins (1974*a*), 35–55.

[4] *Sib. Or.* 3. 46: αὐτὰρ ἐπεὶ Ῥώμη καὶ Αἰγύπτου βασιλεύσει. The suggestion of Lanchester, in Charles (1913), 371, that this may allude to Popillius Laenas' mission to Egypt in 168 BCE, is out of the question. Rome exercised no sovereignty over Egypt at that time. Nor after the bequests of either Ptolemy Apion or Ptolemy Auletes, the other possibilities canvassed by Lanchester.

[5] So Collins (1974*a*), 80–7, citing as parallel Ascension of Isaiah 4: 1. Beliar, however, can have other connotations; see Nikiprowetzky (1970), 138–43.

[6] Collins (1974*a*), 26, implausibly prefers the 2nd cent. BCE on the grounds that Rome was already a world empire by that time. That skirts the significance of the sequence of empires, each kingdom replacing or subduing the previous.

[7] *Sib. Or.* 3. 162–90, esp. 176: λευκὴ καὶ πολύκρανος ἀφ᾽ ἑσπερίοιο θαλάσσης.

verses 350–80 belong more suitably to the late Republic when Roman expansionism and imperial exactions had left deep scars in the east.[8] Yet the oracle that appears next in the text reverts to an earlier time, lamenting the mighty power of Macedon and the sorrows it brings, and looking ahead to its demise.[9] Later, the Sibyl proclaims the dire fate of Italy as consequence not of foreign war but of civil bloodshed, and refers also to a murderous man from Italy, the destroyer of Laodicea. Those verses must recall the Roman Social and civil wars of the early first century BCE and the ravages by Sulla in the east that fell in that very period.[10] Yet the succeeding lines raise the spectre of a previous time, two generations earlier, that witnessed the eradication of Carthage and Corinth.[11] And the Sibyl could also recall a much earlier era, when savage Gauls devastated Thrace in the early third century BCE.[12] One could proceed to passages of more speculative date. But no need. It seems clear that Book III of the Sibylline Oracles constitutes a conglomerate, a gathering of various prophecies that stem from different periods ranging from the second century BCE through the early Roman empire. To postulate a main corpus or a primary redaction reflecting special circumstances does not get us far.[13] The composition has a broader significance.

The ostensible historical pointers in the text require reassessment. Cornerstone for the idea of a principal edition in the second century rests upon three references to a seventh king of Egypt: verses 193, 318, 608. Since he is explicitly described in two of the three passages as 'from the race of the Greeks', the allusion is apparently to a Ptolemaic monarch. Scholars have wrangled over how to calculate the sequence of kings. Does Alexander the Great count as the first or not? Does one include the short and overlapping reign of Ptolemy VII Philopator? The uncertainties have caused some

---

[8] That conclusion is generally accepted, although commentators differ as to whether the lines allude to the Mithridatic war or to Cleopatra's resistance to Rome: cf. Bousset (1906), 271; Peretti (1943), 329–57; Collins (1974a), 57–64. On this, see below.

[9] *Sib. Or.* 3. 381–400.

[10] Ibid. 464–73.

[11] Ibid. 484–8.

[12] Ibid. 508–10.

[13] The conglomerate mixture is reflected also in the confused and overlapping manuscript transmission. The tangled strands permit no neat stemma, suggesting a number of layers built over time by diverse interests and sources. See J. Geffcken (1902a), xxi–liii; Rzach (1923), 2119–22; Goodman, in Schürer (1986), 628–31.

argument over whether 'the seventh king' is Ptolemy VI Philometor
(180–145), Ptolemy VII Philopator (145–144), or Ptolemy VIII
Euergetes (145–116). The first stands as favourite, but near
unanimity, in any case, prevails in identifying the period in question
as the mid-second century.[14] That has engendered the further
conclusion that this work represents the propaganda of Egyptian
Jews to ingratiate themselves with the Ptolemaic dynasty and to
express a common basis for relations between Jews and Gentiles in
Egypt.[15] How legitimate is that analysis?

The first mention of the 'seventh king' causes misgivings right
away. It follows upon the Sibyl's recounting of the rise and fall of
kingdoms. Among them the Greeks are singled out as arrogant and
impious and the Macedonians as bringing a fearsome cloud of war
upon mortals. The God of Heaven, however, will eradicate them,
paving the way for Roman rule, the ascendancy of the many hoary-
headed men from the western sea, whose dominion too will prove
oppressive, whose morals will degenerate, who will provoke hatred,
and who will engage in every form of deceit until the time of the
seventh kingdom when an Egyptian monarch of Greek lineage will
be sovereign.[16] Do these really suit the era of Ptolemy VI or
Ptolemy VII? No *ex eventu* forecast could have set the fall of
Roman power to that period, a time when its might was increasing
and its reach extending. Nor can one imagine the Sibyl (or her
recorder) making such a pronouncement in the reigns of Philometor or Euergetes themselves when its falsity was patent. The idea
collides abruptly with reality.[17] The Sibyl must be looking forward

[14] The conclusion is taken for granted by Lanchester, in Charles (1913), 382. A
fuller discussion by Collins (1974a), 28–32; (1974b), 1–5. See also Rzach (1923),
2127– 8; Fraser (1972), 2. 992; Goodman, in Schürer (1986), 635–6. The sole
dissenter is Nikiprowetzky (1970), 208–17, whose proposal that the seventh king is
Cleopatra has rightly found no takers.

[15] So Collins, in Charlesworth (1983), 356; Collins (1987), 432.

[16] *Sib. Or.* 3. 165–95; see esp. 191–3: μῖσος δ' ἐξεγερεῖ καὶ πᾶς δόλος ἔσσεται αὐτοῖς,
ἄχρι πρὸς ἑβδομάτην βασιληΐδα, ἧς βασιλεύσει Αἰγύπτου Βασιλεύς, ὃς ἀφ' Ἑλλήνων γένος
ἔσται.

[17] Geffcken (1902a), 58, recognized the problem and simply bracketed lines 192–
3, thus removing the seventh kingdom from the passage. Peretti (1943), 178–96, took
a different route, separating out the verses on Roman conquest (lines 175–8), and
seeing the rest of the segment as a denunciation of Macedonian imperialism. Such
dissection, however, is unwarranted and implausible. Geffcken's solution is arbitrary,
and Peretti's reconstruction ignores the problem of the Macedonian realm coming to
an end at the time when Egypt was ruled by a king of Macedonian lineage. The unity
of the whole passage is ably defended by Nikiprowetzky (1970), 209–13. Collins
(1974a), 31–2, argues that an anti-Roman attitude by Egyptian Jews might well have

to a demise of Rome that had not yet occurred. Hence the 'seventh king' can hardly refer to a present or past scion of the Ptolemaic dynasty.

The Sibyl's next reference to a seventh king comes in the midst of numerous woeful prophecies. She dwells on the grievous fate that has either overtaken or will eventually overtake a number of nations. Egypt indeed is among them, with a mighty blow to come, unanticipated and dreadful, in the seventh generation of kings— and then she will rest.[18] The oracle proceeds to detail the evils that will befall numerous other places, reiterating once more that the baleful race of Egypt is approaching its own destruction.[19] In the context of so dire a set of predictions, with the afflictions of Egypt doubly noted, it strains the point to place emphasis upon a single line alluding to a pause in the seventh generation. Nothing in the passage gives any reason to evoke the era of Philometor and Euergetes.[20] Indeed, what is predicted for the seventh generation is dispersal, death, and famine, and only subsequently will it cease.[21] The apocalyptic visions predominate in the long string of verses. A search for historical specificity misses the point.

The third passage is still more problematic. It too lies embedded in an eschatological prophecy. The oracle foresees calamity, war, and pestilence inflicted by the Immortal upon those who fail to acknowledge his existence and persist instead in the worship of idols. Destruction will fall upon Egypt in the time of the young (or new) seventh king reckoned from the rule of the Greeks. And the divine instrument is named: a great king from Asia whose infantry and cavalry will despoil the land, spread every evil, overthrow the

been prompted by Ptolemy Philometor who had reason to feel aggrieved at the Romans. The suggestion carries little conviction. No evidence exists for any animosity on Philometor's part toward Rome, let alone for any prodding of Jews by him for this purpose. Even if the conjecture were right, however, it fails to address the question of how the collapse of Roman power could be set in Philometor's reign.

[18] *Sib. Or.* 3. 295-318. See esp.314–18: ἥξει σοι πληγὴ μεγάλη, Αἴγυπτε, πρὸς οἴκους, δεινή, ἣν οὔπω ποτ' ἐξήλπισας ἐρχομένην σοι . . . θάνατος καὶ λιμὸς ἐφέξει ἑβδομάτῃ γενεῇ βασιλήων, καὶ τότε παύσῃ.

[19] *Sib. Or.* 3. 319–49. See 348: ἴσθι τότ' Αἰγύπτου ὀλοὸν γένος ἐγγὺς ὀλέθρου.

[20] That the allusion in line 316 to a sword passing through their midst refers to civil conflict between Philometor and Euergetes is pure conjecture, made even less substantial by the fact that the line itself is corrupt. The conjecture was offered by Lanchester, in Charles (1913), 384; endorsed by Fraser (1972), 1. 710; 2. 994; Collins (1974*a*), 31; rightly dismissed by Nikiprowetzky (1970), 198. The Sibyl could indeed appeal to biblical authority for civil strife in Egypt; Isaiah 19: 2.

[21] *Sib. Or.* 3. 316, quoted above, n. 18.

Egyptian kingdom, and cart off its possessions over the sea. Then they will bow their knees to God, the great king, the immortal one, while all handmade works collapse in a flame of fire.[22] A standard line has it that the Asian invader is Antiochus IV Epiphanes and the young Egyptian king is Ptolemy Philometor, victim of the Seleucid's assault.[23] Again, however, the effort to find direct historical allusions encounters serious stumbling-blocks. If the Sibyl intended Antiochus IV as the Asian king, her timing would have to be very precise indeed. Seleucid success and deposition of the Ptolemies came as a consequence of Epiphanes' first invasion in 170; the second, in 168, was thwarted by Rome and followed by reinstatement of Ptolemaic authority. An *ex eventu* prophecy would make no sense except in that narrow corridor of time—far too tight a squeeze. The idea of a direct allusion to Antiochus Epiphanes can be discarded. Threats to Egypt from Asia were endemic in Egyptian history and lore. The Sibyl simply fastened upon the traditional foe as anticipated ravager of the land, not a particular monarch, nor an identifiable invasion.[24] The passage also provides little comfort to those who argue that a cordial relationship between Ptolemy Philometor and the Jews and the elevation of Jewish leaders under his aegis justify a dating of the oracle to his reign. On the contrary, the relevant verses hold no brief, indeed hold no hope, for the seventh king. The invasion will come in his time, bringing with it not only devastation and pestilence but the fall of the Egyptian

---

[22] Ibid. 601–18.

[23] See Lanchester, in Charles (1913), 389; Fraser (1972), 2. 998–9; Momigliano (1980), 557. Collins (1974a), 29–30, shrinks from too narrow or definite a judgement on the Asian king, but adheres to the view that Egypt's monarch must be Philometor or Euergetes: if the term νέος in line 608 means 'young', it could suit the youthful Philometor at the time of Antiochus' invasion; if the meaning is 'new', this might be the product of an oracle issued late in either king's reign. Collins leaves the options open. One might even consider the possibility of an allusion to the title of Ptolemy Neos Philopator. Goodman, in Schürer (1986), 636, declines to take a stand.

[24] This is correctly noted by Collins (1974a), 29–30, 39–40, who points to invasions by Hyksos and Persians and to oracular pronouncements in the Potter's Oracle and elsewhere. But he still considers Epiphanes' invasion as a prod for the Sibyl's forecast. On Antiochus' two military expeditions into Egypt, see Gruen (1984), 651–60, with bibliography. Antiochus did, allegedly, acknowledge the power of the Jewish god at the end, as recounted by 2 Macc. 9: 11–17; cf. 1 Macc. 6: 12–13. But this is certainly not alluded to by *Sib. Or.* 3. 616–17, where those who will bend a knee to God are clearly repentant Egyptians. Peretti's notion (1943), 389–93, that the Asian king represents the coming Messiah, drastically misconceives his role in the text—which is that of destroyer, not reclaimer.

kingdom that had been founded by Macedonians.[25] Far better then
to divorce these verses from the particular events that marked the
reign of Ptolemy VI—or anyone else for that matter. The Sibyl
predicts catastrophe for Egyptian idolators, laid low by the hand of
God through the agency of an Asian conqueror, and then redeemed
when they prostrate themselves before the true Immortal. The
model should more properly be sought in something like the
thunderings of Isaiah than in the special circumstances of a
Ptolemaic reign.[26] Once again, the eschatology holds central place
and drives the entire passage. In this context it looks ahead to the
smashing of idolatry, to transformation, conversion, and redemp-
tion. A narrow political interpretation would be simplistic and
distorting.[27]

A noteworthy point demands attention, one missed by all those
who have written on the subject. Designations like Ptolemy VI or
Ptolemy VII may be a convenience for modern scholars, but they
lack ancient authority. The Greek rulers of Egypt nowhere identified themselves by numbers. One will look in vain for such a title in
official documents, whether on stone, papyri, or coinage. Petitions
to the crown do not address the kings in this fashion, nor are they so
referred to indirectly in transactions between private persons. The
Ptolemies, of course, regularly appear with cult titles (Soter,
Euergetes, Philometor, and the like), other epithets of dignity and
honour, and patronymics, but they did not place themselves in a
numerical sequence.[28] Perhaps more striking, our fullest and most
reliable Hellenistic literary source, the historian Polybius, refers to
the Ptolemies regularly and frequently, but never attaches numbers
to them.[29] One can go further still. Jewish sources, contemporary or

---

[25] *Sib. Or.* 3. 608–15: ὁππόταν Αἰγύπτου βασιλεὺς νέος ἕβδομος ἄρχῃ τῆς ἰδίης γαίης
ἀριθμούμενος ἐξ Ἑλλήνων ἀρχῆς, ἧς ἄρξουσι Μακηδόνες ἄσπετοι ἄνδρες. ἔλθῃ δ' ἐξ Ἀσίης
βασιλεὺς μέγας . . . ῥύψει δ' Αἰγύπτου Βασιλήιον. The opposition here between an Asian
ruler and a kingdom founded by Macedonians makes it even less likely that the former
could be a Seleucid. Collins (1987), 431–2, remarks upon 'the enthusiasm for the
Egyptian king in *Sib. Or.* III'. There is certainly no sign of it here. If anything, the reverse.
[26] Nikiprowetzky (1970), 208, rightly points to parallels between Isaiah 2: 18–21,
30: 22–4, and *Sib. Or.* 3. 604–7, 616–23.
[27] Cf. the reference to a coalition of kings organized for a concerted assault on the
Temple; *Sib. Or.* 3. 657–68. No historical circumstance has been suggested or can be
found for that purported episode. Cf. Psalms 2: 1–2.
[28] To take only the most celebrated examples, see the titulature exhibited in the
Canopus decree, and the Rosetta Stone, and Ptolemy Euergetes' will that bequeathed his
kingdom to Rome; *OGIS* 56, 90; *SEG* IX. 7.
[29] See e.g. Polyb. 5. 34. 1: Πτολεμαῖος ὁ κληθεὶς Φιλοπάτωρ; 14. 3–4, 31. 10.

nearly contemporary with the Ptolemaic monarchy, namely 1, 2, and 3 Maccabees, and the Letter of Aristeas, speak of the Egyptian kings—but not by number.[30] The same indeed holds for Josephus' *Antiquitates* which employs cult titles, no numerals.[31] In a word, neither the technical language in documents nor the less formal designations by literary sources, whether pagan or Jewish, employ any numbering system to distinguish the Ptolemies. When the Sibyl makes mention of a seventh king, she could hardly expect her readers to recognize a specific Ptolemy. The number seven possessed high symbolic import for the Jews.[32] It must be understood in that broad and spiritual sense, not as denotation of a royal tenure.

One further passage needs treatment in this connection. The Sibyl describes a dismal period of civil strife, cataclysmic warfare among kings and peoples, seizure of territory and riches, foreign rule over the Greek world, the destructive power of greed for wealth that terminates in utter ruin, death, and devastation. But rescue will come when God sends a king from the sun to put an end to war, slaying some and binding others with oaths of loyalty—an end achieved not by private counsel but by obeying the worthy precepts of the great God.[33] This image too has been associated with the Ptolemies, and 'the king from the sun' reckoned as identical with the 'seventh king'.[34] Precedents and parallels in the Egyptian material ostensibly lend credence to the association. The nearest analogy, however, appears in the Potter's Oracle which looks to a king from the sun appointed by the goddess Isis. And that is an expression of Egyptian nationalist sentiment, certainly not advocacy of Ptolemaic rule.[35] To be sure, connection of the king with the sun might well be appropriated by the Ptolemies too. But the relationship has its roots in Pharaonic imagery and ancient Egyptian religion. These lines in

---

[30] See 1 Macc. 10: 51, 10: 55, 11: 8; 2 Macc. 1: 10, 4: 21; 3 Macc. 1: 1, 3: 12, 7: 1; *Ep. Arist.* 13. 35, 41.

[31] e.g. Joseph *Ant.* 12. 2–3, 11, 118, 235, 243; 13. 62, 79–80, 103, 285, 328, 370. An exception in *C. Apion.* 2. 48: τρίτος Πτολεμαῖος—but this is not a technical designation. Cf. *War* 1. 31.

[32] Cf. Gen. 41; 1 Enoch 91: 12–17, 93: 3–10; and see *Sib. Or.* 3. 280, 3. 728.

[33] *Sib. Or.* 3. 635–56.

[34] A strong argument for this identification is made by Collins (1974*b*), 5–8; (1974*a*), 40–4; (1983), 68–70. Accepted by Camponovo (1984), 344–5. But Collins's claim that 'the identification is inevitable' greatly overstates the case. Momigliano (1980), 556, rightly questions the connection. See also the comments of Nikiprowetzky (1970), 133–7.

[35] See the text in Koenen (1968), 206, lines 38–41.

the Third Sibylline Book represent Jewish adaptation of Egyptian lore to forecast a Messiah who will stamp out strife and restore tranquillity. The 'king from the sun' is an emissary of God, not a Ptolemaic monarch. In short, the standard theory of a central core for the Third Sibyl in the mid-second century is a ramshackle structure on the most fragile foundations.

Similar historical markers have been discerned (or imagined) for the later first century BCE—most notably in alleged allusions to the 'second triumvirate' and to Cleopatra VII, last of the Ptolemies. They do not easily survive scrutiny.

A verse in the early part of the text furnishes the sole basis for finding the 'second triumvirate'—amidst the Sibylline pronouncements. The oracle speaks of a time when Rome will rule over Egypt, when the greatest kingdom of the immortal king will materialize among men, when the holy sovereign will take universal dominion. At that time, inexorable anger will fall upon the men of Latium, and three with woeful destiny will rain destruction upon Rome. And all will perish in their own abodes when a cataract of fire rushes from Heaven.[36] Scholars regularly repeat identification of the cryptic 'three'—with the triumvirate of Antony, Octavian, and Lepidus.[37] But the text itself provides grave difficulties for that hypothesis. The opening line of the passage has Rome exercising dominion over Egypt, an explicit statement that makes sense only after annexation of the land as a Roman province in 30 BCE. But the triumvirate no longer existed at that time: Lepidus had been dropped, Antony was dead, and Octavian unopposed. Furthermore, the forecast that the trio will destroy Rome hardly applies to the triumvirate. Rome stood intact, and the empire had expanded. No *ex eventu* oracle could have uttered such patently false phrases. And a genuine prediction would hardly have conceived Rome's destruction at the hands of the triumvirate after the conquest of Egypt.[38] Nor is it likely that the Sibyl projects three future rulers of Rome who will cause the

---

[36] *Sib. Or.* 3. 46–54: αὐτὰρ ἐπεὶ Ῥώμη καὶ Αἰγύπτου βασιλεύσει . . . τρεῖς Ῥώμην οἰκτρῇ μοίρῃ καταδηλήσονται.

[37] So e.g. Geffcken (1902b), 13–14; Kurfess (1951), 288; Peretti (1943), 342–5. Doubts expressed by M. Simon, in Hellholm (1983), 224.

[38] The remark of Tarn (1932), 142, that once Roman rule was established over Egypt, it could itself be used as a date, is unfathomable. Collins (1997a), 65, rightly sees that the oracle must have been composed after Actium but fails to recognize the implications for any reference to the triumvirate.

destruction of the empire.[39] She foresees the destruction of Rome as the deed of the deathless monarch, the holy prince as sovereign over all the earth, doubtless a reference to the divinity. The three who administer the mournful fate to Rome should therefore be agents of God, not identifiable personages from Roman history.[40] Does Cleopatra appear in the Third Sibylline Book? Many have found her in lines that describe the world as being in the hands of a woman, a world governed and obedient in every regard. The Sibyl goes on to characterize the woman as a widow, reigning over all the universe, hurling gold and silver into the deep, as well as the brass and iron of ephemeral men. Then all parts of the cosmos will be bereft when God rolls up the sky like a scroll and the heavens themselves fall upon the earth, followed by a cataract of fire to burn earth and sea, eradicating daylight and nightfall, as well as all the seasons, a terrible divine judgement.[41] Only guesswork can offer an identity for the 'woman' and the 'widow'. And there has been plenty of that. Many scholars, both early and recent, favour Cleopatra.[42] The reasons fall well short of compelling. Cleopatra, to be sure, was a widow after the death of her brother-husband Ptolemy XIII. But her widowhood was hardly conspicuous at a time when she ruled much of the east together with and largely as a consequence of her consort Mark Antony. Nor is it likely that the widow allusion refers to Cleopatra's association with Isis, on the grounds that Isis lost her husband Osiris every year (only to regain him again) and that Cleopatra was twice widowed. That is far-fetched, and out of tune with the context of the passage. The widow in question rules the world—not simply the lands of the east on the sufferance of a Roman dynast.[43] Only one power fits that description: Rome itself. Characterization of the great city as a widow has parallels in biblical

[39] So Nikiprowetzky (1970), 150–4, who usefully points to the motif of three Roman kings in Jewish apocalyptic.

[40] Note *Sib. Or.* 3. 533–6, which refers to 'five' who will arouse a mighty wrath and who will shamelessly engage one another in frightful and tumultuous war, bringing joy to their enemies but woe to the Greeks. The author evidently blended an echo of Isaiah 30: 17 with an allusion to Roman civil wars. The number 'five', it is clear, lacks any specific denotation here. And there is no more reason to assign specificity to the number 'three' in *Sib. Or.* 3. 52.

[41] *Sib. Or.* 3.75–92.

[42] e.g. Tarn (1932), 142: 'That the widow is Cleopatra . . . seems certain'; Collins (1974a), 66–70; Goodman, in Schürer (1986), 641.

[43] *Sib. Or.* 3. 75–7: καὶ τότε δὴ κόσμος ὑπὸ ταῖς παλάμῃσι γυναικός . . . ἔνθ' ὁπόταν κόσμου παντὸς χήρη βασιλεύσῃ. Indeed κόσμος appears yet a third time in line 81.

prophecies about Babylon.[44] The metaphorical bereavement of the super-power may signify the loss of divine support, presaging an imminent demise, which indeed follows shortly thereafter in the passage. That sense is reinforced by repetition of the widow metaphor in connection with the divine judgement: all elements of the universe will be bereft when God rolls up the heavens.[45] The oracle, like so much else in the Third Book, directs itself against Rome, not Cleopatra.[46]

Another oracle involves an explicit attack on Rome. This too has been identified with Cleopatra, only here she takes the positive role as the avenger of Roman misdeeds. Such at least is the theory.[47] The passage itself makes that conclusion less than obvious. In the Sibylline pronouncement, vengeance will fall upon Rome, a three-fold exaction taken by Asia, previously its victim, now its conqueror, and a twentyfold return in Italian slaves for the Asians once enslaved by Rome, a down payment on a debt of myriads. Rome, the virgin, often intoxicated with numerous suitors, will be wed unceremoniously as a slave. The mistress will frequently snip her locks and, passing judgement, will cast her from heaven to earth and then again from earth to heaven. After destruction, however, will come reconciliation, peace, and prosperity, a time of concord and the flight of all evils.[48] Is Cleopatra the *despoina*, the mistress? Does this represent a Jewish reflection of the Ptolemaic queen's propaganda against Rome? Not a likely inference. The oracle pits Asia against Rome, unambiguously favouring the former and projecting an eventual era of harmony. Depiction of the struggle between Cleopatra and Octavian as one between east and west was, of

[44] Isaiah 47: 8–9; Apocalypse of John 17–18. This was acutely noted by Nikiprowetzky (1970), 146–9.

[45] *Sib. Or.* 3. 80–2: τότε δὴ στοιχεῖα πρόπαντα χηρεύσει κόσμου, ὁπόταν θεὸς αἰθέρι ναίων οὐρανὸν εἰλίξῃ.

[46] The idea of Rome as the referent here was suggested long ago but has found little favour in the last century. See Alexandre (1856), 517; Lanchester, in Charles (1913), 371. Rzach (1923), 2131, rules out Cleopatra and reckons the widow as an apocalyptic figure. The argument of Nikiprowetzky (1970), 146–9, that the widow represents the Messiah or the coming of New Jerusalem, confusingly amalgamates both the world-ruler and the dominion which follows the divine destruction.

[47] So Tarn (1932), 135–41; H. Jeanmaire (1939), 55–61. Collins (1974a), 57–64, questions many of Tarn's arguments, but adopts his conclusion.

[48] *Sib. Or.* 3. 350–80. See esp. 356–60: ὦ χλιδανὴ ζάχρυσε Λατινίδος ἔκγονε Ῥώμη, παρθένε, πολλάκι σοῖσι πολυμνήστοισι γάμοισιν οἰνωθεῖσα, λάτρις νυμφεύσεαι οὐκ ἐνὶ κόσμῳ, πολλάκι δ᾽ ἁβρὴν σεῖο κόμην δέσποινά τε κείρει ἠδὲ δίκην διέπουσα ἀπ᾽ οὐρανόθεν ποτὶ γαῖαν ῥίψει, ἐκ δὲ γαίης πάλιν οὐρανὸν εἰς ἀνεγείρει.

course, the product of propaganda from Rome, a blackening of the shameless and power-mad woman who leads barbaric hordes against the valiant Italians.[49] It is quite unthinkable that Cleopatra herself would embrace that distorted portrait. Egypt had suffered no depradation from Rome, Cleopatra had no reason to seek reparations or exact revenge for past iniquities. The notion that she looked toward conquest of Rome itself rests on a hostile and thoroughly unreliable tradition. The queen's ambitions in fact directed themselves toward revival of the Ptolemaic empire—with the assistance of Rome. Once again, the Sibyl's meaning transcends a specific historical circumstance. The mistress who shears the head of Roma, the newly enslaved servant, may well be Asia itself, a broad and vague allusion to the sufferings of the east at Roman hands, now to be reversed and compensated for many times over.[50] The forecast, plainly a wishful hope for a future that never came to pass, expresses fierce eastern resentment against Roman exploitation and looks ahead to a happier time when the empire will be crushed, its reparations plenteous, and the outcome one of concord. Cleopatra has no place here.

Similar doubts need to be applied to other inferences about historical events or personages lurking behind the Sibyl's dark pronouncements. The very passage just discussed has been ascribed to the time of the Mithridatic wars, an anticipated vengeful retaliation by Mithridates against Romans who had despoiled the east.[51] But Mithridates would hardly qualify as a 'mistress'. And his fearsome war against Romans and Italians would certainly not suit a prediction of subsequent peace and harmony.

Elsewhere, a cryptic oracle regarding Macedonian terrors unleashed upon Asia has stimulated a wealth of scholarly speculation.

---

[49] Cf. Hor. *Epod.* 9; *Carm.* 1. 37; Verg. *Aen.* 8. 675–728; Prop. 3. 11, 4. 6. To be sure, the war of Actium is portrayed as a clash of Europe against Asia also by Philo, *Leg.* 144, a point stressed by Collins (1974*a*), 60. But Philo, whose objective in this section of his work was to contrast the virtues of Caligula's predecessors with his own megalomania, clearly took up the Augustan line and represents no independent Jewish viewpoint—let alone a reflection of Cleopatra's attitude. His account, in fact, omits any allusion to the Ptolemaic queen, depicting the contest as one headed by rival Romans: ἡγεμόνας ἔχουσι καὶ προαγωνιστὰς Ῥωμαίων τοὺς ἐν τέλεσι δοκιμωτάτους. Moreover, Augustus appears not as leader of Rome against a Greek ruler but as champion of Hellenism and civilizer of the barbarians; Philo, *Leg.* 147.

[50] So Peretti (1943), 351–4.

[51] So Bousset (1906), 271; Lanchester, in Charles (1913), 372; Peretti (1943), 329–40; Geffcken (1902*b*), 8–9. Goodman, in Schürer (1986), 636, declines to choose between Mithridates and Cleopatra.

The Sibyl bewails afflictions imposed upon Asia, and even upon Europe, by the horrific Macedon becoming mistress of all lands under the sun, climaxed by the conquest of Babylon. The evils wrought upon Asia are ascribed to an untrustworthy man, clad in purple cloak, characterized as barbaric and fiery, who came to place Asia under a wicked yoke. Ultimately, however, so the Sibyl forecast, the very race he sought to destroy will bring about the destruction of his own race. A still more cryptic pronouncement follows: the destroyer provides a single root which he will cut off from ten horns and will leave another side-shoot; then, after slaying the warrior progenitor of a purple race, he will perish at the hands of his sons, and the side-horn will rule.[52] Opinions divide on the identity of the malignant Macedonian conqueror whose race will perish by the hand of those whom he oppressed. Some opt for Alexander the Great, some for Antiochus IV Epiphanes.[53] Or, as almost all commentators now seem to concur, the original oracle had Alexander as its villain but was then reworked by a Jewish Sibyllist who directed its fire against Antiochus Epiphanes, arch-enemy of the Jews, and saw the collapse of Macedonian power in the internecine warfare of the Seleucid house.[54] Again, however, focus upon historical personages and their actions veers away from the central significance. The purple-clad invader of Asia may well be Alexander the Great, but he is cited as emblematic of Macedonian power and ruthlessness, not with regard to specific deeds of the individual. The one explicit reference to conquest of Babylon should have made that clear to commentators: Alexander did gain control of Babylon, but postured as its liberator, respected its religion and traditions, and treated it with generosity.[55] The Sibyl is concerned with the broader consequences of Macedonian

---

[52] *Sib. Or.* 3. 381–400. The oracle is often divided into two, with a break after line 387. But even if the division is justified, the forecasts are closely related and belong together.

[53] For Antiochus, see e.g. Lanchester, in Charles (1913), 385; Rowley (1926), 324–7; Fraser (1972), 2. 995–6. The argument for Alexander, at least as the initial figure in lines 388–91, was forcefully made by Bousset (1902), 34–41, followed by many in subsequent years.

[54] Peretti (1943), 372–4; Eddy (1961), 11–14; Collins (1974*a*), 27; Goodman, in Schürer (1986), 634. The dispute over whether the first part of the forecast, in lines 381–7, derives from a 'Persian Sibyl', a 'Babylonian Sibyl', or neither one need not be exploited here. See the valuable discussion, with bibliography, by Nikiprowetzky (1987), 474–5, 524–8.

[55] Arrian 3. 16. 3–5, 7. 17. 1–2. See also Ps. Hecataeus in Joseph. *C. Apion.* 1. 192, for a favourable Jewish view of Alexander at Babylon; cf. 2. 43.

dominance, not with historical particulars. By the same token, the narrow interpretation of the oracle's conclusion by seeking to identify individuals in the house of Antiochus Epiphanes has little point. To be sure, the Sibyl here has adopted the image of the ten horns and their offshoot that can be found in Daniel 7: 7–8, but it does not follow that the image carries the same significance—even if we knew for certain to what Daniel does refer. What matters here is the sharp hostility to Hellenic over-lordship in the east, at least as exercised by savage rulers, and the prediction of its violent demise. The thrust of the oracle is out of tune with much else in the Third Book. Knowledge of Daniel implies a Jewish hand at work. But the message contains no hint of divine retribution or intervention. And this is the one segment in the Third Book in which Macedonians, rather than the more usual Romans, are the targets of oracular venom. In so far as Jewish authorship is involved, whether in origin or as redaction, it is best seen as expressing resentment against foreign oppression, wher-ever it manifests itself in the east. The quest for historical specificity has led researchers astray.[56]

A comparable quest for geographical specificity may be equally delusive. The favoured provenance is Egypt, with the Hellenized Jews of Alexandria or Leontopolis as principal sites for authors.[57] The theory connects closely with the idea that a cosy relationship between Jews and the Ptolemies of mid-second-century Egypt finds voice in the utterances of the Third Sibyl. The weakness of that reconstruction has already been indicated above. And the corollary correspondingly falls. Since no unequivocal reference to the rele-vant Ptolemies exists in the text, further speculation about the significance of an alleged Jewish–Egyptian provenance lacks warrant.

In fact, many of the Sibyl's pronouncements would dishearten the devotees of Ptolemaic Egypt. Almost the very opening lines of

[56] See the sensible general remarks of Simon, in Hellholm (1983), 224–5.

[57] The case is made most fully by Collins (1974b), 1–18; (1974a), 35–55. Collins's argument for Leontopolis as the principal site of composition, however, has little force. The absence of any allusion to Leontopolis in the text fatally weakens the idea, forcing Collins to postulate a very narrow corridor of time for the composition: after Onias's arrival in Egypt but before he built the temple at Leontopolis. However, the recent immigration of Onias and his followers from Judaea and their relatively conservative ideology, which Collins himself acknowledges, make them the least likely persons to embrace the quintessentially Hellenic form of Sibylline prophecy to convey their message.

the Third Book denounce Egyptians for their idolatry that includes not only the erection of stone statues to people, but the worship of snakes, and the rendering of sacrifice to cats.[58] The early verses, to be sure, may actually belong to Book II, and hence have no bearing on the attitude of the authors of the Third Sibyl.[59] But it is perhaps not irrelevant that those who ordered the extant edition found ostensible congruence. In any event, later passages are comparably uncomplimentary to Egyptians. When God's wrath falls upon the nations, Egypt will suffer together with others, indeed doubly so.[60] The Egyptians are characterized as a destructive race.[61] The Sibyl brackets them, together with Phoenicians, Romans, and others, as moral transgressors, indulging in homosexual vice.[62] And it is noteworthy that the projected time of peace and prosperity will come *after* the collapse of Egypt, destroyed by an Asian king.[63]

That some verses in the collection stem from Hellenized Jews in Egypt can be readily acknowledged. The denunciations of Egypt noted above belong in that category. So do the lines that give Egypt prominence in the sequence of empires, singling out its royal rule twice.[64] And one may plausibly infer Egyptian provenance for the passage on the 'king from the sun', a Jewish reworking of material rooted in their adopted land.[65] All of this, however, amounts to no more than a fraction of the 829 verses in Book III. Much of the remainder could just as readily derive from Palestinian Jews.[66] And parts indeed need not even be Jewish in origin.[67] In short, it is hazardous to see the centrality of Egypt in the work, let alone Jewish favour toward Ptolemy VI or Ptolemy VIII as stimulus for its composition.[68]

The Sibyl has a wider canvas. Her realm of concern stretches to the world at large, at least the word as she knew it, the lands of the Mediterranean. And there the dominant power was Rome, ruthless, tyrannical, and appalling. Rome is the prime villain of the verses,

---

[58] *Sib. Or.* 3. 29–45.
[59] See Geffcken (1902*b*), 47–53; Bousset (1906), 273–4; Rzach (1923), 2123, 2130.
[60] *Sib. Or.* 3. 314–18, 348–9.
[61] Ibid. 348–9: Αἰγύπτου ὀλοὸν γένος.
[62] Ibid. 596–600.   [63] Ibid. 611–23.
[64] Ibid. 156–61.   [65] Ibid. 619–56.
[66] e.g. *Sib. Or.* 3. 63–74, 97–155, 196–294, 381–400, 489–600, 657–808.
[67] 350–80, 401–88.
[68] A similar criticism with regard to reductive interpretations of the *Oracula Sibyllina*, Book 7 was delivered by Gager (1972), 91–7.

overwhelmingly so. Only misguided scholarly ingenuity has obscured that otherwise conspicuous fact.

The evils of Rome, Romans, and the Roman empire recur repeatedly. A forecast near the outset of Book III issues a severe condemnation. When the imperial power stretches over Egypt, its days become numbered. Despite all the splendid cities with their temples, stadia, fora, and statuary, the empire stands doomed, to be destroyed by the fiery cataract of the Supreme Being who will reign over the earth.[69] The very next oracle directs itself against Beliar from the Sebastenoi, the latter probably signifying the line of Roman emperors and the former perhaps Nero, who will lead men away from God but will perish by divine fire, as will those who put trust in him.[70] There follows the passage in which 'the widow', quite probably Rome, who rules the entire world, will herself be swept away by the mighty wrath of a divine judgement.[71] Not long thereafter in the text, a list of kingdoms culminating in Rome provokes a prophecy whereby the imperial forces of the Roman Republic will wreak widespread destruction only to fall foul of their own arrogance, impiety, and moral corruption.[72] A harsher fate for Rome is proclaimed later in the text: retribution threefold for exactions made from Asia, twentyfold for the numbers enslaved, and ten thousandfold for debts imposed; vengeance will reduce Rome to a mere street.[73] Yet another oracle bewails the devastation and destruction to be wrought by Romans upon the east but also foretells civil war that will tear Italy apart, the land described not as mother of good men but as nurse of wild beasts.[74] Finally, the large barbarian horde, which will devastate the Greeks, rampage, lay waste the earth, enslave and rape the conquered, and place a heavy yoke upon the Hellenes until God unleashes his deadly fire, unquestionably refers to the Romans.[75]

The divine judgement that will eventually blast the Romans to perdition is, of course, a triumphant vindication of Jewish faith.

---

[69] *Sib. Or.* 3. 46–62.

[70] 63–74. On Beliar as Nero, see Collins (1974a), 80–7. *Contra*: Nikiprowetzky (1970), 138–43; cf. Goodman, in Schürer (1986), 640–1.

[71] *Sib. Or.* 3. 75–92. See above.

[72] Ibid. 156–95.

[73] Ibid. 350–64.

[74] Ibid. 464–88; see 469: ἔσσῃ δ' οὐκ ἀγαθῶν μήτηρ, θηρῶν δὲ τιθήνη.

[75] Ibid. 520–44. The suggestion that this may allude to the Gallic invasion of Greece is ruled out by line 530 which states that the Greeks will have no one to give them a little aid in war and to preserve their lives.

Ultimate glory for the Jews is a repeated refrain of the Third Sibyl.[76]
A noteworthy feature, however, needs emphasis here. Whereas the
oracle mounts a heavy assault upon Roman wickedness, no comparable attacks are levelled at the Greeks. To the contrary. The
Sibyl reaches out to the Hellenic world, exhorting its people to
repentance, urging acknowledgment of the true God, and offering
hope of salvation. Oracular verses expose the folly of trust in mortal
leaders and resort to idolatry, proclaiming instead the need to
recognize the great God, thereby to escape the woes that will fall
upon Hellas.[77] A further call to repentance comes several lines later,
prescribing sacrifices, prayers, and righteous behaviour to earn
divine favour.[78] The disasters to befall Greece will eventually be
lifted by God through the agency of a king from the sun.[79] And the
Sibyl subsequently repeats her appeal to unhappy Hellas to abandon haughtiness and embrace the true God—which will bring a
share in the blissful peace to come.[80] In so far as the Third Book
contains negative aspersions upon Greeks, it includes them among
wayward peoples whose failure to see the truth has led them into
arrogance, impiety, and immorality, thus provoking divine vengeance.[81] But Greeks alone are singled out for encouragement to
enter the fold of the true believers.[82]

The gesture of the Sibyl is noble and magnanimous. It should

---

[76] Cf. *Sib. Or.* 3. 211–17, 282–94, 573–600, 669–731, 767–808.

[77] Ibid. 545–72.

[78] Ibid. 624–34. Since these lines follow directly upon a passage that speaks of
Graeco-Macedonians bending a knee to God who then brings about peace and
prosperity, 601–23, the exhortation must be directed to Greeks.

[79] *Sib. Or.* 3. 635–56.

[80] Ibid. 732–61.

[81] Ibid. 196–210, 295–365, 594–600. Only the anti-Macedonian prophecy of lines
381–400, with its parallel to the forecast of Daniel, gives no ostensible hope for
reconciliation. But the reference is to the aggressions of royal imperialists, not to the
Hellenistic people as such. The thesis of Kocsis (1962), 105–10, that the oracles drew
a sharp contrast between the favoured east and the savage west, is simplistic. One
needs only to cite the destructive king from Asia in *Sib. Or.* 3. 611–18.

[82] The Sibyl's hostile comments about Egyptian practices might be thought to
reflect ill upon the Hellenic masters of that land. Not so. The opening verses
unambiguously condemn the idolatry of native Egyptians, worship of snakes and
reverence for cats; *Sib. Or.* 3. 29–45. Later, the baleful race of Egypt whose doom is
nigh is evidently contrasted with the Alexandrians who seem to be put in a different
category; *Sib. Or.* 348–9: ἴσθι τότ᾽ Αἰγύπτου ὀλοὸν γένος ἐγγὺς ὀλέθρου, καὶ τότ᾽
Ἀλεξανδρεῦσιν ἔτος τὸ παρελθὸν ἄμεινον. That the Sibyl did not subsume Greeks
under Egypt is plain from lines 594–600. The cryptic allusions to the seventh king of
Egypt remain elusive, but clearly imply no reproach of the Hellenic dwellers in that
land; *Sib. Or.* 3. 191–5, 314–18, 608. See above.

not, however, be mistaken for a conscious campaign of proselytism. Readership of the Books would consist largely of Hellenized Jews, with but a sprinkling of Gentiles. The message had symbolic import, not a manifesto for missionary activity. It asserted common cultural bonds that could encompass both communities.

The appeal to the Greeks constitutes a striking feature of the text. It may also help to solve a peculiar puzzle. The Sibyl directs her fire against Rome, against the terror, destructiveness, and corruption of the Roman empire. Her verses, of course, are no political clarion call. Efforts to locate the message in precise time and place, with concrete intent and expectation, lead to blind-alleys. The fall of Rome will come only through a cataclysmic divine intervention. But the vitriol against Rome itself demands explanation. Jews did not suffer at Roman hands in the Hellenistic period prior to the advent of Pompey, and rarely thereafter before the time of Caligula. Indeed, they generally enjoyed tolerance, alliance, and signal favour. Why then should a Jewish Sibyl of this era blast the Romans? The question, a difficult and troubling one, seldom even arises in the scholarship. A possible, at least partial, answer may lurk in the features outlined above. Oracular fore-bodings of doom delivered by a Jewish voice through a Greek medium signalled a solidarity between the two cultures. The verbal assault on Rome would suitably fit that context. The Greeks had indeed been victimized by the western power, especially in the later Hellenistic era. Greek resentment bursts out with pointed force in lines preserved by the Third Sibyl herself and plainly deriving from Hellenic circles.[83] Adoption of the anti-Roman line by Hellenized Jews who helped to shape this compilation symbolized the conjoining of Greek experience and Jewish aspirations.

Eschatology is the central ingredient throughout. Reference both to past disasters and to ills still to come issue in forecasts of terrifying divine judgements and usually the glorious elevation of the Jewish faithful. That is surely the significance of the 'king from the sun', not a historical personage but a Messianic figure.[84] And eschatological overtones may be caught also in lines that allude to construction of the Second Temple but also carry deeper meaning

---

[83] The bitterness is unmistakable in *Sib. Or.* 3. 350–80, 464–88, which are surely of Greek origin.

[84] *Sib. Or.* 3. 652–6; see above.

embodied in a king sent by the Lord to deliver judgement in blood and fire.[85]

The message of the Third Sibyl transcends the political realm. Its resonance is religious and cultural. The roots of the Sibyl's utterances reside in biblical prophecy, not the official functionaries who advised kings or participated in cult, but the powerful voices who denounced contemporaries and heralded destruction from the skies: an Amos, a Hosea, or an Isaiah. No less potent in inspiration for the Sibyl was the apocalyptic literature of Hellenistic Judaism: Daniel, 1 Enoch, Jubilees, 4 Ezra, and a variety of other texts, now further illuminated by the Qumran documents. The Sibylline pronouncements fit snugly within that setting, a complex of thoroughly Jewish traditions.[86] At the same time, of course, the authors or compilers of this collection, whether from Palestine or the Diaspora, purposefully and pointedly donned the cloak of the pagan Sibyl. Declarations issuing forth from oracular shrines, subsequently assimilated, expanded, or fabricated in written form, had long been a feature of Hellenic religious culture. They could even take shape as a full scale piece of literature, as in the case of Lycophron's *Alexandra*. Sibylline prophecies constituted an important part of this development, widely circulated in private hands, available for consultation by public authorities, and the basis for literary invention. The authority of the Sibyls spread through much of the Greek world, most especially the prophetess at Erythrae, but also a number of others located at various Mediterranean sites.[87] Jewish intellectuals tapped into the tradition and embraced the

[85] Ibid. 282–94, esp. 286–7: καὶ τότε δὴ θεὸς οὐράνιος πέμψει βασιλῆα, κρινεῖ δ᾽ ἄνδρα ἕκαστον ἐν αἵματι καὶ πυρὸς αὐγῇ. Cf. Peretti (1943), 393–5, whose speculations about the influence of Iranian eschatology, however, need to be taken with caution. The Messianic interpretation of these lines is not in fashion; cf. Nikiprowetzky (1970), 133–7; Collins (1974a), 38–9. Nolland (1979), 158–66, with valuable bibliography, rightly endeavoured to revive it. But his effort to pinpoint it to the early Maccabaean period, despite the absence of any Maccabaean allusion, is unpersuasive. Cf. Collins (1983), 66–8. Nothing in the Third Book gives any hint of Jewish resistance to the Seleucid persecutions. That resounding silence also undermines the thesis of Momigliano (1980), 553–6, that lines 194–5, predicting the future strength of the Jews, refer to the success of the Maccabaean uprising.

[86] This emerges forcefully in Nikiprowetzky's discussion (1970), 95–9, 127–37, 160–76, 248–67. The lengthy and repetitious treatment by Peretti (1943), 363–444, tracing the apocalyptic statements to Iranian eschatology, as exemplified by the Oracle of Hystaspes, is altogether speculative.

[87] On the Sibyls and Sibylline oracles, see Alexandre (1841–56), 2. 1–101; Rzach (1923), 2073–183; Parke (1988), 1–50; Potter (1994), 71–93.

Hellenic oracular form. A Hebrew Sibyl eventually took her place among the venerable female seers acknowledged by pagan writers. Verses in the extant Third Book that concern the tower of Babel, the reign of the Titans, and the myth of Chronos and his sons are attributed to the Sibyl by Alexander Polyhistor already in the first century BCE.[88] By the second century CE Pausanias could make specific reference to a Sibyl of the Hebrews in Palestine alongside the Erythraean, Libyan, and Cumaean Sibyls.[89]

The Jews successfully appropriated the Hellenic medium. The Jewish Sibyl speaks in proper Homeric hexameters. She pronounces her prophecies under divine prodding, a mouthpiece, even a somewhat reluctant one, of the greater power who speaks through her.[90] She has a grasp of Greek mythology and the epic tradition.[91] Indeed she forecasts both the fall of Troy and the Exodus from Egypt.[92] Employment of Hellenic forms, language, and themes in the service of advancing Judaic ideas enlivened the intellectual circles of Hellenistic Judaism. The composers of the Third Sibylline Oracle stand shoulder to shoulder with Ezekiel the tragedian, the historians Demetrius and Eupolemus, and the imaginative reinventors of a Hebraic–Hellenic past like Artapanus, Aristobulus, and Pseudo-Eupolemus.

Preparation for the Eschaton marks a blending of Hebrew and Hellene. The Sibylline declarations extend a hand to Greeks and a promise of divine deliverance—an invitation to link the two heritages. The Jewish authors express a cultural solidarity with Greeks, but one in which the precedence of their own traditions is clear. Greeks who show themselves worthy are invited to partake of the values of the Jews. The provenance of the Third Sibyl makes the point unambiguously. She presents herself as daughter-in-law of Noah, hence a claim on the most distant antiquity and the hoariest biblical and Near-Eastern legacies. The Hellenic connection is a secondary one. The Sibyl moved from Babylon to Greece, there to be associated with Erythrae. But her memory stretches back to the Flood, a divine prescience, infallible as the gift of God.[93] Here is

---

[88] See Euseb. *Chron.* 1. 23 (Schoene).
[89] Paus. 10. 12; cf. Schol. Pl. *Phdr.* 315. See Nikiprowetzky (1970), 37–53; Peretti (1943), 53–69.
[90] See *Sib. Or.* 3. 1–7, 162–4, 196–8, 295–9, 489–91, 698–9.
[91] Ibid. 110–55, 401–32.
[92] Ibid. 248–56, 414–18.
[93] Ibid. 809–29.

appropriation indeed. The Sibyl's origins precede even Babel. She thus asserts a universal heritage, embodying Hebrew traditions and later subsuming the authority of the Erythraean Sibyl, most venerated of the Hellenic prophetesses. Jewish identity stands in the forefront here. The keepers of the faith who had also absorbed pagan learning, literature, and legends claimed a place in both worlds but held firm to their core. The oracular voice promises a happy fate for the Chosen People—and also extends a compassionate embrace to those Greeks touched by their values and ideals.

3

The Hellenization of Jerusalem and Shechem

SETH SCHWARTZ

Everyone knows that an important category of Greek city in the Hellenistic period was the Hellenized native city—a phenomenon especially common in Asia Minor (where Sardis is the best-known example) and in Syria-Palestine. This type of city is of particular interest because it illustrates in the most critical way possible the changing character of ethnicity in the Hellenistic period, for it seems likely that apart from those who, wherever they lived, could plausibly claim Greek ancestry, the prevailing definition of 'Greek' now became formal: a citizen of a city with a Greek constitution was Greek. Everyone also knows, though Jewish historians tend not to think of it in precisely these terms, that the *loci classici* for the Hellenization of native cities are the cases of Jerusalem and Shechem under Antiochus IV. Only here do we have information, however tendentious and incomplete, about the process by which communities actually became Greek.

At this point well-trodden ground ends. Of the two relatively recent discrete discussions of the question of the Hellenized city, one, that of Fergus Millar (1983), provides a careful account of the evidence for the cultural situation in the Greek cities of Hellenistic Phoenicia, and invites us to admire the heady complexity and rich strangeness of its texture. This is a generous gesture, which signals us to draw our own conclusions, but, with all due respect, it is no substitute for analysis. The other main treatment, by Edouard Will (1988), does assume a more analytic attitude, yet ends, as Millar

This paper is a minor artefact of the generosity of the King's College (Cambridge) Research Centre, written while I was a member of its Early Christianity Project. I would like to thank the Convenors, Martin Hyland and Iain Fenlon, the managers, and my colleagues, Catherine Hezser, Keith Hopkins, Wolfram Kinzig, and Markus Vinzent.

implicitly does, by retaining an essentialist view of what it meant to be Greek. By this I mean the view that Greekness consisted of a large and exclusive set of normative patterns of behaviour readily identifiable as Greek because they were characteristic also of classical Greece; or, to put it less formally, Millar and Will are typical in believing that we know a Greek when we see one.[1] I would argue, however, that the main importance of the cases of Jerusalem and Shechem is to suggest ways in which, under Macedonian rule, being Greek changed.

There is needless to say a speculative quality to such an argument, given the poverty of the evidence. But I would like to take the speculation several steps further by addressing the implications of one aspect of the new Greekness. If, as I will argue, Greekness was now essentially a public and formal property, some preservation of the native culture, for which there is Hellenistic evidence, must have been taking place elsewhere than in the public sphere. Let me be still more abstract: in the last millennium of antiquity in the eastern Mediterranean, there were several cases of surprisingly radical cultural transformation, which however in each case somehow coexisted with or concealed a tendency towards profound cultural conservatism. Hellenization in the third century BCE, Christianization in fourth and fifth CE, and Islamization in the seventh and eighth, each brought about drastic changes in language, cultic behaviour, political ideology. I would like to argue that they all also produced temporarily a gulf between public and private which served as the mechanism for preservation of elements of the older cultural systems, and, as the gulf narrowed, as the norms of public and the practices of private life were inevitably contaminated, for the incorporation and naturalization of old elements in the new systems.

Before taking up this question, though, let us return to earth, and look briefly at the familiar cases of pre-Maccabean Jerusalem and Shechem. First, Jerusalem: 2 Maccabees (4: 7–20) describes how soon after 175 BCE Jason, having usurped the high priesthood of Jerusalem, petitioned (and bribed) Antiochus IV for the right to establish, 'under his own authority', a gymnasium, an ephebate, and a citizen body at Jerusalem (I am intentionally being vague about this so as to avoid the old problem of the meaning of *tous en*

---

[1] See also Sherwin-White and Kuhrt (1993), 141–9.

Hierosolymois Antiocheis anagrapsai (4: 9); I am slightly more convinced by Tcherikover's interpretation than Bickerman's, but am still troubled by the vagueness of 2 Maccabees' wording if what it meant to say was 'to give Jerusalem a Greek constitution and rename it Antioch', as well as by what, in that case, verse 19 might mean).[2] In any case, the ruler of the city, still its high priest, responded to the city's new status by sending *theoroi* (ambassadors) to a panhellenic festival in Tyre (4: 18–20). If the crucial verse does mean what Tcherikover said it does, then Judaea was now transformed from an autonomous *ethnos* (people) centred on a temple, and ruled by a privileged priesthood, into a city-plus-territory with a Greek constitution, with the temple now merely housing the municipal cult of the city; the cult itself was unchanged. It was only in 168 that a more zealous high priest altered it, or, if you prefer, that the king imposed cultic change on a largely unresistant Judaean upper class,[3] but even then, the religion introduced was only part Greek. Festivals of Dionysos were celebrated (2 Macc. 6: 7), but the patron-god of Greek Jerusalem, named Zeus Olympios, was perhaps worshipped in the form of an aniconic stela, and the temple was almost certainly frequented by sacred prostitutes—both practices at odds with Greek custom.[4] The book of Daniel's punning denunciation of this cult indicates that the god of Jerusalem was also called Baal-Shamim (11: 31). So, for the first seven or so years of its existence, the Greek city of Jerusalem continued its traditional cult, and subsequently, the religion introduced was a Graeco-Syrian hybrid.

The second account is closely related to the first: when, according to Josephus (*Ant.* 12. 257–64), the traditional Jewish cult was abolished in Jerusalem, the rulers of the Samaritan city of Shechem petitioned Antiochus for the right to reform the municipal cult so as

---

[2] See Tcherikover (1958), 152–74; Bickerman (1979), 38–42, arguing that Jason established not a Greek city but a Greek corporation within the still Jewish city of Jerusalem. See also Le Rider (1965), 410–11, supporting Tcherikover's argument on the basis of such common Seleucid coin legends as *Antiocheon ton en Ptolemaidi*, where the reference is clearly to a Greek city, and not a Greek corporation in a native city; Millar (1978), 10; Habicht (1976), 216–17. Verse 19: 'Jason . . . sent as *theoroi* men who were Antiochenes from Jerusalem [or, as *theoroi* from Jerusalem men who were Antiochenes], carrying three hundred silver drachmas . . .' This is, on the face of it, difficult to reconcile with Tcherikover's view. Perhaps the author of 2 Maccabees himself misunderstood what his source, Jason of Cyrene, had written.

[3] See 2 Macc. 6: 1–9; Bickerman (1979), 83–8.

[4] See Bickerman (1979), 60–75.

to make Zeus Xenios the patron-god of the city. (I am assuming, by the way, that the letter is basically genuine, notwithstanding the powerful arguments of Rappaport.) But they also asked to retain their traditional laws, provided with an *interpretatio graeca* and altered in such a way as to obscure the laws' connection with those of the Jews. The king responded by welcoming the Shechemites' adoption of 'Hellenic customs' (*hellenika ethe*; Joseph. *Ant.* 12. 264; the expression is also used of Jerusalem in Antiochus V's rescission of the Hellenization, 2 Macc. 11: 24).[5] What resulted in both cases were cities whose Hellenism was in part notional: Jerusalem was still governed by a high priest and a board of *gerontes* (elders) (2 Macc. 4: 18, 44), just as Phoenician cities in the same period were still ruled by their *dikastai* (judges);[6] the municipal religion in both Jerusalem and Shechem was at first basically the traditional one, and even later in Jerusalem was not precisely Greek. In sum, then, the *hellenika ethe* of these Greek cities consisted of nominally Hellenized religion, and political structure, combined with (at Jerusalem certainly, at Shechem possibly) a gymnasium and ephebate.

We cannot be sure that the same process occurred also in such other Hellenizing cities as Sardis, Tyre, Sidon, and Gaza, but the supposition that something similar did explains the significant continuities in religious and political life listed by Fergus Millar in his discussion of Phoenician cities, and by Sherwin-White and Kuhrt (1993: 180–4) in their discussion of Sardis. Indeed, such continuities may have been even more conspicuous in the other cities than in Jerusalem, where the zeal of the petitioners, or of the king, eventually led them to introduce changes more radical than what was normally required to make a community 'Greek'—a fact which may help explain the failure of the Hellenization of Jerusalem (about the fate of Shechem, where the reforms were more moderate, we can only speculate).

It is worth pausing for a moment to consider the character of these Greek cities. Here were cities which seem to have received few settlers of ethnic Greek origin. The cities eventually looked more or less Greek, but not entirely so, because there is little reason to believe that many of them were substantially rebuilt in the early

---

[5] For fuller discussions of this episode, see Schwartz (1993), 9–25; Rappaport (1990), 373–96, arguing that the letters recorded by Josephus are forgeries.
[6] Millar (1983), 62, 67.

Hellenistic period, so that many pre-Hellenistic structures remained; indeed, many cities of the Greek east did not acquire a properly 'Hellenic' appearance until they came under Roman rule. We know, however, that after a destructive invasion in the late third century BCE Sardis was redesigned according to the so-called Hippodamian plan, a typical sign of a Greek city. Temples, to extrapolate from Dura-Europus and Aï Khanoum, sometimes featured the superimposition of some Greek elements on a non-Greek design, but were often left unchanged from their pre-'Greek' state.[7] Even the *public* institutions of these cities often were scarcely changed in *substance* from what they had been previously, apart from the important introduction of Greek education, and the *private* behaviour of the citizens will at first have changed even less. Indeed, Phoenician inscriptions of the Hellenistic period give the disquieting (though misleading) feeling that deep down, nothing had changed.[8] In what sense then were these places Greek?

First of all, there is no question that despite the problems in recognizing them as such, the citizens of the Hellenized cities were in their own eyes, in the eyes of their rulers, and in those of their enemies, Greeks, who conducted their lives according to Greek customs, and lived in cities with Greek constitutions. They participated in panhellenic festivals and instituted panhellenic festivals of their own. Thus, the very nature of Greekness changed. It was not simply that now outsiders could join up (as Cohen emphasized):[9] this had always been true in a very, very limited way; it was that becoming a Greek now required a communal declaration of adherence accompanied by what from our perspective were usually small changes in public behaviour, so 'Greekness' could accommodate significant preservation of pre-Greek behaviour. Yet (*contra* Kuhrt and Sherwin-White) this new Greekness was not superficial or trivial, because by becoming Greek, a community reordered its religious, cultural, political, life along a new ideological axis. I may add that it also reordered its economic life: precisely because of its public character, Hellenism—involving the construction and maintenance of gymnasia, hippodromes, theatres, bathhouses, maybe new temples—cost lots of money. The classic expression of this reordering is 2 Maccabees' description of the behaviour of the

---

[7] See Sherwin-White and Kuhrt (1993), 149–87.
[8] See Donner and Röllig (1962–4), 1. §§ 40–60, with commentary in ii. 57–64.
[9] S. Cohen (1990), 204–23.

young priests after Jason's reforms (2 Macc. 4: 14–15) 'the priests
were no longer eager to perform their duties at the altar but made
light of the temple and neglected the sacrifices in their haste after
the gong sounded (*vel sim.*) calling them to participate in the illicit
entertainment in the palaistra. *Setting at nought their hereditary
distinctions, they put the highest value on Greek honors.*[10] This is of
course a polemical account, ignoring as it does the fact that the cult
apparently continued undisturbed for several years after Jason's
reform, obviously because the priests preserved it. Some of the
priests of Jerusalem, that is, like the priests in other Hellenizing
cities, found ways to be simultaneously traditionalists and Greeks.

The Hellenization of a city, then, provided its citizens with a new
set of cultural options, which partly supplemented and partly
replaced the old (for there is surely *some* truth to 2 Maccabees'
statement that traditional honours were devalued in Jason's Jerusalem). These new cultural options—participation in athletics, acquisition of rhetorical skills, for instance—were in form unmistakably
'old Greek'.

Yet the new Greekness functioned in two different ways to
preserve elements, displaced and altered, of traditional cultures.
Now I assume that when one, or several, of the Phoenician cities
retained the title *dikastai* for one of their magistracies, few people,
after the first generation, were necessarily aware that anything
distinctive, or at any rate distinctively Phoenician, was being
preserved; but the preservation of the traditional cults in the
Hellenized cities may have actually functioned to keep alive a
significant consciousness of a special past.[11] Certainly the priests
preserved pre-Hellenic languages and myths (even if the latter often
had incorporated layers of Greek interpretation)—how else are we
to understand the survival of the Phoenician language and, in the
work of Philo of Byblos, of fragments of Canaanite mythology,
albeit stoicized and euhemerized?[12] Once Hellenized, of course, this
mythology took its place in the common élite culture of the Hellenistic world, and thereby changed it, yet it retained simultaneously an
irreducible distinctiveness.

Another way the new Greekness may have preserved elements of
the traditional cultures was by driving them indoors, underground,

[10] I follow here the translation of Goldstein (1984), 217, with nn. at 230–1.
[11] So Millar (1983), 64–5.
[12] See Attridge and Oden (1981), 3–9; Schwartz (1995), 19–23.

and to the margins, which it did by insisting on its own predominance in public discourse. Here speculation begins in earnest,
because we know so little about private behaviour—about preservation of local types of sexual behaviour, cuisine, medical/magical
practice, even of pre-Greek languages. I would argue that the
apparent speed and thoroughness of the Hellenization of the cities
was enabled in part by the fact that the very public and formal
character of Greekness allowed the change to be less drastic than it
might seem.

If I am right about the heightened sense of the private created by
the diffusion of Greek culture in the third and second centuries BCE,
then Hellenization was the first of several cases of large-scale and
radical cultural transformations in the high and late antique
Mediterranean and Near East which I believe all follow a roughly
similar pattern, for reasons which I admit I do not know. First,
smallest-scale in demographic terms, and most obscure may be the
Judaization of Palestine under the Hasmoneans, perhaps a sort of
counter-Hellenization, which must have consisted primarily of a
Judaization of public life—closure of temples, of markets on the
Sabbath, and so on.[13] We know, once again, too little about private
life to know for certain that it was left alone at first, but I think it
must have been; there is no reason to suppose Herod's courtier
Costobar was unique among the Idumaeans in his private devotion
to the ancestral god Qos (Jos. *Ant.* 15. 253–8); perhaps the new
excavations at Marisa and the newly found Hellenistic documents
from the town will help us detect other hidden survivals of Edomite
practice in post-Maccabean Judaism (aside from the case of burial
in special burial slots (*kokhim*)).[14]

Still more striking, because much more is known about it, is the
case of Christianity. Owing to constraints of space and knowledge, I
will focus on only one aspect of the changes introduced by the
Christianization of the Roman empire. Peter Brown (1995) has
recently emphasized that in the fourth century the Roman élites,
whether Christian or pagan, were still bound together by their
devotion to *paideia*, classical culture. This began to change at the
very end of the century—perhaps at the moment when Christian

---

[13] See in general Cohen (1990).
[14] For the time being see Kloner (1991), 70–85; *Hadashot Arkheologiyot*, 99
(1993), 79–80; 101–2 (1994), 102–4; on the Idumaean origin of burial in *kokhim*,
see Oren and Rappaport (1984), 149–51.

demographic predominance, combined with the consolidation of theological consensus, allowed a burgeoning orthodox church to help bring about a change in public culture. In the fifth and sixth centuries, the character and appearance of the cities of Asia Minor and Syria-Palestine, which had been basically stable since the third century BCE, once again began to change. The city councils began to disappear, and with them the amenities which the city councillors had traditionally been responsible for maintaining—the theatres, public baths, needless to say the temples, and eventually even the massively popular hippodromes.[15] The grand public *agorai* (marketplaces) with their colonnades and monuments were built over and replaced with winding alleys containing shops. In short, the classical city, in the fifth and sixth centuries, gave way to what is conventionally but incorrectly thought of as the Muslim city.[16] One thing that happened was that the character of the public culture changed; the curial classes and their Graeco-Roman pagan culture gave way to an élite of great landowners, bishops, and bureaucrats, who supported mainly churches and associated public welfare funds. It was not only theatres and *agorai* which were shut down and built over: the great houses, too, with their lavishly decorated semi-public atria, where the city councillors had entertained their clients, were now enclosed, and many of the wealthy are thought to have moved out to their country estates. I would argue that this change conforms to the pattern whereby a conversionist cultural system works by creating an unpoliced private space, in which fragments of previous systems are preserved until they can be safely injected into the now well-established new system.[17]

The Hellenization of the cities of Asia Minor and Syria-Palestine certainly exhibits these features only in a relatively weak form. Hellenism was in some ways more malleable, could more freely absorb suitably dressed-up elements of pre-Hellenic cultures, could, through its interest in preserving traditional cults, actually even allow for significant preservation of pre-Greek lore as a (rather devalued) part of Greek urban high culture. Furthermore, the Macedonian rulers themselves did not actively promote Hellenism

---

[15] The classic account is Jones (1964), I. 737–57.

[16] See Whittow (1990), Kennedy (1985).

[17] I refrain, due to ignorance, from discussing the Muslim city, despite its evident relevance. I am nevertheless indebted to Dr Basim Musallam for stimulating discussion of this issue, and of many others.

as an integrating principle in their kingdoms, merely made clear the fact that they considered it the cultural ideal, and zealously patronized it when it cropped up on its own. It was only the Romans who utilized this newly created urban culture as a way of holding their empire together. Consequently, the public–private divide that the Hellenism of the Hellenistic cities generated, if any, is less gaping than that created by Christianity and Islam, and perhaps by Judaism in second-century BCE Palestine.

4

Josephus' Tobiads: Back to the Second Century?

DANIEL R. SCHWARTZ

As an illustration of the use of Jewish evidence for the study of Graeco-Roman history, this chapter will discuss something which did *not* happen in one of the particularly lively junctures of that history. I refer to the first few decades of the second century BCE, when the Roman republic, having just completed the long and difficult Second Punic War in the western Mediterranean, found itself free to get involved in the east.

This development was especially troublesome for Seleucid Syria, then ruled by Antiochus III, who had just completed long and successful campaigns in Asia and Arabia, thus earning himself the title 'the Great'; in 200 BCE, only a year or two after Zama, he had defeated the Ptolemaic army and annexed Coele-Syria, including Palestine. After this, in the early 190s, with nothing left to do in the east, Antiochus began to invade the mainland of Europe, eventually making his way into Greece. It was, therefore, highly unfortunate for Antiochus that precisely at this time Rome had become free to deal with the east, starting off with its success in the Second Macedonian War. Indeed, results followed quickly: a Roman victory over Antiochus at Thermopylae (191 BCE) was followed by a Seleucid withdrawal into Asia Minor. There, late in 190, Rome successfully completed its 'Bellum Antiochum' with a resounding victory at Magnesia. In the ensuing Treaty of Apamea, correspondingly, Rome imposed severe restrictions upon the Seleucid army, heavy war indemnities (which were to weigh heavily on the Seleucids for more than a decade), and other humiliations.[1] No wonder that Seleucus IV, who succeeded his father a year or two after Apamea, is said to have been 'do-nothing (*apraktos*) and weak

---

[1] For the events reviewed in this paragraph, see the relevant chapters of Will (1982) and of Astin *et al.* (1989). On the Treaty of Apamea: Mørkholm (1966), 22–8. On the indemnities it imposed: Le Rider (1993).

due to his father's suffering' (Appian, *Syriake* 66). Jerome, similarly, roundly dismisses him as having done nothing worthy of Syria
or his fathers (*In Danielem* 11. 20).

Against this background, we come to our question about what did
not happen. As noted above, Antiochus conquered Coele-Syria
from the Ptolemies in 200 BCE. We may now add that this event, in
the Fifth Syrian War, brought to an end a century of Ptolemaic rule
there, which had been punctuated by four earlier Syrian wars, all of
which had ended with the same status quo ante of Ptolemaic rule.[2]
That is, rule over Coele-Syria had been an issue between the two
neighbouring Hellenistic dynasties for a century. Why, then, during
the first decades of the second century, when Antiochus was first
throwing all of his efforts into the northern Mediterranean, and later
when he and his son and successor, Seleucus IV, were so weakened
by Magnesia and Apamea, did Ptolemaic Egypt do nothing by way
of revanche? Why was there no Egyptian attempt to regain Coele-
Syria?

In the standard works and monographs we find only one answer,
namely, the fact that in 193 BCE, when preparing for his clash with
Rome, Antiochus III had married off his daughter Cleopatra I
'Syra' to Ptolemy V Epiphanes, who ruled Egypt 204–180 BCE.[3]
However, with all due respect for that lady's charms, one would
normally expect that there were some other terms to the agreement.
At a time of such obvious Seleucid weakness, at a time when eastern
Seleucid provinces and Armenia were successfully detaching them-
selves from Seleucid suzerainty, why would Ptolemy V just twiddle
his thumbs?[4]

To this puzzle from the world of Hellenistic Realpolitik, we will
add another from Polybius, Livy, and Josephus. Polybius' account
of the role of Coele-Syria in the Sixth Syrian War is not very clear:
on the one hand he states that the land had been ruled by the

---

[2] See Heinen (1984).
[3] On this marriage see, in general, Will (1982), 2. 190–2, and Seibert (1967), 65–6.
[4] On the eastern provinces and Armenia, see Yarshatar (1983), 303, 307, 512–13.
Mørkholm (1966), 29, noting that 'it would only have been natural for the Egyptian
king to use the opportunity offered by the Syrian defeat to make an attempt at
recovering the lost province', continued to deduce that 'as we hear of no Egyptian
endeavours in that direction, we may assume that the internal troubles in Egypt at the
time were too serious . . .' But this type of excuse sounds hollow, and Mørkholm's
note (ibid., n. 39) refers only to a revolt which ended already in 186. Of course, there
are always internal problems of one sort or another; at times foreign campaigns may
even be useful ways of dealing with them . . . Cf. below, n. 43.

Seleucids since the battle of Panium in the days of Antiochus III, but on the other hand he says that Antiochus IV 'was struggling to defend the country as one belonging to him' but Ptolemy VI 'was not disposed to abandon these places to Antiochus' (Polyb. 28. 1, trans. Paton (Loeb)). If Antiochus IV was ruling the country pure and simple, how could Ptolemy VI consider abandoning it? Of course, it could be that all Polybius means is that Ptolemy VI was attacking Coele-Syria because he did not want Panium to constitute a definitive Ptolemaic abandonment of the country. But that too is not so simple, for the war began with campaigns by Antiochus IV into Egypt, not with a Ptolemaic attack upon Coele-Syria. Must we assume that Polybius viewed Antiochus' moves as pre-emptive?[5]

Moreover, note that Livy, in the context of his review of the situation in the east around 171 BCE when Rome was getting involved in the Third Macedonian War, states that Antiochus IV thought of exploiting Roman involvement elsewhere in order 'to raise disputes about Coele-Syria in order to have a cause for war (against Egypt)' (*ambigendo de Coele Syria causam belli se habiturum*: Livy 42. 29. 5). Here too we must ask the same question: if Antiochus was himself the ruler of Coele-Syria, pure and simple, what disputes could he hope to raise? Scholars who ask this question either reject Livy's statement out of hand or suggest it is out of place. But such treatment is never quite satisfactory. Moreover, Livy is quite explicitly supported by Josephus' opening statement in his *Jewish War* (1. 31), which refers to a dispute raised by Antiochus Epiphanes against Ptolemy VI concerning Coele-Syria; although Josephus' account here is usually disregarded, the reasons have nothing to do with the definition of the dispute as one raised by Antiochus Epiphanes about Coele-Syria.[6]

Obviously, both of our questions—why did Ptolemy V do nothing to regain Coele-Syria, and what did Livy and Josephus mean by disputes Antiochus IV could raise about Coele-Syria—could easily be resolved by the suggestion that Ptolemaic Egypt had indeed received back, from the Seleucids, some measure of their lost interests in that province. It would be that which kept Egypt

---

[5] This is, indeed, Mørkholm's position (1966), 67–8.

[6] For discussion and references concerning Livy, see Otto (1934), 30–1, n. 4 and 40–1, n. 2. As for Josephus, *War* 1. 31–3, see Tcherikover (1959), 392–5; in this attack on Josephus, just as in the Hebrew essay on which it is based, no notice is taken of the detail which interests us, apart from correcting the text from 'all Syria' to 'Coele-Syria'.

quiet as long as Rome had the upper hand over Syria, and it would be that which Antiochus could contest when he thought Rome was not in a position to interfere.

Now, the fact of the matter is, that Josephus indeed reports just such a Seleucid concession. At *Ant.* 12. 154, just after his account of Antiochus III's conquest of Coele-Syria and his edicts concerning the Jews, Josephus reports that when Cleopatra Syra was given in marriage to Ptolemy her dowry was 'Coele-Syria, Samaria, Judaea, and Phoenicia'. This seemingly broad statement is followed, in the very next lines, by details about how the taxes from these regions were divided between Cleopatra and Ptolemy, so it is clear that the general statement must be limited accordingly.[7] That is, as Cleopatra's dowry—i.e. as a means of keeping Egypt quiet in contemplation of the coming clash with Rome, as Appian notes (*Syr.* 5)— Antiochus gave away not only his daughter but also the tribute of Coele-Syria etc. This is the context into which Josephus next introduces his long story of the Tobiads, who collected the taxes of Coele-Syria for the Ptolemies (§§ 160–236).

Here, then, is what could easily answer both of our opening questions: the Seleucid conqueror of Coele-Syria had allowed its income to revert to Ptolemy V. But Josephus' statement is rejected out of hand, usually with virtually no argument, by all contemporary scholars. Bengtson brands it 'eine Erfindung des Josephus', to which Seibert adds only 'sicher'; Gruen says it is 'almost certainly false' and Orrieux asserts Josephus knew it was false; Walbank proclaims it 'improbable', referring (as Orrieux) to Will, who says that nothing confirms it.[8] As if the burden of proof were on those

---

[7] For the presumption that reasonable exegesis requires that the seemingly sweeping statement of § 154 be limited by the reference to tribute in § 155, see esp. Cuq (1927), 148. So, similarly, Wilcken (1894), 2466: 'Als Mitgift erhielt sie die Gefälle mehrerer Städte in Koilesyrien, Iudaea und Phoinikia (Jos. ant. XII 154–155)'; elsewhere (in Droysen (1894), 433) Wilcken emphasizes, as Cuq, that the reference in § 155 to the division of the tribute 'genauer charakterisiert' the promise mentioned in § 154. Among those who deny the truth of Josephus' claim we nevertheless frequently find the same understanding of it; so, among others, Bengtson (1944), 161 n. 2; Seibert (1967), 66 n. 74; Will (1982), 192; Walbank (1979*a*), 356.

[8] The references for Bengtson, Seibert, Walbank, and Will are in n. 7; Bengtson liked 'Erfindung' and repeated it (1977), 479–80 n. 5. As for Seibert's 'sicher', cf. Kennard (1945/6), 281. The other references: Gruen (1984), 2. 684 n. 63, and Orrieux (1986), 8–9. The most detailed discussion I know is Mago's (1907), 47–9; it too rejects the notion of such a concession. What is interesting about Mago's discussion, in the present context, is that it makes no mention of the Tobiads.

who believe an ancient source rather than on those who would reject it.

There are, indeed, three arguments which are commonly adduced against Josephus' claim. Let us examine them.

First, Appian (*Syr.* 5) and Porphyry (*ap.* Jerome, *In Danielem* 11. 17 = *GLAJJ* ii. 464l) say Antiochus III gave Coele-Syria as Cleopatra's dowry;[9] since, unlike Josephus' statement, there is no subsequent detail limiting the matter to taxation, the obvious interpretation refers to full rule. That is obviously untrue, however, for we have—albeit meagre—epigraphic and literary evidence for the Seleucid governors of Coele-Syria during this period,[10] and Polybius (28. 1. 3), writing of events c.170 BCE, explicitly states that Coele-Syria and Phoenicia had been ruled by the Seleucids ever since Antiochus III's victory at Panium (200 BCE). Josephus refers, as we have seen, not to rule in general but only to taxes, but scholars have associated Josephus' modest statement with the sweeping implication of the statements by Appian and Porphyry and thrown them all out together.

Second, according to Polybius (28. 20. 6–10), Antiochus IV—in a speech before Greek envoys after the successful conclusion of his first campaign into Egypt in 170/169 BCE—himself denied that his father had agreed to give Ptolemy V Coele-Syria as his daughter's dowry, and Polybius adds that Antiochus convinced not only himself, but also his audience, that he was right. Surprisingly enough, Polybius' reference to Antiochus' rhetorical success is often taken as evidence that the denial is truthful, and that only mendacious Alexandrian propagandists had concocted the claim.

This is an important illustration of the fact that the Tobiads were not very prominent in scholarly consciousness when he wrote (1907), a decade before the publication of the Zenon Papyri. Once those papyri were published, the Tobiads became very prominent (see e.g. the bibliographies assembled by Tcherikover in *CPJ* i. 118 n. 4 and by Marcus in vol. 7 of the Loeb *Josephus*, 767–8); as we shall see, it was those papyri which were taken as justification for drastically abbreviating the debate.

[9] Compare Josephus' *phernes onomati* (*Ant.* 12. 154) to Porphyry's 'dotis nomine' (and note that the Loeb translation of the latter, which Stern reprints in *GLAJJ*, misleadingly renders 'nomine' by 'professedly'). The similarity of phrase leads one to suspect that both are based on a common source, for which the likely candidate is Polybius. Polybius' own account of 196–192 BCE (Book 19—Olympiad 146) is lost, but see Walbank (1979a) who notes that the section of Livy which reports the marriage (35. 13. 4) is based on Polybius' lost account. The claim that Coele-Syria was given to Ptolemy V as Cleopatra's dowry also appears in various later chronicles; see *PWRE* I. 21 (1921), 738.

[10] See esp. 2 Macc. 3–4; Bengtson (1944), 161–4.

However, given Polybius' usual antipathy toward Antiochus IV,[11] his political engagement on behalf of the Ptolemies in their struggle with him and his consistently positive attitude toward Ptolemy VI,[12] and his friendship with Demetrius I (see Polybius 31. 11–13), who had every reason to despise his uncle Antiochus, it is likely that Polybius' statement that Antiochus convinced 'not only himself . . .' is to be read as ironic.[13] Moreover, the denial is just what is to be expected from a Seleucid king, and in any case, as Jouguet drily remarked, statements by generals at the head of victorious armies, as Antiochus IV was, are usually quite convincing . . .[14]

Third, and most important for us in the present context, Josephus is usually thought to be confused about the Tobiads. He places them in the early second century BCE, in the days of Ptolemy Epiphanes, but today you will not find anyone who leaves them there. All assume they belong to the mid-to-late third century BCE, when all agree the Ptolemies ruled Coele-Syria.[15] Accordingly, it is explained that Josephus thought the story concerns the second century and therefore invented his story of Cleopatra's dowry in order to account for Ptolemaic taxation after the Seleucid conquest. However, this widespread rejection of Josephus seems to be based on very little, as we will indicate in eight points:

1. Any such rejection of Josephus should suggest what it was in his source which led him to misplace the story. However, I know of only two such suggestions, both stated most conveniently by Orrieux. First, the story relates to a Queen Cleopatra; since there were none such before the second century, the name would have led Josephus to place the story in that century. Second, Josephus reports at *Ant.* 12. 178 that Joseph the Tobiad referred to the Ptolemaic king and queen as co-guarantors for the tribute; Josephus could see this as confirming the old Ptolemaic claim concerning the tributes of Coele-Syria. Orrieux assumes that Cleopatra's name was

[11] See Welwei (1963), 68–76; Mørkholm (1966), 181–4.

[12] See Walbank (1979b), 184–5. Walbank terms Polybius and his father the pillars of 'an Egyptian pressure group in Achaea'.

[13] Mago (1907), 49, includes among his arguments the fact that Polybius, despite his pro-Ptolemaic attitude and opposition to Antiochus IV, 'tace completamente, almeno nei frammenti che possediamo, sull' autenticità del famoso trattato'. I submit that 'not only himself' is in fact quite loud.

[14] Jouguet (1937), 222. Similarly, Hoffmann noted in this connection that, under the circumstances, it is understandable that Antiochus 'nicht an jenen Rechtsvertrag erinnert sein wollte' (1873), 26 n. 1.

[15] On the precise dates posited, see below, n. 24.

wrongly inserted into the story by someone who thought it was the name of all Ptolemaic queens, and he also assumes that reference to the splitting of tribute was in fact only 'un artifice rhétorique'. That is, in both cases Orrieux admits that Josephus' deductions were reasonable; what he denies is the reliability of the data upon which Josephus worked—but his denial is based on nothing more than a prior belief that the story belongs to the third century. On 'Cleopatra', see also the third point below.

2. The main reason to reject Josephus is the assumption that Ptolemaic taxation must indicate Ptolemaic rule.[16] However, Josephus claims it need not, and we do know of cases of kings giving away the income of cities or territories as dowries or the like.[17]

3. Another reason is the fact that some manuscripts add 'Euergetes, who was the father of Philopator' to 'King Ptolemy' at *Ant.* 12.158 and 'Euergetes' to 'Ptolemy' at § 163; if accepted, this would point us to Ptolemy III Euergetes (246–221 BCE), a possibility supported by the later reference to the accession to the Seleucid throne of Seleucus Soter (§ 223), which brings us to 226–223 BCE. In general, however, short identifications of particular rulers among homonyms are not always very reliable, when not supported by context, whether in ancient or modern works.[18] Indeed, in the case of Ptolemy 'Euergetes', other witnesses which omit the text in question were preferred by all modern editors (Naber, Niese, Reinarch, Marcus); as Niese notes, if the Vorlage had identified the king as Ptolemy Euergetes, Josephus would have placed the story prior to his account of the Fifth Syrian War.[19] That is, the

---

[16] Orrieux's recent discussion offers an especially explicit instance of such a pronouncement being accepted as the first and last word of the discussion: 'Le fermier général des taxes des Syrie-Phénicie mises en adjudication à Alexandrie n'a pu remplir ces fonctions qu'à l'époque de la domination ptolémaïque' (Orrieux (1986), 8). Of course, in normal circumstances taxation and rule go hand in hand, but intermarriage between competing royal families can make for abnormal circumstances.

[17] See e.g. 2 Macc. 4: 30 and Justin 38. 5. 3. Similar cases are cited by Cuq (1927), 147–8, and by Welles (1962), 151. Cf. *OGIS* 225.

[18] Note, for a case identical to ours, Derfler's statement that 'Seleucus III Soter ruled Syria from 187–175 BCE' (Derfler (1990), 23 n. 43). This comes after his discussion of Antiochus III and before that of Antiochus IV, and no one would argue that the byname is to be preferred to the dates and the context.

[19] See Niese's note ad *Ant.* 12. 158 in his editio maior. Reinach, in his note ad loc. to Chamonard's 1904 French translation, goes so far as to call 'Euergetes, Philopator's father' a 'glosse absurde'. It is frequently instructive to compare the

Daniel Schwartz

addition of 'Euergetes, the father of Philopator' and 'Euergetes' in some witnesses may be understood as a learned correction inserted by scribes motivated by arguments similar to those followed by modern sceptics.[20] Moreover, the addition in § 158 is very clumsy and its very repetition in § 163 tells against it, for after the first identification plain 'Ptolemy' should suffice, as it does throughout the rest of the narrative (§§ 165, 166, 170, 172, 178 etc.).

The weakness of this argument from 'Euergetes' is further pointed up by comparison with an opposing argument: in his account of the Tobiads Josephus frequently—and in all the witnesses—names the Egyptian queen 'Cleopatra' (*Ant.* 12. 154, 167, 185, 204, 217), a name which points us to a period no earlier than that of Cleopatra Syra. Scholars who doubt Josephus here monotonously repeat the argument that Josephus (or his source) erroneously inserted the name as a corollary of the original sin of misassigning the Tobiad story to the second century, when all Egyptian queens were called 'Cleopatra'—unless, as Orrieux (above, no. 1), they assume the mistake was in Josephus' source and this is what misled him. But although 'Euergetes' is less common than 'Cleopatra' and hence less likely to have been inserted thoughtlessly, it does not seem responsible to depend securely on a royal byname which appears only twice and in only some witnesses, while blithely explaining away the queen's name, which is much

judgements made by editors and translators, who are relatively unconcerned by historical considerations but are, after all, the ones most familiar with the texts with which they are dealing, their style and their witnesses. For a similar case, see Schwartz (1992), 226 n. 31.

[20] Gressmann (1921), 667 n. 4, referring only to 12.158, asserts that the words are original but Josephus overlooked them because he was otherwise convinced, erroneously, that the material applied to the days of Ptolemy V, but this leads us from the frying pan into the fire, for why was Josephus so convinced? Maybe he had some good reason? Similarly, Stern (1962/3), 42 [29], who states that 'there is no reason to assume that the text has been corrupted and that the words "Euergetes, father of Philopator" are an interpolation', refers in his note to Tcherikover (1959), 458 n. 32. But all that Tcherikover offers is the remark that 'it would however be wrong to ascribe to an interpolator words that have no particular point[;] Josephus satisfactorily explained the payment of tribute to the Ptolemies instead of to the Seleucids by his story of Cleopatra's dowry (*Ant.* 12, 154–5) and the pointless addition of the name "Euergetes" can change nothing in this narrative'. He too thus moves from the frying pan into the fire, admitting that Josephus' explanation is (i.e. could have been) satisfactory and that the name 'Euergetes' changes nothing. For while Tcherikover's conclusion is that it is original, one could just as easily conclude that it is secondary, added by a scribe who, like so many moderns, was not satisfied by Josephus' explanation.

more secure in the text.[21] Our suggestion, we underline, was not that 'Euergetes' was inserted thoughtlessly, but, rather, that an erudite scribe made the error while trying to improve the text.

As for the reference to Seleucus 'Soter' at § 223, after giving him that byname Josephus immediately proceeds to identify him precisely as 'the son of Antiochus the Great' (Antiochus III)—but that Seleucus' byname was not Soter, but, rather, Philopator. We must, therefore, choose here between the byname and the detailed identification—a difficult choice. Recall, in this connection, that the story about Joseph begins after a narrative and documents concerning Antiochus III and ends—shortly after this reference to Seleucus 'Soter'—not only with the death of Seleucus (this time without byname—§ 234), but also with the notice, in § 235, of the death of Ptolemy Epiphanes (180 BCE) and the accession of 'Antiochus surnamed Epiphanes' (175 BCE). Similarly, note that Josephus says (§ 234) that Hyrcanus was active in Transjordan during seven years under Seleucus—which fits Seleucus IV (187–175 BCE) but is impossible for Seleucus III Soter, who reigned only 226—223 BCE. In other words, the context of §§ 223–36 (the end of the story) is definitely that of the sons of Antiochus III, and to allow the appearance of 'Soter' in § 223 to put the end of the story back to the 220s would be unwise. While it does correspond to the earlier references to Ptolemy 'Euergetes', it might be—if not a mere slip—no more than another learned correction meant to bring some consistency into the story.

4. A very specific chronological reason is often given for rejection of Josephus' placement of the Tobiad story. Josephus twice says that Joseph's career lasted twenty-two years (§§ 186, 224), and also reports that Joseph's career was followed by that of his son Hyrcanus, which in turn lasted seven years, during the reign of Seleucus IV, and ended with his suicide upon Antiochus IV's ascent to the throne (§§ 234–6), i.e. in 175 BCE. However, Josephus places the beginning of Joseph's career at the time of the wedding of Ptolemy V and Cleopatra Syra, and that event is placed—by Livy and Porphyry—in 193 BCE; clearly, one cannot fit the Tobiads'

---

[21] And certainly—*pace* Orrieux (1986), 8—there is no justification to point to § 206, where Hyrcanus tells the king that he had been Joseph's benefactor (*euergetēs*), as evidence that the king was in fact named Euergetes; every Hellenistic king was happy to be described in such terms. (Orrieux also refers to § 163 in this connection, but I see no reason.) I owe to Professor Erich Gruen the suggestion that the greater frequency of the name 'Cleopatra' than 'Euergetes' might be significant.

twenty-nine years into 193–175 BCE. Hence, it is argued, Josephus must be confused, so scholars are free to attempt to improve upon his placement of the story.

This argument is methodologically unsound. For Josephus, as opposed to Livy and Porphyry, did not place the royal marriage in 193 BCE; he placed it right at the outset of Ptolemy V's reign, which was in 204 BCE.[22] Josephus has the Fifth Syrian War breaking out already at the end of Ptolemy IV's reign and concluding at the beginning of that of Ptolemy V, and he has the marriage immediately following the Seleucid victory. Note that, in Josephus' narrative, the accounts of the conquest (*Ant.* 12. 129–37) and the marriage-cum-tax-concession (§ 154) are separated only by some documents, which take up no historical time; in §§ 137 and 153 Josephus explicitly brackets the documents as an excursus. The truth of Josephus' chronology of the war, which contradicts that of Polybius, need not concern us here;[23] what is important, for the assessment of Josephus' Tobiad chronology, is that Josephus placed the wedding *c.*204 BCE, and it is irrelevant, in this context, that Livy and Porphyry place the wedding more than a decade later. Now, looked at from our perspective, it is impossible not to be impressed by the simple fact that precisely twenty-nine years separate Ptolemy V's accession to the throne (204 BCE) from that of Antiochus IV (175 BCE). Josephus, it seems, was not at all confused about the placement of the story in this period: although he may have misdated the war and the wedding, he knew exactly which Ptolemaic king he meant. Are we really so sure we know better?

5. In connection with the latter point, we may note that those who would reject Josephus' placement of the story usually accept his data concerning the length of Joseph's and Hyrcanus' careers; consequently, they have invested much energy into finding the precise places in the third century into which their twenty-two and seven years may be fitted.[24] Such scholars also think they know why Josephus misplaced (as they hold) the story in the second century:

[22] See Samuel (1962), 108–14; Walbank (1979*a*), 784–5.

[23] It is, in fact, usually given very short shrift; see e.g. Holleaux (1942), 319 n. 1. The passage does not figure at all in a more recent detailed study of the war's chronology: Taylor (1979), 28–50.

[24] See e.g. the tables in Tcherikover (1959), 130, and Goldstein (1975), 101, also Stark (1852), 415–16 and Stern (1962/3), 43–5 [30–2]. Tcherikover has Joseph's twenty-two years spanning somewhere *c.*230–220 until *c.*205–200; Goldstein, 227/224–205/202; Stark, *c.*229–207; and Stern, *c.*240–218 BCE.

since his source assigned its heroes twenty-nine years which ended with Antiochus' rise to the throne, Josephus must have calculated backwards from 175 BCE. In fact, they argue, the source's data need not be taken to refer to two consecutive periods of twenty-two and seven years; apart from simply positing an error, the usual suggestion is that Josephus telescoped two sources, of which the first dealt with a third-century Joseph ben Tobias and the second with a later member of the family.[25] Such telescoping explains, for example, Josephus' account at the end of *Antiquities* Book 11, where material concerning Sanballat I is combined with material concerning Sanballat III, thus eliding a century;[26] could it not explain the confusion here as well?

The answer, apparently, is 'hardly', precisely because of the differences in comparison with the case in *Antiquities* Book 11. There we have independent epigraphic evidence for the different Sanballats, obvious splicing of sources, and Josephus' obvious ignorance concerning the length of the Persian period, which means he was unaware of the problems he created. In our case, in contrast, we have no evidence for the existence of more than one Joseph or Hyrcanus, no convincing case—as D. Gera has shown—for the use of separate sources,[27] and good evidence, cited below (no. 6), that Josephus was at home with the royal chronologies of the period.

Moreover, it seems clear that Josephus did not find both of his two data, twenty-two and seven years, in his source. Both references to Joseph's twenty-two years seem clearly to have been added by

[25] For this theory, see Bikerman (1938), 29–30. Bikerman made no attempt to distinguish the two sources in detail, presumably depending on Otto and Momigliano, cited in n. 27. However, those theories have the second source begin at § 223 or § 228, which poses a serious difficulty to Bikerman's theory: can we really imagine that the Hyrcanus of §§ 186 ff. is different from the one of §§ 228 ff.?

[26] See Schwartz (1990).

[27] See Gera (1990), 31, 35–6. Similarly Stern, in a more recent discussion of our story, changed its name from 'The Story of Joseph the Tobiad' (as in his 1962/3 article) to 'The Story of the House of Tobias', and emphasized that the whole story has Hyrcanus at its centre: 'The story of Joseph ben Tobias, who is described to a certain degree as a prototype of his son, serves [only] as a sort of background for the praise of his son' (Stern (1982/3), 229). For the main statements of the two-source theory, see Otto (1914), 527–9, and Momigliano (1975), 607–9. Both take §§ 223–36 to be based on a source or sources distinct from that which supplied the preceding material—but §§ 223–4 are a potpourri of details Josephus supplied to bring the reader up to date, §§ 226–7 have nothing to do with the Tobiad story, and §§ 228–9 are basically only a Wiederaufnahme of the narrative broken off at § 222.

Josephus to material supplied by his source. The first such reference, in §186, introduces the birth of Hyrcanus which came 'under the following circumstances'; as has frequently been shown, such introductions by Josephus are usually his own composition, used for splicing in a new source or a new section of a source already in use.[28] Similarly, the second reference to Joseph's twenty-two years (§224) might easily be Josephus' own contribution, for it comes in the midst of a brief but pious eulogy for Joseph which not only conflicts with the mundane tone of the rest of the story[29] but also is sandwiched among a few other odds and ends, which Josephus put in to catch up with parallel events. In contrast, the reference to Hyrcanus' seven-year career very probably was supplied by Josephus' source, not only because seven is a common round number in stories like this, but also, and especially, because the story has been shown to play frequently with motifs from the story of the biblical Joseph, and 'seven years' is standard there.[30]

Our conclusion is that Josephus learned from his source only the length of Hyrcanus' tenure. If he nevertheless states the length of Joseph's, then it must be a result of his own calculation, based upon his assumption, demonstrated above, that the two careers must be fitted into the years between 204 and 175 BCE. In other words, it is not the case that Josephus was led to the reigns of Ptolemy V and Seleucus IV by the chronological data in his source: twenty-nine years leading up to the accession of Antiochus IV. Rather, his certainty that the material applied to those kings led him to generate one of his two main chronological data.[31]

6. On the positive side, note that Josephus, who placed the story after his detailed account of the Fifth Syrian War and Ptolemy Epiphanes' ascent to the throne, was quite well informed about the chronology of Hellenistic kings. At *Ant.* 12. 11, for example, he

[28] See Williamson (1977), 50–5; also Schwartz (1992), 271 n. 76.

[29] As noted by Otto (1914), 529. On the generally secular tone of the story, see Stern (1982/3), 229.

[30] See esp. Gera (1990), 31–3. For 'seven years' in the Joseph story, see Genesis 41; for its general use as a round number, see Bergmann (1938), 364–5. In contrast, twenty-two does not figure at all in Bergmann's article.

[31] Readers who remain unconvinced about leaving the story of the Tobiads in the 2nd cent. may at least appreciate being released from the necessity of finding precisely twenty-two years for Joseph in the third, just as scholars have long abandoned the quest for a reconstruction which can account for all of Josephus' data about the relative ages of the story's personae; these are simply the baggage of romance. See Orrieux (1988), 135–8.

reports that Alexander the Great reigned for twelve years, Ptolemy I Soter for forty-one, and Ptolemy II Philadelphus for thirty-nine; all of these data are correct. Similarly, he knew 200 years went by between Alexander's conquest of Palestine and the beginning of John Hyrcanus' rule (*Ant.* 13. 256),[32] and even that 481 years and three months separated the Babylonian Exile from the coronation of Aristobulos I (ibid. § 301)—these figures too are very precise.[33] Hence, we should be very wary of rejecting Josephus' testimony concerning Hellenistic kings as if it were the result of a massive chronological error.

7. It seems that the real reason for the current unanimity with which scholars reject Josephus' placement of the Tobiad story is merely a common pitfall in the history of scholarship: when a new datum is discovered, scholarly enthusiasm for new combinations allowed by the new find all too often exaggerates its importance and allows it to upset more than its rightful share of previously held views.[34] I refer, in our case, to the 1918 discovery of the Zenon Papyri, which clearly place a rich Tobias in Transjordan, and in contact with the Ptolemaic government, in 259 BCE.[35] This datum was certainly important, in so far as it fits into other evidence for the continuity of the Tobiads.[36] But scholars wanted more: this Tobias had to be the father of Josephus' Joseph ben Tobias, and so the latter's career had to belong to the next decades.[37] However, the fact

[32] This is not at all affected by the discovery of numismatic evidence that Hyrcanus' destruction of Mt. Gerizim, reported here, in fact took place a decade and a half later than Josephus thought; see Barag (1992/3).

[33] In the latter instance, Josephus in fact refers to the Jews' return from Babylonia. However, as the late Prof. Menahem Stern once explained orally, the point of departure here is actually the destruction of the First Temple—which marked the departure into Babylonian captivity—in 586 BCE, which makes more sense than the return from Babylonia, since (*a*) it was the destruction which interrupted Jewish monarchy, and (*b*) the month of the destruction is known, while that of the return from Babylonia is not. Given that correction, and Aristobulus' tenure *c.*104 BCE, the period stated by Josephus is quite accurate.

[34] Cf. Schwartz (1990), 175.

[35] See Tcherikover (1957), no. 1 (259 BCE), also ibid. nos. 2, 4, 5 of 259 and 257 BCE.

[36] For which see esp. Gressmann (1921); Mazar (1957).

[37] The assumption that Zenon's Tobias was the father of Josephus' Joseph, and that the latter—despite Josephus' dating—belonged to the 3rd cent., was promulgated, emphatically, as early as 1920/1: Vincent (1920), esp. 182–202; Gressmann (1921), 667–8. Vincent (1920), 200 n. 1, compares the Zenon Papyri's correction of Josephus' dating of the Tobiads to the Elephantine Papyri's correction of Josephus' dating of Sanballat *et al.* at the end of Joseph. *Ant.* Book 11. But although the

is that we know of Tobiads for centuries prior to the third century
BCE and of 'sons of Tobias' in the second century BCE as well (*Ant.*
12. 239–40), in the same region and with the same general
characteristics (see n. 36), so the discovery of epigraphic evidence
for any particular Tobias cannot, by itself, pin down the dating of
one mentioned in the literature.

8. Finally, a recent numismatic observation of possible interest:
according to Georges Le Rider, after Antiochus III conquered
Coele-Syria and Phoenicia, the Attic standard did not supplant
the Ptolemaic standard there as might have been expected; the two
standards coexisted and soon enough the Seleucids too began
minting there according to the Ptolemaic standard.[38] Le Rider did
not make much of this point, but it seems obvious that it could well
be explained by a reconstruction which has the region remaining
fiscally Ptolemaic in this period—as Josephus said.

A few years after the great J. G. Droysen repeated without any
doubt at all Josephus' account of Cleopatra's dowry,[39] J. C. C.
Hofmann—citing and building upon eighteenth-century predecessors[40]—opened his 1835 Erlangen dissertation on the Sixth Syrian
War with the following thesis:

Coeles Syriae et Phoenices et Palaestinae incolae post foedus ab Antiocho
Magno cum Ptolemaeo Epiphane initum nec Syriae neque Aegypti regibus
satis obnoxii ab Antiocho Epiphane ad pristinam obedientiam redacti
sunt.[41]

Hofmann supported this thesis, in the following pages, by a review
of the evidence for Antiochus III's conquest of Palestine and for
subsequent Seleucid rule of Palestine, on the one hand, and of
Josephus' evidence for Cleopatra's dowry and the Tobiads, on the
other. The result is, as stated, that the situation of Coele-Syria etc.

scholarly world reacted similarly, the cases are in fact very different; see above, at
nn. 26–7.

[38] Le Rider (1993), 54.

[39] Droysen (1894), 360 (first published in 1831).

[40] See Prideaux (1808), 186, where Josephus' story is said to be 'a clear proof of
the contrary' (of the notion, based upon Polybius and 2 Maccabees, that the
Seleucids ruled Coele-Syria throughout this period); also Jahn (1800), 394–7.

[41] Hofmann (1835), 1: 'The inhabitants of Coele-Syria, Phoenicia and Palestine,
which after the treaty between Antiochus the Great and Ptolemy Epiphanes had been
sufficiently subject neither to the kings of Syria nor to those of Egypt, were reduced
by Antiochus Epiphanes to full submission.'

was ambiguous during the reigns of Ptolemy Epiphanes and Seleucus IV. It was this lack of clarity and certainty which would make for the appearance of pro-Ptolemaic and pro-Seleucid factions there, and, eventually, for the suicide of Hyrcanus, a prime supporter of the Ptolemies, when Antiochus Epiphanes attempted to bring Seleucid clarity to the situation.[42]

The present paper was born, basically, out of a sense that modern historians have, in this case, been too quick to think they know better than their colleague of nineteen hundred years ago. For it seems to me that, with all due respect for the Zenon Papyri, nothing much has changed, or should have changed, since the days of Droysen and Hofmann.[43] While the situation of Coele-Syria which they posited was less than clear, and while, given the textual difficulties, we too cannot be entirely certain about the placement of Josephus' story of the Tobiads, nevertheless, there are in the real world historical situations which are less than clear, and there are historical questions which historians can answer with less than total certainty. With regard to such questions, it is imprudent to run to discard the testimony of our sources. Perhaps today, in other words, almost eighty years after the discovery of the Zenon Papyri, historians might take a new look at the subject and, while leaving those papyri in the third century, where they were found, leave Josephus' story where he put it—in the second, and receive with more of an open mind his account of Cleopatra's dowry. If that will help explain Ptolemaic passivity, Livy 42. 29. 5, and Josephus, *War* I. 31, so much the better.

---

[42] See Joseph. *Ant.* 12. 236. Supporters of Ptolemy are also mentioned at Joseph. *War* I. 31–2 and in passages from Porphyry preserved by Jerome, *In Danielem* 11. 13–21 (= *GLAJJ* ii nos. 464l and 464n).

[43] And Wilcken (above, n. 7). The fragmentary inscription published by Isaac (1991), which he kindly brought to my attention after the lecture on which this chapter is based, does not seem to change anything in this context. Even if it more clearly indicated that the 'Sidonians of Jamnia' had assisted Antiochus III and IV, there is no obvious relationship between that and the question whether the tribute of Coele-Syria had been going to Egypt—just as, for that matter, there is no clear relationship between Ptolemy V's *bon mot*, as to where he might be able to get money for a campaign to Coele-Syria (Diodorus 29. 29 and Jerome, *In Danielem* 11.20 = *GLAJJ* ii. no. 464m), and the thesis offered in this paper. As long as one admits Syria was ruling Coele-Syria at the time, such evidence as this does not affect the question of tribute allocation.

PART II

Social Integration?

5

Jews, Christians and others in Palestine: The Evidence from Eusebius

BENJAMIN ISAAC

Demography is one of those topics which are as important as they are frustrating to those interested in numbers in the ancient world. The absence of information is such that modern specialists consider any effort at serious study an idle undertaking. Palestine is known to have been populated by pagans, Jews, and Christians in the Roman and Byzantine periods. I shall not be dealing here with problems of social identity, nor will I attempt to reach any conclusions about numbers, which would seem an unprofitable enterprise in the absence of hard facts. My aim is to raise a related question that should at least be asked, even if no clear-cut answer can be given at this stage. What was the distribution of the various population groups in Palestine: pagans, Jews, and Christians? The situation in the cities has been discussed in several works and there are various sources. Avi-Yonah is, indeed, confident enough to give concrete numbers.[1] Even so we do not know much about the physical aspects. It is generally admitted that larger cities such as Caesarea had mixed populations, but this is information which derives from literary sources and we have no clear idea of what it meant in practice.[2] The excavations at Sepphoris give us a glimpse of a surprisingly mixed city centre in a town which the sources might

---

[1] Avi-Yonah (1962), 16–20. He asserts that, after the Bar Kokhba war, there were fifty-six Jewish communities (i.e. non-mixed villages) in Galilee; see also 133, 224, 241 f. Id. (1977), ch. 3, 'Population', pp. 212–21, esp. 219–21: 'Numbers'. Alon (1980–4), 750–7, tends less to cite specific numbers, but he is fairly confident that he can make valid statements about the relative strength of the various communities. Abel (1967), does not discuss these questions at all. The most recent treatment, Schwartz (1986), covers southern Palestine: Schwartz seems to allow for the existence of mixed communities, for instance in the area of Beth Guvrin (97, 107).

[2] For Caesarea, see now Vann (1992) and several papers in Humphrey (1995).

have led us to believe was overwhelmingly Jewish.[3] Other important towns, such as Lydda and Beth Guvrin, have been explored less, and we cannot know whether systematic excavations, where possible, would add new information or raise new questions. There is, in any case, a clear awareness among scholars that most Roman and Byzantine cities had mixed populations to some extent at least.[4]

Even less is known about the situation in the countryside. Did the various groups live together in the same villages, or did each have their own villages?[5] To what extent were there regional patterns that can be traced? How did these develop over time? These questions are essential to any effort at understanding social relationships. It is usually assumed that, while most cities had mixed populations, the villages were monocultures inhabited by representatives of a single ethnic and religious group.[6] Yet it must be admitted that little thought has been given to the nature of the evidence for this assumption and its implications. It is, in principle, quite possible that many villages had a mixed population. The distribution of pagans and Christians, for example, must have depended on the manner in which Christianity spread in the rural parts of Palestine during the late Roman and Byzantine periods. If conversion took place more often on an individual than a group basis, many villages must inevitably have been inhabited by both unconverted pagans and converted Christians. It is usually asserted—and there is good evidence to support this—that the Jewish population of Palestine was considerably reduced by the time of the Muslim conquest.

[3] Alon (1980–4), 751: '. . . Jews *were* the overwhelming majority in those towns.' Avi-Yonah (1977), 218: 'Sepphoris-Diocaesarea in the fifth century was still purely Jewish.' A historical monograph, Miller (1984), does not discuss the presence of gentiles in the city. Miller seems to assume that there were no Christian inhabitants there before they are actually attested in the 5th cent. (p. 4 with n. 19). For the recent excavations: Meyers, Netzer, and Meyers (1986), 4–19; Netzer and Weiss (1994).

[4] Alon (1980–4). For Lydda, Oppenheimer (1988), 115–36; Schwartz (1991).

[5] Sartre (1991), 389 f.; Millar (1993), 348–51, 374–7, are cautious and do not express an opinion on the distribution of social groups in rural Palestine.

[6] Avi-Yonah (1962) does not say so explicitly, but the assumption is implicit throughout, for instance, on pp. 132–4; in Avi-Yonah (1977), 215–19, he refers frequently to 'Jewish settlements', 'Jewish villages'. He assumes (215, 219) that the Roman government made specific, regional decisions about the ethnic composition of the population. There is no evidence that the Roman authorities tried to do this, or that it could have if it wanted. Incidentally, on p. 217 Avi-Yonah assumes that the units mentioned in the *Notitia Dignitatum* were still ethnic in character. This is erroneous, for the old ethnic names may still be used for units manned with locally recruited troops. Alon (1980–4) discusses the distribution of the population exclusively in regional terms.

Since the population as a whole saw a huge increase during the Byzantine period[7] we have to consider the possibility that the Jewish population decreased less in absolute numbers than in proportion to the vastly increased gentile population. Again, we must ask how Christianization worked in Palestine. Were entire villages taken over? Was there a gradual, individual process at work? One point to note briefly at this stage is the significance of synagogues and churches in rural settlements. Villages which boasted of such buildings were not necessarily inhabited by representatives of one group only.

It is not the aim of this paper to discuss these problems in general, but rather to focus on a unique source which, I claim, is not sufficiently understood and is worth closer scrutiny, namely the *Onomasticon* of biblical place-names by Eusebius. This is a mine of information about Palestine in the Roman and Byzantine periods of a kind which does not exist for any other part of the empire. It is unique because it is the only text which is concerned solely and consistently with regional matters. It contains more than 900 lemmata, which refer to twenty-nine cities and hundreds of villages. Eusebius mentions the location of settlements along twenty roads and knows of the presence of military garrisons at eleven sites. His aim in the work is to focus not primarily on the cities, but on biblical sites, most of which were villages and small places. Thus while cities regularly serve as a point of reference, the setting of the work is essentially rural, a rare feature in classical texts. Of course the work has been studied intensively by scholars interested in the Holy Land,[8] but it is not a book which has drawn much attention from historical geographers of the Roman empire. Yet it is a rare source, giving us an insight into the level of detailed geographical knowledge available locally in a provincial capital rather than at the centre of the Roman empire. It has been cited most frequently for its information about administrative matters and specific sites, but

---

[7] This may be seen in any of the publications of the 'Archaeological Survey of Israel', published by the Israel Antiquities Authority. The increase in settlement in the area between Lydda and Jerusalem is discussed by Fischer, Isaac, and Roll (1996), part V, pp. 301 ff.

[8] The work is used extensively in all the works about the historical geography of the Holy Land, cited above. Specific studies: Klostermann (1904, introd., pp. vii–xxxiv; Kubitschek (1905), 119–27; Noth (1943), 32–63; Barnes (1975), 412–15. Matters of method: Avi-Yonah (1977), 127–9; criticized by Isaac and Roll (1982), 11–13.

there is little genuine discussion about the nature of the document as such, the sources which Eusebius used, and his geographical methods. In the following pages I shall attempt to show that the *Onomasticon* if properly interpreted has more to tell us about the distribution of population groups in Palestine in the third century than it has been given credit for by most scholars.[9]

Among the large number of villages that Eusebius mentions there is a fairly small group which he qualifies in some manner. Thus he describes thirty-three as 'very big villages' (μεγίστη κώμη) and three as 'big villages' (κώμη μεγάλη). He refers to eleven 'villages of Jews' of which seven are 'very big'. Three villages are inhabited 'entirely by Christians' (ὅλη Χριστιανῶν). Two of these are also 'very big' villages. Eusebius further mentions four 'villages of Samaritans' (κώμη Σαμαρέων) or villages 'founded by the Samaritans from Babylonia'.[10] In the entire work he does not mention any specifically 'pagan' villages. The term (τὰ ἔθνη) only occurs when he refers to three rural sanctuaries as being 'still venerated by the pagans'.[11] Galilee is also described as 'belonging to the gentiles', but that derives from Matthew and thus indirectly from Isaiah.[12]

The first question to be asked is why so few villages are assigned to specific groups: only eighteen out of the hundreds of villages which Eusebius mentions in his work. There are several possible explanations. It could be assumed that he provides random information, correct in itself, but not significant in its relationship to the other villages which he also mentions in his work. If this were the case nothing could be deduced from negative information, from the fact that he does *not* assign a village to a specific group. In other words, he describes a few villages as Christian while there were many others, also mentioned in the work, which he could and

---

[9] I have discussed the administrative information contained in Eusebius in a paper, 'Eusebius and the Geography of Roman Provinces', in Kennedy (1996), 153–67. I will discuss these matters systematically and extensively in a joint book with Aharon Oppenheimer.

[10] The expression ταύτην ἔκτισαν οἱ ἀπὸ Βαβυλῶνος Σαμαρεῖται is almost certainly just a reference to 2 Kings 17: 30. An interesting misunderstanding is the village of 'Nerigel' (138. 16), which Eusebius derives from the mention of the god Nergal in the text of Kings. However, Socho (see below) was a genuine Samaritan village. For Bainith (58. 3) he also seems to have in mind a specific village called Baithanne. Eusebius is critical of the Samaritan tradition regarding Mt. Gerizim and Ebal (Gaibal) (64. 12).

[11] The oak of Mamre: 6. 8; Mt. Hermon: 20. 11; Galgala: 64. 24.

[12] Γαλιλαία τῶν ἐθνῶν (116. 7; 120. 3); Matt. 14. 5. 3; Is. 8. 23. 5.

should have included among the Christian villages. His failure to do so could have been due to inconsistency or ignorance. If we are to accept the proposition that Eusebius' information about Jewish and Christian villages was the result of an entirely random selection nothing further could be deduced from the material, except that Eusebius' description might be true for the relevant settlements. However, this is not a likely hypothesis, for it does not agree with other aspects of Eusebius' *Onomasticon*. As I have argued elsewhere, there is a clear and demonstrable pattern in the references to garrisons, roads, and city territories, all of which represent valued and consistent contemporary information.[13] While this is an obvious fact in the case of the garrisons and roads, the conclusion regarding city territories is based on a rather complex argument which cannot be used in support of considerations about other aspects of the work. Nevertheless it can safely be said that Eusebius, where he provides contemporary information, does so in a consistent manner.

A second claim could be that Eusebius does not provide a representative sample, since he only refers to villages identified with biblical places. This too is an unsatisfactory explanation, for the number of places which he mentions is still very large in absolute terms. Even if he gives the names of only one-fifth of the villages existing in Palestine in his time, the ratio would not change drastically. Among thousands of settlements only fifteen would have been Christian. A third possibility is to assume that the information is representative in some way and requires an explanation in its own right.

Before we pursue this further we ought to consider whether there is any correlation between the evidence from Eusebius and other material. Apart from the evidence in Eusebius, what else can we know about villages? We should consider other written sources, notably rabbinic literature, and the question of what we can deduce from the presence in a settlement of an early church or synagogue as regards the composition of the population.

The first question is whether places which Eusebius knows as Jewish are mentioned as such in rabbinic sources. In any comparison between information in rabbinic material and Eusebius it is important to note that the latter almost certainly represents a narrow

[13] Kennedy (1996).

time-span. Since his information about cities and army units derives exclusively from the late third or the early fourth century, the same may be assumed for his statements about villages. Rabbinic literature, on the other hand, developed over centuries.

The first thing we must note here, then, is that there is little correlation between Jewish villages recorded by Eusebius and those occurring in the rabbinic texts. Of ten villages described as Jewish by Eusebius, only four are mentioned in rabbinic literature: Kefar Dagon,[14] Naaran,[15] En Geddi, and Naveh in Arabia.[16] There are also villages which occur in rabbinic sources and which Eusebius mentions without describing them as Jewish: Mikhmas,[17] Zoar,[18] Haifa,[19] and many sites in the north. We may add that Jericho is mentioned in rabbinic literature as a place typically inhabited by gentiles, as opposed to nearby Naaran.[20] This approach clearly does not get us any further, for there are good possible explanations as to why there might be little correlation between the two sources: rabbinic literature does not single out places inhabited exclusively by Jews, but refers to them for other reasons, apart from the exceptional passage reflecting the reality of the fourth to fifth century which mentions a number of pairs of neighbouring gentile and Jewish places: Halamish and Naveh, Sussita (Hippos) and Tiberias, Castra and Haifa, Jericho and Naaran, Lod and Ono. Although of varied importance these places were apparently all remarkable for the fact that they were predominantly Jewish or

---

[14] t. Ohol. 3. 9.

[15] Lev. R. 23. 5 (ed. Margulies, p. 533); Lam. R. (Buber) 1. 17, p. 91; Cant. R. 2. 2 (5). Naaran is mentioned also in later sources, discussed by Mayerson (1984), 51–6 = (1994), 216–21; the synagogue found there dates to the 6th cent.: *NEAEHL* iii. 1075 f.

[16] See the rabbinic sources cited in the previous note. For the remains of a synagogue at Naveh, see below.

[17] *On.* 132. 3: Large village. m. Men. 8: 1, indicating that it produced fine flour. Note also a Hebrew inscription on a coffin from the village: *ZDPV* (1914), 135 f. (*CIJ* ii. 1191).

[18] t. Sheb. 15: 7, ed. Lieberman, p. 198. Near the site a Jewish cemetery has been found, cf. *TIR* 263, s.v. Zoora; Schwartz (1986), 111 f.; Sartre (1993), 133–7, nos. 150, 106. Near Zoar was Mahoza which is mentioned frequently in the Babatha archive; cf. Lewis (1989). At that time (early 2nd cent.) it was inhabited by both Jews and Nabataeans.

[19] Haifa: Euseb. *On.* 108. 31; rabbinic sources cited in n. 14.

[20] Loc. cit. Note the presence of a group of important sages recorded in t. Ber. 4. 16, ed. Lieberman, p. 21. This shows that Jericho was either not entirely gentile, or not at all times, yet another indication that we should not blindly rely on sources which seem to suggest that specific places were inhabited exclusively by one group.

gentile. There is also an interesting reference to Kefar Nahum, described in one source as a place where there was a presence of 'minim' in the period of the Bar Kokhba revolt.[21] Apparently it was inhabited by Jews, interspersed with sectarian elements. The village is known for its synagogue, the date of whose erection is disputed.[22] New Testament Capernaum is also mentioned in a well-known and particularly relevant statement made by Epiphanius in his story about the *comes* Joseph. According to Epiphanius, writing in the last quarter of the fourth century, Joseph obtained permission from Constantine to build churches 'in the cities and villages of the Jews, where nobody has been able to build churches, because there are no Hellenes, Samaritans or Christians among them. This remains the case particularly in Tiberias, in Diocaesarea, which is now called Sepphoris, in Nazareth, and in Capernaum, that there are no gentiles among them.'[23] It must be stressed that this is a dubious source, but, taken at face value, it would confirm that the absence of gentiles in settlements inhabited by Jews is the exception rather than the rule. Epiphanius here mentions the two main cities of Galilee and two villages in which the presence of Christians would have been particularly desirable, from his point of view, because of their prominence in the Gospels. In any case, these two explicit contemporary statements about the ethnic and religious separation or mix in Palestinian towns and villages support rather than contradict the assumption that the different elements of the population usually lived together in the same settlements.

When we consider the presence of synagogues in rural settlements we should, of course, refer only to those firmly dated to the period under consideration. This excludes many places, for the majority of synagogues are dated to a much later period. Again, this

---

[21] Eccles. R. 1. 8 (4). Euseb. *On.* 120. 2 merely mentions that it is an extant village in 'Galilee of the Gentiles'.

[22] Hüttenmeister and Reeg (1977), i. 260–9; Taylor (1994), 'The question of the synagogue', 290 f. with up-to-date bibliography and discussion. If the synagogue dates to the 4th–5th cent., this may not be relevant for the period to which Eusebius refers.

[23] Epiphanius, *Panarion* 30. 4–12 (*GCS* 25. 1. 347): κόμητα γὰρ αὐτὸν κατέστησε, φήσας αὐτῷ αἰτεῖν πάλιν ὃ βούλεται· ὁ δὲ οὐδὲν ᾐτήσατο πλὴν τοῦτο μέγιστον χάρισμα τυχεῖν παρὰ τοῦ βασιλέως τὸ ἐπιτραπῆναι [καὶ] διὰ προστάγματος βασιλικοῦ οἰκοδομῆσαι Χριστοῦ ἐκκλησίας ἐν ταῖς πόλεσι καὶ κώμαις τῶν Ἰουδαίων, ἔνθα τις οὐδέποτε ἴσχυσεν προστήσασθαι ἐκκλησίας διὰ τὸ μήτε Ἕλληνα μήτε Σαμαρείτην μήτε Χριστιανὸν μέσον αὐτῶν εἶναι. τοῦτο δὲ μάλιστα ἐν Τιβεριάδι καὶ ἐν Διοκαισαρείᾳ τῇ καὶ Σεπφουρὶν καὶ ἐν Ναζαρὲτ καὶ ἐν Καπερναοὺμ φυλάσσεται ⟨τὸ⟩ παρ' αὐτοῖς [τοῦ] μὴ εἶναι ἀλλόεθνον.

approach is not very productive. Synagogues have been found in villages which Eusebius mentions, but does not describe as Jewish, for instance Apheka/Fiq,[24] Maon in Judaea,[25] and Gabatha (Gevat).[26] Kana[27] may also belong to this category.[28] Did Eusebius not know these were Jewish settlements? Or does he not describe them as Jewish because they had a mixed population? There are quite a few villages which Eusebius describes as Jewish for which we do have contemporary corroborating evidence: Anim (Anaia),[29] Carmel(?),[30] En Rimmon (Eremmon),[31] Eshtemo(a),[32] En Geddi,[33] Nineve/Nave.[34] In the case of the Samaritan villages this may be true for the village of Socho (modern Shuweika).[35] There are villages which Eusebius describes as Jewish for which we have no other evidence, literary or archaeological, of their Jewishness in

[24] Hüttenmeister and Reeg (1977), i. 2–4 (2nd–3rd cent.).

[25] *On.* 130. 12; the synagogue: *NEAEHI* iii. 942–4 f. (4th–7th cent.).

[26] *On.* 78. 3: village in the territory of Diocaesarea. Hüttenmeister and Reeg (1977), i. 137 f. mention the discovery there of a pillar with a menorah and a stone with Jewish symbols. Hüttenmeister notes that this does not prove there was a synagogue, which is true, but it does demonstrate a Jewish presence in the area.

[27] In the case of Kana it is impossible to say whether a synagogue was indeed discovered at the site which Eusebius had in mind since there are various places with related names and problems in identification: Schmitt (1995), 115 f.

[28] For Kapharnaoum (Kefar Nahum) see below. Khorazin may also be a special case. Eusebius, *On.* 174. 23, describes it as 'now deserted'. The excavations are said to have confirmed that the settlement with its synagogue were partially destroyed in the early 4th cent.: *NEAEHL* i. 301–4. The Babylonian Talmud refers to it, but in a context related to the period of the Second Temple: b. Men. 85a.

[29] Euseb. *On.* 26. 9–13; *NEAEHL* i. 62, s.v. Horvat 'Anim (4th–7th cent.). Note that there are two neighbouring villages of this name. The other, a smaller village, mentioned also below, is described as Christian by Eusebius, ibid.; *Mart.Pal.* 10. 2 (*GCS* 9, p. 931) thus notes the two villages of Anaia as one Jewish and one Christian. As pointed out to me by Susan Weingarten, it might be relevant that he does *not* say this about the two villages of Socho (156. 18), where an underground hideaway has been found (upper site) as well as a church (lower site); see references in *TIR* 234, s.v. Socho I.

[30] *On.* 92. 20: Jewish; 118. 5: garrison. Remains of a synagogue at Kh. Kirmil, possibly brought from there to Yatta: Hüttenmeister and Reeg (1977), i. 253.

[31] *NEAEHL* iv. 1284 (3rd–4th cent.).

[32] *NEAEHL* ii. 423–6; Hüttenmeister and Reeg (1977), i. 117–21 (4th–5th cent.).

[33] *NEAEHL* ii. 399–409 (late 2nd/early 3rd cent. till Islamic conquest); Hüttenmeister and Reeg (1977), i. 108–114. For Naveh in talmudic sources, see above.

[34] Hüttenmeister and Reeg (1977), i. 336–9. Full references in Reeg (1989), 433–5; Schmitt (1995), 266. See also above, n. 15.

[35] It is mentioned in the Samaritan Chronicle, *REJ* 44 (1902), 225–7. Abel (1967), ii. 467 s.v. Socho (3); Hüttenmeister and Reeg (1977), ii. 668. Note that this is a different site from the two villages of the same name, mentioned above, n. 29.

this period: Akkaron/Eqron,[36] Ietta,[37] Thala,[38] Dabeira.[39] The same is true for the Samaritan village of Tharsila in Batanea (*On.* 102. 4).[40]

It is clear therefore, that we cannot solve these problems by simply combining or mixing the archaeological evidence with that from Eusebius, even when the two refer to the same period. Other literary sources are sometimes helpful, but the rabbinic material can be no more a basis for systematic comparison with the evidence in Eusebius than the archaeological remains. What we can do is to keep an open mind in considering the material and watch out for indications of the existence of mixed communities, e.g. in rabbinic and patristic sources, through the distribution of dated inscriptions.

My suggestion is that the overwhelming majority of villages had a mixed population: pagan, Jewish, Christian, and Samaritan. Eusebius would have considered this the norm and found it worth mentioning only if a settlement was purely Jewish, Christian, or Samaritan; purely pagan settlements would have been of no interest to him. This, if true, is important. Jews and gentiles would have lived side by side both in the cities and in the countryside. The parallel midrashic sources which mention well-known pairs of neighbouring settlements inhabited by gentiles and Jews respectively have been cited above.[41] It could be argued that the point is emphasized because this was not the usual pattern. When did this pattern develop? After one of the two revolts? In any case, around 300 CE very few villages could be described as homogeneous. It will be clear that Eusebius—whatever the precise date of the *Onomasticon*—wrote before the Christianization of Palestine gained decisive momentum. This is not to deny the impact of the Jewish

---

[36] *On.* 22. 9. This is an ancient site where extensive excavations of the biblical period have been undertaken (*NEAEHL* iii. 1051–9, s.v. Miqne, Tel). These have not produced information on the Late Roman/Byzantine village; cf. *TIR*, p. 56, s.v. Accaron.

[37] Ietta (*On.* 108. 8) or Iutta, modern Yatta, was a bishopric by 450 (ACO ii, 1, 2 (p. 103): Μαρκιανὸς ὁ εὐλαβέστατος ἐπίσκοπος Ἰωτάνης; ii, 2, 2 (p. 70)), cf. Abel (1967), ii. 366 f., s.v. Jouttah; *TIR* 155. A church has been noted there, but no synagogue.

[38] Thala almost certainly should be identified with the excavated site of Tel Halif, a flourishing settlement in the Late Roman and Byzantine periods: *NEAEHL* ii. 558 f.

[39] *On.* 78. 5–7 (Dabaritta). A church, but no synagogue is reported to have been found there, cf. *TIR* 106.

[40] Avi-Yonah (1976), 100: modern Tsil?

[41] Above, n. 15. Two of the five Jewish settlements mentioned in these sources are also mentioned by Eusebius as Jewish.

presence in Galilee in this period or afterwards. If this situation continued into the following centuries it has consequences for our understanding of the presence of synagogues in rural settlements. Synagogues clearly provide evidence of a prosperous Jewish presence in villages where they are found, but they do not prove the absence of gentiles in such communities.

6

Where were the Jews of the Diaspora buried?

DAVID NOY

It is generally accepted that in the first centuries BCE and CE the dead in the city of Rome and in most of the Roman empire were almost invariably cremated,[1] although other practices were followed on the fringes of the empire, e.g. embalming and mummification in Egypt, secondary burial in ossuaries in Judaea. In the second century CE, starting in the city of Rome in the time of Trajan and Hadrian and gradually moving outwards into the provinces, there was a drastic change of practice: cremation was replaced by inhumation. From the third century, inhumation was the norm almost everywhere. The change is well documented, although no wholly satisfactory explanation has been offered: an alteration of fashion seems more plausible than any fundamental revision of religious beliefs.[2]

There are isolated examples of inhumation in the 'cremation period' at Rome.[3] M. Varro, who died in 26 BCE, appears to have been buried in an earthenware sarcophagus 'in the Pythagorean style'.[4] In the Vatican necropolis, four inhumation graves were found which date from some time between the reign of Vespasian and the mid-second century, and the 'Tomb of the Egyptians' (Tomb 2, designed almost entirely for inhumation) may have a

I am grateful to Dr V. Hope for discussion during the preparation of this paper.

[1] e.g. Nock (1932), 323–4.

[2] Nock (1932). Turcan (1958) stresses the continuity of inhumation among e.g. the Etruscans and in Asia Minor, and the philosophical ideas which made it more attractive in the 2nd cent.

[3] Toynbee (1971), 113: two 1st-cent. CE loculi in the Tomb of the Scipios. Ibid. 117: a 1st-cent. BCE chamber-tomb on the Via Caelimontana which seems to have been used for inhumation first and then for cremation. Cf. Davies (1977), 17; Morris (1992), 43. Nock (1932), 323, refers to some possibly Augustan sarcophagi. Pliny, *HN* 7. 54. 189, states that Sulla (d. 78 BCE) was the first member of the gens Cornelia to be cremated. Statius, *Silvae* 5. 1. 226–7, says that Domitian's secretary Abascantus decided to have his wife inhumed rather than cremated.

[4] Pliny, *HN* 35. 160: 'fictilibus soliis condi'.

similar date and indicate the wish of a group of immigrants to maintain the practice of inhumation.[5] At Pompeii, one inhumation was found.[6] It is possible that some dating of graves has been done by archaeologists on the assumption that inhumation was not practised at this period: inhumations, which may be more difficult to date than cremations anyway, would automatically be assigned to a later period unless there is evidence to the contrary.[7] Morris (1992: 45–6) acknowledges that columbaria (buildings with niches for large numbers of funerary urns, usually operated by *collegia* (clubs) or by *familiae* of slaves and ex-slaves) were only available to a minority,[8] but concludes 'that cremation was probably virtually the only rite used at Rome in the first century AD'.

Outside Rome itself, the predominance of cremation was certainly never absolute. For example, in some parts of Sicily (e.g. Lipari, Messina, Agrigento), inhumation was the usual practice in the first and second centuries CE; there may have been a tendency for the rich to use cremation and the poor inhumation.[9] In some parts of Gaul, too, inhumation was practised on a significant scale in the first and second centuries.[10] At Naples, inhumation was normal in the Augustan period.[11]

It should be added that knowledge of what happened to the very poor is extremely limited. The poor may in some cases have been able to use the claims of patronage or family relationship to get spaces in the tombs of the better-off, but there must have been huge numbers of people with no access to the sorts of grave which archaeology usually discovers. In the city of Rome, common pits

[5] Toynbee and Ward Perkins (1956), 51–5, 145–8; cf. Morris (1992), 57–9. The Tomb of the Egyptians may, however, be of a later date, after the general change to inhumation. One of the four inhumation graves has a libation-tube and an altar-like structure, and is presumably pagan; the others have no indication of religious affiliation.

[6] At tomb 33 in the necropolis outside the Porta di Stabia; recorded by M. della Corte in *NS* (1916), 302.

[7] Morris (1992), 62, notes that cremations often provide datable urns whereas inhumations without grave-goods provide no internal dating clues at all. Ashby (1907), 83, refers to the finding at Tavolato on the road to Marino (near the Via Latina) of 'many late burials, the bodies being covered with pent roofs which bore stamps of 123 AD'. Presumably the use of inhumation is what caused him to reject the idea that the burials themselves might be datable to soon after 123.

[8] Ashby (1907), 26, mentions a columbarium on the Via Latina with some 'poorer inhumation graves', but it is not clear if these were contemporary.

[9] Wilson (1990), 128–36.

[10] Morris (1992), 50.

[11] Audin (1960), 322.

(*puticuli*) south of the Esquiline Gate were used for the bodies of the poor at least until the time of Augustus.[12] Corpses also seem to have been thrown into the moat by the *Agger*; in 1876, Lanciani found a mass of remains which he thought could represent at least 24,000 bodies.[13] Patterson (1992: 16) suggests that the use of inhumation rather than cremation indicates that those buried were either the victims of epidemics or were too poor to afford the 'standard funerary customs of the time'. Such pits were probably used in Italian towns too, although there may have been a change to mass cremation of the poor in the first century CE.[14] Martial 8. 75 describes what happens to the body of a relatively poor man (he does however own one slave): 'the unhappy pyre (*rogus*) receives a thousand such.' Bodel (1994: 114 n. 194) suggests that the impracticability of providing enough *puticuli* for the bodies of the poor actually motivated the change to cremation in their case.

At the Isola Sacra, the necropolis of Portus, scattered among the carefully arranged house-tombs of the prosperous were unmarked graves, graves marked only by amphorae, and burials in large wine jars. The bodies were usually cremated. Many of the adjacent elaborate tombs date from the period of transition from cremation to inhumation.[15]

According to a late source, Nerva paid a burial allowance of HS 250 to the Roman plebs. It is not known if this practice continued after his death; its institution suggests a recognition of the problem of how the poor were to obtain decent burial.[16] Joining a burial *collegium* was not an option available to those who did not have enough to pay a monthly subscription.

Graves which now appear unmarked were of course not necessarily so originally; they may have had markers made of perishable material, e.g. wood. Failure to mark a grave, or the use of what appear to be low-cost burial methods, do not *necessarily* indicate the

---

[12] Bodel (1994), 38–54 discusses the evidence and the excavations of Lanciani. He believes that the area which Maecenas turned into gardens had already ceased to be used for corpses, but that bodies were being disposed of elsewhere in the area; hence the reference to 'a field sad with white bones' in Horace, *Sat.* 1. 8. 14–16.

[13] Lanciani (1888), 64–7; Davies (1977), 17; Hopkins (1983), 208.

[14] Morris (1992), 42.

[15] Toynbee (1971), 101–2.

[16] Degrassi (1962); Hopkins (1983), 211. Degrassi believes that it was abolished by Trajan as part of his retrenchment programme.

poverty of the deceased or the commentators; there may be other reasons for avoiding funerary ostentation.[17]

For the Jews of the Diaspora, three types of burial arrangement were possible, each of which may be applicable to different times and places:

1. They were buried in the communities where they had lived, in their own burial areas.
2. They were buried in the communities where they had lived, in burial areas used by people of any religious or ethnic group.
3. Their remains were transported to Palestine for burial.

It seems that the third option was not used by European Jews. Aristobulus II, having been exiled from Judaea, was poisoned in 49 BCE after having been sent by Julius Caesar from Rome to Syria, and his corpse was preserved in honey and later sent back by Mark Antony for burial in a Hasmonean tomb;[18] however, he was not really a Jew of the Diaspora, but only a temporary exile in special circumstances. Epitaphs from Jerusalem and Jaffa in the first centuries BCE and CE name people who originated in the Diaspora, e.g. the family of Nicanor of Alexandria at Jerusalem. The epitaphs of Vitus of Alexandria at Tiberias and Abraham of Pharbaithos (in the eastern Nile Delta) at Khirbet Hebra are undated, and are probably of the second century CE or later, like those of various Egyptians at Jaffa.[19] However, none of these provide certain evidence of people who lived in the Diaspora and were buried in Palestine; they may have moved to Palestine during their lifetime.[20] The only European Jew involved seems to be the proselyte Miriam of Delos.[21]

Gafni (1981: 99) believes that the first known example of the remains of a Diaspora Jew being brought to Palestine (probably Beth She'arim) is that of Huna the Exilarch in the time of R. Judah the Prince. During the third century CE, burial at Beth She'arim seems to have been considered desirable for some Jews in Asia

---

[17] Cannon (1989) provides a reminder that the simplicity of a tomb does not necessarily correlate with the poverty of its occupant; see further below.

[18] Josephus, *War* I. 184; *Ant.* 14. 124.

[19] *JIGRE* 145–53.

[20] Gafni (1981), 98. Jews buried at Rome who are recorded as coming from e.g. Aquileia or Mauretania are much more likely to have been immigrants to the city than to have been taken there after their deaths, so it would be wrong to assume that Jews of Diaspora origin buried in Palestine were only taken there after their deaths.

[21] *CIJ* ii. 1390.

Minor, but it would have been logistically impossible for Diaspora communities to send all their dead there. Rabbinic teaching on the desirability of burial in Palestine (as an expiation of sin and as a means of hastening resurrection) seems to date only from the third century.[22] Thus, the practice of burial in Palestine, which cannot have been an option for most Diaspora Jews anyway, seems to have developed only at the time when the Jewish catacombs of Rome were being used most heavily.

From the late second century CE, the first option was standard for the Jews of Rome, using catacombs which appear to have been exclusively Jewish,[23] and methods which were similar but not entirely identical to those used by contemporary Christians (and pagans). However, the latest research suggests that the catacombs were not in use before the late second century, making their appearance roughly contemporary with the general change from cremation to inhumation. The dating of the catacombs by Rutgers *et al.* is based on the building techniques, brick stamps and wall-paintings.[24] The inscriptions too are consistent with such a date. It is possible that the material on which the dating is based displaced what was there earlier, and in the case of the Monteverde catacomb reliance must be placed on notes written and objects removed before the catacomb was destroyed in the 1920s. However, if the catacombs were in use before the late second century, it can only have been on a small scale. Yet there was already a large Jewish community in Rome in the early first century CE, numbering at least 30,000, and perhaps much more,[25] with many hundreds of deaths each year.

For Rome before the late second century, and even later for other European Jewish communities which never had their own cata-combs, both the first and the second option are possible. There are no more than seven clearly Jewish epitaphs from western Europe which can be dated with any degree of confidence to before the third century:

1. *JIWE* i. 7: Aquileia, first century BCE, Latin. This is not certainly an epitaph.

---

[22] Gafni (1981), 102–3.

[23] Rajak (1994), 239, casts doubt on an exclusivity which rests more on presumption than on conclusive argument.

[24] See particularly Rutgers (1990). Dating to the 3rd cent. was already suggested by Testini (1966), 48.

[25] Various estimates (or guesses) are collected by Solin (1983), 698–701.

2. ibid. 14: Ostia, first–second century CE, Latin. From an area of necropoleis, but its exact provenance is unknown.
3. ibid. 18: Castel Porziano, second century CE, Latin. From a burial area; refers to a plot 18 × 17 ft. (about 5.5 × 5 m.).
4. ibid. 23: Marano, near Puteoli, first century CE or later, Latin. This is not certainly an epitaph.
5. ibid. 26: Naples (?), 70–95 CE, Latin. Exact provenance unknown.
6. ibid. 188: Villamesías, Spain, first–third century CE, Latin. Exact provenance unknown.
7. *JIWE* ii. 553: Rome, second–third century CE (?), Latin. Exact provenance unknown.

None of these makes use of any Jewish symbols; they are identified as Jewish only by the content of the epitaphs, usually the use of a designation like *Ioudaios* or of a mainly Jewish title like *archisynagogos*. *JIWE* i. 18 refers to a burial plot granted by the Jewish community (probably of Ostia). It was discovered along with a number of pagan epitaphs, and there is no evidence that a separate area used only by Jews existed. All these 'early' epitaphs occur in isolation; nowhere have two identifiably Jewish epitaphs been found together.

The dearth of Jewish epitaphs in western Europe before the third century requires explanation. Were Jews not producing epitaphs at all, or were they producing epitaphs which are now indistinguishable from non-Jewish ones?

The questions of where the Jews of Rome were buried before the late second century and why there are so few earlier epitaphs have not been discussed in much depth. Leon (1960), relying on what now seems to be erroneously early dating of the catacombs, apparently saw no need to ask them at all. Williams (1994: 176–7), following Leon, asserts that 'many graves (e.g. those in the earlier part of the Monteverde) never bore an epitaph at all'. In fact, most graves throughout Monteverde had no recorded epitaph, and even if one area could plausibly be identified as 'earlier', the state of our information would not justify any statement about the prevalence of epitaph-less graves there in comparison with other parts of the catacomb.

Solin observes that the catacombs increase the chances of Jewish inscriptions both surviving and being identifiable; he supposes that, earlier, Jewish families would acquire plots in pagan burial areas and might come to dominate parts of them.[26] Vismara seems to envisage separate burial areas for Jewish inhumation, but does not try to explain why none have been found, even though she supposes that Jews would have used distinctive symbols at this period too.[27] Rutgers points to the possibility of Jews using cremation but also to the absence of evidence for Jews in the columbaria (see below). He notes that the Vigna Randanini catacomb was apparently based on several hypogea which merged.[28]

The existence of separate Jewish burial areas before the catacombs seems on the whole fairly unlikely. Jews elsewhere and Christians at Rome apparently did not object to sharing burial areas with pagans in the first and second centuries, and Jews in many places adopted the forms of tomb and the methods of commemoration most generally favoured in their cities.[29] Jewish families or larger groups may have had their own hypogea, like those suggested at Vigna Randanini, but entirely Jewish cemeteries probably did not yet exist in western Europe. Individual Jews had their own surface plots, as in *JIWE* i. 18, but these were situated among non-Jewish plots. At Tlos in Lycia at the end of the first century CE, Ptolemaios son of Leukios built a cemetery (ἡρῷον; presumably more than an individual tomb in this case) for the Jews of the city, but this was a private benefaction with no known parallel, and did not necessarily accommodate a very large number of burials.[30]

Many epitaphs from the catacombs are identified as Jewish by context or by symbols and formulae which only came into use in the third century, not by the criteria of terminology like *Ioudaios* on which the earlier inscriptions are identified. No one would presume that an epitaph reading 'Aurelius Bassus (had this) made for Aemilia Theodora' (*JIWE* ii. 206) was Jewish if it had not been found in a Jewish catacomb.

[26] Solin (1983), 707–8 n. 264c.

[27] Vismara (1986), 359.

[28] Rutgers (1990), 143; (1995), 53.

[29] Williams (1994), 174–5 and Price (1994), 180–4 (Jews in Asia Minor and Egypt); Fasola and Fiocchi Nicolai (1986), 1154 (Christians generally); Rutgers (1992), 109–14 (Christians at Rome and Jews in Italy and the East); Ferrua (1991), 159 (Christians).

[30] *CIJ* ii. 757, discussed by Strubbe (1994), 102–3. Strubbe's arguments for the existence of other exclusively Jewish cemeteries in Asia are not convincing; his suggestion that Jewish curses are mainly aimed at other Jews is plausible but is entirely dependent on his assumption that exclusive Jewish areas existed.

The writing of anything more than the deceased's name and patronymic was fairly unusual on Judaean ossuaries, and the composition of epitaphs was by no means characteristic of all areas and levels of the Roman world. Many rich graves were not marked by epitaphs,[31] or at least not by epitaphs on stone. The most prominent tomb at Beth She'arim, which may be that of R. Judah the Prince, has no surviving inscription.[32] Although rabbinic sources indicate that graves were normally marked to prevent ritual defilement, this was not necessarily done by means of an epitaph.[33] When Jews at Rome began to use sarcophagi in the catacomb period, small and crudely inscribed epitaphs were sometimes written on elaborate and presumably expensive sarcophagi.[34]

If the Augustesian and Agrippesian synagogues at Rome were founded at or soon after the time of their apparent eponyms,[35] they no doubt had title-holders before the third century, but these either did not have their titles recorded in their epitaphs or left no epitaphs at all. The Jews of Ostia were using titles like *archisynagogos* in the first or second century. A pagan epitaph from Rome referring to a *proseucha* seems to belong to the first or second century,[36] also suggesting the existence of synagogues (presumably with title-holders) by that date.

The early Jewish epitaphs from western Europe are all in Latin. This is consistent with the assumption that other minority groups at Rome, e.g. Syrians, used Latin for epitaphs which were going to be placed in generally accessible burial areas, regardless of what language they spoke at home.[37] *JIWE* i. 26, with its request not to violate the inscription, seems to belong in a generally accessible area; there is nothing similar in the Jewish catacombs.

It therefore seems plausible that before the time of the catacombs Jews were usually buried among non-Jews and rarely had epitaphs

---

[31] Hopkins (1987), 114.

[32] Finegan (1992), 322.

[33] Safrai (1976), 780. The discussion in b. M. Kat. 5b–6a largely envisages graves which are liable to be ploughed up; stones painted with lime are to be used as markers.

[34] Rajak (1994), 234–6. Cf. the similarly irregular script found on ossuaries, suggesting that the names were inscribed by family members rather than professional stone-cutters (Hachlili (1988), 99).

[35] The synagogue of the Hebrews may have been older; Leon (1960), 149, argues that it must have been the first Jewish congregation at Rome.

[36] *JIWE* ii. 602.

[37] Kaimio (1979), 173.

on stone (see further below). If most Jews at Rome were really as poor as writers like Juvenal imagined, the option of individual commemoration was probably not available to them anyway. Their bodies would have been disposed of in the same way as those of the pagan poor, in common graves. In the catacombs there seems to have been a conscious effort to keep bodies separate from each other. This was not always Jewish practice, however. For example, in a late first-century BCE tomb at Jerusalem, eighteen secondary burials were found together in one pit (with no inscription).[38]

MacMullen (1983) discusses the 'epigraphic habit'. He sees it as a sign of identification with the dominant culture, spreading during the second century and reaching its peak in the late second and early third centuries. Meyer (1990) puts it in the context of changing attitudes to Roman citizenship in the provinces. Similar considerations may be relevant at Rome itself. It is impossible to know what proportion of the Jewish community at Rome held Roman citizenship before 212. Ex-slaves would normally be citizens; other immigrants normally would not. If the two groups intermarried, citizenship may have diminished rather than increased within the community.

According to Josephus, 'The pious rites which (the Law) provides for the dead do not consist of costly obsequies or the erection of conspicuous monuments.'[39] There seems in general to have been a degree of ideological hostility to excessive display at funerals; for example, it was said that Rabban Gamaliel was buried in garments of linen to stop a trend towards excessive expenditure on clothing the deceased.[40]

Cannon (1989) proposes a model of ostentatious 'mortuary behaviour' beginning with the élite and gradually being imitated by the rest of society, followed by a tendency towards restraint also beginning with the élite. If the provision of a Roman-style epitaph can be seen as ostentatious in this context, the practice may have begun with 'élite' members of the Jewish community at Rome, including title-holders in synagogues. The prevalence in the

---

[38] Strange (1975). Burial of the poor at Jerusalem was evidently a problem, since, under the revolutionary government before defeat in 70, public funds were used to pay for the removal of 115,880 corpses of paupers without relatives during the siege, according to Josephus, *War* 5. 568.

[39] Josephus, *C. Apion* 2. 205.

[40] b. Keth. 8b.

catacombs of epitaphs commemorating such people would thus be explained; they were among those most eager to take up the epigraphic habit. However, the fact that the epitaphs were in Greek much more often than in Latin shows that in taking it up they gave it a particular twist of their own: the expected readership was a very restricted one, not the users of the main roads who were supposed to stop and look at many epitaphs at Rome.

Burial among non-Jews, without an epitaph, is likely to have been the destiny of most deceased Jews in Europe before the third century. It seems quite plausible that the practice of inhumation was generally maintained throughout the period when cremation was predominant. If elaborate tombs and epitaphs were not in vogue, the absence of a datable archaeological record is not surprising. Inhumations are known to have been mixed with cremations at sites such as Isola Sacra and the Vatican necropolis. This is usually attributable to the transition period between the two rites, but it is possible that it was actually a more prolonged practice.

However, there is no reason to presume that everyone was treated in the same way. Many Jews in Rome in the first centuries BCE and CE were slaves or ex-slaves. Many slaves and ex-slaves had their remains buried in the columbaria of their *familiae* or their burial *collegia*. If Jews did not require separate burial areas, it would be natural for them to take their places in the columbaria along with their *colliberti* (fellow ex-slaves). However, columbaria seem to have been designed exclusively for the remains of those who were cremated; some were later adapted to make room for inhumations, but this was a consequence of the change in general burial practice, not something planned when the columbaria were designed. The possibility that cremation would have been used for some Jews at Rome cannot be dismissed out of hand.

Comments on cremation in various Jewish literary sources show that it was generally disapproved,[41] and there is no conclusive archaeological evidence of its use by Jews at this period. A freed-woman named Iunia Sabbatis put up an epitaph for her patron L. Iunius Amphio, herself, and their successors, in the Monumentum Marcellae at Rome,[42] and this would have marked a place for cremation urns, but she cannot be regarded as certainly Jewish.

---

[41] *JIGRE* 32; no literature shows Jews actually using cremation, but there is enough ambiguity to show that it was not necessarily rejected absolutely.

[42] *CIL* vi. 4779.

Tacitus[43] observed that the Jews 'bury corpses in Egyptian fashion rather than cremate them'. The reference to 'Egyptian fashion' probably results from the context of a comparison of Jewish and Egyptian religion rather than indicating that Tacitus really thought the Jews practised mummification; the force of the whole passage is the difference between Jews and Romans. If Tacitus had any accurate information about how the Jews dealt with their dead, he may well have derived it from the Jews of Rome. Jewish burial practices were evidently not regarded as sufficiently unusual to attract comment from any other pagan writer.

However, Nock notes a number of cases where people whose names suggest that they were immigrants to Rome from the east (Egypt,[44] Syria, Parthia) were cremated during the early empire,[45] even though it was not their native custom. It is possible, if unprovable, that some Jews at Rome, particularly ex-slaves attached to columbarium-owning households, would have adapted to the local custom in the same way. Jews practising cremation might be among those least likely to have distinctively Jewish names or designations, so there would be nothing recognizably Jewish about their epitaphs. The very poor probably had no choice about what was done to their deceased relatives' remains; the bodies of poor Jews probably ended up in the *puticuli* along with those of non-Jews.

The development of separate Jewish burial areas seems to be a relatively late phenomenon. The idea that the Jewish catacombs were the model for the Christian ones[46] is now invalidated by the dating of the Jewish ones; the two types seem to have developed simultaneously.[47] The growth of some Christian catacombs around the tombs of martyrs and of the Beth She'arim catacombs around the tomb of R. Judah the Prince do not seem appropriate models for the Jewish catacombs of Rome; no Roman Jews are known of sufficient prestige to provide a similar focus. It is also not possible to maintain that the practice of the Roman Jews was wholly

---

[43] *Hist.* 5. 5.

[44] Toynbee (1971), 41–2, refers to three mummies found at Rome (a mid-2nd-cent. CE one from the Via Cassia, and two from the Via Appia), but the importation of this practice was clearly exceptional.

[45] Nock (1932), 329–30; the Egyptians may, however, have been Egyptian Greeks and therefore not departing from their native custom. Audin (1960), 526, notes that initiates of Mithras, Isis, and Cybele used cremation at this time.

[46] As suggested by e.g. Finegan (1946), 358.

[47] Stevenson (1978), 12.

modelled on what happened in Palestine. Although there are signs of Palestinian influence (particularly the use of *kokhim* in one part of Vigna Randanini),[48] there were no pre-existing Palestinian models for the sort of catacombs developed at Rome. They did not have Italian models either, although some of the necessary techniques were developed in the extraction of building materials and the installation of *condutture* for collecting rainwater in underground Rome.[49] Earlier underground burials by pagans in Italy, e.g. at Anzio up to the second century BCE, were only on a very small scale compared to the Jewish and Christian catacombs; small hypogea were still being developed around Rome in the fourth century CE.[50] Closer precedents could be found in the east, at e.g. Alexandria and Palmyra,[51] but there too the tendency was to use adjacent hypogea of limited size, rather than huge complexes like the Roman catacombs.

Several alternative (not necessarily mutually exclusive) explanations for the development of the catacombs seem possible. The general change from cremation to inhumation in the second century may have encouraged Jews to seek additional ways of distinguishing their burials, by using exclusive sites with distinctive symbolism. Increased demand for land as the result of the general change to inhumation, a practice which required more space, may have been the stimulus for some groups to find different ways of using such surface areas as were available. Alternatively, there may have been a substantial growth in the size of the Jewish community at Rome which made previous burial arrangements insufficient.

Christian catacombs were expected to provide for the very poor,[52] and presumably Jewish ones did so too. The large numbers of loculi for which no epitaphs survive, and those with epitaphs consisting simply of the deceased's name scratched or painted on the plaster, perhaps catered for the poor; however, they may simply have been for those who most desired to avoid ostentatious

---

[48] The use of *kokhim* (burial slots cut into the walls at floor-level, at right-angles to the main gallery) rather than *loculi* (burial slots parallel to the gallery) occurs at Rome only at Vigna Randanini (Rutgers (1995), 61–4); it was normal in the Jerusalem area from *c.*150 BCE to *c.*150 CE (Finegan (1992), 297, 302).

[49] Pergola (1986), 342.

[50] Fasola and Fiocchi Nicolai (1986), 1184–5; Rutgers (1995), 52. Testini (1966), 48–9, stresses the local precedents for the Christian catacombs: underground Etruscan tombs, columbaria, and galleries under the Forum Romanum.

[51] Pergola (1986), 343.

[52] Stevenson (1978), 11–12.

commemoration, irrespective of what they could afford. If provision for the poor was a purpose, rather than a consequence, of the catacombs' development, it would suggest that some communal organization was involved. Williams (1994) shows that there is no evidence for the involvement of synagogues, but suggests the existence of burial societies encouraged by wealthy members of the community. Someone, either a communal organisation, an entrepreneur or an individual benefactor, must have owned the surface area beneath which each catacomb was dug.

There is virtually no information about the processes by which the Jewish catacombs were developed. The layout of the Villa Torlonia catacombs suggests considerable pre-planning, and Fasola (1976) was able to establish the relative chronology of various parts. Vigna Randanini, however, shows no sign of planning at all and uses the available space quite inefficiently. There is evidence for at least one possible family cubiculum there,[53] and the cubicula may in general have been used by individual families. There are no Jewish inscriptions referring to the purchase of spaces in the catacombs, whereas a number of Christian inscriptions record such purchases, sometimes from individual *fossores*;[54] this may indicate a different system of allocating spaces, but may be no more than a consequence of the relative scarcity of Jewish inscriptions. At Beth She'arim the burial society sold spaces to purchasers; there is no evidence of how other Jewish burial societies in the east operated, and they may in any case have been influenced more by local practice than by what Jews did elsewhere.[55] There are also many Christian inscriptions which record the deceased's acquisition of the tomb while still alive, but these are absent from the Jewish catacombs. The Roman Jews may have rejected the Christian and pagan practice of preparing one's own tomb; they certainly rejected the practice of recording it.[56]

The impact of an increased demand for land because of the

---

[53] *JIWE* ii. 237–9: epitaphs of three sisters. At least two were found in Cubiculum 6, but this does not *necessarily* mean that the family owned the whole cubiculum. The epitaphs are painted rather than inscribed on marble plaques, suggesting either limited finances or limited interest in epigraphic niceties.

[54] Guyon (1974); Conde Guerri (1979), esp. pp. 138–52.

[55] Hachlili (1988), 103; Reynolds and Tannenbaum (1987), 29–30; Trebilco (1991), 79–80. The evidence which Trebilco cites for a 3rd-cent. society at Acmonia seems much less conclusive than he claims.

[56] The practice had plenty of biblical precedent: e.g. Jacob (Gen. 50: 5), Amon (2 Kings 21: 26), Asa (2 Chron. 16: 14).

general change to inhumation may be less appropriate to the Jewish than to the Christian catacombs. Comparison of Vigna Randanini with the Christian catacombs of the Via Appia suggests that the Jews felt less pressure than the Christians to maximize their use of space.[57] The Jewish catacomb has lower and wider galleries, uses less wall-space for burials, and does not have one level running below another.

Growth in population size seems to be the explanation for the development of the Christian catacombs accepted by Stevenson (1978), 13, but a substantial growth in Jewish numbers at this time would be surprising. Fuks (1985) notes the possible arrival of Jewish slaves in large numbers after the Bar-Kokhba revolt, but it seems unlikely that the influx then was larger than that in 71 CE.[58] Conversions to Judaism may have increased the size of the community, but surely not to the extent that this was happening among Christians. Natural increase in the number of Jews at Rome seems unlikely; unless the Jews at Rome had a very different demographic profile from the rest of the city's population (which is possible, given the Jews' aversion to family limitation), they would probably have needed a substantial rate of immigration just to maintain the community's size.

In the second century, there was a general trend towards making tombs more private—enclosing them behind walls rather than having them fully open to the view of passers-by. The idea of communal burial areas underground seems to be a logical extension of this, following the mainly above-ground example of the columbaria.[59] However, if the view proposed earlier is accepted, i.e. that Jews had previously tended to be inhumed in largely non-Jewish burial areas, then the general change to inhumation would have left no obvious distinction between a Jewish burial and a non-Jewish one. If such distinction was considered desirable, the growth of epigraphic symbolism, e.g. the use of the menorah on tombs, might be explained. I have argued elsewhere that the use of Greek in the catacombs at a time when Christian inscriptions were moving

[57] Pergola (1986), 343, notes that there seems to have been no pressure on space when the Christians began to reuse *arenari* for burials: the tombs were large, widely spaced and irregularly arranged.

[58] Jerome, *In Hieremiam* 31. 15. 6 (*CCSL* 74, p. 307), refers to huge numbers of prisoners in both revolts, but only mentions their reaching Rome under Vespasian.

[59] Von Hesberg (1992), 42–4; Williams (1994). Rutgers (1995), 51, discusses the provision of underground extensions for some tombs during the 2nd cent.

towards Latin may in part have been another way of providing Jewish distinctiveness.[60] The change to inhumation in the wider society seems to be the most plausible explanation of changing Jewish practices.

The phenomenon of Jewish catacombs containing large numbers of epitaphs may therefore result from a combination of the following:

1. The Jews of Rome, starting with their community leaders, 'got the epigraphic habit'.
2. They also felt an increased need to differentiate their burials from those of non-Jews.
3. Some sort of communal or entrepreneurial organization developed for making use of a limited amount of available land, and the catacombs were dug.

[60] Noy (1997).

PART III

Similarities?

7

Graeco-Roman Voluntary Associations and Ancient Jewish Sects

ALBERT BAUMGARTEN

I

Alongside the institutions of the state, armed with the power to coerce, the Graeco-Roman world knew a variety of voluntary organizations, such as guilds, clubs, and cult fellowships, in which people chose to be members. These groups filled many different roles in the lives of their participants, supplying an assortment of personal and social needs, but at the heart of most of them was a bond forged and reinforced by commensality.[1] Jews of ancient Palestine were divided into sects—that is, groups which were opposed to a greater or lesser extent to the mainstream institutions of their society at some point in their history[2]—which some of them elected to join, such as Pharisees, Sadducees, and Essenes. These played a significant part in their lives, a place so important that Josephus felt that his account of the Jewish past would be incomprehensible if his reader were not aware of the nature of these groups, hence he devoted a substantial excursus to them (*War* 2. 119–66). The contribution of the way of life laid down by these groups to individual identity, and hence to the national political and religious life of Jews, was thus considerable.

These two blocs of social foundations, Graeco-Roman and Palestinian Jewish, as will be discussed more fully below, were brought into connection with each other by both Philo and Josephus, apparently in the hope that the Graeco-Roman varieties,

---

[1] On the power of common eating and drinking to create and strengthen social bonds see e.g. the essays in Douglas (1987).

[2] In the terminology followed in this paper, Pharisees, Sadducees, and Essenes were sects. For a discussion of this definition of sect see Stark and Bainbridge (1985), 23. See now Baumgarten (1997), 5–11.

better known to their readers, would help illuminate the Jewish examples. When modern scholars come to evaluate these analogies we note first that the comparison between Graeco-Roman voluntary associations and Jewish sects is multi-faceted on both sides of the entities being compared.[3]

The mass of organizations which ancient authors gathered together under the heading of Graeco-Roman voluntary associations comprised a fair variety. Thus Solon's law, quoted in *Dig.* 47. 22. 4 (Frag. 76a Ruschenbusch), mentioned the validity of actions by pseudo-kinship political groups such as tribes, as well as by true voluntary associations, such as sacred bands (*thiasoi*), dining clubs, or groups formed for the purpose of trade or even piracy. Athenaeus, *Deipn.* 5. 185c–186a, centuries later than Solon, noted a diversity of forms of commensality, including tribe and deme dinners, those of sacred bands, of brotherhoods, and of priesthoods, as well as those of philosophic schools such as the Diogenists, the Antipatrists, or the Panaetiasts. Furthermore, as modern scholars have come to recognize, Greek varieties of voluntary association had a history, varying over time.[4] Moreover, they should be distinguished from forms of voluntary association prevalent in Graeco-Roman Egypt, in the Hellenistic East, or in the Latin-speaking Roman world.[5]

Nor was the ancient Jewish side monolithic. These sects differed in the degree of their opposition to the mainstream institutions of Jewish society in Palestine of their day. The extent to which they demanded severance of all ties between themselves and the larger society, a severance often enforced by purity regulations, also varied from one group to another. In the terminology of Wilson, to be adopted below, some were reformist sects, others introversionist sects.[6]

---

[3] My perspective is different. Nevertheless, it is a pleasure to acknowledge my debt to Weinfeld (1986). See also Mason (1992).

[4] See the excellent summary in Fisher (1988*a*), 1167–97.

[5] On the varieties of such groups from one part of the Mediterranean world to another see Herrmann *et al.* (1978), cols. 83–155. On the distinctiveness of groups in Graeco-Roman Egypt see Nock (1972), 430–42. On associations in the east see Fevrier (1931), 201–8; Greenfield (1974), 451–5; Teixidor (1981), 306–14. See also the discussion of the neo-Babylonian *kiništu/kinaštu* 'the collegium' of a temple, or the *puḫrum* (assembly) of the temple city in Weinfeld (1973), 74–5. On Roman organizations see Fisher (1988*b*), 1199–225.

[6] Wilson (1973), 18–26. This distinction is identical to the one offered by Sanders (1977), 425–6, between party and sect. The former sort of group retains some sense

The diversity which we recognize on both sides of the comparison might seem to doom such an endeavour in advance, either to impossibility or to insignificance. How can two sets of entities, each set so multiform, usefully be compared to each other? We might therefore be tempted to shun such an undertaking. Nevertheless, ancient authors such as Philo and Josephus thought such correspondences meaningful and helpful for their readers, and made such analogies between Graeco-Roman voluntary associations and Jewish sects. For that reason, we should not avoid the task of investigation. This study will therefore be devoted to analysis of the similarities and differences between the two sorts of groups. As the lead here is taken from Philo and Josephus the emphasis will be on a comparison between Graeco-Roman voluntary organizations and the Jewish sects they discussed—Pharisees, Sadducees, and Essenes—and in particular on the Essenes, the only group examined by Philo, and the one described in greatest detail by Josephus.[7] One point shared by many of these institutions, Graeco-Roman and Jewish, was commensality. The analysis below will therefore often focus on issues such as what food members of different groups ate, with whom, how frequently, and under what conditions. These aspects of life, apparently trivial, will provide a significant insight into the nature of social identity.[8]

II

According to Philo (*Hyp.* 11. 1), the Essenes lived a life of *koinonia* (fellowship).[9] They were organized *kata thiasous* (in groups), and in

of connection with others outside its limits, believing that these outsiders still form part of the nation and are capable of correction (hence reformist). The latter sort has given up hope of ever mending the ways of outsiders, and has turned in completely on itself, no longer caring for the fate of those Jews beyond its members.

[7] As I have argued that Qumran evidence has no privileged place in discussion of the Essenes and vice versa, the focus below will be on the Essenes as they appear in classical sources. See Baumgarten (1994*b*), 121–42; Baumgarten (1996*a*), 9–20. For a slightly different perspective on these issues, but reaching a conclusion I share wholeheartedly, see now Goodman (1995), 161–6.

[8] See e.g. Douglas (1984); Dumont (1979); Goody (1982). For an application of these perspectives to other historical material see Meens (1995), 3–19, esp. 15–16.

[9] The latter was a word with an important intellectual pedigree. It had been employed by Aristotle to describe voluntary associations, *Eth. Nic.* 8. 9, 1160[a]8–20, but was not used by organizations themselves, Herrmann *et al.* (1978), col. 85.

hetairias (associations),[10] with bands of comradeship and common meals (*Hyp.* 11. 5). Philo called their way of life a *proairesis* (a 'purposeful choice') (*Hyp.* 11. 2), in which membership was based on choice, not birth (*Hyp.* 11. 2).

The evidence of Josephus overlaps at least in part. The Essene manner of life, according to him, did not differ at all from that of the so-called Ctistae among the Dacians; in fact, it was as close as it could be (*Ant.* 18. 22). The Pharisees were similar to Stoics (*Vita* 12). The Jews as a whole, he reported, were divided into either three or four philosophies (*War* 2. 119; *Ant.* 18. 9, 11), or *haireseis* (sects) (*War* 2. 137; *Ant.* 13. 171).[11]

Philo and Josephus employed similar terms: *proairesis* vs. *haireseis*, but that may be an accident of language, rather than a meaningful indication that both authors were thinking along the same lines. In general, Philo seemed to be thinking more of analogous groups in social/religious realms, while Josephus seemed to be thinking more in philosophical terms.

What could an ancient reader conclude from these comparisons? He would understand that as a group organized *kata thiasous*, the Essenes were an organization that met together for a common meal under religious auspices. This conclusion was accurate enough, as far as it went, but as even Philo was aware and as he explained, Essene common life was much more extensive and intensive than that among the analogous Graeco-Roman groups. The meals of the guild of Zeus Hypsistos, in Egypt of the first century BCE, were held once a month.[12] The Iobacchi, whose regulations are known in detail from *SIG* [3] 1109,[13] ate together only once a month, as well as on the anniversary of the foundation of the group and other festivals. We know of the eating clubs of Hellenistic Syria from their denunciation by Posidonius (Frag. 62a,b *ap.* Athenaeus, *Deipn.* 12. 527e–f):

the people in the cities, at any rate, because of the great plenty which their land afforded (were relieved) of any distress regarding the necessaries of

---

[10] Perhaps the latter term was a reflection of the fact of some internal differentiation among the Essenes. Cf. Josephus on the four orders of Essenes (*War* 2. 150).

[11] The latter term was also employed in Acts to refer to the Pharisees (26: 5), the Sadducees (5: 17), and was applied by Jews to Christians (24: 5, 14), although its use for Christians by Jews was probably derogatory.

[12] See Nock (1972), 414.

[13] Translation in Weinfeld (1986), 51–4.

life; hence they held many gatherings at which they feasted continually, using the gymnasia as if they were baths, anointing themselves with expensive oils and perfumes, and living in the *grammateia*[14]—for so they called the commons where diners met—as though they were their private houses, and putting in the greater part of the day there in filling their bellies—there, in the midst of wines and foods so abundant that they even carried a great deal home with them besides—and in delighting their ears with sounds from a loud-twanging tortoise shell, so that the towns rang from end to end with such noises.

Regular common meals seemed to have been a feature of these groups, but this was a matter of choice. A member of such a club *elected* to have his meals there. He had a home elsewhere, where he could have eaten any food (according to Posidonius, that is what he *should* have done). He took food home from the eating club as a matter of self-indulgence.

In the Roman world, the Bacchic associations outlawed in 186 BCE made slightly more rigorous demands of their members.[15] One of the major complaints against innovation in the Bacchic cult in 186 BCE, which made the latter suspect in the eyes of senators, was that instead of three days of initiation per year there were now five per month (Livy 39. 13. 9).[16] These associations had oaths of loyalty enforced by gods and human sanction (Livy 39. 13. 5; *CIL* i. 581). The group was persecuted by the state, at which time some members committed suicide (Livy 39. 17. 5), yet another indication of a high degree of commitment.

All this, however, should be contrasted with the Essenes. Their meals were not occasional (Philo, *Hyp.* 11. 5): Essenes *only* ate together, every day of the year. The Essene meal was exclusive, open to members only (Joseph. *War* 2. 129), as a matter of purity.[17]

---

[14] On the meaning of this obscure term see below, p. 107. Posidonius did not expect his reader to understand the term, as his comment on the name of these clubs indicates.

[15] The literature on the subject is extensive. I have consulted the following: Bruhl (1953), 82–116; Cantarella (1987), 127–8; Cova (1974), 82–109; Festugière (1954), 79–99; Frank (1927), 128–32; Kraemer (1992), 42–9; McDonald (1944), 26–31; Pallier (1982), 929–52. See also Cancik-Lindemaier (1996), 77–96.

[16] Other major complaints were the involvement of men in a cult previously reserved for women, perhaps also a membership crossing social orders. From the time of Augustus on, groups which met too frequently were prohibited. See Nock (1924), 106; see further Herrmann *et al.* (1978), cols. 110–13.

[17] Cf. the Demotic religious association of embalmers known from Berlin Papyrus 3115, who punished a potential member who after years of participation did not accept full membership by prohibiting other members from working, eating, or

Essenes had no other food, other than that prepared under the auspices of the movement (*War* 2. 143). All other food was marked with the social order, with which the Essenes were at odds. An Essene had no home but his group. Thus Essenes not only ate together, but they also had common property and practised celibacy (e.g. *War* 2. 120–2). The Essenes, as I have argued in detail elsewhere,[18] were very near to being fully introversionist, as opposed to their analogies in the Graeco-Roman world, which were much more closely identified with the mainstream institutions of the social context in which they lived. Moreover, an Essene had no identity but as a member of his movement. He had sacrificed his personality to a greedy institution,[19] which demanded his sexual activity, his property, and which, while it encouraged him to give charity to strangers in need, did not even allow him to give presents to relatives without the permission of the leaders of the order (*War* 2. 134). His body functions were severely restricted, and he was forbidden to defecate one day a week (*War* 2. 147–8).

Turning to Josephus, his comparisons, as noted above, were normally made in a philosophical direction (I leave aside the unsolvable puzzle of who the Ctistae were): the Pharisees were like Stoics in their belief in divine providence, or Jewish schools were similar to *haireseis* among philosophers. What might these analogies have meant to an ancient non-Jewish reader? That reader should have concluded that the Jewish sects were groups of literate men, centred on an intellectual/ideological agenda, around which their life revolved. Appropriately, as is well known, Josephus stressed the beliefs of the different groups in his description of them (*War* 2. 119–66). At least some such Greek groups lived together and had a common way of life, in which shared meals played a large part (Athenaeus, *Deipn.* 5 cited above). Perhaps that side of Jewish sectarian life was also intended to be illuminated by Josephus in his assertion that these Jewish groups were philosophies. Finally, philosophical schools were often engaged in harsh mutual debate or polemic. Perhaps the comparison suggested by Josephus

drinking with the man who had refused to pay up. This, however, was a practical sanction, an economic matter: since he had not paid he could not enjoy the privileges of membership. See further Weinfeld (1986), 25.

[18] See Baumgarten (1994*a*), 182–3.

[19] On sectarian life as effacing individual identity see Coser (1974), 103–16. Coser focuses his comments on individuality as expressed in sexuality. His conclusions, however, can and should be extended to all aspects of human self-expression.

was intended to help make the disagreements on points of doctrine between Pharisees and Sadducees to which he occasionally referred (e.g. *Ant.* 13. 297–8) more comprehensible to a Greek reader.

To take up these points in greater detail, among the various philosophical groups whom Josephus might have had in mind, as especially close to the Jewish groups in way of life and outlook, were the Epicureans.[20] Mentioned by Josephus for their denial of all forms of prophecy (*Ant.* 10. 277; see also Diog. Laert. 10. 135), and for shunning politics (Joseph. *Ant.* 19. 32), their form of organization was particularly analogous to that of Jewish sects.[21] Indeed, one distinguished contemporary scholar of ancient philosophy has called them a sect.[22] Epicureans swore an oath on entry to be faithful to the way of life taught by Epicurus (Philodemus, *Peri Parresias* 45. 8–11): 'We will be obedient to Epicurus, according to whom we have made it our choice to live.'[23] They paid an *equal* annual contribution for the upkeep of their school and master (Fr. B 41),[24] stressing their roles as equal partners in the enterprise. That contribution was conceived as a first fruits' offering to the holy body of Epicurus (Fr. B 26). They ate a simple diet of bread and water (Diog. Laert. 10. 131), occasionally indulging in thin wine (Diog. Laert. 10. 11).[25]

The members of this school further believed that true security was possible only in a community of friends, safe from its neighbours (Diog. Laert. 10. 154). Only there could physical and mental serenity be achieved. Within the confines of this community they taught new members, who were organized in various orders of seniority, rebuking them as necessary.[26] Slyness and secretiveness were considered the worst offences against the friendship they were trying to establish (Philodemus 41. 1–4). Reporting of misdemeanours committed by fellow students was approved as an act of

---

[20] On the possible analogy with the Pythagoreans see Burkert (1982), 1–22. On the possible analogy with medical schools see von Staden (1982), 76–100.

[21] On this subject see esp. De Witt (1936), 205–11.

[22] Rist (1972), 12.

[23] See also Seneca, *Epist.* 25. 5: 'Sic fac omnia tamquam spectet Epicurus.'

[24] Fragments of Epicurus cited according to Bailey (1926).

[25] This did not stop their opponents from denouncing them as gluttons. See e.g. Diog. Laert. 10. 6: Epicurus had to vomit twice a day because of his over-indulgence, or he spent a whole mina daily on his table.

[26] See the discussion in De Witt (1936), 206–7, based primarily on the testimony of Philodemus. De Witt's interpretation of Philodemus was accepted by Rist (1972), 10 n. 2.

genuine friendship and failure to report such a person stamped a man as 'an evil friend and a friend to evil' (Philodemus 50). The environment was such that even seniors had to accept constructive criticism when it came from their inferiors (Diog. Laert. 10. 120; Philodemus X^a. 1–5 and X^b. 11–13). We are told that students were once rebuked for wearing Greek cloaks (Philodemus 31. 4–8), which suggests that the group may have had a quasi-uniform.

While Epicureans did not share their property, they refused this step because it implied a lack of trust in each other. Rather, Epicurus preferred total confidence, in which members of the group retained their private possessions, but nevertheless made them available for the life of the community (Diog. Laert. 10. 11). A wise man, according to Epicurus, would avoid politics and marriage, as distractions and potential sources of pain (Diog. Laert. 10. 119; see also Joseph. *Ant.* 19. 32), although there were female members of the group, with whom Epicurus was reputed to have been involved, hence the adherents were not celibate.[27] In this manner, according to the testimony of a number of ancient authors (Diog. Laert. 10. 9; Numenius, *ap.* Eusebius, *PE* 114. 5, 727d–728a), the members of this school managed to preserve and transmit their doctrine free of internal strife and schism for several centuries, an achievement of which they were duly proud.[28]

The similarities between this way of life and that ascribed by Josephus and Philo to the Essenes are significant. There too we find oaths of entry (Joseph. *War* 2. 139), of loyalty to the authorities (*War* 2. 140), as well as the requirement to be a permanent spy on the activities of fellow members (*War* 2. 141). In a move probably intended to contain schism, the new Essene swore to transmit doctrines exactly as he had received them (*War* 2. 142). The Essene had a uniform, which consisted of a white garment worn at sacred meals and a hatchet used to bury waste when defecating, both received on entering the group (*War* 2. 131, 137, 148). Admission was a gradual process (*War* 2. 137), the candidate climbing the grades of membership at different levels (*War* 2. 150), until he reached a point where he lived a life removed from that of fellow Jews (Philo, *Hyp.* 11. 1; Joseph. *War* 2. 124–6),

[27] On female members of the group and their experiences see Rist (1972), 10–11.
[28] See Malherbe (1982), 47–8. As Malherbe reminds us, ibid. 47, one should be careful not to exaggerate the unchanging nature of Epicurean doctrine over time. As a living institution the teachings of the school did change. See further De Lacey (1948), 12–23.

separated from his own family, even requiring permission to help them financially (*War* 2. 134). Rebuke must have been a regular aspect of life among the Essenes, particularly during the probationary period when the new member was being taught and tested on his willingness to live in accordance with the rules of the group (*War* 2. 138).[29] Finally, property was held in common (Philo, *Hyp.* 11. 4; Joseph. *War* 2. 122), and marriage shunned (Philo, *Hyp.* 11. 14; Joseph. *War* 2. 120, 160–1).

Nevertheless, in spite of these similarities, Essene life was different. Epicureans met infrequently, once each month, in celebration of the birth of the founder, and on other holidays (Diog. Laert. 10. 18). Their restricted diet was a matter of practical necessity, advantageous for a healthy life (Diog. Laert. 10. 131). Essenes, by contrast, as discussed above, ate every meal together (Philo, *Omnis Probus* 86). Again, as discussed above, all food outside the confines of their group was forbidden to them. They shared all aspects of their lives, having sacrificed themselves, as we saw above, to a greedy institution. Accordingly, Philo was right to trumpet that: 'In no other community can we find the custom of sharing roof, life and board more firmly established in actual practice' (*Omnis Probus* 86).[30]

Indeed, as Philo implied, to find more exact equivalents of Essene behaviour in the Graeco-Roman world we must turn our attention to the realm of imagination, to Greek utopias. Iambulus' 'Children of the Sun', for example, came close to the way of life attributed to the Essenes:[31] they divided sharply (in their own ways) between purity maintained on the inside and the impure world on the outside. They ate *all* meals together (Diod. Sic. 2. 59. 5), living in perfect equality and harmony (Diod. Sic. 2. 58. 7). Some of the means of achieving these goals were different among the 'Children of the Sun', others the same. Thus, they were *not* celibate, but shared all women and raised children in common, thus avoiding strife, which would impede the life of fellowship (Diodorus Siculus 2. 58. 1; cf. Philo, *Hyp.* 11. 16).

[29] For Qumran equivalents see now Eshel (1994), 117–18.

[30] A perverse spirit leads me to the suggestion that perhaps the much-vaunted Epicurean lack of schism was due to the fact that contact between members was so restricted and the group made such relatively light demands of its adherents. Had contact been more intensive and/or the degree of insistence greater, perhaps the Epicureans might not have been able to maintain their strife-free life.

[31] On Iambulus and the Essenes see Mendels (1979), 205–22.

The greater intensity of Jewish sectarian life was not only characteristic of the Essenes, but also of the Pharisees. The latter, compared by Josephus to the Stoics, were in the reformist category of sect,[32] much less at odds with the mainstream institutions of their society, in fact sometimes controlling them. Nevertheless, Pharisaic practice concerning the consumption of food confirmed the boundaries they drew around themselves, separating themselves off from the rest of Jewish society. While that separation was not as extreme as that of the Essenes, reflecting the less acute sense of antagonism to the social structure as a whole, it was still substantial.[33]

A passage in the Gospel of Mark (7: 4) contains a detail which has received surprisingly little attention in studies of the Pharisees: 'when they come from the marketplace, they do not eat unless they purify [*rhantisontai*; some MSS read *baptisontai* = immerse] themselves.'[34] This practice is explicitly different from that mentioned in the previous verse, the washing of hands prior to eating, but like the former it would seem to come from the Pharisaic *paradosis*, the collection of laws not mentioned in the Bible but observed by the Pharisees. Immersion of the self prior to eating has no biblical source. As such it was an ideal candidate for inclusion in the *paradosis* of the Pharisees. In fact, such immersion by the Pharisees is not mentioned in any rabbinic, apocryphal, or pseudepigraphic source.[35] The practice does appear, however, in one other place in

[32] For the Pharisees as a reformist sect according to Wilson, see Saldarini (1988), 286.

[33] In the discussion below I will not appeal to rabbinic sources discussing the *haverim* (= 'associates'), as the relationship between these and the Pharisees is a matter of dispute.

[34] I understand the verb in middle plural as referring to the Pharisees purifying themselves by immersion, on coming from the market, rather than some objects, bought in the market. This understanding of *ean mē rhan/baptisontai* is natural when following *ean mē . . . nipsontai*. Cf. the discussion and literature cited in Guelich (1989), 365. On *rhantisontai* as meaning purification by immersion compare Heb. 10: 22, and see the discussion of the meaning of the verb in the middle voice in BAG, *s.v.*

[35] See further Str.–B. ii. 14, where no parallels are listed. In the elaborate description of a Jewish meal based on rabbinic sources in Str.–B. ivb. 611–39 there is also no mention of purification prior to eating. The fact that this Pharisaic practice is mentioned in no rabbinic, apocryphal, or pseudepigraphic source is inadequate reason to reject its historicity. The nature of our evidence on Jewish sects, as has recently been stressed by Goodman (1995), 162, is such that there is relatively little overlap between the information provided by various sources. We should therefore not expect them to confirm each other regularly. Moreover, neither the rabbis nor Josephus were especially interested in the halachic usages of the Pharisees. Rabbis saw the Pharisees as rather distant predecessors, about whom they preserved

the New Testament, in Luke 11: 38. A Pharisee, apparently thinking that Jesus belonged to his group,[36] invited him to dinner. When Jesus 'did not first immerse himself (*ebaptisthē*) before dinner',[37] his host was shocked. As the story is told from the perspective of the followers of Jesus, it ends with Jesus rebuking his host. Had it been told from the point of view of the Pharisees it might have ended with Jesus being asked to leave.

The reasons Pharisees immersed themselves on returning from the market, before eating, are not specified in these passages, hence we can only speculate. I think it fair, however, to conclude that such immersion was deemed necessary because Pharisees believed that they had contracted impurity while in the market, from 'bumping into' people of indeterminate status, Jewish and/or non-Jewish. Eating could only take place after the elimination of this impurity,[38] and in the company of others who were also pure (lest an impure person present reintroduce the impurity which had just been removed by immersion, which would then start the cycle going again, and prevent the Pharisee from eating).

This interpretation of Pharisaic practice is illuminated by one partial illustration of the New Testament passages quoted to be found in rabbinic sources, in texts already noted by Buechler at the beginning of the century but since then somewhat over-looked.[39] y. Sheb. 6. 1. 36c, with a parallel in t. Ohal. 18: 18 reports on the purification of Ashkelon. It is a story about R.

relatively little information, while Josephus stressed the doctrinal side of the group. To find the New Testament standing alone as witness to Pharisaic halacha should not deter us from accepting that testimony as historical.

[36] Only understanding the invitation as having been extended under a misapprehension of Jesus's affiliation will explain the astonishment of the host at Jesus's behaviour, which will follow.

[37] Some translations, e.g. Deilitsch's into Hebrew, render this passage as if Jesus had failed to wash his hands, notwithstanding the explicit use of *ebaptisthē*, and the omission of all mention of hands in the Greek. See also Fitzmyer (1985), 947 who struggles to make this passage refer to washing hands only, against its explicit meaning. I take this testimony of the gospels to reflect Pharisaic practice in the 1st cent., whether or not it is explicit evidence for incidents in the life of the historical Jesus.

[38] This suggestion was already made by Str.–B. ii. 14. It does not seem that this immersion was done as preparatory to entering a higher degree of sanctity, such as the immersion of already pure priests before beginning service in the Temple, or of Essenes before their meal. The passage in Mark seems to specify that this immersion was necessary because the Pharisee was returning *from the market* to eat. Had he not been in the market the immersion might not have been necessary.

[39] Buechler (1956), 187–93.

Pinhas b. Yair, an ascetic and extreme pietist active at the time of R. Judah I.[40]

Ashkelon was declared to be within the holy land, benefiting from being considered not defiled by gentiles, on the testimony of R. Pinhas b. Yair.[41] He declared that 'we used to go to the market place, come home, immerse ourselves and eat *terumah*' (in the parallel in t. Ohal. 18: 18, 'offer the passover sacrifice').[42]

That R. Pinhas b. Yair, as a priest,[43] was eating *terumah* is credible enough. The payment of agricultural taxes to priests was observed throughout the period of the Mishnah and Talmud.[44] That anyone was offering the Passover sacrifice around the year 200 CE is less clear; perhaps R. Pinhas b. Yair's testimony referred to the past, as suggested by Buechler.[45] However one understands it, R. Pinhas b. Yair's statement established that even someone as stringent as he did not consider Ashkelon impure gentile land. After returning from Ashkelon all one needed to do before consuming *terumah* or eating the Passover was immerse. Full-scale purification from corpse uncleanness was not needed. Immersion, however, was necessary because one might have 'bumped into' someone impure in the market, probably a non-Jew in Ashkelon.[46]

What then of the discrepancy between the two versions? Did priests 'really' eat the Passover or *terumah* after immersing following a visit to Ashkelon? From my perspective, it is unnecessary to resolve this disagreement between the versions of R. Pinhas b.

---

[40] I have discussed these sources in detail in Baumgarten (1981), 161–70, and Baumgarten (1983*a*), 242–5.

[41] In a separate vote, taken later, Ashkelon was granted a paradoxical status. Although part of the land of Israel on matters of purity, it was deemed a gentile enclave within that territory, hence its produce was exempted from requirements of *terumah*, the tithe, and the sabbatical year. This aspect of the decisions taken is not the focus of concern here. For a discussion of that facet of the sources see the studies mentioned in the previous note.

[42] According to Buechler (1956), 192 n. 1, the tradition concerning R. Pinhas b. Yair was originally one in which he testified concerning the eating of the Passover sacrifice after visiting Ashkelon. This tradition was then transformed by the *amoraim* into one concerning *terumah*. This complication seems unnecessary.

[43] On the question whether R. Pinhas b. Yair was a priest see Buechler (1956), 192 n. 1.

[44] In addition to Buechler (1956), 179–244, see Safrai (1965/6), 304–28 (1966/7), 1–21. The Rehov inscription, erected centuries after the destruction of the Temple, is another sort of proof that these laws were being observed. See Sussmann (1973/4), 88–158.

[45] Buechler (1956), 189.

[46] On the interpretation of the passages offered here see Lieberman (1939), 160.

Yair's statement. It is enough to conclude that the account of his testimony, according to which some priests went to Ashkelon, immersed, and then ate *terumah* seemed plausible enough to be retold and preserved.

This may have been the model of stringent behaviour by exceptionally scrupulous priests which the Pharisees of Mark 7: 4 were imitating. As has been argued often by others, these Pharisees were raising the level of holiness in their lives by behaving as if they were priests (cf. the Nazirite, who also raised the sanctity of his life by taking on some of the obligations of serving priests),[47] treating their ordinary food as if it were subject to some of the restrictions on sacred food consumed by priests.[48]

As noted above, the purity boundary maintained by the Pharisees was less extreme than that of the Essenes. A member of the former group could go to the market, presumably to buy his food there, while the latter was restricted to food prepared under the auspices of his group. The Essene had no home other than the sect, while the Pharisee could apparently invite Jesus to his home (*par' autōi*). Unlike the Essene meal, which was exclusively communal, the Pharisee and Jesus seem to have been eating alone. Nevertheless, even the more moderate regulations of the Pharisees demanded a far greater degree of stringency concerning commensality, with regard to purity, than was found among Graeco-Roman voluntary associations. If the conjectures above are correct, Pharisees could only eat with other Pharisees, or with those who maintained their standards (perhaps only temporarily). A purity barrier divided them from other Jews.[49] None of the real Graeco-Roman groups (as opposed to utopias) were marked by such exclusivity.

---

[47] For this interpretation of the Nazirite see further Baumgarten (1996c). The idea that the level of sanctity in one's life can be raised by taking on all or part of the life style of those in a higher place in the hierarchy has its equivalents in a number of other traditions. See Dumont (1979), 192.

[48] The Pharisees as priests *manqués* has been one of the ongoing themes in the writing of Neusner on the topic. See e.g. Neusner (1971), iii. 288. For a summary and critique of Neusner's position see Sanders (1990), 131–254. If the argument developed above can be sustained my conclusion would favour Neusner. See further Harrington (1995), 42–54; Hengel and Deines (1995), 41–51.

[49] Might this way of life have been the reason the Pharisees called themselves separatists? See Baumgarten (1983b), 411–28.

III

When we check the comparison between Graeco-Roman voluntary associations and Jewish sects suggested by Philo and Josephus we find similarities and differences. There are some ways in which the correlation illuminates important aspects of the Jewish groups, while there are others in which it hides what may have been most distinctive about the Jewish movements, both Essenes and Pharisees. This result is, in fact, not all that surprising. Virtually all comparative analysis, when well done, reveals similarities as well as differences, of varying degrees of significance.[50]

What then can we gain from such comparative inquiry? What can we learn that we do not, or should not, already know? I would suggest that several aspects of Graeco-Roman voluntary associations overlap with those of the Jewish sects in such a way as to suggest one piece of an answer to a larger question of some grander consequence. That is, one of the puzzles which intrigued ancient Jews as well as modern scholars is why ancient Jewish sectarianism flourished at the time it did (the Hasmonean era, in my view).[51] What circumstances favoured this result, what was the connection between context and consequence? The ancient rabbis answered this question, as usual in their works, in interpersonal terms, as the result of the misunderstanding of the saying of a master by his disciples.[52] We moderns expect to find other sorts of answers to such questions, as detailed and nuanced as possible. Some insight into one part of that complex answer is offered, I suggest, by the comparison between Graeco-Roman voluntary associations and Jewish sects.

Graeco-Roman voluntary associations were *urban*, and there is some evidence that the same was true of the Jewish sects. Josephus testified that the Essenes had centres in every town (*War* 2. 124). Philo was less clear: Essenes lived in cities and villages of Judea (*Hyp.* 11. 1), but elsewhere (*Omnis Probus* 76) he wrote that the Essenes avoided cities. In the view of modern scholars, Jerusalem and the Temple were the main focus of sectarian activity.[53]

[50] See Bloch (1967), 44–81; Sewell (1967), 208–18.

[51] The date of the rise of ancient Jewish sectarianism has been much disputed. For a presentation of my view see Baumgarten (1995), 54. See also Baumgarten (1997), 15–27.

[52] See Aboth de Rabbi Nathan 5 (26, Schecter), and discussions of this and similar sources in Cohen (1980), 1–11; Baumgarten (1995), 52–6.

[53] Cohen (1984), 43–6.

What then of Pliny's testimony (*HN* 5. 73) placing the Essenes in a distinctly non-urban setting, on the west side of the Dead Sea, or the discovery of the remains of the Qumran community more or less in the place indicated by Pliny?[54] Pliny's account contains a sentence which has received less attention than the rest of his comments:

Day by day the throng of refugees is recruited to an equal number by numerous accessions of persons tired of life and driven thither by the waves of fortune to adopt their manners.

Membership levels at the city of the Essenes, according to Pliny, remained high in spite of the fact that there was no reproduction because of new recruits who came there as refugees, tired of life, from elsewhere.[55] The source of these refugees, I suggest, was the city. Thus Pliny's Essenes began their lives as city-dwellers, and it was their dissatisfaction with city life which brought them to the Essene settlement, below which lay Ein Gedi.

A similar argument can be made for the Qumran sect. The obscure comments on their history at the beginning of CD nevertheless make it clear that this movement began in Jerusalem, and only reached the desert at a later stage in its existence, as explained in 1QS ix. 19–20, at the time of the 'preparation of the way into the wilderness'.

Next, the role of literacy in the Graeco-Roman groups. According to Posidonius, the eating clubs of Syria which he denounced met in the *grammateia*. While the meaning of the phrase is obscure, the likelihood that it has something to do with letters and literacy is high.[56] Inscriptions erected by voluntary associations all over the Graeco-Roman world provide abundant incontrovertible evidence

---

[54] It is probable that Pliny's Essenes were the Qumran community. But were they the same as the Essenes of Philo and Josephus? Must we accept Pliny, a non-Jew, who probably never visited Palestine, and whose geographical account is quite confused (for these conclusions concerning Pliny see *GLAJJ* i. 465–6), as a reliable guide to the intricacies of Jewish sectarian identity, capable of making fine distinctions between groups? See above, n. 7.

[55] Membership levels, according to Pliny, remained constant, because they were replenished by new recruits, but for whom they would have declined. Pliny did not specify the reason for this potential drop in membership levels. One obvious possibility, however, was deaths. Perhaps another cause of decreases in membership numbers was defections. Compare Josephus' description of his period of floating between groups, *Vita* 10–12.

[56] See Kidd (1988), 301.

of the place of literacy in the lives of these groups. To have one's name inscribed on a record of contributors was an incentive to raise contributions in a building campaign for a gymnasium in Halicarnassus in the third century BCE.[57] The regulations of the Iobacchi specified that a new member was required to apply to join the group in writing. On acceptance, he was registered in writing on the rolls, and received a written certificate attesting to his new status. The record of regulations of the Guild of Zeus Hypsistos, known to us from a papyrus, came from a draft made by an official of the club for his use.[58] According to the by-laws of the burial society of Lanuvium, Italy (Dessau, *ILS* 7212, 136 CE), a new member was warned to 'read the by-laws carefully', so that he knows the exact privileges accruing to him on membership lest, later, he find cause for complaint or bequeath a lawsuit to his heirs.[59]

The role of knowledge of reading and writing in Jewish groups was also significant. The Essenes, according to Josephus, had books which they transmitted to their new members, and which the latter were sworn to preserve carefully (*War* 2. 142). Qumran members had round-the-clock Torah study sessions going every day of the year. A member should know how to read in order to be able to participate in this activity (1QS vi. 6). There is also a high evaluation of writing in sectarian texts such as Jubilees and the Damascus Document. Jubilees emphasized repeatedly the fact that certain laws were written in heaven on high and were eternal (e.g. 6. 24, 31). What was written and hence ordained by God was to be distinguished from what might be invented—even by an angel, not to mention a human being—from his heart (6. 35). Enoch was the

---

[57] See Forbes (1933), 48–9. Ibid. 6–10, Forbes presents a list of all *Neoi* inscriptions known to him. For a sample of Greek inscriptions erected by voluntary associations of all sorts see *SIG* [3], 1095–120. One of the themes found in virtually all cases is that one aspect of enacting the decision taken was to have it recorded as an inscription. In the instance of the Iobacchi, *SIG* [3] 1109, after the new regulations had been promulgated they were acclaimed with the cry that they should now be inscribed.

[58] Nock (1972), 415.

[59] Literacy plays a similar part in the groups formed by newly literate urbanites in contemporary Africa, educated out of subsistence agriculture, who create associations organized to run activities during the brief period when they return home for the holidays. See Goody (1987), 141–7; Anderson (1991), 118–20. Such groups are typically called 'Young Men's Associations of X', emphasizing their role as the advanced intelligentsia of the area, who control the means of modernization. This fits well with the role assigned by Nock to Graeco-Roman voluntary associations, as agents of change and adaptation, discussed below.

first human to discover writing, while both he and Noah wrote books (4. 17, 23; 10. 13), books which were later quoted by Abraham in his parting words to Isaac (21. 10). The written library passed down from Abraham was ultimately deposited with Levi (45. 15). Finally, the righteous man was written down on high, attesting to his status (2. 20; 30. 20–3; 36. 10). A similar situation prevails in the Damascus Document from Qumran. In at least three places (iii. 3; iv. 4–5; xiv. 4), to be written down among the righteous was to attain the highest rank possible. To be *written* among one's brothers was a formula for becoming a full member of the Qumran community (1QS vi. 22).

Graeco-Roman voluntary associations were instruments of religious innovation, and a means for the introduction of new cults. In the words of Nock, they were an 'opportunity for evolution of new religious ideas',[60] a place where people who had sensed a problem and discovered a common solution came together. Jewish sects played a similar role: they too were a place where people who had created and/or found common answers to dilemmas posed by the new circumstances of the second century BCE came together.

What might these problems have been in each of the cultural contexts which we have been comparing? In the instance of the Graeco-Roman groups it is an old conclusion, already proposed by Rostovtzeff: voluntary associations had a special appeal for uprooted and dispossessed urbanites, now finding themselves a bit adrift in cities of the Mediterranean world.[61] Political life of the *polis* no longer supplied a meaningful pursuit under the rule of the Hellenistic monarchies, hence people turned to voluntary associations.[62] These needs had been much less acutely felt prior to the Hellenistic period, prior to the dispersal of Greeks in the wake of the conquests of Alexander the Great, and prior to the rise of the Hellenistic kingdoms, hence these groups became prominent from the Hellenistic era onwards. The flowering of these groups in the Hellenistic era and thereafter has been noted by many authors on the topic.[63]

The considerations above lead to a suggestion to be explored: as more or less the same sort of people, of equivalent background, and in similar circumstances, were involved in Graeco-Roman voluntary

[60] Nock (1924), 105.   [61] See Rostovtzeff (1941), ii. 1064.
[62] See e.g. Fisher (1988a), 1195.
[63] See e.g. Herrmann *et al.* (1978), col. 94; Fisher (1988a), 1194.

associations and Jewish sects, perhaps the reasons for the attract-
iveness of the Graeco-Roman groups might also help explain the
rise of Jewish sects. That is, perhaps something about the experience of literate urbanites, somewhat adrift in a metropolitan
setting, will provide part of the solution to understanding how
and why the Jewish groups flourished at the time they did. If this
proposition could be confirmed, the benefit of the comparison of
the Graeco-Roman and Jewish groups would be significant. As is
regularly the case in successful comparative studies, a point clearer
on one side of the comparison will have suggested a fruitful line of
investigation on the other.[64]

IV

The proposal made above has much to recommend it from yet
another perspective. The importance of the place of the city, and
the role of new immigrants to an urban environment, have been
indicated in studies of the origin of sectarian movements at other
times and places. Its role has been noted in seventeenth-century
Britain,[65] as well as in modern Iran.[66] Uprooted and dislocated
people who find new meaning in their lives from the direction given
them by some religious master, whose teachings concerning the
'correct' way to live in accord with their tradition help fill the void in
their lives, play a role in the explanation of the growth of
fundamentalism all over the contemporary Middle East.[67]

V

The argument presented in this paper can now be brought to a
conclusion. The same sorts of people were involved in Graeco-
Roman voluntary associations as in Jewish sects, perhaps for some

[64] Nevertheless, one important possible difference between the Graeco-Roman
and Jewish examples should be noted. Perhaps the loss of political independence was
an important factor on the Graeco-Roman side, while Jews of the 2nd cent. BCE were
confronting the thrill of regained independence.

[65] See Thomas (1971), 153. Compare similar remarks made by Hill (1975), 38–9.

[66] See Arjomand (1988), 91.

[67] See Kupferschmidt (1987), 411. In Egirdir in Turkey, a provincial town of
9,000–12,000 inhabitants, with a strong tradition of toleration, the Tappers found
that those few religious extremists in town were largely people of recent village origin.
See R. and N. Tapper (1987), 61.

of the same reasons. Perhaps the expressions which these similar people gave to their analogous distress in their differing cultural contexts were not exactly identical.[68] Nevertheless, hypothesizing that the circumstances of dispossessed new urbanites had something to do with the rise of ancient Jewish sectarianism yields a conclusion which in fact agrees with explanations of the rise of sectarianism in other historical circumstances and hence is quite tempting. The solution at this stage is still incomplete. To complete it, at the very least one would need to find evidence—direct and indirect, to the extent possible—for a migration from the cities to the towns, and to Jerusalem in particular, in the second century BCE and thereafter, and for the distress that experience might have caused. The combination of circumstances above is enough, in my opinion, to encourage one to start looking.[69]

[68] See n. 64.

[69] For a discussion of this aspect of the evidence see Baumgarten (1996*b*). I have since attempted to unite these perspectives in Baumgarten (1997), 143–51. Among the works that have appeared on the general topic of this paper since it was written, I should note the important collection of essays in Kloppenborg and Wilson (1996).

8

Antichrist among Jews and Gentiles

WILLIAM HORBURY

Antichrist seems as native to Christianity as the devil with horns and a tail. This impression receives learned support in much recent scholarship. Thus G. C. Jenks, C. E. Hill, and L. J. Lietaert Peerbolte all contend that the figure of Antichrist is a Christian development. In earlier years, by contrast, it had been considered originally Jewish by Wilhelm Bousset, Moritz Friedländer, Louis Ginzberg, and Israel Lévi. Then, however, Paul Billerbeck (1926), concisely summarizing a wealth of material, urged that, despite appearances, there was virtually no contact in substance between ancient Jewish literature and the New Testament on Antichrist; in Jewish sources the messiah had political opponents, but the Christian Antichrist was a religious figure.[1] More recently Stefan Heid, in a book finished in 1990, accepted that Bousset was fundamentally right. A contrast between Christian and Jewish sources, in some ways recalling that drawn by Billerbeck, has nevertheless returned to prominence. For Jenks (1991), Hill (1995), and Lietaert Peerbolte (1996) the expectation of an enemy specifically opposed to the messiah first occurs among the earliest Christians, rather than among the non-Christian or pre-Christian Jews. Pre-Christian traditions, it is urged, refer to an eschatological tyrant, a final attack by evil powers, or an accompanying false prophecy, rather than a messianic opponent who can properly be termed Antichrist.

Yet, just as Belial with horns now looms up hauntingly in Qumran texts (see 11Q Apocryphal Psalms^a, col. iv, lines 6–7), so it may be asked again, a hundred years after Bousset, whether Antichrist is not pre-Christian and Jewish as well as Christian. With regard to the Jews in the Roman empire this question frames itself

---

[1] Billerbeck in Str.–B. iii. 637–40, on 2 Thess. 2: 3.

more precisely. In the early empire, was Antichrist a Jewish counter-part of Greek and Roman notions concerning the great enemy of a saviour king? If so, Jews and gentiles would have shared, in this as in many other respects, a broadly similar pattern of hopes and fears for the future.[2]

I. THE WICKED ONE

First, was an Antichrist already envisaged by Jews in the early Roman empire? They might be expected to have imagined such a figure, because biblical texts which were important in messianic hope naturally emphasize victory over enemies; see for example three passages which were all later connected with an arch-enemy of the messiah, Num. 24: 17 (the star from Jacob smites the corners of Moab), Isa. 11: 4 (with the breath of his lips he shall slay the wicked), and Ps. 2: 2 (the kings of the earth rise up, and the rulers take counsel together, against the Lord and against his anointed). Moreover, from the Persian period onwards it was expected that a tyrannical king would oppress Israel and the nations just before the decisive divine victory. This thought is already suggested by the placing of the prophecy of Gog and Magog in Ezekiel 38–9, after the prophecies of a David to come and the revival of the dry bones, and before the description of new Jerusalem; and the expectation is developed or alluded to in Dan. 7: 8, 24–7; 8: 9–11, 23–6, on the little horn which signifies a king of fierce countenance; Ass. Mos. 8. 1 ('regem regum terrae', cf. Ps. 2: 2 'kings of the earth'); and 2 Esdras 5: 6 ('et regnabit quem non sperant qui inhabitant super terram'). The time-honoured representation of oppressive rulers or kingdoms as monstrous beasts often marks this line of thought, as in Daniel and later on in Revelation. An influence of the expectation of an evil king on the texts associated with messianic victory is suggested by Ecclus. 36: 12 in the Hebrew textual tradition ('destroy the *head* of the corners of Moab', cf. Num. 24: 17, Jer. 48: 45, and Ass. Mos. 8. 1 '*king* of the kings of the earth'); but it cannot simply be assumed that oracles which speak of many enemies of the messiah, like the psalms cited above, had at the time of the Roman principate generally been interpreted as also indicating one great anti-messianic overlord.

---

[2] A similar observation is made on different grounds by Downing (1995), 196–211.

Of course such a messianic opponent was envisaged by Jews later on. In the Byzantine period he is the subject of the legend of Armilus the wicked, attested in the early seventh-century book *Zerubbabel* and elsewhere. Here Armilus slays messiah son of Joseph, and is himself slain by messiah son of David, as prophesied in Isa. 11: 4 ('with the breath of his lips he shall slay the wicked').[3] Elements of this story, without the name Armilus, can be identified in midrash and piyyut. So the possibly fifth-century poet Yose ben Yose, in his New Year composition *ahallelah elohay* which incorporates the series of *malkhuyyoth* texts, writes (line 55)

> . . . the wicked one shall be *shaken out* [Job 38: 13],
> but one has set righteousness for his feet [Isa. 41: 2], and he shall be crowned with KINGDOM.[4]

Here Yose seems to reflect the notion of Antichrist—'the wicked one', in line with Isa. 11: 4—being removed by the messiah of righteousness; note that the plural 'wicked ones' of Job 38: 13 have become singular. Compare a probably earlier midrash found in Lev. R. 27. 11 = Pes.R.K. 9. 11, in Midrash Tehillim 2. 4 (on Ps. 2: 2), and elsewhere, in the name of the third-century haggadist R. Levi, on Gog-and-Magog (speaking as a single figure) planning war 'against the Lord and against his messiah', as envisaged in Ps. 2: 2. This messianic psalm could indeed be called 'the chapter of Gog and Magog', followed by 'the chapter of Absalom' (Ps. 3, ascribed in its title to the time of Absalom's revolt), as can be seen from a comment on the juxtaposition of the two psalms repeated by Abbahu of Caesarea in the name of his mid-third-century teacher Yohanan, who settled in Tiberias (b. Ber. 10a); this designation of Ps. 2 presupposes that the messiah's enemy is Gog-and-Magog. The messianic antagonist is similarly assumed in a famous explanation of the closed Mem in the prophecy 'of the increase of government' in Isa. 9: 6(7), cited as given by Bar Kappara (early third century) in Sepphoris; the Holy One sought to make Hezekiah the messiah, and Sennacherib Gog-and-Magog (b. Sanh. 94a). At the time of this explanation, the conception of Gog-and-Magog as the messiah's opponent needed no special justification. These three

---

[3] Text in Jellinek (1967), 54–7; the related midrash *Signs of the Messiah*, as reprinted by Jellinek, ibid. 58–63 from *Abqat Rokhel* (Amsterdam, 1696), includes a note that Armilus is 'he whom the nations call *anticristo*' (Jellinek, ibid. xxii, 60). For the dating of the Armilus legend in the time of Heraclius see Sharf (1971), 54.

[4] Text in Mirsky (1977), 94, discussed by Horbury (1981), 162–5.

midrashim citing third-century teachers together suggest that war between Gog-and-Magog and the messiah will have been a familiar and uncontroversial expectation in Caesarea and Galilee under the Jewish patriarchs by the end of the age of the Severi.

Nevertheless, even as early as this, the possibility of Christian influence on Jewish messianic hopes cannot be ruled out. Jewish notions of an opponent of the messiah are commonly thought to be less well attested, or not attested at all, at the beginning of the Roman imperial period. The earliest full descriptions of Antichrist, identified by that name, are Christian, and they come from sources of the second and third centuries—Irenaeus, Tertullian, Origen, and the exegetical works attributed to Hippolytus. Moreover, the first attestations of the Greek word *antichristos* are Christian, being found—here without fuller explanation or description—in two of the three Johannine epistles of the New Testament, probably written towards the end of the first century (1 John 2: 18, 22; 4: 3; 2 John 7). The 'antichrists' are those who deny that Jesus is the messiah (1 John 2: 18–23); their emergence fulfils the familiar teaching that 'Antichrist is coming'. Probably they led their followers into or back to the majority Jewish community;[5] but even if they are to be understood simply as the founders of a separate party within the Christian body, their leadership will still have had a political significance for the Christian community which suits the traditional depiction of the messianic opponent as a ruler. Accordingly, the emphasis on false teaching in these Johannine passages on Antichrist should not be sharply contrasted with the emphasis on oppressive rule in the traditions on the messianic opponent—which themselves include the motif of false teaching, in the conception of the beast with the mouth speaking great things (Dan. 7: 8).[6]

Antichrist, then, was certainly an important early *Christian* conception. Nevertheless, the Christian references to him include much to suggest that, like the figure of the christ or messiah, he derived from pre-Christian Judaism in its Greek and Roman setting. This view is consonant with the lack of explanation of the Antichrist figure in the New Testament, and it is supported by Jewish sources

---

[5] So O'Neill (1966), 5–6, 46–8, 65, followed by Lampe (1973), 261–2; Hengel (1989), 57–63 prefers to take the denial as referring to a docetic christology like that of Cerinthus, as suggested by 1 John 4: 7 and 2 John 7 on coming 'in flesh'.

[6] Such a contrast is drawn e.g. by Billerbeck in Str.–B. iii. 637–8; Hill (1995), 100; Lietaert Peerbolte (1996), 343.

from the end of the Second Temple period which describe an Antichrist-like figure without using this term, naming him rather as the wicked one, Gog, or Beliar. These sources can be said to bridge the gap between the biblical passages already noted, which attest the expectations of messianic victory and of a final arch-enemy of Israel without explicit interconnection between them, and the rabbinic passages also noted above, which suggest that the notion of a great messianic opponent was familiar under the Jewish patriarchate in the third century.

Against this background it can be seen that the technical Greek term *antichristos*, although it is known only from Christian sources, need not necessarily be Christian in origin. It is true that the distribution of the word can readily suggest that it is a Christian coinage. *Antichristos* first occurs in the Johannine epistles, and it is not used by other Greek Jewish or early Christian writings which speak of an identical or similar figure, notably the Sibylline Oracles (but *antichristos* is somewhat inconvenient for their metre), 2 Thess. 2: 1–13, Revelation 11–20, the Didache and Justin Martyr; it next occurs in Polycarp and Irenaeus—second-century authors who knew the Johannine writings. Hence a specifically Johannine origin for the word has been regarded as a strong possibility.[7]

Yet, in the Johannine epistles *antichristos* is not treated as a new word, but as belonging to a teaching which is already current—'Antichrist is coming' (1 John 2: 18, cf. 4: 3); and the gospel of John, which is very close to the epistles in style and vocabulary, attests for the first time one or two other words which were probably non-Christian Jewish technical terms, notably the Hellenized Aramaic *messias* and the Greek *aposynagogos*, 'excluded from assembly' (John 1: 41; 4: 25; 9: 22; 12: 42; 16: 2). *Christos*, used both in John and elsewhere in the New Testament, was likewise taken over from the contemporary Jewish vocabulary. The same may well have been true of *antichristos*. Comparable Jewish uses of compounds with *anti-* are exemplified by ἀντίδικος, in Ben Sira's grandson's rendering of the prayer for the crushing of the arrogant enemy in Ecclus. 36: 7, or the verb ἀντιβασίλευω in Josephus' depiction of John of Gischala as a rival sovereign over against the remainder of the Zealot party (*War* 4. 395), or ἀντίθεος, in Philo's warning against the season of good fortune which is 'against God' and put in the place of God (Num. 14: 9 LXX, as interpreted in *Post. C.* 122–3).

---

[7] Hengel (1989), 171–2 n. 69, citing R. E. Brown.

(Is Philo here thinking in part of current associations of Fortune with the supreme deity, as seen in Horace, *Od.* 1. 34–5 and elsewhere?)

Even the technical term 'Antichrist', therefore, is by no means clearly of Christian origin. However that may be, the figure which the term describes—the great enemy to be slain by the messiah—is probably pre-Christian. In his argument for this view, Bousset pointed especially to the passage in the twelfth chapter of the book of Revelation describing how the great red dragon seeks to devour the man-child borne by the woman clothed with the sun; building on H. Gunkel's interpretation of Rev. 11–12 as a fragment of a myth of the messiah, and noting also that much developed exegesis is presupposed in the second-century and later Christian texts on Antichrist, Bousset urged that an 'antichrist myth' was also known at the time of the New Testament writers.[8] Criticism has fastened on his inferences from Christian evidence, including relatively late material, to a connected myth envisaged as in circulation at the time of Christian origins; but perhaps too little credit has been given to the support for his view found in Jewish sources of the Second Temple period, notably the Septuagint, the Sibylline Oracles, 2 Esdras and 2 Baruch, and the Qumran texts.

First, messianic expectations of this period included a judgement scene in which the messiah condemned and executed his great adversary. This scene was associated with an exegesis of Isa. 11: 4 'but with righteousness shall he judge the poor, and reprove with equity for the meek of the earth: and he shall smite the earth with the rod of his mouth, and with the breath of his lips he shall slay the wicked'. In the LXX the Hebrew of the second part of the verse is rendered 'he shall smite the earth with the word of his mouth, and with a breath through the lips shall he remove the impious'. In the context of chapter 10 the wicked one in question can readily be understood as a threatening king, Sennacherib in Isaiah's time or the great foe of the messiah yet to come. The application of Isa. 11: 4 to the destruction of a special future enemy is of course found in the New Testament. Thus a judgement scene is presupposed with allusion to this verse in 2 Thess. 2: 8 'then shall be revealed the lawless one, whom the Lord Jesus shall remove by the breath of his mouth, and shall destroy by the epiphany of his advent'; and Isa. 11: 4 is also vividly pictorialized in Relevation, where the enemies of the

---

[8] Bousset (1896), esp. 15, 152–90, 214–17, 247–9.

two witnesses are destroyed by fire from the Lord's mouth (Rev. 11: 5), and the conquering messiah has a sword coming out of his mouth (Rev. 1: 16; 2: 13, 16; 19: 15, 21). In the vision of Rev. 19: 11–21 the messiah judges in righteousness (verse 11, cf. Isa. 11: 4), and with the sword of his mouth he is to smite the nations (verse 15, cf. Isa. 11: 4); the beast who leads the kings of the earth (cf. Ps. 2: 2, Ass. Mos. 8. 1) and his false prophet would be slain by it, as their followers are, if the two leaders were not preserved to be cast into the lake of fire (verses 19–21, cf. Isa. 11: 4 'he shall slay the wicked').

These Christian texts of the first century in 2 Thessalonians and Revelation evidently presuppose a scene built on Isa. 11: 4. This point gives the passages a unity which would not be recognized if they were simply classified according to their descriptions of the opponents. Their shared dependence on Isa. 11: 4 suggests the existence of a prophetically based myth of the messiah and his adversary, on the lines suggested by Gunkel and Bousset, and their early date underlines the likelihood that it is originally Jewish; but on the basis of this evidence alone the possibility that an antichrist myth first emerged in the intense messianism of the rise of Christianity would still remain.

Yet the judgement scene associated with this passage of Isaiah is also attested in non-Christian Jewish sources of the same period. Thus in the apocalypses of Ezra and Baruch, to be dated not long after the destruction of Jerusalem by Titus, the messiah, taking his stand on mount Zion, first rebukes, and then destroys, the fourth kingdom—here the Roman empire. The sequence of reproof and execution found in both apocalypses once again follows Isa. 11: 4 ('judge . . . and reprove . . .: smite the earth . . . and . . . slay the wicked'). In the Ezra-apocalypse the kingdom is personified individually in the eagle-vision of chapter 11, but emphasis later falls on the nations and the multitude who support its oppressive rule (see 2 Esdras 11: 36–46; 12: 30–3; 13: 4–11, 27–8, 35–8). The influence of Isa. 11: 4 'with the rod of his mouth, and with the breath of his lips', and of the understanding of it attested in the LXX 'with the *word* of his mouth', is seen in the motif of destruction by the messiah's voice, which is also the law (2 Esdras 12: 1–3; 13: 4, 10–11, 38). (This emphasis on the godlike power of his voice also approximates the description to contemporary praise of rulers.)[9] In the Syriac

---

[9] Compare Acts 12: 22 'the voice of a god, and not of a man' (Agrippa I), with

apocalypse of Baruch, on the other hand, the destruction of all the hosts of the fourth kingdom is reported first; the stream and the vine of Baruch's dream-vision destroy the forest first of all, and finally the great cedar which is its last survivor (2 (Syriac) Baruch 37–9). This vision is inspired by passages including Ps. 80: 15–18, but also, notably in the present context, Isa. 10: 34 (a verse followed immediately by Isa. 11: 1–4) 'he shall cut down the thickets of the forest, and Lebanon shall fall by a mighty one'—Lebanon, on the exegetical convention followed here, standing for a gentile king.[10] In the interpretation of Baruch's dream, correspondingly, the last leader of the fourth kingdom is finally singled out and brought to mount Zion for the reproof and execution suggested by Isa. 11: 4; 'my messiah will charge him with all his iniquities . . ., and afterwards he shall put him to death' (2 (Syriac) Baruch 40: 1–2). Here there is close resemblance to the execution of the beast and the false prophet by the judgement of the messiah in Rev. 19. Thus—to view the apocalypses of Ezra and Baruch together—the conception of a single messianic opponent is not absent from 2 Esdras, where it is adumbrated by the contest between the lion and the eagle; but it takes particularly clear and concrete form in 2 Baruch, which seems to envisage the messiah as putting the Roman emperor to death. Both apocalypses are shaped by Isa. 11: 4, considered—as is evident especially from 2 Baruch—in its larger context.

A brief depiction of this messianic judgement scene is given in a third source close in date to the two apocalypses. *Sib. Or.* 5. 101–10. Here the conqueror of Persia who attacks Egypt from the west grows formidably great and threatens 'the city of the blessed', like the he goat from the west in Dan. 8: 5–12; but 'a king sent from God against him | shall destroy all great kings and mighty men; | and so shall there be judgement upon men from the Immortal' (lines 108–10). As in 2 Esdras, the end of 'him' is less emphasized than the general destruction of his kings and warriors, but it is clear that the messiah has one great adversary. The description based on Daniel leads to a judgement scene at Jerusalem like that associated

---

Tac. *Ann.* 16. 22, on Nero (Thrasea Paetus never sacrificed 'pro salute principis aut caelesti voce') and other passages discussed by Loesch (1933), 18–24.

[10] The influence of Isa. 10: 34 here is brought out by G. Vermes in Vermes *et al.* (1992), 90; on the conventions followed in the interpretation of 'Lebanon' see Gordon, ibid. 93–4 (urging that in 4Q 285, discussed below, it is simultaneously equated with 'king' and 'nations').

with Isa. 11: 4, a verse which is recalled, without any detailed correspondence, by the emphasis in lines 108–10 on judgement and destruction of foes after the victory of the God-sent king over his enemy at Jerusalem. The Sibylline passage is also broadly compatible with the myth of Nero's return, which is utilized below in lines 137–54. This point indicates the similarity, noted further below, between the Jewish conception of a messianic adversary and non-Jewish expectations in the Roman empire.

Further attestation of this messianic judgement scene are found in the Dead Sea Scrolls. First, in a fragment which has been attributed to the Rule of War (4Q 285, fragment 5), in the course of a continuous exegesis of Isa. 10: 34–11: 5, it is said that 'there shall slay him the Prince of the Congregation, the Branch of David'. The foe to be slain by the Davidic messiah is unnamed because of lacunae, but will be connected with the Kittim mentioned in a surviving phrase; probably he is 'the king of the Kittim' who leads the enemy army in the War Scroll (15. 2).[11] The scene imagined then corresponds exactly with that described in 2 (Syriac) Baruch. Comparably, the Blessing of the Prince of the Congregation prays, once again taking up Isa. 11: 4, that with the breath of his lips he may slay the wicked (1QSb col. 5, lines 24–5). This slaying is mentioned yet again in the fragmentary commentary on Isa.10: 33–11: 5 in 4Q 161.[12] Here the 'high ones of stature' (10: 33) are 'the mighty men of the Kittim'(line 5), and 'Lebanon' in 10: 34 seems likely again to be their chief or king, although the relevant text is lacking (beginning of line 8); later in this fragment (lines 16–18) 'he shall slay the wicked' is interpreted of the branch of David who will slay 'his [en]emy' (singular).[13] The description of his rule and judgement includes a mention of Magog (line 20), which recalls the role of Gog and Magog as the foe of the messiah, already noted in connection with rabbinic interpretation of Ps. 2.

Still other biblical passages were probably drawn into this scene in contemporary exegesis, for example Ps. 68: 30–1 on the gifts

---

[11] For text and discussion see Vermes and Gordon in Vermes *et al.* (1992).

[12] Allegro (1968), 13–15, and pl. v; translation also in F. García Martínez (1994), 186.

[13] *'w]ybw* (line 18) is taken by Allegro and García Martínez as a defectively written plural and rendered 'his enemies', but the more straightforward rendering 'his enemy', in the singular, seems preferable against the background sketched above. Vermes and Gordon do not discuss this question in their comments on 4Q 161 in Vermes *et al.* (1992).

brought by kings and the rebuke administered to 'the beast of the reeds', who seems to be linked with the Kittim in a fragmentary commentary on Ps. 68 (1Q 16).[14] In midrash and piyyut this beast is Rome; so, in a poetic account of the succession of the four Danielic kingdoms, 'to the beast of the reeds then he sold the land' (Yose ben Yose, *'anusah le 'ezrah*, line 23).[15] Now in an exegesis of Ps. 68: 30–1 attributed to the early third-century Ishmael b. Jose b. Halafta (who himself is said to have repeated it as something that 'my father said') Rome is rebuked by or in the presence of the messiah—who has accepted gifts from the other gentile monarchies (Exod. R. 35: 5, on Exod. 26: 15; b. Pes. 118b). In this probably tannaitic interpretation the judgement scene considered above seems to have been linked with the old and widely-attested scene in which the messiah receives gifts from the nations; for the latter see Ps. Sol. 18: 31, 2 Esdras 13: 13, cf. Ps. 72: 10–11, Isa. 66: 20; Ber. R. 78: 12, on Gen. 33: 11 (quoting Ps. 72: 10); Midrash Tehillim 87: 6, on verse 4 (quoting Isa. 66: 20). In the dream-vision of 2 Esdras 13: 1–13 the two scenes are already connected, through a messianic interpretation of Isa. 66: 5–24; and with the Qumran material in view it may be suggested that they were also linked in the Second-Temple period on the basis of Ps. 68: 30–1.

These passages do not comprise all the Qumran material relevant to discussion of Antichrist.[16] Thus the present writer thinks that the figure called 'son of God' in the Aramaic prophecy in 4Q 246 is probably once again the expected evil king.[17] Similarly, the conflict between Melchizedech and Melchiresha (see 11Q Melchizedek, 4Q Amram (in Aramaic) and 4Q 280) can be interpreted with fair probability as one between angelic spirits who take human form as the messiah and his great opponent.[18] These positions cannot be

[14] So J. T. Milik in Barthélemy and Milik (1955), 82.

[15] Mirsky (1977), 108; the context is summarized in Horbury (1981), 151.

[16] Lietaert Peerbolte (1996), 258–89 gives a valuable survey, including interpretations of the 'son of God' and Melchizedek texts which differ from those mentioned below, but not including discussion of the texts on a messianic judgement scene which have just been considered.

[17] See Vermes (1992), 301–3 (probably the last ruler of the final world empire). Collins (1995), 154–72, prefers a messianic interpretation.

[18] Collins (1995), 176 understands Melchizedek as an angelic saviour, not a messiah. The view that Melchizedek is a messianic figure, put forward by J. Carmignac and others, is freshly argued by Rainbow (1997). I am grateful to Dr Rainbow for allowing me to see a preliminary form of his article. This view of Melchizedek would be consistent with the ancient opinion that, together with Elijah, king messiah, and the priest anointed for war, Melchizedek is one of the 'four smiths'

presented here, but the argument does not depend upon them. The view that a messianic opponent was envisaged in the Second Temple period is supported, rather, by the less-discussed scene of messianic judgement of 'the wicked one' which some Hebrew texts discovered at Qumran share with Jewish prophecies known through Christian transmission. In the exegesis represented in the first three Qumran texts, Isa. 11: 4 was regularly interpreted as referring to the execution of 'the wicked', probably the ruler of the Kittim, by the branch of David. This interpretation was also connected with other scriptural passages, including the prophecy of Gog and probably also Ps. 68, as suggested by 1Q 16 in the light of 2 Esdras and the midrash. This understanding of Isa. 11: 4 will therefore have been familiar among Jews at the beginning of the Herodian period. It will have influenced both the Christian and the Jewish texts from the end of this period which have just been considered—2 Thessalonians, Revelation, and the apocalypses of Ezra and Baruch. Moreover, it had already helped to shape an imagined scene of messianic judgement, found again in the Fifth Sibylline Book, which can properly be called an element in a myth of the messiah and his arch-enemy. This story could also be attached to other biblical texts, as the rabbinic passages on Gog discussed above have shown, and from the Second Temple period onwards it was sometimes linked with the related scene in which the messiah receives tribute from the nations.

As a pendant to what now appears as a regularly envisaged Isaianic scene one may note Jerome's allegation that Bar Kokhba pretended to breathe fire by a trick (*Adv. Rufinum* 3. 31). Probably this reproduces a Jewish tradition hostile to Bar Kokhba, once again with allusion to Isa. 11: 4; compare the talmudic legend that he was slain because the rabbis saw that he did not fulfil Isa. 11: 3 'he shall not judge by the sight of his eyes' (b. Sanh. 93b).

From among other evidence pointing in the same direction as the judgement scene of the 'wicked one' of Isa. 11: 4, two further old identifications of the messiah's adversary may be briefly outlined. First, as already noted, Gog-and-Magog constitute his foe in rabbinic interpretation current in the third century; and in the fragmentary 4Q 161, representing exegesis known during the Herodian period, Magog is named in the context of the messiah's

of Zech. 2: 3–4 (1: 20–1) who come to cast down the horns of the nations who threaten Judah (Pes. R. K. v 9, and elsewhere).

rule over all the nations.[19] The likelihood that the name is connected here with opposition, in line with rabbinic exegesis and with Targum Ps.-Jonathan on Num. 11: 26, cited below, is strengthened by Septuagintal references to Gog. Thus in the third century BCE Num. 24: 7 was rendered in the LXX (presupposing $mg(w)g$ for MT $m'gg$) 'there shall come forth a man . . . his kingdom shall be higher than Gog'. Here Gos is already the messianic opponent. In the prophets, the end of Amos 7: 1 is rendered 'behold, one locust was king Gog' (presupposing gwg where MT has gzy). This oracle could be understood of Sennacherib's invasion (so Jerome), but in the light of Num. 24: 7 LXX it seems likely that the translator took it of a future adversary. Comparably, Amos 4: 13 LXX includes the phrase 'announcing to men his messiah' (presupposing $mšhw$, cf. MT $mhšhw$). Both these Septuagintal renderings in Amos fit the messianic close of the book (9: 11–15).[20] On a distinct but closely related line of interpretation, the third Sibylline book, in a passage reflecting Jewish Egypt perhaps during the second century BCE, locates 'the land of Gog and Magog' in Ethiopia (cf. Ezek. 38: 5) and predicts its doom as a 'house of judgement' drenched in blood (*Sib. Or.* 3. 319–21).

The wide early circulation of the understanding of Gog-and-Magog as the enemy to be destroyed by the messiah is further confirmed by its occurrence in the prophecy of Eldad and Medad according to the Targum: 'Gog-and-Magog and his forces go up to Jerusalem and fall into the hand of king messiah' (Num. 11: 26 in Neofiti and the Fragment Targum). 4Q 161, if rightly restored, similarly says that the Kittim or their leaders 'will be given into the hand of his great one' (fragments 8–10, line 8). Pseudo-Jonathan at Num. 11: 26 on 'the king from the land of Magog' who is overlord of other kings and princes is comparable with and longer than Neofiti and the Fragment Targum, but does not specify the messiah. Its phrasing, however, confirms that 'Magog' in 4Q 161 should be understood primarily of the land, as in Ezek. 38: 3 and

---

[19] Material on Gog-and-Magog is gathered by Billerbeck in Str.–B. iii. 638 (on 2 Thess. 2: 3), 831–40 (on Rev. 20: 8–9), and Perez Fernandez (1981), 282–6.

[20] According to the Greek of Codex Vaticanus (B), Ecclus. 48: 17b, on Hezekiah, runs 'and he led Gog into their midst'. Γώγ is probably an inner-Greek corruption of Γίων 'Gion' (see Hart (1909), 219–20), but it suggests knowledge of the close connection in Jewish thought between Hezekiah and the messiah, illustrated above from Bar Kappara's saying in b. Sanh. 94a. As Hezekiah's captive, Gog is the messianic adversary.

Sib. Or. 3. 319. The prophecy of Eldad and Medad mentioned in Pseudo-Philo's *Biblical Antiquities* (20. 5, exactly corresponding to an earlier prophecy on Joshua in the Targums on Num. 11: 26) and quoted in Greek in the Shepherd of Hermas (*Vis.* 2. 3, 4, roughly corresponding to a phrase in Pseudo-Jonathan on the king from Magog) may well have included a version of this oracle on Gog. The identification of the great messianic adversary as Gog is therefore continuously attested in Jewish sources from the Septuagint Pentateuch to the Targums and rabbinic literature, and 4Q 161 can be understood in connection with this series of interpretations.

A second old identification of the messianic opponent names him Beliar. Belial or Beliar has of course become the name of an archdemon in Qumran texts, the Testaments of the Twelve Patriarchs, and elsewhere, often with the emphasis on deception found in biblical texts using *beliyya'al* (e.g. Deut. 13: 14); but in *Sib. Or.* 3. 63–74 and in the *Ascension of Isaiah* 4. 1–18 (a Christian insertion following the pattern of the messianic judgement scene) Beliar also takes the form of an earthly leader. Thus the Sibyl predicts that Beliar will come forth from the Sebastenoi to lead many astray by delusive miracles, including raisings of the dead; but when the divine threats come near to fulfilment, he and his followers will be burnt up by a fiery power from the deep (*Sib. Or.* 3. 63–74). J. J. Collins, following the view that the Sebastenoi are the line of the Augusti, takes the passage as alluding to the return of Nero, which is well attested elsewhere in the Sibyllines, as noted above.[21] He rejects the alternative interpretation of Sebastenoi as inhabitants of Sebaste (Samaria), urging that there is no parallel in Jewish writings for the notion of a Samaritan anti-messiah.

Yet the Samaritan interpretation has much to be said for it. It fits the hostility towards Samaritans evident in the later Second Temple period, for example in Ben Sira (50. 25–6), Ps.-Philo (*Biblical Antiquities* 25. 10–11, on idolatrous images of 'the holy nymphs' buried at Shechem) and Josephus; this hostility is linked with Beliar in the *Ascension of Isaiah*, 2. 1–3. 12 (a probably Jewish portion of the work), where a Samaritan false prophet accuses Isaiah under Manasseh, who serves Beliar. Moreover, despite the apparent lack of Jewish reference to a Samaritan 'anti-messiah', Josephus (*Ant.* 18. 85–6) describes the leader of a Samaritan uprising under Pontius

---

[21] J. J. Collins in Charlesworth (1983), 360; his interpretation is followed by Lietaert Peerbolte (1996), 336–8.

Pilate as a deceiver who claimed to show the hiding-place of the sacred vessels deposited by Moses, according to a tradition which is satirized in the allegation about hidden idols in Ps.-Philo, as cited above;[22] figures like this Samaritan leader could exemplify the seductive deception attributed to Beliar 'from the Sebastenes'. There is nothing in this Sibylline passage itself to suggest the Nero myth, but on the other hand it agrees with Jewish expectations; the raising of the dead is associated with the days of the messiah in the Qumran 'messianic apocalypse' (4Q 521, 3, lines 1 and 12), and Beliar's destruction by fire from the sea recalls the fire sent forth (cf. Isa. 11: 4) by the man who comes up from the sea and flies with the clouds in 2 Esdras 13: 3–4. The passage need not then be dated after Nero, but could be tentatively ascribed to the Hasmonaean or Herodian period, since it probably assumes the status of Beliar as an archdemon. Like its early Christian counterpart in *Asc. Isa.* 4, however, it presents a Beliar incorporate who could justly be compared with a messiah, as occurs implicitly when St Paul asks 'What is the concord of Christ with Beliar?' (2 Cor. 6: 15).

It is noteworthy that 2 Thess. 2: 8, quoted already, calls the evil opponent to be slain by the messiah not 'wicked' ($\dot{\alpha}\sigma\epsilon\beta\acute{\eta}s$, as Isa. 11: 4 LXX), but 'lawless' ($\ddot{\alpha}\nu o\mu os$); this choice of adjective is probably influenced by the contextual use of the noun $\dot{\alpha}\nu o\mu\acute{\iota}\alpha$ in the phrases 'man of lawlessness' and 'mystery of lawlessness' (2. 3 and 7), but that in turn recalls the noun used to render Belial in the LXX Pentateuch ($\dot{\alpha}\nu\acute{o}\mu\eta\mu\alpha$, Deut. 15: 9). Probably therefore Beliar lies just beneath the surface here.

In this name the associations of false teaching and seduction to idolatry are uppermost, but they are compatible with the portrait of a king or leader, like Manasseh in the *Ascension of Isaiah* or the Samaritan leader under Pilate in Josephus.

The great foe to be slain by the messiah was therefore a familiar figure in Jewish biblical interpretation of the Second Temple period. His execution was central in a widely-attested scene of messianic judgement, which was shaped especially by exegesis of Isa. 11: 4. This scene has long been known from the New Testament (2 Thessalonians and Revelation) and from 2 Esdras, 2 Baruch and

---

[22] Other references to this Jewish allegation based on Gen. 35: 4, including Ber. R. 81: 4 (idols hidden beneath the Samaritan temple), are gathered by Hayward (1990), 176–80.

the Fifth Sibylline, but its Jewish origins and its familiarity in the pre-Christian period have been confirmed by interpretations of Isaiah in Hebrew texts discovered at Qumran. This material further suggests that, as later happened in rabbinic interpretation, the scene of the messiah's victory over his adversary could be linked with the scene in which he receives offerings from the gentile nations. Gunkel and Bousset were right, therefore, in positing a myth of the messiah and his opponent, in the sense of a number of scenes which were regularly depicted and linked.

The opponent was above all the last leader of the fourth kingdom, in some cases clearly the Roman emperor. He could be named as Gog, in an interpretation of Ezek. 38–9 which goes back at least to the Septuagint Pentateuch and independently attests that the messiah's adversary was familiar in exegesis of the Second Temple period. The naming of the adversary as Beliar brings out the motif of seduction which in any case belongs to the portrait of the evil king (Dan. 7: 8, etc.); the 'political' and the 'religious' opponent are not so clearly differentiated as Billerbeck suggested, and the Christian Antichrist, as is noted below, retains markedly political traits.[23] The portrait of the messiah, as noted in passing, comparably receives motifs from current political flattery. The 'wicked one' of Second Temple Jewish exegesis is continuous with the opponent later attested in rabbinic interpretation, but he is also continuous with the Christian Antichrist—as is evident from the New Testament examples of the messianic judgement scene, and from Christian adoption and elaboration of the anti-Roman apocalypses of Ezra and Baruch and the Sibylline Oracles. Antichrist therefore came to belong to specifically Christian expectations and conceptions of the Roman empire; but he is an originally Jewish figure, and in the early imperial period he symbolizes Jewish dissent from Roman assumptions of *imperium* granted *sine fine*.

II. TITAN

Such Roman assumptions were also, however, touched by fears expressed through myths which closely resemble Jewish prophecies of opposition to the heaven-sent king. This point has already begun

---

[23] Hence the church fathers whom Hill (1995), 99–101 views as combining separate emphases on false teaching and on political power could be regarded rather as continuing both sides of a single pre-Christian Jewish tradition.

to emerge from the Sibylline Oracles, where the messianic opponent fits readily into the general Sibylline theme of *bella, horrida bella*. The same point was already expressly made in the ancient world, where resemblances between biblical tradition and mythology were often noted,[24] by observers who scrutinized the Christian expectation of Antichrist. Thus, from within the Christian tradition, elements in this expectation were compared with the myth of the Titans and the giants which Philo discussed, as just noted, in connection with the giants of Gen. 6: 3. 'Titan' is regarded as the most plausible interpretation of the number of the beast in Rev. 13: 8 by Irenaeus, writing towards the end of the second century. Not only (he notes) does TEITAN add up to 666, but it is thought to be a divine name, being often applied to the sun; it has a show of vengeance which suits a figure claiming to vindicate the oppressed; and it is a royal, or rather a tyrannical name (Irenaeus, *Haer.* 5. 30. 3).

Here Irenaeus clearly shares the political interpretation of the myth of the war of the Titans. Pretenders to the throne, *tyranni* or *adfectatores tyrannidis*, were familiar in the Roman empire.[25] In Hesiod's *Theogony* the Titans are Chronos, father of Zeus, and his brothers and sisters. Chronos, aided by the vigilance of the other Titans, swallowed his children, but Zeus and others survived; Clement of Alexandria (*Protr.* 2. 15) relates how the Titans tore the child Dionysus in pieces. The Titans struggled with Zeus and the Olympians for power, aided by giants, but were thrown down. The sun is called 'Titan' (often in Roman poetry, e.g. Virgil, *Aen.* 4. 119) as son of the Titan Hyperion (Hesiod, *Theog.* 371). The name Titan also individually belonged (according to a rendering of the myth given by Euhemerus and incorporated into *Sib. Or.* 3. 97–154) to a brother of Chronos, who fought with him for the kingdom when their father died. A Latin version of Euhemerus, made by Ennius, is quoted by Lactantius, who also knew the version in *Sib. Or.* 3 (Lactantius, *Div. Inst.* 1. 14). Hesiod links the name with *tisis*,

---

[24] See e.g. Philo, *Gig.* 58, on Gen. 6: 4 (Moses did not follow the myth of the giants); on Christian traditions, 2 Peter 1: 16 (again claiming independence of myth); on the other hand, Justin, *I Apol.* 22 (if you accept analogous myths, you can accept Christian teaching), and Tertullian, *Apol.* 21. 14 'recipite interim hanc fabulam, similis est vestris'.

[25] For these expressions see HA Avidius Cassius 5. 1 (Aemilius Parthenianus wrote a history of *adfectatores tyrannidis*, including Avidius Cassius), Pescennius Niger 1. 1 (those whom other men's victories made *tyranni*).

vengeance (*Theogony* 209). Rulers were associated with the sun, as Augustus had been,[26] and praised as avengers; so Pliny (*Panegyric* 35–6) stressed that Trajan provided *ultio* against informers. The giants similarly were avenging the wrongs of the Titans and their mother Earth (in Claudian, *Gigantomachia* 27 she addresses the giants as *exercitus ultor* (avenging army)). Antichrist therefore appear to Irenaeus—who has based his description on Daniel, quoted at length, as well as 2 Thessalonians and Revelation— above all as a plausible pretender to power, a figure recalling the Titans who tried to storm Olympus.

The resemblance between the Antichrist myth and the myth of the Titans was also noted at about the same time, perhaps under Marcus Aurelius, by Celsus, the pagan critic of Christianity.[27] He says that the Christian doctrine of the devil and 'Satanas', and the teaching of Jesus that Satan will appear like himself and will manifest great and glorious works, usurping the glory of God, rests on a misunderstanding of the enigmas of the Greek myths of a divine war. He specifies 'the mysteries which affirm that the Titans and Giants fought with the gods, and . . . the mysteries of the Egyptians which tell of Typhon and Horus and Osiris' (Origen, *C. Cels.* 6. 42). These myths of course overlapped in their theme of contention for the throne, and had in common the figure of Typhon or Typhoeus, slain by Zeus in Greek mythology but also identified with the Egyptian Seth (Plutarch, *Isis and Osiris*, 371b). The Greek gigantomachy also had a long history in art, including the altar of Pergamum. In literature, comparably, the *Titanomachia* was a lost member of the epic cycle, and the Titans and the giants occupy surviving Greek poets from Hesiod onwards, and Latin writers from Ennius to Claudian (both cited above). Geographically, the legend was linked especially with volcanic areas of Asia Minor (the district of Catacecaumene near Philadelphia, Strabo, *Geog.* 13. 4, 11), Sicily and Campania; the battle of the giants took place on the Phlegraean Fields in Campania, and Typhon was buried alive beneath Cumae, Procida, Ischia, and Etna (Pindar, *Pyth.* 1, epode 1; Virgil, *Aen.* 9. 715–16).

---

[26] So Apollo, Augustus's patron, and Sol—linked but not necessarily identical— are both invoked by Horace, *Carmen Saeculare*, lines 1 and 9 (Phoebe . . . alme Sol). Irenaeus does not quote the Sibyl, but he may perhaps also have had in view the oracle Sib. 3. 652 'and then God will send a king from the sun', later quoted as a prophecy of Christ by Lactantius, *Div. Inst.* 7. 18, 7.

[27] On the date of Celsus' work see Chadwick (1965), pp. xxvi–xxviii (on balance, probability lies with a date in the period 177–80).

Celsus in this passage alludes directly or indirectly to Rev. 12: 8, on the casting out of the devil or Satanas, and to Christ's prophecy of those who will arise and give signs and wonders to lead astray (Mark 13: 21–3). Origen in his reply therefore deals both with Satan, on the basis of Revelation here, and with Antichrist, as suggested by Christ's prophecy. Celsus has urged that all this Christian material is a misunderstanding of what he takes to be the profoundly significant myths of the Titans and of Typhon and Osiris. His point of course has its place in a broader argument among pagans, Jews, and Christians over the allegorization of mythology. In the present context, however, it is notable as a pagan identification of mythological counterparts to the Antichrist myth, converging with the contemporary inner-Christian association of Antichrist and Titan found in Irenaeus.

The resemblances between Typhon in particular and the evil king as attested in Daniel are richly documented from both Greek and Egyptian legend by J. W. van Henten; he shows that the Danielic depiction of Antiochus IV has been influenced by the originally Egyptian stereotype of a 'Typhonic king', but in the course of this argument he brings out the significance of Typhon as a symbol of threat to order and sovereignty in the wider Greek world under the Hellenistic monarchies and later.[28] In the present context it is only necessary to note the continuance and development of such symbolism in the early Roman empire.

First, the probable influence of Sibylline oracles on the Augustan poets should be recalled. When Virgil made the Sibyl of Cumae Aeneas' guide to the underworld, he indicated among other things a debt to Sibylline writings. Individual oracles circulated in Rome, and a form of what is now the third Sibylline book was known there by the middle of the first century BCE.[29] Against the dark background of the civil wars at home and the Parthian threat in the east, Virgil in his early work invoked the hopes of 'Cumaean song' in the Fourth Eclogue, possibly but not plainly drawing on the Jewish prophecies of prosperity in *Sib. Or.* 3 as preserved (lines 18–25, 28–39 in the Eclogue have been compared with *Sib. Or.* 3. 619–24, 743–59, 787–94). At about the same time Horace, in *Epodes* 16. 1–14, appears to echo the third Sibylline book in language as well as in

---

[28] Van Henten (1993), esp. 228–36.
[29] Parke (1988), 143–4 (Alexander Polyhistor used *Sib. Or.* 3).

his more characteristically Sibylline theme of woe.[30] Rome is falling through her own strength in the civil wars, 'suis et ipsa Roma viribus ruit' (line 2, cf. *Sib. Or.* 3. 364 Ῥώμη ῥύμη 'Rome a mere alley' or 'Rome a ruin'). The ashes of the City will be trampled by a barbarian victor, mounted and no doubt Parthian, who will scatter Roman bones; 'barbarus heu cineres insistet victor . . . ossa Quirini (nefas videre) dissipabit insolens' (lines 11–14). Mythical imagery is lacking, but the nightmare of the fall of Rome at the hand of an eastern foe corresponds to woes which were to be developed in the later Jewish Sibyllines by integration with the expected return of Nero from the east, as noted above (see *Sib. Or.* 4. 119–22, 137–9; 5. 143–8, 361–4, and compare the Antichrist of *Asc. Isa.* 4. 2–4 'a lawless king, the slayer of his mother'). The Sibyl had incorporated Greek mythology, including Euhemerus' version of the war of the Titans, as noted above; these prophetic passages from Virgil and Horace show, on the other hand, how fully the poets who commended the Augustan peace and at once became classical in the empire (Virgil was soon read at the outposts of empire, Masada and Hadrian's Wall) shared the thought-world of the Greek Jewish prophecies heralding the messiah and his adversary.

Second, the myth of the Titans and giants was brought into connection with the figure of a saviour-king—Augustus—in the longest of Horace's group of 'Roman odes' (*Carm.* 3. 4. 37–80). A resemblance to the Jewish and Christian Antichrist myth emerges strongly. The Muses aid Caesar with their gentle counsel, Horace writes; and we know that Jupiter, the just ruler of the universe, overthrew the impious Titans with a thunderbolt—'scimus ut impios | Titanas immanemque turbam | fulmine sustulerit caduco' (lines 42–4). Here, according to the convention of court poetry, Jupiter stands for Augustus, who in the following fifth ode of the third book is hailed as the 'present god' come to reign here in earth on Jupiter's behalf (*Carm.* 3. 5. 1–4). Yet, in one of the most striking statements of the fourth ode, Jupiter had been terror-struck; 'magnum ille terrorem intulerat Jovi | fidens iuventus horrida brachiis' (lines 49–50). The force of the prominently-placed 'great terror' is brought out with spirit in Philip Francis's English version:

---

[30] Macleod (1983), 218–19.

> . . . the fierce Titanian brood
> Whose horrid youth, elate with impious pride,
> Unnumbered, on their sinewy force relied;
> Mountain on mountain piled they raised in air,
> And shook the throne of Jove, and bade the Thunderer fear.

This fear is consistent with the formidable character which Typhon bears in other poets, notably in the Egyptian motif of the flight of the gods before him, a flight which in Ovid includes Jupiter.[31] Nevertheless, Jupiter, the slayer of Typhon, usually stands his ground; in Pindar's first Pythian ode, which is similarly supporting a ruler and influenced this ode of Horace,[32] the punishment of Typhon is central (his body stretches underground from Cumae to Etna), and there is no mention of any fear on the part of Zeus. In Horace here Typhoeus is mentioned (line 53), but the fear is inspired by the collective appearance of the Titans and giants. Their terrifying impact remains startling, therefore, and recalls the formidable aspect of the messianic opponent and his followers, notably the sometimes monstrous form which stands for a king of fierce countenance, as in Dan. 7–8. Moreover, the general symbolism of the myth as used in Horace is comparable with that of the messianic judgement scene; both involve the omnipotent deity and his vice-gerent, and in both the evil power which would usurp rightful sovereignty is overthrown.

I can then perhaps say with Horace (*Carm.* 3. 4. 69–70) 'testis mearum centimanus Gyas | sententiarum'. To summarize, a myth of a messianic opponent, in the sense of regularly envisaged and interconnected scenes in which the opponent figures, appeared in the first part of this study to have been current among Jews from before the time of Pompey and throughout the Roman period. Its specifically anti-messianic focus was strong enough to warrant Bousset's term 'antichrist myth'. It could include an emphasis on false teaching as well as usurpation. Despite the contrast between Christian and Jewish views drawn in much study of antichrist, Christian notions of antichrist derived from Jewish tradition. Jewish tradition on this subject also, however, had many points of correspondence with non-Jewish expectations current in the Greek and Roman world. The myth of the Titans and the giants was picked out by both Christian and pagan observers as particularly close to

---

[31] Ovid, *Meta.* 5. 321–31, quoted with other texts by van Henten (1993), 228–31.
[32] Fraenkel (1957), 276–85.

the antichrist myth. In the Greek age the figure of Typhon symbolized a threat to rightful monarchy, and influenced the Danielic depiction of Antiochus IV, as J. W. van Henten showed. With the Roman empire in view, it can be added that in the late Roman republic and the principate the Augustan poets entered into the thought-world of Jewish messianic and anti-messianic prophecy especially through the medium of Sibylline literature. Against this background, finally, the treatment of the Titans in Horace's longest Roman ode has suggested that it may not be out of place to speak of antichrist among gentiles as well as Jews in the Roman empire.

9

Rhetoric and Assumptions: Romans and Rabbis on Sex

MICHAEL L. SATLOW

When we examine the contact between Jews and non-Jews in the Graeco-Roman world, we ask two sets of questions. First, we seek to describe the similarities and differences between the various groups. Second, we attempt to explain the significance of these similarities and differences. The first task, that of description, appears on the surface to be relatively straightforward. Scholars have compared synagogual architecture and organization, Jewish social and communal institutions, Jewish linguistic usage, rabbinic literature, philosophy, science, and law to their non-Jewish counterparts.[1] It does not take long, however, to discover that straightforward description is hardly straightforward. In rabbinic literature, for example, how is one to understand a concept that accords with that of the Stoics; a legal institution found also in the *Digest*; a hermeneutic similar to those of Alexandrian dream interpreters; a medical 'truth' shared by classical doctors? Even if we are able, as we rarely are, to trace direct contact and influence, how should we interpret this data? Do we maintain a model of binary opposition between 'pure Judaism' and 'external influence', and attempt to plot various communities along this spectrum? Will we begin by asking why are there as many similarities as we appear to find, or why there are not more similarities? In this short paper, I will focus on one small problem that, I think, illuminates these methodological issues of both description and analysis.

Rabbinic dicta and documents can be used historically as more than just compilations of isolated facts that can be separated and reprocessed. They are, perhaps primarily, rhetorical works. These

---

[1] The literature on this topic is vast and includes, of course, many of the essays in this volume. For some examples, see Levine (1987); Lieberman (1942; 1950); Cohen (1966).

works seek to persuade. If we assume, as is likely, that at least in
Roman Palestine in the third century CE the rabbis had little juridical
power and sometimes marginal influence, then we can better
understand the rabbinic need to persuade.[2] Jews will become
rabbinic Jews or follow those norms that may have been uniquely
rabbinic only to the extent that they are persuaded and convinced
that they should. Moreover, even if the rabbis had more authority
than is now sometimes thought, their ability to persuade Jews to
observe those norms that are out of public view—sex, for example—would still depend upon their rhetorical ability.

For rhetoric to work it must build upon and appeal to common
assumptions. Arguments make no senses to those who hold differing fundamental assumptions: there would not even exist criteria by
which to judge whether the argument is good or bad. For example,
an argument that homosexuality is bad because the Bible says so
would be incomprehensible to one who either did not know what
'homosexuality' was, or to one who did not accept the authority of
Scripture. If we then accept that the rabbis are making arguments
that are based on shared deep assumptions, we can attempt to
unearth these assumptions. What arguments did different groups of
rabbis employ in order to persuade their intended audience(s), and
what are the presuppositions of these arguments? How do rabbinic
and non-rabbinic, indeed non-Jewish, assumptions relate?

Rabbinic dicta on sexuality demonstrate how this relationship
between rhetoric and assumptions works. In order to illustrate this
process, I will examine three different, but related, subjects:
homoeroticism, the concept of 'wasted seed', and rabbinic ideals
of masculinity. Since I have already published somewhat technical
articles on each of these topics, I will here summarize my conclusions on these topics and attempt to show how they can help us
better to understand the relationship of Jew to non-Jew in the
Graeco-Roman world.[3]

Let me begin with a comment on methodology. My goal is to
unearth the assumptions underlying rabbinic rhetoric. Since it is the
nature of assumptions to remain buried, one can rarely find a
'smoking gun', a statement in which an ancient writer detaches
himself (all of our authors appear to be men) from the discourse far

---

[2] Cf. Levine (1989), 127–33; Neusner (1969–70), 2: 282–7, 3: 220–9.
[3] I refer the reader to these articles for full discussion and annotation for each of
these topics: Satlow (1994a; 1994b; 1995; 1996).

and long enough to note what he or his colleagues are assuming. My method has been to collect all the relevant rabbinic data and test different groupings of this data for what appear to me to be deep similarities.[4] The method is hardly objective, and when I also compare these materials to those of non-Jewish authors, interpenetration of categories might suggest a certain circularity. Nevertheless, I think that there is merit to the enterprise, and that it can produce some suggestive, even compelling, conclusions.

Were the rabbis confident that they were addressing an audience that fully accepted the authority of Scripture, there would be far less rabbinic commentary on male homoeroticism than actually exists.[5] In fact, the rabbis do not simply cite Leviticus 18: 22 and 20: 13, which both clearly (from the rabbinic perspective) prohibit anal intercourse between men: they exhibit a far more complex set of assumptions about what it means for a man to engage in homoerotic activities.[6] Dicta attributed to Palestinian rabbis, even when found in the Babylonian Talmud, all exhibit instead particular anxiety about the man who allows another man to penetrate him anally. For these rabbis, the underlying assumption is one of gender-boundaries. A man who allows another man to penetrate him is thought both to feminize himself and to succumb to sexual urges beyond what God deemed appropriate.

Males who were sexually penetrated were considered humiliated. An example of this attitude can be found in a Palestinian tradition:

It is written, 'May [the guilt] fall upon the head of Yoab . . . May the house of Yoab never be without someone suffering from a discharge or an eruption, or a male who handles the spindle, or one slain by the sword, or one lacking bread,' [2 Sam 3: 29]. 'A male who handles the spindle'—this is Yoash, '. . . they inflicted punishments on Yoash, ' [2 Chron. 24: 24]. Taught R. Ishmael: This teaches that they appointed over him cruel guards who never knew a woman and they would abuse him the way one abuses a

---

[4] For sexuality, the documentary approach—what does each discrete rabbinic document say about sexuality or an aspect of sexuality?—yields far less coherent results than the approach I have taken here. See Satlow (1995), 10–11, 328–30.

[5] The rabbis had no category like our own 'homosexuality'. They understood that some people engaged in sexual activities with others of the same gender, but did not have a label for those who were sexually attracted to members of the same gender. For a discussion of the modern conception of 'homosexuality', see Halperin (1990).

[6] These verses might not be as 'clear' as the rabbis thought. See Olyan (1994).

woman. Just as when it is said, 'Israel's pride will be humbled before his very eyes,' [Hos. 5: 5]. [Read instead:] 'And he will abuse Israel's pride before his very eyes.'[7]

The tradition identifies the later king Yoash, a descendent of Yoab, as the referent of the prophecy 'the male who handles the spindle', one like a woman. To be like a woman, the midrash says, means to be penetrated. The physical penetration of Yoash does more than torture him, it humiliates him. Although the setting of the midrash is 'exceptional'—penetration is used in a prison setting as a form of abuse—rhetorically the message is clear. Penetration, emphasized by the implied reference to the sexual frenzy of the guards, is equated with 'feminization' and humiliation.

This sentiment, linking penetration, feminization, and power, can be seen even more clearly in a Palestinian midrash. Referring to Esau, Israel laments to God, 'is it not enough that we are subjugated to the seventy nations, but even to this one, who is penetrated like women?'[8] This tradition assumes that a man who is penetrated cannot rule like a man. Here, as in other places in rabbinic literature, Esau probably represents Rome. Israel, seeing that homoerotic intercourse occurs in Rome, complains that Rome, in effect, has no right to rule not because Romans are engaged in homoerotic intercourse *per se*, but specifically because they allow themselves to be penetrated. By allowing themselves to be penetrated, they sacrifice their 'maleness', a prerequisite for power.

Palestinian rabbis deemed male homoerotic intercourse to be a sign of excess: one who goes beyond the God-given bounds of sexuality approaches the slippery slope of loss of control that inevitably leads to idolatry. Accusations of gentile male homoerotic intercourse are part of the broader concept of gentile sexual lechery, which itself is representative of the gentile's denial of God's covenant.

Gentile lack of sexual self-control is seen as so strong that some rabbinic sources advocate keeping one's male children away from gentile men. Ishmael is identified with the three transgressions of murder, idolatry and *'arayot*—where *'arayot* is identified as referring both to general sexual promiscuity and to homoerotic intercourse. According to a passage in the *Sifra* which atomizes Lev. 18: 3, 'Just

---

[7] y. Kidd. 1: 7, 61a. All translations are mine.
[8] Ber. R. 63: 10 (ed. Theodor and Albeck, 693).

as "the practices of the Canaanite", [who] are steeped in idolatry, *'arayot*, murder, homoerotic intercourse and bestiality, so too "the practices of the Egyptians".[9] We see the connection of male homoeroticism with other horrible offences, but here the source highlights the proclivity toward these things as inherent character-istics of both the Canaanites and the Egyptians, i.e. gentiles. The lemma, Lev. 18: 3, introduces the long list of prohibitions that includes the incest restrictions, homoerotic intercourse, and bes-tiality. Yet absent from the biblical list are murder and perhaps idolatry. This suggests that biblical interpretation alone does not lie behind this text. Rather, the rabbis create the gentile as the antithesis of the Jew and all that is godly: he or she exercises no self-control, surrendering to the first impulses of violence and lust. Homoeroticism becomes, for the rabbis, just one example of this ungodly lust.

To those familiar with the Roman rhetoric on male homoeroti-cism, this discussion will sound familiar. Roman authors too excoriated the male who allowed himself to be anally penetrated, also because he was seen as feminizing himself. The act of penetration, though, was not the sole source of this perceived feminization: excessive or wanton sexual activity of all sorts was seen by Roman philosophers, moralists, and doctors as a loss of self-mastery. 'Control', be it of oneself or others, was a character-istic that élite Roman men gendered as masculine. Losing self-control is equivalent to losing one's claim to manhood.[10] Thus, although the Palestinian rabbis of the third and fourth centuries discuss homoeroticism with reference to the appropriate biblical verses, their assumptions about homoeroticism do not derive from the Bible. Underneath these rabbinic traditions lurks the same complex attitude as exhibited in Roman sources. For a man to allow himself to be penetrated was tantamount to him 'effeminizing' himself, a prospect viewed with loathing by (at least) the male élite of antiquity. Similarly, for a man to engage in homoerotic inter-course was seen by both Palestinian rabbis and Romans as a sign of loss of self-control and thus feminization.

The shared assumptions between rabbis and Romans on homo-eroticism is highlighted when compared to the assumptions on the same topic of Babylonian rabbis. It is striking that nearly all the

[9] Sifra Ahare 9: 8 (ed. Weiss 85c–d).
[10] Cf. Dover (1974); Richlin (1992); Corrington (1992).

rabbinic dicta on homoeroticism are attributed to Palestinians. Where Babylonian rabbis do contribute to this discussion, not only are their dicta usually short and marginal, but they sometimes appear to misunderstand the assumptions that underlie the Palestinian sources upon which they are commenting. For example, Palestinians, invoking the biblical prohibition on cross-dressing (Deut. 22: 5), forbid a man to pluck his hairs. The prohibition appears to have been aimed at the pathic. In the Babylonian Talmud, however, the redactor explains this prohibition as due to the fear that a man, by appearing like a woman, will slip disguised among women and consort with them.[11] If I am correct that the original discussions assumed the subject to be the male pathic, then the redactor did not understand the sexual assumptions and anxieties that originally informed this Palestinian tradition. Babylonians, who might not have shared the cultural assumptions of feminization that underlie both Roman and Palestinian rabbinic dicta on homoeroticism simply misinterpreted the dictum.

I am arguing that on a fundamental level élite Roman men could have understood the assumptions of Palestinian rabbis on male homoeroticism, whereas Babylonian rabbis could not have. This phenomenon is not limited to male homoeroticism: it can also be seen in rabbinic discussions of male self-arousal.

The rabbis, both Palestinian and Babylonian, like the Romans, put great stock in self-control. Sexual desire was seen as one of the primary threats to that self-control. Hence, it is not surprising that the rabbis frequently and consistently condemn self-arousal and male masturbation. To arouse oneself sexually was equivalent to opening the door to the 'evil impulse', losing control not only for the moment but more importantly starting one down the undisciplined path that would ultimately lead to idolatry. For Palestinian, and many Babylonian, rabbis, male masturbation was not considered wrong because of its ends—the 'wasteful emission' of semen that resulted—it was wrong only because it was a means to loss of self-control. In this attitude, these rabbis did not differ from Roman authors, all of whom saw such activity as shameful for precisely the same reason.[12]

Only when we get to the Babylonian materials, and really only the redactor's contribution at that, do we see the emergence of a

[11] b. Naz. 59a.
[12] Cf. Satlow (1994*b*), esp. 162–8.

concept of the 'wasteful emission of semen', *šikbat zera' lĕbaṭalah*, a phrase that appears, with very few exceptions, only in the redactorial layer of the Babylonian Talmud. This concept casts a new understanding not only on male self-arousal, but on a number of otherwise discrete sexual activities. Homoeroticism, for example, which Palestinian sources never associate with the concept of the wasted emission of semen, is grouped by the redactor of the Babylonian Talmud with other non-procreative activities. In cases where this concept appears in traditions in the Babylonian Talmud that have parallels in rabbinic documents redacted in Palestine, the concept of 'wasted emission of semen' is always lacking in the Palestinian parallel.[13] One striking example is the well-known passage in the Tosefta of the three kinds of women who can, must, or should use a *mok*, some kind of barrier contraceptive. In the middle of this tradition, R. Meir comments on proper sexual activities with a woman who is nursing one's own child: 'all twenty four months he threshes inside and winnows outside', that is, practises coitus interruptus. Whenever this tradition is cited in the Babylonian Talmud, R. Meir's statement is suppressed.[14]

Neither Palestinian rabbis nor Romans would have understood the idea of a 'wasteful emission of semen'. Semen was seen as potential, not actual, life with no true value in and of itself. This is why Palestinian rabbis had no scruples about all forms of non-procreative sex. A Roman doctor would have understood R. Meir better than the redactor of the Babylonian Talmud.

A less clear, but no less interesting, example of shared assumptions occurs within the determination of which characteristics are necessary to turn a 'male' into a 'man'. What, for the rabbis, constitutes 'manliness'? Within rabbinic literature, there are very few occurrences of phrases equivalent to our own 'be a man', which would indicate clearly what traits are expected of men. Where the phrase does occur, it is always associated with Torah study. At the end of a passage that details the characteristics necessary for successful Torah learning, the Mishna states, 'in a place where there are no men, try to be a man'.[15] The only other place that the expression is found is in a statement in the Babylonian Talmud

---

[13] Cf. Satlow (1994*b*), 150–7.
[14] See t. Nidd. 2: 6 (ed. Zuckermandel, 642–3); b. Yeb. 12b, 34b, 100b; b. Ket. 39a; b. Nidd. 45a; b. Ned. 35a.
[15] m. Ab. 2: 6 (ed. Albeck, 4: 359).

attributed to Bar Kappara, interpreted by the anonymous commentator ad loc. to mean that when one is in a place that has no scholars, there one should teach, but in a place where there are those who are wiser one should refrain from teaching. 'To be a man', in these passages, means at least to teach (and by implication, to study) Torah.[16] Another Palestinian tradition links 'being a man' to liturgical expertise.[17]

If Torah study defines masculinity for the rabbis, the acquisition of it requires the virtue of self-control. In contrast to a Gentile man or woman, or even a Jewish woman, a Jewish man, according to the rabbis, possesses the ability to fight off the *yeṣer hara'*, evil impulse. All the rabbinic condemnations of female Torah study base themselves on the assumption that because a woman does not have the requisite amount of self-discipline, she will use her Torah knowledge for ill. Rabbi Eliezer's famous prohibition on teaching one's daughters Torah, for example, is based on the fear that if a woman gains Torah knowledge she will be partially immunized from the effects of the *soṭa* ordeal.[18] Her knowledge of her immunity to this test for the suspected adulteress will lead her to adultery. A more extreme example is a Palestinian tradition that expresses fear that a woman will use her knowledge of Torah to seduce unwary men.[19]

For the rabbis, then, *to be a 'man' means to use that uniquely male trait, self-restraint, in the pursuit of the divine through Torah study*. For the rabbis, being a 'man' is the opposite of being a woman. A man, unlike a woman, could exercise the kind of self-control that allows for a life of the mind, a life not constructed as open to women. This conclusion appears to hold for all rabbis, early and late, Palestinian and Babylonian, and cuts cross all rabbinic documents. More importantly, it is identical to the constructions of manhood exhibited within earlier Jewish wisdom literature, Philo, and Greek and Roman authors.[20] This view does not appear to have been intended for or shared by either most Jews or most Romans. Rather, the rabbis, and Greek and Roman philosophers, moralists, and doctors, all had a common understanding of 'manhood'.

---

[16] t. Ber. 6(7): 24 (ed. Lieberman, 1: 40); b. Ber. 63a.

[17] Lev. R. 23: 4 (ed. Margulies, 532).

[18] m. Sot. 3: 4 (ed. Albeck, 3: 240). [19] y. Sot. 3: 4, 19a.

[20] See Satlow (1996). On Greek and Roman constructions of masculinity, see Musonius Rufus 12. 3; Juvenal 2. 54–6; Richlin (1992), xii–xxxiii, 81–143, 287–90, and the sources indicated on p. 246 n. 35; Richlin (1993).

Up to this point, I have attempted to describe the shared sexual assumptions of élite Greek and Roman men and (especially Palestinian) rabbis. If this description is accurate, what does it mean? I suggest that these observations have broad repercussions for how we approach the problem of similarity and difference between Jews and non-Jews in Roman Palestine. The influence of the Greeks and the Romans on Palestinian rabbis went far beyond the occasional practice, linguistic oddity, or legal institution: many of the assumptions that generated Palestinian rabbinic rhetoric on sexuality almost certainly derived from those of the Greeks and Romans. Although Palestinian rabbinic rulings on sexuality occasionally differ from their Greek and Roman equivalents, all share fundamental thought-categories and assumptions. To talk of particular points of 'Hellenistic influence' thus largely skirts around the issue. Whether or not particular customs or practices are consciously adopted or rejected by the Palestinian rabbis, their fundamental way of thinking at least about sexuality is virtually identical to those whom they label the 'other'.[21] It would be interesting to see if the same claim would hold for rabbinic assumptions about other issues.

Ultimately, there is nothing startling about this conclusion. Too frequently the *a priori* conclusion—that there were two basically pure and opposite cultures that confronted each other—has been used to shape the descriptive analysis, which of course then circles back to reinforce the conclusion. If the rabbis themselves employed a category like 'Romanization', seeing Judaism in fundamental conflict with an opposing culture, then we could at least note their use of a model of culture conflict as a part of rabbinic historiography. But unlike the author of 2 Maccabees, the rabbis, to my knowledge, never did this. The rabbis might fight bitterly against political subjugation and particular Roman institutions and practices, but on one level the fight was internal, among people who could hear and understand each other if they were inclined to try.

Modern anthropologists have noted that most Mediterranean societies share several societal characteristics.[22] Many of these characteristics concern constructions of sexuality. The same, I

---

[21] This, perhaps, should not surprise us. The 'other', as Jonathan Z. Smith suggested, often gains the position precisely as a result of their proximity. See Smith (1985).
[22] Cf. Gilmore (1987).

think, is true for antiquity. The rabbis, and probably non-rabbinic Jews as well, were part of a Mediterranean culture, not an Arab or Eastern one.[23] Precisely when this shift occurred might still be an important question, but by the rabbinic period it was long finished.

[23] If such a culture even existed. Curiously, even Millar, who argues against the existence of an Arab or Eastern culture at this time, subscribes to the view that Jewish 'culture' was in conflict with surrounding non-Jewish culture. See Millar (1993), esp. 337–86.

10

Gambling in Ancient Jewish Society and in the Graeco-Roman World

JOSHUA SCHWARTZ

INTRODUCTION

It is a commonplace among historians, and particularly historians of games and gambling, that games of chance have existed in most societies, from ancient to modern and from primitive to complex.[1] The study of Jewish society has shown that the Jews were not immune to the attractions of gambling. It is the purpose of our present study to examine this phenomenon in Jewish society during the Second Temple, mishnaic, and talmudic periods and to try and determine whether the common view cited above indeed reflects this ancient Jewish society.[2]

Our undertaking is not without difficult problems. First, the relevant literary traditions are found mostly in rabbinic literature which by its nature was not composed for the historian of any subject including games and gambling. Moreover, the rabbinic traditions on gambling sometimes seem to be making a conscious effort to camouflage particulars of the phenomenon, giving only enough details to elucidate the halachic background but no more, and it will often be necessary to learn from what has been omitted.

Also, it is not always easy to determine exactly which activities mentioned in ancient sources involved gambling. There were clearly games or pastimes such as dicing which were connected with gambling behaviour, but there were also games that required dice which had nothing at all to do with gambling.[3] The opposite could also be true. Thus, nuts were usually a plaything associated

---

[1] See e.g. Jones (1973).
[2] See esp. Landman (1966/7; 1967/8) and the bibliography cited there. To this should be added the new studies of Bazak (1968) and Warhaftig (1972).
[3] Pennick (1988) and Murray (1952).

with innocent children's games, but they often served the gambler, both adult and child.

Moreover, the sources are not always clear as to who is playing. Non-gambling play of children can become gambling in an adult play situation. Also, it was theoretically possible to gamble or bet on anything and wages could also be of a verbal nature, unconnected with any equipment or physical actions by those betting.

Lastly on matters of source material, any study of social phenomena based on the study of rabbinic literature should, of course, attempt to evince clear-cut chronological development and geographic venue. The limited number of gambling sources, however, do not make this simple and sometimes it will be necessary to generalize from one time to another within the Second Temple, mishnaic, or talmudic periods or from Palestine to Babylonia and *vice versa*.

Fortunately, rabbinic literature is supplemented by a small amount of archaeological material relevant to gambling. However, this material is also somewhat problematical. It is, for instance, notoriously difficult to distinguish between playthings of adults or children and miniature objects devoted to other purposes. Thus, whether a small round disk is a theatre ticket or a game-counter can be of great importance for our purposes.[4] Also, it is not always possible to determine the ethnic background of a find and whether it was used by Jews or not.

There is one more source of relevant material at our disposal. The Jewish traditions and archaeological remains obviously cannot be examined in a vacuum. Many games and pastimes of the Graeco-Roman world found their way into ancient Jewish society, although there were also many cases of independent parallel development. In any case, a cautious use of the Graeco-Roman material can help us learn about Jewish gambling games. We shall, therefore, briefly discuss a number of aspects of gambling in the ancient world which were relevant to gambling in ancient Jewish society.

GAMBLING IN THE GRAECO-ROMAN WORLD

Discussion here will be limited to dice, astragals, and board-games. I shall also examine some of the social implications of gambling

---

[4] See e.g. Alfoeldi-Rosenbaum (1971) and Bieber (1961), 90, 246 ff. and figs. 320, 812*a–k*, 813*a–f*, 814*a–c*, 815*a–b* (= theatre tickets).

behaviour in this world, and particularly those aspects with direct bearing upon Jewish society.

According to Greek legend, dicing was devised by the Lydians during the siege of Troy as a means of diverting attention from the suffering of starvation.[5] It soon became quite popular in Greek[6] and Roman society, becoming in fact the most popular Roman recreational activity.[7] 'Dicing' games were probably first played with astragals[8] and then later on with dice.[9] Whether with astragal or dice, dicing was regarded as serious business.[10]

Many other forms of gambling were associated with board-games.[11] The majority of these games used either dice or astragals, although some could be played without this equipment.[12] They were relatively easy to play and could in fact be played almost anywhere, with simple or more complex gameboards even being inscribed on stones in courtyards, markets, or other areas in the public or private domain.

In spite of the popularity of many of these games, it is not always easy to reconstruct them. A number of Greek games were called by generic terms, some of which also took on specific meanings. *Petteia*, for instance, refers to games played with *pessoi* (i.e. 'pieces' or 'men') but came to refer to 'battle-games'. *Kubeia*, a term which usually referred to dicing, also took on the meaning of 'racing' board-games and finally meant all kinds of board-games, signifying that most of them were played with dice.[13]

A number of games were mentioned by name in Graeco-Roman literature. Rabbinic literature, however, does not cite gambling games specifically by name and this, as we shall see, may be quite significant. It is likely, though, that some of these games were played in Jewish society, and therefore I shall make brief reference to a few of these gambling games.

---

[5] Herod. 1. 94. In general see Lamer (1927).

[6] Garland (1990), 126, 142.

[7] Vaeterlein (1976), 7–13.

[8] The *astragalus* is technically the hucklebone, lying close above the *talus* which is the heel-bone. Sometimes knuckle-bone is used in both ancient and medieval literature.

[9] David (1962), 9.

[10] See e.g. Plato, *Republic* 374c.

[11] On board-games in general see e.g. Lamer (1927), cols. 1900–2029; Murray (1952) and Bell (1979). On Graeco-Roman board-games see esp. Austin (1934), (1935), and (1940).

[12] Austin (1934), 25. [13] Ibid.

One such Greek game, for instance, was *poleis* or 'cities' (Pollux 9. 98), a battle-game with pieces called 'dogs' moved along lines of the board (the 'city'). This game was apparently identical or at least similar to the Roman battle-game *latrunculi* or *ludus latrunculorum* and was not played with dice. Another game was called *diagrammismos* or *grammai* ('lines') (Pollux 9. 97) and was apparently played with dice and gaming pieces.[14] Another Roman game was *ludus duodecim scriptorum*. Similar to earlier ones that existed in Egypt, this game was of the backgammon type, and was played with the help of dice on a board marked with letters. An apparently more advanced form of it, popular during the Byzantine period and afterwards under different names, was *alea* or *tabula*.[15] Another Roman board-game was an early form of what later was called *marelle*, 'merels', and 'three men's morris'. A square was intersected by four lines which all passed through the centre of the square and the purpose of the game was to move pieces on vacant points until one managed to reach the centre.[16] There were undoubtedly other games not mentioned in the sources such as the 'mancala' games which I shall discuss later on.[17]

Gambling was, of course, a social phenomenon; one never gambled alone. It is important to remember, however, that not all aspects of gambling or gambling behaviour actually originated as gambling. Thus, what modern society might attribute to mathematical randomness, the ancients would often attribute to the gods.[18] Astragals and dice were occasionally used in place of lots for the purpose of divination. At various sites in the Graeco-Roman world, it was possible to gain a glimpse into the future by casting astragals and checking the results with standard lists or tables.[19] Although technically this was not gambling, in popular consciousness this became associated with 'gambling of the gods'. Thus, dicing might

---

[14] Austin (1940), 266–7.

[15] Austin (1934) and (1935). *Alea* literally meant dice, but like *kubeia* began to take on additional meanings. On this game see also Murray (1952), 31 ff.

[16] Austin (1935).

[17] See Murray (1952), 7. Mancala (from the Arabic *naqala*—to move) games, usually having a board with two rows of cup-shaped depressions or holes in which pieces were moved or arranged, date for the most part to the Muslim period and afterwards. A few examples of these games from Palestine, however, may date to the Roman–Byzantine period.

[18] Pennick (1988), 31–6.

[19] Heinevetter (1912), esp. 30–1.

have become identified as a 'pagan' game, something which could have aroused opposition in Jewish society.

There were also a number of external factors associated with gambling which might have been important for the Jews. Thus, many aspects of dicing and gambling took on or presupposed skills and knowledge widespread in the Graeco-Roman world.[20] There were occasional allusions to literature and mystical numerology and a great many of these games took on marked Graeco-Roman guises, even if those guises were not really necessary.

The venue of these games could also have been problematical. As we mentioned, many could have been played almost anywhere, but they were often associated with taverns or brothels, not something about which the rabbis, for instance, would have been happy.[21]

Much of this also bothered Graeco-Roman society. To begin with, even those who liked gambling considered it to be a waste of time.[22] Second, it was possible to lose huge sums of money.[23] It was, of course, also possible to win large sums of money, but the resultant changes in the socio-economic structure could be a cause for concern.[24]

Gambling also aroused negative behaviour. Plain greed was often accompanied by displays of cheating, lying, and violent behaviour.[25] Sexual tension was a common side-effect of many types of gambling, whether it took place in the brothel or anywhere else.[26]

There was also the matter of obscene language on many boards and counters used for gambling. The popularity of these types of games in military circles might partially explain the language.[27] However, even if scatological comments were absent, there was also the matter of representations of gods, goddesses, rulers, and the like on some of the counters or boards.[28] All of this did not bode well for an easy reception of gambling in Jewish society.

Worst of all perhaps was that children often imitated their parents

[20] Purcell (1995).
[21] Lanciani (1892).
[22] The Greek world linked gaming with wastrel aristocratic youth. There were unfavourable comments but not universal condemnation as was the case in the Roman world. See Purcell (1995), 6–16.
[23] Purcell (1995).
[24] Ibid. 9–10.
[25] Lanciani (1892), 97-105. Cf. Purcell (1995).
[26] Schmidt (1977), 51–2.
[27] Purcell (1995), 26.
[28] Alfoeldi-Rosenbaum (1971).

and other adults and began, albeit usually surreptitiously, to engage in gambling play with certain of their own toys, eventually graduating to full-scale dicing at a rather early age.[29] Parents clearly disapproved of their children gambling and would not hesitate to punish them,[30] but it was not easy to catch them since, as we have mentioned, some of the gambling equipment could be used for other pastimes.

Some gambling might have been excused: technically, children may have had more spare time and thus their gambling might have been considered less of a waste of time, while women and the elderly either never had or no longer had official responsibilities which gambling could have turned into 'dereliction of duty'. There were, however, many in Roman society who despaired of the decaying moral fabric of that society and particularly of Roman youth and adolescents, caused to a great extent by their engaging in gambling and other questionable pastimes. All the negative factors mentioned above probably explain why gambling was officially forbidden in the Roman world except on the occasion of the Saturnalia. At other times one could be prosecuted if caught dicing, although the popularity of gambling made it a very hard law to enforce.[31] The Greeks, however, had fewer problems and despite some grumblings most people could engage in gambling to their hearts' content.[32]

GAMBLING IN JEWISH SOCIETY

Compared to the amount of Graeco-Roman material, there are few rabbinic traditions on gambling, which itself says something about respective attitudes towards this pastime. The two sources traditionally considered as setting the tone and attitude towards gambling in ancient Jewish society are m. R.Sh. 1: 8 and m. Sanh. 3: 3. At first glance, they appear to be quite similar. This, as we shall see, was not so. Because of their importance, we cite them in their entirety:[33]

---

[29] Lanciani (1892).
[30] Martial 14. 18.
[31] Purcell (1995), 14–15.
[32] Ibid. 7.
[33] The translations, with minor revisions, are based upon Danby (1933), 189 and 385 respectively.

1. These are they that are ineligible: *ha-mesaheq be-kubiya'*, a usurer, pigeon-flyers (= *mafrihei-yonim*), traffickers in seventh year produce (= *sheviit*), and slaves (m. R.Sh. 1: 8).

2. And these are they that are not qualified: *ha-mesaheq be-kubiya'*, a usurer, pigeon-flyers, and traffickers in seventh year produce[34] . . . R. Judah said: This applies only if they have no other trade, but if they have some other trade then they are not disqualified (m. Sanh. 3: 3).

The first source deals with one specific matter of testimony, i.e. those who were not permitted to testify regarding the New Moon. The second tradition deals with testimony in general and with some of the categories of those whose testimony was not acceptable. *Mesaheq be-kubiya'* has usually been explained or translated as 'dicer' or 'dice-player', based on the clear-cut etymology of *kubiya'*,[35] and 'pigeon-flyers' were also connected with gambling.[36] It has always been assumed that gambling was a serious matter.[37] Surprisingly, the Mishnah gave no reason for the prohibition against dicing.

There are many differences between the two sources. The most striking difference between the two traditions is that the statement of R. Judah which limits the disqualification of 'dicers' to those who do it for a living, appears only in m. Sanh. and not in m. R.Sh. This, as we shall see, may be quite significant.

Also, we have so far translated *mesaheq be-kubiya'* as 'dice-player', the literal translation. Was this, however, the intention of the Mishnah or was 'dice-player' a euphemism for 'gambler'? Moreover, the disqualifications pronounced in the Mishnah were based on rabbinic law and not Torah law. Just how evil, therefore, were 'dicers' and the other types of reprobates mentioned above?

To answer these questions it is necessary to discuss another tradition which brings dicing into a clearer perspective. As we saw above, dicing in the ancient world was also connected with divination. Lots, although apparently not astragals or dice, were also used by Jews for purposes of divination and the rabbis seemed to

---

[34] A number of versions and manuscripts add 'slaves' as appears in m. R.Sh. 1: 8. This textual problem, however, is beyond the purview of our discussion.

[35] LSJ, s.v. *kubeia*, p. 1004.

[36] It is doubtful that pigeon-flying was actually a form of gambling. Constraints of space make it necessary for us to deal with this matter in a different forum.

[37] See e.g. Landman (1966/7), 20: 'Thus, the Mishnah declares dicing as infamous.'

have had nothing against such 'random mechanics'.[38] Indeed, nowhere in rabbinic literature is there any reference to dicing as a form of pagan or cultic activity. Thus, 'games of chance' need not have been forbidden in spite of the occasional questionable use of the 'tools of chance' in the Graeco-Roman world.

The question then is whether dicing and gambling had other characteristics in addition to their randomness, and whether those other characteristics might have aroused the objections of the rabbis. m. Shab. 23: 2 addresses this question and in our view contains the earliest contextual reference in rabbinic texts to dicing and gambling. The tradition states:

A man may reckon up the number of his guests and his savoury portions by word of mouth but not from what is written down. And he may cast lots with his children and with his household at a meal (for the several portions) provided that he does not intend thereby to allot a large as against a small portion [which is forbidden] on the grounds of playing dice [*mshum kubiya'*]. They [= priests in the Temple] may cast lots on a Festival-day for the Hallowed Things (offered on a Festival-day), but not for the portion.[39]

The tradition deals with a meal taking place on the Sabbath and a householder dividing up the food. There seems to be some type of 'game' which is permissible, just as long as it does not turn into *kubiya'*. The difference between 'tools of chance' and the types of games described above is not great. The 'game' is allowed; the minute it becomes gambling, though, it is forbidden. In the case of the passage cited from m. Shab., there are clearly no actual dice involved.

The source, though, is far from straightforward. Thus, the reference to dice-playing does not contain any explanatory information and assumes knowledge of relevant details. This would hardly strengthen our contention that m. Shab. 23: 2 is the earliest contextual passage in the chain of *kubiya'* traditions in the Mishnah. It is important to remember, though, as we have already pointed out, that no *kubiya'* traditions provide information as to the mechanics of dicing or any other form of the game. The rabbis who preserved those traditions did not want to make it any easier to engage in these pastimes and apparently assumed that everyone was

---

[38] Rabinovitch (1973).
[39] Translation in Danby (1933), 120.

familiar with the basics. The key to the early dating of the context is the end of the passage, which reflects late Temple times and the division of sacrificial meat through the casting of lots.[40]

There is still, though, the matter of the Sabbath. It is clear that the intention of m. Shab. 23: 2 was not to forbid gambling on the Sabbath and permit it at other times. This, however, appears to be precisely the point. The passage strengthens the decision against dicing in general by associating it with the Sabbath. Someone who is not particular about the kind of board-games he plays during the week will undoubtedly be guilty of transgressions on the Sabbath and this is what the passage seeks to prevent, even if it is only a minimum option.[41] Perhaps this may have been all that was necessary.

Thus the first stage of the *kubiya'* tradition is reflected in m. Shab. 23: 2, which assumed the existence of non-gambling forms of table games which were permitted and other gambling games which were forbidden. The reasons for the prohibition were never stated and complex halachic arguments were used to make dicing appear to be a more serious legal offence than it really was.

Similar arguments were used by the rabbis when dealing with dicing in the case of the serious matters dealt with in m. R.Sh. 1: 8: the entire religious calendar was dependent upon the correct establishment of the New Moon, so characters of questionable moral fibre had to be disqualified, even if the legal justification was minimal, and there was no room for any differentiation between the professional and casual dicer. In our opinion, it is likely that m. R.Sh. 1: 8 reflects conditions soon after 70 CE or at the end of the first century and beginning of the second century CE.

m. Sanh. 3: 3, which focuses on testimony in general, belongs to the final stage of the formulation of these traditions.[42] This is the most elaborate formulation regarding those disqualified from testimony. The statement of the Ushan sage R. Judah dates this passage to the middle or to the latter part of the second century CE. It is not clear from the passage whether R. Judah, who differentiates between professional and casual gamblers, disagrees with views of the other rabbis cited, who still would disqualify every gambler, or whether he qualifies the statement of those rabbis. What is important is that there was now a view that casual dicing was not all that

---

[40] Cf. Rabinovitch (1973), 25 ff. [41] Goldberg (1976), 383–5.
[42] Cf. m. Shebu. 7: 4. In this mishnah, the list serves as a standard literary device.

bad. Was this because there were fewer casual gamblers and it was only the professional who posed a threat, or because there was a real change in attitude and the casual dicer was no longer considered to be pernicious? Perhaps both reasons were true. We shall, of course, examine this matter further.

R. Judah's view, however, and the social realities reflected in it were liable to cause confusion. *Kubiya'* was a difficult term and could mean many things. When everything was forbidden, then an all-inclusive interpretation of *kubiya'* was acceptable. If, however, there was a trend to permit, or at least not to forbid, certain games, then it was necessary to spell out clearly exactly what was involved.

t. Sanh. 5: 2 (p. 423, ed. Zuckermandel)[43] attempts to do just that, but exchanges one difficult word for another. The tradition defines *ha-mesaheq be-kubiya'* as 'he who plays with *psephasim*'. *Psephos* was literally a pebble, but in the gaming world its primary meaning was 'dice'.[44] Thus t. Sanh. 5: 2 explicitly states that the prohibition applies to dice. However, *psephos* could also refer to gaming pieces,[45] and thus the tradition also seems to be commenting on board-games, permitting their casual play, even for stakes, while prohibiting play by the professional. The advantage of this word was that it could refer also to board-games without dice, something that may not have been clear regarding *kubeia*, which after all literally meant dice.

t. Sanh. 5: 2 then goes on to make a general statement about the intention of the Mishnah: 'one who plays with *psephasim* and one who plays with shells of nuts or pomegranates, he is not accepted again (= as a witness) until he breaks his *psephasim* or rips up his (gambling)notes and is examined and makes complete repentance.' This statement does a number of things. First it adds to the list gambling games which are not connected with dicing or board-games. Second, it proves that the prohibition refers to the professional. Thus, the former gambler is not accepted as a witness until he breaks his dice and/or game counters and the like so that he will not play under any circumstances. He must also rip up any outstanding notes of those who owe him money. None of this would make sense regarding the casual gambler.

---

[43] See also y. Sanh. 3: 6 (21a); y. R.Sh. 1, 9 (57c–d) and b. Sanh. 25b.
[44] Lamer (1927), cols. 1939–40. MS Erfurt for t. Sanh. 5: 2 reads *tyfasym*, but this is obviously incorrect. See the sources cited in n. 43.
[45] Ibid.

We have suggested that the view of R. Judah was based on a shift in attitude towards the occasional gambler who was no longer considered evil and that the occasional enjoyment of gambling should no longer invalidate one's legal standing *vis-à-vis* testimony. An interesting tradition seems to imply that such casual dicing may have even reached some levels of rabbinic society, albeit in Babylonia. Thus, a tradition in b. Kidd. 21b regarding third-century CE Babylonia, tells of rabbis at the academy of Samuel in Nehardea playing with astragals; such games on an adult level were usually in a gambling framework.[46] Nowhere, however, does the tradition even hint at any opposition to this.

We have so far tried to pinpoint changing trends in attitudes towards gambling, yet have not pointed out exactly what the Rabbis considered objectionable. Only a single tradition in the Babylonian Talmud actually attempted to do this. The reticence of the Palestinian tradition is surprising, perhaps indicating once again that lack of information may reflect a conscious trend to avoid publicizing this pastime in Palestine, while the Babylonians may have been less wary of the evils of gambling. Unfortunately, the explanations in b. Sanh. 24b are not terribly helpful:

What [wrong] does the dice player do? Rammi b. Hama said: [He is disqualified] because it [= gambling] is an *Asmakhta*, and *Asmakhta* is not legally binding. R. Shesheth said: Such cases do not come under the category of *Asmakhta*; but the reason is that they [= dice players] are not concerned with general welfare (trans., ed. Soncino, pp. 142–3).

The two sages mentioned are both Babylonian and fairly late. *Asmakhta* refers to 'fictitious' contracts wherein each side promises to pay the other should certain conditions prevail, but nobody ever expects these conditions actually to exist. This was considered to be a form of theft.[47] The second reason, 'not being concerned with the general welfare', is so broad that it could refer to just about any type of questionable activity. It is hard to imagine, though, that the opposition to dicing in the mishnaic traditions discussed above revolved around problems of legal fictions or around an amorphous objection that could have included many types of activities. The silence of the Palestinian tradition is also quite telling. As we have

[46] The game is called *'iskomadari* (= *'iskandari*) which derives from astragal and has, therefore, been interpreted as a game of chance. See Krauss (1910–12), iii. 113.
[47] Lifshitz (1988), 19–23, 81–3.

suggested, everyone apparently knew that something was wrong with dicing, but from a purely legal standpoint, there was not much that could be said about precisely what that was.

The Palestinian Talmud may not give its own reasons why dicing was forbidden, but it does mention dicing in a number of other interesting contexts such as the comment of Rabban Simeon b. Gamaliel in y. B.K. 5: 6 (5a) that it is '*kotizmi*' (= *kottismos* = dicing) to pay more for a 'fruitful' handmaiden, since she may die in childbirth.[48] Rabban Simeon clearly uses a dicing metaphor with no indication that there is anything wrong with gambling or dicing apart from the fact that it might be a bad investment; his short statement, though, is of great significance for the understanding of attitudes towards gambling. Rabban Simeon b. Gamaliel was a contemporary of R. Judah and his casual use of the metaphor would seem to imply what we have already suggested, i.e. a more liberal attitude towards casual dicing in the mid to late second century CE.

As we mentioned above, the liberal attitude towards the casual dicer was accompanied by a more stringent attitude towards the professional or compulsive gambler. A story in y. Ned. 5: 4 (39b) has been interpreted as referring to a professional or compulsive dicer who apparently tried to desist from his (profitable?) habit but to no avail. His conscience now weighed heavy and he wished to be absolved of his oath, but R. Yudan b. Shalom refused once he discovered that gambling was involved.[49]

A number of other sources refer to the professional or compulsive dicer. None are complimentary and this is hardly surprising. Thus t. B.B. 4: 7 (pp. 141–2, ed. Lieberman) stated that if one sold a slave to his fellow and he was found to be a (professional) dicer, then the sale was still valid, implying that it was unusual to buy a slave who was a dicer. Slave society was apparently not considered to be inherently corrupt or immoral. It is also interesting to note that the tradition hints at a possible relationship between dicing and becoming a slave, probably through falling into debt. However, since the passage indicates that few slaves were compulsive gamblers, it would seem likely that there was no widespread phenomenon of dicers under financial pressure selling themselves or being sold into slavery.

The professional or compulsive gambler is mentioned a number

---

[48] Lieberman (1991), 227–8.   [49] Landman (1967/8), 35 ff.

of other times together with thieves.[50] Thus, a tradition in b. Hull. 91b relates how when the angel wrestling with Jacob asked to be released because the dawn was at hand (Gen. 32: 27), Jacob accused him of being either a thief or a dicer (*kubyustos*). It is hardly surprising that a professional gambler might have feared the rising sun and discovery by creditors. It is not clear, though, whether the tradition reflects the situation in Jewish society since, after all, Jacob was wrestling with the guardian angel of Edom, usually identified with Rome,[51] and perhaps the source is actually reflecting Roman social reality.[52]

Thus, the few traditions which seem to refer to the professional or compulsive dicer do not seem to reflect any widespread phenomenon in Jewish society, and indeed, the traditions mostly appear in relation to non-Jewish society. Nor do the Jewish sources connect this type of dicer with other forms of libertine behaviour, such as the tavern or brothel, as was the case in the Graeco-Roman world.

The rabbinic material examined up to now has either been halachic in nature or rooted in halachic tradition. This type of material, as we have stated, avoided moralizing, whether because there was no legal basis for this or, as we have also suggested, because there may not have been a pressing need for it. Later aggadic literature was apparently not bothered by lack of legal foundation. Thus, for instance, Tanhuma Noah 20 (p. 24a–b, ed. Buber) mentions dicing together with prostitutes, gladiatorial games and magic and accuses the non-Jew Bilaam of using all these practices to corrupt Israel.[53] Perhaps what the Tanhuma explicitly states here is what the rabbis really thought or feared, but did not or could not say within a halachic framework. Bilaam, of course, did not succeed, perhaps indicating that contemporary attempts to contaminate Israel were no more successful. The tradition then did not indicate a pressing need for moralizing because of an increase in gambling, but rather a willingness to use that tactic as a preventive measure.

Another example of such moralizing is found in Seder Eliyahu Rabba, chapter (15) 16 (p. 77, ed. Ish Shalom) which mentions

---

[50] Midrash on Psalms 26: 7.   [51] Herr (1971).
[52] Yalkut Shimoni, Eqev, §847. See also b. Bekh. 5b and y. Sanh. 1, 6 (19d).
[53] Purcell (1995). Cicero mentions the gambler with such dubious types as gluttons, procurers, prostitutes, drunkards, debauchers, and the like.

dicers together with those who lend with interest, apostates, and defilers of the Divine name and does not allow dicers to bequeath their (ill-gotten) property to their children. This, however, might be in keeping with the moralizing tone of the book, but not in keeping with halacha, even if the tradition is probably referring to professional gamblers.[54]

One last source remains regarding the morality of gambling. Up to now, all of the Jewish gambling traditions have dealt with gambling within some type of game framework. It was, of course, possible to wager on any type of event, phenomenon or activity. Needless to say, this type of activity is difficult to track down. Fortunately, a case of taking wagers is mentioned in b. Shab. 30b–31a (= Avot d'Rabbi Nathan, Version A, chapter 15, p. 60, ed. Schechter). The tradition refers to the days of Hillel, theoretically the end of the Second Temple period, but more likely reflects some time in the period of the Talmud. The story tells of two men who made a wager with each other as to which could make Hillel angry. One went to try, but he could not incense Hillel, and finally out of desperation cursed him. Hillel explained that keeping one's composure was more important than winning a wager.

This tradition is amazing. Nowhere is there even the slightest hint that the two protagonists of the story should not be engaging in gambling. The rabbis probably realized that some aspects of human nature simply could not be changed. This was reality and as long as it did not get out of hand and become obsessive or 'professional', then there was no reason to undertake a lost cause in fighting it.

ARCHAEOLOGY AND THE JEWISH GAMBLER

Archaeological remains provide some additional evidence. Finds from Palestine indicate a long history of gaming with dice and astragals as well as the playing of many forms of board-games,[55] but the relatively small amount of material also clearly indicates that these pastimes were never as popular as they were in the Graeco-Roman world.

Dice, astragals, game-boards, equipment, and other finds relevant to gaming have also been discovered from the Persian,

---

[54] Elon (1988), 1408.
[55] Huebner (1992), 43–60 on astragals, 61–6 on dice, and 67–85 on board and related games.

Hellenistic, and Roman periods. We briefly mention some of the non-Jewish finds in Palestine to serve as a basis for comparison with the Jewish material.

We have seen, for example, that gambling pastimes were popular in military circles. Thus, astragals found in the area of the Antonia fortress in Jerusalem most likely belonged to Roman soldiers who had served there or in the vicinity.[56] Roman soldiers probably also gambled on game-boards cut into the pavement floor in the Monastery of the Sisters of Zion,[57] or on the game-board incised into the floor of the gate-complex of the Damascus Gate, or even on the two game-boards inscribed on limestone at Qumran.[58] The soldiers' gambling probably did little to endear them to the Jews, but this was hardly the main basis for the relationship between the Jews and non-Jewish soldiers and undoubtedly most of the military gambling took place when the soldiers were off-duty and had little to do with the Jewish population. It is highly unlikely that they gambled together with Jews.

The Jewish material is of different types, although it is not always easy to prove that it was used by Jews. Thus, the limestone dice from Hellenistic period Gezer or sheep-bone astragals from the upper strata there of what MaCalister called the 'Maccabean Castle' might have been used by Jews if they indeed date to the period after the city had been conquered by Simon the Hasmonean.[59] The same might be true about 'draught boards' from the Hellenistic period and small and well-polished pins of porphyry and ivory found in the stratum of the same date. Slabs intended for games similar to those found at Gezer were found in Tel Zakariya in the Shephelah and since this area was Jewish during a good part of the Second Temple period, there is a strong possibility that these boards belonged to Jews.[60]

[56] De Sion (1955), 120–1 and pl. 44. The astragals are placed on a board-game cut into the central courtyard. The military attribution of these astragals is based on de Sion's now generally unaccepted view that the Monastery of the Sisters of Zion is to be identified with the Antonia. Thus, for instance, the identification as a guard room of a room in which many astragals were embedded is also questionable.

[57] Ibid. 119–42 and pls. 44–8. The most famous game found there was the Game of the King (= *Basilikos*).

[58] De Sion (1955), 129. The boards have not yet been published and, according to de Sion, probably were incised by Roman legionnaires who came to the site after June 68 CE.

[59] MaCalister (1912), 301, 303.

[60] Ibid. 306.

However, only one find from the Hellenistic period can be attributed with absolute certainty to Jewish use. Thus, an irregular rhomboid-shaped die with rounded edges was found in Jason's Tomb in Jerusalem.[61] The dots of the die were placed in such a manner that a two could be interpreted as a three; in other words the die was 'loaded'.

The question of cheating is important: we have seen above that cheating was common in dicing circles in the Graeco-Roman world. The 'loaded' die in Jason's Tomb was not the only one found in remains from Palestine of the Second Temple period, but probably the only one that was definitely 'Jewish'.[62] Can the crooked die from Jason's Tomb tell us anything about contemporary Jewish life and mores? Jason's Tomb is dated to the early first century BCE and usually considered to be the tomb of an upper-class Sadducean family. Obviously, a single 'loaded' die does not make all Sadducaeans cheats. However, finding the die in an upper-class tomb would most likely indicate that dicing was more widespread in the Hellenized circles of Jerusalem than in lower socio-economic strata.

There are also remains from Herodian times. N. Avigad, who excavated the Upper City of Jerusalem, usually identified with the richer neighbourhoods of that city, uncovered a bone die that was probably used for gambling by upper-class Jews who lived there.[63] Avigad also discovered a number of discs in a Herodian period building. The small discs, between 2.6 and 3 cm. in diameter, were identified by Avigad as theatre tokens,[64] but we have seen above that such discs or 'tesserae' were more probably game counters.[65] These finds should perhaps be understood together with the die found in the Armenian Garden excavations of A. D. Tushingham, not far from the areas excavated by Avigad and inhabited by the same social strata and dated by Tushingham to the 'late Jewish period' (= often Herodian).[66] This, together with Avigad's finds, would seem to indicate that the upper classes of Jewish society in

---

[61] Rahmani (1967), 90, pl. 24d, p. 96.

[62] A bone die from the citadel of Beth Zur could never throw a five. Sellers dates the die to the Hellenistic pre-Hasmonean period, probably indicating that it was used by a Seleucid soldier stationed there who was not terribly honest. Sellers (1933), 61–2 and fig. 56: 4.

[63] Avigad (1980), 193, fig. 224.

[64] Ibid. 200, fig. 239.

[65] See n. 4.

[66] Tushingham (1985), 58.

Jerusalem engaged in gambling.[67] It is also possible that some of the similar tesserae from Caesarea were connected to board-games played by the upper crust of Jewish society in that city.[68]

There was also another segment of Jewish society which apparently engaged in gambling. We have already seen above that dicing and gambling were popular among soldiers, and Jewish soldiers apparently were no exception. Thus, a die was found at Masada in a casemate wall of a room used as a dwelling by the Sicarii.[69] This is reminiscent of the Greek tradition which attributed the origins of dicing to the Trojan War, devised as a means of diverting attention from the suffering of starvation. The Sicarii at Masada may have had food, but they certainly did have other fears, which some dicing may have temporarily allayed. It is also possible that the wooden gaming counters found in the 'Cave of Horrors' in the Judaean Desert and possibly belonging to Jewish soldiers fighting in the forces of Bar-Kokhba in the revolt against Rome (132–5 CE) served the same diversionary purposes.[70] It is still far from clear, however, as to how widespread this phenomenon actually was among Jewish soldiers.

Archaeological remains pertaining to Jewish gambling from the Roman–Byzantine period are also quite meagre. A number of dice were discovered from Roman period Sepphoris.[71] It is impossible, of course, to prove that they were used by Jews, but based on the nature of the city at this time, this would not be all that unlikely and the same is true regarding a number of games inscribed into pavement slabs discovered there. Thus, three such games composed of double rows of depressions have been found incised in pavements of Sepphoris.[72] One was found in the courtyard of what

[67] Two 'boards' (?) are inscribed on a Herodian period street slab right in front of the Warren Gate. It is difficult to know who put them there.

[68] Hamburger (1986), 187–204. See Huebner (1992), 85 n. 139 who interpreted them correctly as game counters. Some of the tesserae had Jewish motifs (194 §§ 85, 86).

[69] Yadin (1966), 145.

[70] Aharoni (1961), 22 and pl. 8.

[71] This is based on information supplied by James Strange, Douglas Edwards, and Stuart Miller.

[72] The dating of such finds is somewhat problematical. Most excavators have tended automatically to date the games to the Muslim period. Some scholars, though, have begun to re-date some of the games to the late Roman or Byzantine periods. Most of the material on games from Sepphoris is based on information I have received from Marianne Sawicki and James Strange of the University of South Florida Excavations at Sepphoris.

has been identified as a shop floor while another turned up on work surfaces at the aqueduct to the east.[73] Although 'mancala' games of this sort were popular among the Arabs, they did exist earlier and thus it is possible that they were carved in the Roman–Byzantine period and that their initial usage dates to 'Jewish' Sepphoris.[74] There are, however, still many unknowns in the games described above, such as whether there was any special significance in games carved into shop pavements.[75]

Two circular game-boards were also found in the pavement of the courtyard of the building to the east of the synagogue at Capernaum,[76] perhaps implying that gambling took place within or near sacred precincts;[77] such activities would also not have been alien to the nearby church or monastery.[78] Other board-games have been found in Byzantine period Palestine, but it is unlikely that they were 'Jewish'.[79]

CONCLUSIONS

It is possible to make a number of tentative conclusions based on the archaeological and literary material combined. There was a sharp decline in the amount of gambling material discovered in Palestine from the Hellenistic, Roman, and Byzantine periods as compared with the remains of the bronze and iron ages, indicating that dicing and gambling were not as popular later on as they had been earlier. This might be understandable regarding the Jews, but is somewhat puzzling regarding the non-Jewish population. Perhaps these non-Jews were not all that Hellenized after all, at least *vis-à-vis* gambling games.

Also, the meagre finds of Jewish dice and astragals are extremely telling. This is especially important in light of the total lack of such

---

[73] This information is also from Marianne Sawicki. Initially, the complex was dated to periods of Arab rule in Palestine, but Byzantine trash and fragments would point to an earlier date in the Byzantine period.

[74] Murray (1952), 158–204.

[75] Sawicki (1997).

[76] Corbo (1970), Tavola 1.

[77] Huebner (1992), 84.

[78] Ibid.

[79] e.g. a game-board for a game similar to checkers was scratched on the jamb stone of a door in Byzantine Jerusalem. Similar games have been found in Nessana, Haluza, and a few other sites in the south; here too, it is unlikely that they were used by Jews.

finds at Jewish *necropoleis* such as Beth Shearim and Joppa and compared with the tremendous amount of dice and astragals found in grave sites in the Graeco-Roman world. All this might support our contention that the more liberal attitude towards casual gambling in Jewish society during the Roman period was the result of minimal interest in this pastime as well as the fact that casual gambling did not seem to attract large numbers of adherents to the ranks of the professionals.

Also, the difference between the types of finds might be indicative of changes in gambling trends in Jewish society. In the Hellenistic and Herodian periods, dice and astragal games seemed to have been more common. Afterwards, board-games became popular, although dicing did not totally disappear. t. Sanh. 5: 2 explained the term *kubiya'* in the mishnaic sources as *psephas,* which could mean both die and game counter. The choice of this phrase then could reflect the increasing popularity of board-games, both with and without dice.

It should also be pointed out that none of the archaeological material found can be connected specifically with either women or children. Taken together with the fact that all of the Jewish literary traditions we have examined refer to adult males, it is possible that such gambling as did take place in Jewish society within the frameworks we have examined was basically a matter for adult males and not women and children. The conservative nature of Jewish society probably imposed sufficient social restrictions on such activity by women or children. This was quite different from the situation in Graeco-Roman society.

There were a few trends, though, that were common to the Jewish world and Graeco-Roman society. Jewish soldiers, for instance, engaged in certain kinds of gambling games, just like their non-Jewish counterparts. At first glance this might seem quite natural, since many scholars have seen soldiers as natural practitioners of gambling activities, but if certain gambling games were identified too much with Graeco-Roman society, then Jewish soldiers could hardly have engaged in them without arousing antagonism. However, since many of the gambling games were 'universal' and since the material we have regarding Jewish soldiers relates to periods of dire straits, there might have been problems of a more pressing nature than whether the particular Jewish soldiers in question were engaging in games that were too Greek or Roman or, if they did, whether they did so too much.

Also, the majority of the 'civilian' Jewish gambling remains were found in an urban setting and a number seem to relate to the upper classes, indicating that a good deal of Jewish gambling took place in an urban upper-class setting, as was the case in the Roman world. Gambling required capital and spare funds were not often available in the rural sphere or among the poor.[80]

It would appear then that both literary traditions and material remains indicate that gambling was not a widespread phenomenon or problem in Jewish Palestine during the Second Temple, mishnaic, and talmudic periods, although there were enough instances of both casual and professional gambling to cause some concern. The literary traditions have shown that the initial strict attitude towards all types of gambling eventually gave way to a more liberal one towards casual gambling. The professional gambler was another matter. The rabbis continued to fight against this phenomenon with all the means at their disposal.

Can all this tell us anything about Jewish society? Since attitudes and behaviour in this respect were different in the Middle Ages and afterwards, there must have been something unique about the Judaism of the Second Temple, mishnaic, and talmudic periods.

Modern research has shown that two factors in particular contribute to a low rate of gambling: home-centredness and work-centred leisure.[81] Both are relevant for ancient Jewish society. Thus, regarding the first, the importance of home and family is well known in the traditions of ancient Judaism and hardly needs to be expanded upon here. The second factor also relates to time spent out of the house. This does not mean leisure at the actual physical place of work. Rather, it is important to remember that as far as the rabbis were concerned, the ideal pastime was the study of Torah. This should have been one's 'work'. Since this was not usually possible, then it should have been at least one's leisure. This too would curb gambling. Also, both factors could provide the social interaction and intellectual challenge that gambling often offered[82] while at the same time guaranteeing a good deal of social control.

All this, however, does not explain why it was only in the Second Temple, mishnaic, and talmudic periods that Jewish gambling was

---

[80] Purcell (1995), 17. This is, of course, not to say that there was no gambling in lower socio-economic circles.

[81] Downes (1976), 89–95.

[82] Bruce and Johnson (1992).

limited. The two values mentioned above undoubtedly existed in later Jewish society. One possibility is that the negative characteristics of gambling in the Graeco-Roman world made more of an impression on the Jews than similar phenomena in the non-Jewish world made on later Jewish society. Another possibility, though, goes right to the heart of the nature of ancient Jewish society. It has been established that gambling varies inversely with the sway exerted by any normative culture, which would almost automatically have been opposed to gambling.[83] The attitude of the rabbis to gambling was certainly dictated by their views in general on religious and moral guidelines for society. Thus, their success regarding gambling might well reflect power and success in other similar spheres. This, of course, still requires much further study.

[83] Downes (1976), 69–88.

11

The Rabbis and the Documents

HANNAH M. COTTON

Dedicated to the memory of my teacher and friend
Abraham (Addi) Wasserstein

On 2 December 127 CE Babatha daughter of Shim'on had her
guardian, Judah son of Eleazar Khthousion, write the following
sworn subscription to her land declaration, submitted in Rabbath-
Moab on the occasion of the census held in the Roman province of
Arabia by the governor, Titus Aninius Sextius Florentinus: 'I,
Babatha daughter of Shim'on, swear by the genius (*tyche*) of the
Lord Caesar that I have in good faith registered as has been written
above. I, Judanes son of Eleazar, acted as guardian and wrote for
her.' This subscription has survived only in its Greek translation in
the verified copy of Babatha's land declaration.[1] Seven months
earlier, around 25 April, another Jew, whose name has not been
preserved, but whose patronymic is Levi, thus X son of Levi,
because he was illiterate had his sworn declaration written for him
by the Nabataean Onainos son of Sa'adalos.[2] The wording is almost
identical: 'I, X son of Levi, swear by the genius of the Lord Caesar
that I have in good faith registered as written above, concealing
nothing.'[3]

We find similar oath formulas in census returns of the fourteen-
year census cycle in Egypt, the κατ᾽ οἰκίαν ἀπογραφή.[4] The oath does

It is my pleasure to thank my friend Professor David Wasserstein for his incisive
criticisms.

[1] Βαβθα Σίμωνος ὄμνυμι τύχην κυρίου Καίσαρος καλῇ πίστει ἀπογεγράφθαι ὡς
προγέγραπτ[τα]ι. Ἰουδάνης ἐπιτρόπευ[σ]α καὶ ἔγραψα ὑπὲρ αὐτῆς, *P.Yadin* 16, ll. 33–5
in Lewis (1989), 67.

[2] See Cotton (1995*b*), 34–8.

[3] ['Ο δεῖνα] Λειουου ὄμνυμι τύχην Κυρίου Καίσαρος κ[α]λῇ πίστει ἀπογεγράφθαι ὡς
προγέγραπται μηθὲν ὑποστειλάμενος in Cotton (1993*a*), 117, ll. 2–3 = *eadem*
(1995), 176 = *DJD* xxvii, no. 61.

[4] On which see Hombert and Préaux (1952) and Bagnall and Frier (1994).

not appear on all declarations: the presence or absence of the oath
depends entirely on local custom.[5] The oath is by the reigning
emperor or his *tyche* as well as by local divinities. We do not possess
an example of a Jew affixing an oath by the *tyche* of the emperor to a
census declaration from Egypt, but we do have an example of a Jew
from the Fayyûm, Soteles son of Josepos, affixing an oath by the
emperor to the notification of the death of his son (Josepos), which
he is submitting to the authorities.[6] It is true that *tyche* is not
mentioned here. However, the editors of the *Corpus Papyrorum
Judaicarum* are right to argue that this omission is not 'on account
of the Judaism of Soteles', but is explained by the fact that 'the
Roman oath "by the genius of the emperor" was not yet familiar in
Egypt'. And at any rate 'an oath by the emperor presupposes his
superhuman origin, which contradicts the principles of Judaism'.[7] It
would seem that the Jews of this period were less conscious—even
oblivious—of the religious implication of an oath by the emperor or
by his *tyche* from the standpoint of a monotheistic Jewish theology.
It is not necessary to assume that they felt coerced into using the
formula. One's expectations of what Jews would or would not do at
certain periods of their history are often belied by the evidence.
Babatha and X son of Levi swore by the *tyche* of the emperor as a
matter of course. In this as well as in their other contacts with the
authorities, they simply followed local custom.[8]

It could be objected that those Jews who swear by the *tyche* of the
emperor are Hellenized Jews. This is patently not true of the men
and women who people the Babatha archive and the archive of
Salome Komaïse daughter of Levi, the sister of the declarant
mentioned above.[9] On the contrary: they sign and subscribe in
Aramaic, and when they need their contracts written in Greek, they
employ scribes.[10] And even the latter are not very proficient in
Greek. Perhaps the most glaring example is a deed of gift from the

---

[5] Hombert and Préaux (1952), 125.

[6] Σωτέλης Ἰωσήπου ὁ πρωγεγραμένος ὠμνύω Αὐτοκράτορα Καίσα[ρα Νέρουαν] Τραιαν[ὸν] Σεβα[στόν], *BGU* iv. 1068 = *CPJ* ii. 427, ll. 18–24 (101 CE).

[7] *CPJ* ii. 214, on ll. 18 ff.

[8] It may be suggested that this was facilitated by another social phenomenon described by Lieberman (1984), namely the abusive use of the practice of oath taking in daily life in Palestine.

[9] See Cotton in Cotton and Yardeni (1997), 160–2.

[10] For scribes in the Babatha archive see *P.Yadin* 11: Iustinus; *P.Yadin* 14, 15, 17, 18: Theenas son of Simon; *P.Yadin* 19: X son of Simon; *P.Yadin* 20–7: Germanus son of Joudah.

archive of Salome Komaïse daughter of Levi.[11] The scribe pays no attention whatever to case endings and gender.[12] He cannot be said to know the language; he translates from the Aramaic word for word and literally. At times the Aramaic *Urtext* is so close to the surface that the text can be understood only when translated back into the original Aramaic. For example: in lines 6–9 the mother, Salome Gropte, declares: 'I acknowledge that I have given you as a gift from this day and for ever my property in Maḥoza, which items are listed as follows: a date orchard called the Garden of Asaʿadaia with its water [allowance], once a week on the fourth day, for one half-hour.' The Greek reads:

ὁμολογῶ ἐνενοχ[έ]ναι σοι εἰς δόσιν ἀπὸ τῆς σήμερον δόσιν αἰωνίου τὰ ὑπάρχοντά μοι ἐν Μαωζας ἃ εἴδη ὑποτεταγμένα· κῆπον φοινεικῶνος καλούμενον γανναθ Ἀσαδαια σὺν ὕδατος αὐτῆς ἐφ᾽ ἡμερῶν ἑπτὰ εἰς ἑπτὰ ἡμέραν τετάρτῃ ἡ[μ]ιωρ(ί)αν μίαν.

My proposed translation into Aramaic is based entirely on the Aramaic deed of gift written for Babatha's mother, Miriam, by her husband in 120:[13]

אנא יהבת לכי מן יומא דנה ולעלם מתנת עלם דאיתי לי במחוזא... כדי כתיבין גנת תמריא די מתקריא גנת חצדיתה? אסאדיה? וענימיה יום ארבעה בשבת פלגות שעה...

The use of Greek in my opinion is to be explained by the desire to make the deed of gift valid and enforceable in a Greek-speaking court, such as that of the governor of the province. Babatha, for example, as well as her opponents, were in the habit of approaching this court on their own initiative, as any reader of the Greek part of the archive immediately discovers.[14] Another reason could be the need to deposit the deeds in a public archive, similar to what we know to have been the case in Egypt, where public archives were used to deposit private documents; having been registered there, these documents could later be produced in court as evidence.[15] We have a reference to such archives in the Babatha archive. A deed of gift by Judah son of Eleazar Khthousion to his daughter from his

---

[11] See Cotton (1995*a*), 183–203 = *DJD* xxvii, no. 64.

[12] See text and apparatus in Cotton (1995*a*), 185–7 = Cotton in Cotton and Yardeni (1997), 206–7.

[13] *P. Yadin* 7, published in Yadin, Greenfield, and Yardeni (1996), 11. 1–5 = ll. 30–6; ll. 14–16 = ll. 50–4. I am grateful to the editors for allowing me to see and use the text in advance of publication.   [14] See Cotton (1993*b*), 106 ff.

[15] See Cockle (1984), 116; see also Burkhalter (1990).

first wife concludes with: 'And whenever Shelamzion summons the said Judah he will register it with the public archives.'[16] Again, in a deed of concession of inherited property, Besas son of Yeshu'a and Julia Crispina promise Shelamzion to register with the public archives in her name at her expense a courtyard in Ein-Gedi which had belonged to her paternal grandfather.[17] In both cases, since the property is located in Ein-Gedi, it is likely that the public archive operating in Greek is to be located there. A fragmentary papyrus from the same archive tells us that Babatha's late husband had registered date-groves in her name in the *apographe*.[18] *Apographe* here—as we can see from what follows—cannot refer to the census,[19] and thus must refer to an official registration of property, presumably in the public archives.

That Jews registered their contracts with the public authorities is neither surprising nor unknown. We hear in the rabbinic sources of these 'non-Jewish archives'—ערכאות הגויים, in which the term ערכאות is simply a transliteration of the Greek word ἀρχεῖα. That these were frequently used by Jews we learn for example from m. Gittin 1: 5: 'Any deed is valid that is registered in the registries of the gentiles (ערכאות הגיים), although witnessed by gentiles, except a deed of divorce or a deed of emancipation. R. Shim'on [*c*.130–60] says: "These, too, are valid; they were mentioned [as invalid] only when they were prepared by unauthorized people (נעשו בהדיוט)".' The language of the deed is not important as we learn from t. Baba Bathra 11: 8: 'They change the language of deeds from Hebrew to Greek and from Greek to Hebrew and make it valid' (ועושין לו קיום בית דין).[20]

There are several discussions in the rabbinic sources on the validity of contracts made in Greek, on the use of gentile witnesses, courts and archives. Sometimes such activities are explicitly forbidden. I have been able to find only two tannaitic passages which explicitly discourage Jews from using gentile courts. These two passages are not unrelated. The harsh language employed by the

---

[16] ὅταν δὲ παραγγείλει Σελα⟨μ⟩ψιοῦς τῷ αὐτῷ Ἰούδατι, τευχίζ{ζ}ει αὐτὴν διὰ δημοσίων, *P.Yadin* 19, ll. 25–7.

[17] ταυτὴν δὲ τὴν αὐλὴν ὅπου ἂν βουληθῇς τευχίσω σο[ι] διὰ δημοσίων, σοῦ διδούσης τὸ ἀνάλωμα, *P.Yadin* 20, ll. 34–6.

[18] ἀπεγράψατο Ἰούδας Ἐλεαζάρο[υ Χθουσίωνος] ἀπογενομένου σου ἀνὴρ ἐπ' ὀνόματός σου ἐν τῇ ἀπ[ο]γραφῇ κήπους φοινικῶνος ἐν Μαωζᾳ, *P.Yadin* 24, ll. 4–6.

[19] So Lewis (1989), 105–7.

[20] Lieberman (1988), 168–9: 'the court approves the translation.'

rabbis in the prohibition on using gentile courts may well indicate that the Jews *did* use them; no less is implied when the rabbis used conciliatory language and allowed what was in common use to have validity under Jewish law.

It is a remarkable fact that no court, Jewish or non-Jewish—apart from that of the Roman governor of Arabia—is mentioned in any of the documents from the Judaean Desert—a great many of which are legal documents. We should not jump from this to the conclusion that the governor's court was the only court in operation in a Roman province. Still the absence of others is disturbing, especially in view of the host of references in rabbinic sources to courts of different sizes in towns and villages.[21]

Non-Hellenized Jews were using the Greek language—sometimes a very faulty version of it—in their contracts, for a variety of reasons: perhaps in the absence of Jewish courts and archives; perhaps in order to leave their options open: with their contracts written in Greek they could go to the court of their choice, Jewish or gentile—perhaps that of the Roman governor. But we can go further than this: not all the contracts are written in faulty Greek, nor are they all literal translations from the Aramaic, as is the deed of gift in favour of Salome Komaïse daughter of Levi cited above. Some of them use a language not different from the *koine* used in the papyri from Egypt. Even the script is similar, and this in itself is significant.[22] The external resemblance is paralleled by internal similarities: not only the Greek script and Greek diplomatics but often the very phrases, the entire ethos of the Greek contract was taken over by the Jewish scribes. Thus we find deeds of sale, petitions, land registrations, receipts, mortgages, promissory notes, and even marriage contracts, all of which bear a striking resemblance to their Egyptian counterparts.

What makes a contract Jewish is not its language, content, or particular ingredients. Jewish civil law, as we have it in the tannaitic and later sources (as well as in the Pentateuch), was not created *in vacuo*, but absorbed very many local, or, better, regional traditions which are reflected in its rules. But unless we wish to describe everything used by Jews as Jewish, we need to find some criteria which will distinguish what is Jewish from what is not. I have not

---

[21] Schürer, Vermes, and Millar (1979), 184–8; Alon (1984), 553–7; Gulak (1929), 54 ff.; less sceptical is Safrai (1995), 76 ff.

[22] See Crisci (1996).

found a better definition for what is Jewish than that such material eventually received halachic sanction, and is present in the halachic sources. Conversely, what is not there, or explicitly forbidden, I would designate non-Jewish. I wish to emphasize that in the period reflected in most of the documents from the Judaean Desert—after the destruction of the Temple in 70 and before the end of the Bar Kokhba Revolt in 135/6—Jewish civil law was in the process of being created in the rabbinic schools, but had yet to receive its final shape—let alone the authority it was to acquire after its formal redaction at the end of the second century CE. Thus to say that Jews are using 'non-Jewish' contracts is to say no more than that the legal usage reflected in the documents is not in harmony with what eventually came to be normative Jewish law. The diversity and fluidity manifested in the documents from the Judaean Desert are the best evidence we have, I believe, for the state of Jewish law and the authority exercised by the rabbis at the time.

Objections could be made to my exclusive reliance on these documents to evaluate the state of Jewish law and the authority exercised by the rabbis at this time. Three points need to be made in defence of my position.

First, the Jews represented in the documents from the Judaean Desert are not a fringe group, even if the presence of their documents in the caves of the Judaean Desert was caused by the upheaval resulting from the outbreak of the Bar Kokhba Revolt and is thus limited both in place—to those parts of Judaea and the province of Arabia that were near the caves—and in time—to the period 70–135/6 CE. These are Jews from villages as scattered as Maḥoza and Mazra'a in the southern part of the Dead Sea area in the Province of Arabia, Sophathe[..] from the Peraea in Trans-Jordan, which belonged to the province of Judaea, Ein-Gedi near the Dead Sea, Yaqim and Aristoboulias in the area south-east of Hebron, Bethbassi near Herodium, Galoda in eastern Samaria, and Batharda in southern Samaria. They are by no means restricted to one locality. I maintain, therefore, that they are representative of Jewish society as a whole in the period under discussion. They present a faithful picture of the realities of life at the time that they were written.

Second, any notion of a distinction between Jews from the province of Arabia and those from Judaea should be dispelled; we are talking about areas which are very close to each other (a day's walk or two days at most between the furthest destinations), and where borders had very little inhibiting effect on movement. The official names, Arabia, Judaea, and Syria-Palaestina, represent artificial divisions which did not seem to matter very much in reality. The archives amply demonstrate that the Jews living in Arabia and the Jews living in the province of Judaea belonged to a single Jewish society whose internal ties overrode provincial boundaries: they disregard the provincial boundaries in their residence, marriages, and property holdings.

Lastly, the Jews represented in these documents come from densely populated Jewish areas, from the heartland of the Bar Kokhba Revolt, a religious and national movement. Many of the Greek documents were written close to the time when the revolt broke out—a revolt which was carefully prepared some years in advance. In fact the very presence of the documents in the caves demonstrates their owners' participation in the revolt. The writers of these documents cannot and should not be regarded as assimilated Jews.[23]

I should like to illustrate the state of fluidity in the legal habits and traditions manifest amongst Jews in the period between 70 and 135 through one kind of contract: the marriage contract. I choose this particular contract for several reasons. First of all because we have by now no less than eight (perhaps nine) such contracts from the Judaean Desert.[24] Second, because it is in the sphere of marriage law that rabbinic traditions claim to go back to a period long before the destruction of the Temple, and by implication to have become normative by the time of our documents. I refer to the artificial reconstruction of how the biblical *mohar* was transformed from an immediate payment, a bride-gift to the wife's father, into an 'endowment pledge, a divorce payment', which was due to the wife upon the dissolution of the marriage, and as such written in to the marriage contract, the *ketubba*. The traditional and almost

---

[23] See above.

[24] (1) *DJD* ii, no. 20, i or ii cent. CE, Ḥardona, Aramaic; (2) *DJD* ii, no. 115, 124 CE, Bethbassi, Judaea, Greek; (3) *P.Yadin* 10 (Yadin, Greenfield, and Yardeni (1994)), 125–8 CE, Maḥoza, Arabia, Aramaic; (4) *P.Yadin* 18, 128 CE, Maḥoza, Arabia, Greek; (5) *XḤevlṢe Gr* 2 (Cotton (1994) = *DJD* xxvii, no. 69), 130 CE, Aristoboulias, Judaea, Greek; (6) *P.Yadin* 37 (= *DJD* xxvii, no. 65), 131 CE, Maḥoza, Arabia, Greek; (7) *DJD* ii, no. 116, first half of 2nd cent. CE, unknown place, Greek; (8) *DJD* ii, no. 21, i or ii cent. CE, unknown place, Aramaic; perhaps also (9) *DJD* xxvii, no. 11, i or ii cent. CE, unknown place, Aramaic.

universally accepted view is that the process reached its conclusion when Shimʿon b. Shetah—who was active in the first half of the first century BCE—put into the *ketubba* a clause to the effect that the husband's entire property is held liable for the payment of the *mohar*. We find the story in several versions.[25] I use the term 'artificial' to describe this process deliberately, since I believe that among other things this narrative was constructed to account for the fact that the term *mohar* simply disappeared from current usage. In the earliest *ketubboth*, that of Babatha published recently and that in *DJD* ii, no. 21, the payment in question is referred to simply, but equivocally, as 'the money of your *ketubba*'—כסף כתבתך.[26] Third, and lastly, I choose the marriage contract because the *ketubba*, the Jewish marriage contract—unlike other contracts—includes, in addition to financial arrangements, formulae which place it solidly within a Jewish framework and under the sanction of Jewish law. I refer of course to the formula 'that you will be my wife according to the law of Moses and the Jews'—די תהוא לי לאנתה כדין משה ויהודאי—a formula that we find in the opening lines of two almost contemporary Aramaic marriage contracts, *DJD* ii, no. 20 and *P.Yadin* 10 (see n. 24, nos. 1 and 3 respectively).[27]

The three Aramaic marriage contracts from the Judaean Desert reveal to us that the rabbinic marriage contract had indeed by then developed its own special form. But had it become normative? Surely not. Not one of the five marriage contracts written in Greek can be said to be a translation of an Aramaic *ketubba*. All of them resemble both in spirit and in phraseology contemporary Greek marriage contracts from Egypt.[28] The crucial formula 'that you will be my wife according to the law of Moses and the Jews' is absent from all of them.

I have laid much emphasis in the past on the fact that whereas the *ketubba* is centred around the sum of money that the husband pledges to the wife, which was once called *mohar* and is now called (by the rabbis) *ketubba*, the Greek marriage contract is an acknowledgement by the groom that he has received the dowry from the

---

[25] b. Ket. 82b; y. Ket. 8. 11, 32b; t. Ket. 12. 1; Friedman (1986), 257 ff.; Geller (1978), 227–37; Archer (1990), 159–63.

[26] *P.Yadin* 10, l. 16 (Yadin, Greenfield, and Yardeni (1994), 78) and *DJD* ii, no. 21, l. 10.

[27] *DJD* ii, no. 20, l. 3: ד[י תהוא לי לאנתה כדין מ]שה ויהודאי (revised reading of Ada Yardeni); *P.Yadin* 10, l. 5: לאנת]ה כדי]ן משה ויה]ו[דאי [.......].

[28] See Cotton (1994), 68 ff. for a detailed survey of the Egyptian parallels.

bride or her family.[29] I have now come to believe that the difference is more apparent than real. I am not sure that I fully understand the expression 'the money of your *ketubba*' in the documents. If the fictitious *mohar* is meant, then it must be said that it is treated in the very same way as what we may call the 'gentile' dowry is treated: the husband's entire property is put in lien to secure the return of that money on the dissolution of the marriage, and it is stipulated that the wife's sons will inherit that money, if she dies before the husband. There is nothing whatsoever in the text of *DJD* ii, no. 21 and in *P.Yadin* 10—where the phrase 'the money of your *ketubba*' occurs—which forces us to think that 'the money of your *ketubba*' is the rabbinic fictitious *mohar*, rather than the dowry of the Greek marriage contracts.[30]

I have been able to find only one exception to the 'non-Jewish character' of the Greek marriage contract between Jews, i.e. the absence of features in them which set marriage contracts between Jews apart from marriage contracts between non-Jews. I have in mind the stipulation that the sons will inherit the dowry or *ketubba* money of their mother. This stipulation is present in all four marriage contracts from Wadi Murabba'at, both Aramaic and Greek (*DJD* ii, nos. 20, 21, 115, 116),[31] in the Aramaic *P.Yadin* 10 (Babatha's *ketubba*),[32] as well as in the Greek marriage contract from Aristoboulias (*DJD* xxvii, no. 69). Sometimes it is accompanied by the phrase that the daughters are to be provided for out of the husband's property (*DJD* ii, nos. 20, 21, *P.Yadin* 10 and *DJD* xxvii, no. 69). The specific clauses which distinguish between male and female children are attested so far only in the Jewish marriage contract tradition, and, it seems, already in the early mishnaic period. The phrase 'The sons inherit and the daughters are provided for'— הבנים ירשו והבנות יזונו (m. Ket. 4: 6) is said there to have been expounded on by R. Eleazar b. Azariah, a second generation Tanna (90–130 CE), and thus must have existed for a while.

[29] Cotton (1994), 82 ff.

[30] Bickerman (1976), 212–15, in fact comes very close to suggesting that 'the money of the *ketubba*' may refer to the dowry; cf. Levine (1979), 85; Satlow (1993), 137 ff.: the documentary marriage contracts support Satlow's claim that 'The rabbinic *ketubah* payment was a rabbinic innovation of around the late first century CE', 146.

[31] Cf. Cotton (1994), 80–1.

[32] See the editors' comments on ll. 11–14: Yadin, Greenfield, and Yardeni (1994), 93 ff.

It cannot be denied, therefore, that this particular clause unites marriage contracts between Jews written both in Greek and in Aramaic. However, these clauses are absent from *P. Yadin* 18 (from the Babatha archive) and from *DJD* xxvii, no. 65 (from the archive of Salome Komaïse daughter of Levi). Furthermore, the order of the relevant clauses concerning provision for the children in the case of the prior death of the wife, and sometimes without reference to it, varies a great deal.[33]

The stipulation that the daughters are to be fed and clothed may have replaced an earlier one which provided for all children to be fed and clothed from the father's property.[34] This original situation is reflected in one of the two Greek marriage contracts from Wadi Murabba'at (*DJD* ii, no. 115) as well as in the two marriage contracts from Arabia, both of which use almost identical terminology: 'with his undertaking to feed and clothe both her and the children to come in accordance with Greek custom upon the said Judah Cimber's good faith and peril and security of all his possessions, both those which he now possesses in his said home village and here and all those which he may in addition acquire.'[35]

It should also be pointed out, though, that the provision concerning male children as heirs to their mother's property had entered Jewish law under the influence of other Near Eastern traditions, where—unlike the situation under Jewish law—the wife's children were her heirs. The provision certainly contravenes the biblical law of inheritance which made the husband sole heir to his wife's property; upon his death all his sons, including those from another woman, would divide his property equally between them. Thus the provision for male sons to inherit their mother's dowry or her *ketubba* was meant to protect male sons in polygamous marriages against the loss of part of their mother's property to sons of another woman.[36] This can be safely read in *DJD* ii, no. 116, ll. 4–8: '[And if Salome] dies [before Aurelius], the sons that she will have from him will inherit her dowry and the things written

---

[33] Cf. Cotton (1994), 80–1.

[34] Friedman (1986), 369.

[35] ἀκολούθως αἱρέσει τροφῆς καὶ ἀμφιασμοῦ αὐτῆς τε καὶ τῶν μελλόντων τέκνων ἑλληνικῷ νόμῳ ἐπὶ τῆς τοῦ αὐτοῦ Ἰούδα Κίμβ[ε]ρο[ς] πίστεως καὶ κινδύνου καὶ πάντων ὑπαρχόντων ὧν τε ἔχει ἐν τῇ αὐτῇ [πα]τρίδι αὐτοῦ καὶ ὧδε καὶ ὧν ἐπικτήσηται, *P. Yadin* 18, ll. 16–18 = ll. 49–51; almost identical phrasing in *DJD* xxvii, no. 65, ll. 9–10.

[36] Friedman (1986), 380–2; Falk (1952).

above . . . [in addition] to inheriting all of Aurelius' property together with their future brothers [from another woman].'[37]

I have deliberately emphasized the variation, the lack of uniformity, even when the provisions seem unique to marriage contracts between Jews; this needs to be emphasized even more with regard to provisions which disappeared from the later *ketubba* tradition.[38] There was no normative, authoritative and uniform marriage contract which Jews knew that they had to use. Neither may we assume that for every marriage contract in Greek which diverges from the rabbinic *ketubba* which has been preserved, a 'kosher' Jewish Aramaic *ketubba* has been lost. Obviously the Jews who wrote these documents felt free to use the legal instrument that seemed to them most effective.

We can perhaps take this argument one step further and question the assumption that a written marriage contract was a *sine qua non* for the conclusion of marriage between Jews.

In *DJD* xxvii, no. 65 (=P.Yadin 37), which we now know to be the marriage contract of Salome Komaïse daughter of Levi of the archive mentioned above, we find the following clause: 'Yeshuʿa son of Menaḥem, domiciled in the village of Sophathe[..] in the district of the city of Livias of the administrative region of P[eraia] agreed with Salome also called Komaïse [daughter of Levi], his wife who is from Maḥoza, [that they continue] life together *as also before this time*.'[39]

In his introduction to the papyrus Lewis quite rightly cites the parallel of the 'unwritten marriage' ἄγραφος γάμος recorded in Egyptian papyri,[40] a union which was 'sometimes later converted by a written contract into ἔγγραφος γάμος'. But he rejects this interpretation in favour of an *interpretatio Hebraica*: 'Close as the parallel may be, however, . . . the expression "as also before this time" more likely implies that the bride and groom had been living together since the day of their betrothal, in keeping with a

---

[37] *DJD* ii, 116, ll. 4–8: [ἐὰν δὲ ἡ Σαλώμη πρὸ τοῦ Αὐρηλίου] τὸν βίον μ[ε]ταλλάξει υ[ἱού]ς οὓς ἂν ἕξει ἀπ' αὐτ[οῦ . . . κληρονομήσουσιν] τὴν φερνὴν καὶ τὰ πρ[ογε]γραμμένα [*c.*40 letters missing] τῆς τοῦ Αὐρηλίου οὐ[σ]ίας πᾶσα[ν κλ]ηρονομίαν μεθ' ὧν ἂν ἔξωσιν ἀ[δ]ελφῶν.

[38] e.g. the need to provide for all children.

[39] ὡμολογήσ]ατο Ἰησοῦς Μαναήμου τῷ[ν ἀπὸ κώμης c. 8 letters] Σοφφαθε [. .] . . . περὶ πόλιν Λιουιάδος τῆς Π[εραίας c. 9 letters πρὸς(?) Σαλ]ωμην καλουμένην Κ[ομαϊσην Αηουειου τὴν] γυναῖκα Μ[α]ωζηνὴν ὥστε αὐτούς {ὥστε α[ὐτούς} c. 17 letters] . . . συμβιῶσ [c. 14 letters] αὐτῆς ᾧ[c κ]αὶ πρὸ τούτου τοῦ χρόνου, ll. 3–6.

[40] Cf. above all Wolff (1939).

Jewish practice of the time when the bride was an orphan and a minor.'[41]

We now know a great deal more about Salome Komaïse: she was indeed an orphan in 131, but not a minor. Already in 127 (if not before) she had been married to Sammouos son of Shim'on who represented her in the deed of renunciation.[42] Yeshu'a son of Menaḥem of DJD xxvii, no. 65 is her second husband. In 129 she received a gift from her mother, unaccompanied, so far as we can tell, by either a husband or guardian.[43] Thus putative minority cannot explain their having lived together before the contract was drawn up, even if we assume that they followed Jewish customs—an assumption unwarranted by the marriage contract concluded between them: this marriage contract, in which the groom undertakes to follow Greek law and custom in providing for her and the children to come, cannot be described as a Jewish *ketubba*.[44] Neither can I accept the suggestion propounded recently that we have here a case of premarital cohabitation peculiar to and common in Judaea.[45] This so-called radical approach assumes just as does the 'apologetic approach' of Lewis that by this time there existed a coherent and operative system of Jewish law which had already become normative. In this system 'a man may not keep his wife even one hour without a *ketubba*' (b. B.K. 89a), and life together without a *ketubba* must be branded 'premarital cohabitation' or 'sex out of wedlock'. If we go by halacha, DJD xxvii, no. 65 is not the *ketubba* which would turn 'premarital cohabitation' into a proper Jewish marriage. Lewis's original suggestion of 'unwritten marriage'—ἄγραφος γάμος—is surely the right solution.

Thus even the writing of a marriage contract had not yet become the norm. Yeshu'a son of Menaḥem from the Peraea and Salome Komaïse daughter of Levi from Maḥoza had been married for a while by the time their marriage contract was written, as the verb συμβιόω demonstrates: the verb does *not* mean 'to live together' in the modern sense of experimenting at life together before finalizing

[41] Lewis (1989), 130.
[42] Cotton (1995a), Doc. III, pp. 177–83 = DJD xxvii, no. 63.
[43] Cotton (1995a), Doc. IV, pp. 183–203 = DJD xxvii, no. 64; but the occasion did not call for the presence of a husband in the role of a guardian.
[44] σὺν αἱρέσει τροφῆς [καὶ ἀμφιασμοῦ αὐτῆς] τε καὶ τῶν καὶ τῶν μελλόντῳ[ν τέκ]νῳν νόμ[ῳ ἑλληνικ]ῷ καὶ ἐλλ[η]νικῷ τρόπῳ (ll. 9–10); see Wasserstein (1989), 117 ff. against Katzoff in Lewis, Katzoff, and Greenfield (1987), 241 f.; Katzoff modified his views in (1991), 173–4.   [45] Ilan (1993).

the bond, but is used in Egyptian papyri to describe life together in wedlock. Likewise the adjective σύνβιος means 'spouse' and συνβίωσις means 'marriage'. The two last terms are used in these very senses in *DJD* ii, no. 115 which is a contract of remarriage, where we read: 'Eleaios son of Shim'on from the village of Galoda of Akrabatta . . . an inhabitant of Batharda of Gophna came into a written agreement with Salome daughter of Yoḥanan Galgoula, who used to be his wife (σύνβιον) . . .' and later: 'For the sake of marriage (σ[υ]νβιώσεως χάριν) now the same Eleaios son of Shim'on agrees to be reconciled and take again Salome daughter of Yoḥanan Galgoula as wedded wife' (ll. 2–5).[46]

There are other branches of personal law, such as the law of succession[47] and the law of guardianship,[48] in which similar discrepancies between the documents and halachic law are apparent, and the incursion of other legal systems can sometimes be seen and sometimes be assumed. For an appreciation of the polyethnic society of Aramaic-speaking people, into which these documents fit—a society whose cultural, social, and legal life absorbed many and various elements from different sources, only one of which was Hellenism—one should consult two recent studies by Abraham Wasserstein, to whose memory this paper is dedicated.[49] Rabbinic law itself acquired its shape in the same environment: that it reflects the documents is only to be expected. We should be wrong, though, to assume without compelling proof that the documents reflect the still-to-be-codified halacha. These documents are the raw material of which life is made, and on which the rabbis wished to put their own stamp.[50]

---

[46] ἐξομολ[ογ]ήσα[το καὶ σ]υνεγράψατο Ἐλεαῖος Σίμωνος τῶν ἀπὸ κ(ώμης) Γαλωδῶν τῆς περὶ Ἀκραβαττῶν οἰκῶν ἐν κώμῃ Βαιτοαρδοις τῆς περὶ Γοφνοῖς πρὸς [Σα]λώμην [Ἰ]ωά[νου Γαλγ]ουλα προγενομέ[νην] αὐτοῦ Ἐλαίου σύνβιον . . . σ[υ]νβιώσεος χάριν. νυνεὶ ὁμολογεῖ ὁ αὐτὸς Ἐλαῖος Σίμω[νος] ἐξ ἀνανεώσεος καταλλάξαι κ[αὶ] προσλαβέσθαι τὴν αὐτὴν Σαλώ[μην Ἰω]άν[ο]υ Γ[αλγο]υλὰ εἰ[ς γυναῖ]κα γαμετήν, *DJD* ii, no. 115, ll. 2–5.

[47] Cotton and Greenfield (1994); Cotton (1997) and (1998).

[48] See Cotton (1993*b*).

[49] Wasserstein (1989); Wasserstein (1995).

[50] Lapin (1995), using as a test case the mishnaic tractate *Baba Meṣi'a* is able to show that mishnaic economic and contract law is not reflected in the literature of the Second Temple period, nor in the documents which postdate the destruction. I am grateful to Professor Lapin for letting me see his manuscript in advance of publication.

12

Jewish Penal Authority in Roman Judaea

AHARON OPPENHEIMER

The discovery of the Babatha archive and the legal documents it contains has once more brought to the fore the question of the role played by Jewish law in the Land of Israel at the time of the Mishnah. For example, one of the documents, which relates to the year 124 CE, provides evidence that the *boule* of Petra appointed legal guardians for Babatha's son after the death of his father.[1] This incident raises several questions. For example, did the family have the option of a hearing in a Jewish court? Would they have turned to such a Jewish court had they lived elsewhere—for example, in one of the heavily settled Jewish areas in Judaea or Galilee? However, such questions are merely of secondary importance as compared to the more basic issues. How far did the Roman government recognize local law in the provinces in general, and in Judaea (and later Syria-Palaestina) in particular? And how far did they authorize the local legal system to sentence offenders to various different punishments?

In the Jerusalem Talmud we find the following story:

It happened that the authorities sent two army men (*stratiotai*) to learn Torah from Rabban Gamaliel. They learned Scripture, Mishnah, Talmud, *halakhot* and *aggadot*. Finally they said to him: all your laws are fine and praiseworthy except for these two things—that you say that a Jewish woman should not act as midwife for a non-Jew, but a non-Jewish woman may act as midwife for a Jew; and similarly, a Jewish woman may not nurse the child of a non-Jewish woman, but a non-Jewish woman may be wet-nurse for a Jewish woman, with her permission. What is stolen from a Jew is prohibited, but what is stolen from a non-Jew is permitted. Then and there Rabban Gamaliel made an enactment that it is forbidden to steal from a non-Jew, so as not to profane the Divine name. If the ox of a Jew gores the ox of a non-Jew it is not liable [to a penalty] etc. In this case we do

---

[1] Lewis (1989), no. 16; Isaac (1992), 62–75.

not inform the Roman authorities. In spite of this they had not reached the Ladder of Tyre before they had forgotten everything [they had learned].[2]

There can be little doubt that the activities of the men sent by the Roman authorities, as detailed in this source, are connected with the recognition given to the Jewish legal system in the days of Rabban Gamaliel (at the turn of the first and second centuries CE), for they concentrate on examining questions concerned with the attitude of Jews towards non-Jews and are particularly concerned with laws which discriminate against non-Jews. Rabban Gamaliel's immediate response, laying down a rule which forbids robbing a non-Jew, shows quite probably that if he had not acted in this way he would have endangered his legal authority. The 'forgetfulness' which the Roman representatives are said to have displayed from the moment they crossed the borders of the Land of Israel is undoubtedly a legendary accretion, but through this we learn that they were presumably not representatives of the governor in the Land of Israel, but from the government in Syria. This detail corresponds well with a parallel source in Sifre Deuteronomy, where the text says that the Roman representatives came to Rabban Gamaliel at Ushah.[3] It is understandable that it would be easier for an official embassy coming from Syria to meet the Jewish leader during one of his tours of inspection at Ushah in Galilee, rather than travel south to Yavneh. (There is no evidence at all for the suggestion made by some scholars that the main rabbinic assembly had already moved to Ushah even before the Bar Kokhba Revolt.)[4] We can also connect this incident with the statement that 'Rabban Gamaliel went to have permission granted him from the governor in Syria',[5] even if no one has yet clarified exactly what this 'permission' or authority, which was given to him by the Roman government in Syria, actually was. It is doubtful if we can deduce from this, as

---

[2] y. B.K. 3: 4b. Note that Rabbi Akiva's method rules out stealing from a non-Jew from first principles (b. B.K. 113a–b; and cf. Midrash Tannaim [Hoffman] on Deut. 20: 14, p. 121).

[3] Sifre Deuteronomy 344 (ed. Finkelstein), p. 401 and n. 2.

[4] Scholars who are of this opinion relate the move to the period between the 'War of Quietus' (the events in Palestine parallel to the Diaspora Revolt in the time of Trajan) and the Bar Kokhba Revolt. See e.g. Urbach (1973), 66–9. By this time it is most unlikely that Rabban Gamaliel was still alive. For a complete refutation of this theory see Alon (1984), 462–5, and for Rabban Gamaliel's custom of travelling from place to place, Oppenheimer (1988), 8–18.

[5] m. Eduy. 7: 7.

Shmuel Safrai has suggested, that the province of Judaea was in some way or other subservient to the more important province of Syria,[6] but the juxtaposition of events is certainly evidence of some sort of connection between the two.

We must note also that, according to the talmudic story, the inspection of the Jewish legal system was carried out by people from the army—the Jerusalem Talmud calls them *istratiotot* where Sifre has *sarditi'ot*, but both these versions are clearly forms of the Greek *stratiotes*, a soldier. Evidently these were thought of as soldiers who dealt with internal security, an area which came under the jurisdiction of the Roman army.

Another passage in the Jerusalem Talmud refers to some sort of audit of the Jewish courts as early as the days of Rabban Yohanan b. Zakkai:

Aganatus the governor asked Rabban Yohanan b. Zakkai: Do you stone the ox and put his owner to death? (Ex. 21: 29) He said to him: The partner of a brigand is like a brigand. But when he went out his pupils asked him: Rabbi, you put him off with a straw, what do you say to us? He said to them: It is written, the ox shall be stoned and his owner shall also be put to death. The death of the ox [must be] like the death of his owner, for the death of the owner is tied to the death of the ox. For just as the death of the owner requires investigation by twenty-three [judges], so does the death of the ox require investigation by twenty-three [judges].[7]

It is doubtful whether we can learn from this that in the time of Rabban Yohanan b. Zakkai (in the aftermath of 70 CE), there was already some Roman recognition of the Jewish legal system, for the conversation described is like a large number of such conversations recorded throughout rabbinic literature, between a governor or emperor on the one side, and Rabbi Joshua b. Hananiah or Rabbi Akiva on the other. These conversations do no more than note Roman interest in Judaism, and most of their details belong to the legendary sphere. However, the conversation we are looking at here does deal with the question of legal penalties. In this context, it is interesting to note the general attitude of the rabbinic sages who, following Scripture, attribute legal liability to animals as well as

---

[6] Safrai (1962), 216–22. See too Stern (1981).
[7] y. Sanh. 1. 19b. On Rabban Yohanan b. Zakkai's answer to his pupils, see *Mekhilta de-Rabbi Simeon b. Yochai, Mishpatim*, 21: 29 (ed. Epstein–Melamed), p. 181.

humans, requiring investigation by a 'small Sanhedrin' of twenty-three members. This follows the rule already laid down in Mishnah Sanhedrin, which deals with the following case:

Cases concerning capital offences [are decided] by twenty-three [judges]. A beast that commits or suffers unnatural intercourse [is judged] by twenty-three, as it is written: 'Thou shalt slay the woman and the beast' (Lev. 20: 16), and again it says 'And ye shall slay the beast' (Lev. 20: 15). The ox that is to be stoned [is judged] by twenty-three, as it is written 'The ox shall be stoned and its owner shall also be put to death' (Exod. 21: 29). The ox is put to death in the same way as the owner is put to death. Similarly, the wolf, the lion, the bear, the leopard, the panther or the snake [that killed a man]—their death is decided upon by twenty-three [judges]. Rabbi Eliezer says: The first to kill them wins. Rabbi Akiva says: Their death is decided upon by twenty-three [judges].[8]

It would seem that, at least theoretically, according to the opinion of the anonymous rabbinic authority cited first in this text, and of Rabbi Akiva who agrees with him, the punishment for animals was to be determined by a 'small Sanhedrin' of twenty-three, which was to sit in towns or the centres of toparchies. However, it appears that, in reality, the authority to rule in capital cases was given to the Great Sanhedrin of seventy or seventy-one judges. We can presume that an animal which injured a man, or was involved in unnatural intercourse, was not actually brought for searching cross-examination before any court pending its punishment at the end of the full judicial process. It is reasonable to assume that this legal ruling is one of those which are theoretically practicable, but in practice theoretical. This is not the case with the death penalty itself, as we see from the evidence of Rabbi Judah b. Bava, 'that a cock was stoned in Jerusalem because it killed a person'.[9] This cock pierced the brain of a baby, and the sages condemned it to the death by stoning which is demanded by Scripture and by the legal rules for 'ox which gores', from the viewpoint that 'what is written is the usual case': in other words, Scripture deals with the most common event, so that we can deduce from the regulations about an 'ox which gores' that what is meant is not necessarily an ox, but all other animals as well, which are liable to the same penalty.

The most far-reaching tradition on the recognition of Jewish

---

[8] m. Sanh. 1: 4; cf. Mekhilta de-Rabbi Simeon b. Yochai (loc. cit. n. 7 above). On this subject see Urbach (1972), 37–48; Lipsius (1905).

[9] m. Eduy. 6: 1; cf. Mekhilta de-Rabbi Simeon b.Yochai (loc. cit. n. 7 above).

jurisdiction can be found in the evidence of Origen, on the right to judge capital cases which was given *de facto* to the Nasi (the Jewish Patriarch). This evidence is found in Origen's letter to Julius Africanus, where it is used to answer his query as to whether the story of Susanna and the Elders, one of the additions to the Book of Daniel in the Septuagint, is to be considered a forgery.

> And even now, under Roman rule, when the Jews pay the *didrachma* in tax, the Ethnarch acts as the authority for the Jews, and, as it were with the connivance of the Emperor, he is in no way different from a king over his people. For cases are tried surreptitiously according to the [Jewish] law, and people are even condemned to death, albeit not entirely openly, but certainly not without the knowledge of the Emperor.[10]

Origen stresses that he is relying on direct evidence obtained as a result of living in the Land of Israel, and indeed he was in the country towards the end of the patriarchate of Rabbi Judah ha-Nasi, between 215–19 CE. In spite of the doubts cast on this evidence by many scholars, and the variety of suggestions, some stranger than others, proposed to cope with it,[11] there is no real reason to doubt its veracity, nor that the title 'ethnarch', like the title 'patriarch' in other Greek and Latin sources, referred to the *nasi* mentioned in rabbinic texts. Rabbi Judah ha-Nasi's status *vis-à-vis* the Jews and the Romans is entirely in keeping with the silent delegation of power to judge in capital cases.

This fits the evidence of judicial autonomy granted to free communities under Roman rule elsewhere.[12] The question which remains unanswered is, on what sort of offenders Rabbi Judah ha-Nasi used his legal authority. Is this source talking about cases brought to court of *anyone* accused of a crime which carried the death penalty? Or does it deal with some sort of field court-martial which condemned to death an offender whom Jewish law allowed to be attacked by zealots without full legal process, such as an *agent provocateur*? It is interesting to note that Origen attributes the authority to condemn people to death exclusively to the Nasi without mentioning any Jewish law court.

We know that there was a sort of police force associated with the

---

[10] *Ep. ad Africanum*, 14 (*Patrologia Graeca*, ed. J. P. Migne, xi, 82–4). See also Katz (1936).
[11] For an analysis of the letter with full bibliography, which raises doubts as to the authenticity of the picture it describes, see Habas-Rubin (1991), i. 64–71; ii. 265–73.
[12] Colin (1965), ch. 2.

Patriarch which helped to carry out court orders. The open presence of such a body is evidence that the Romans recognized the authority of its jurisdiction. The following evidence comes from Midrash Ecclesiastes Rabbah:

When a person came before Rabbi [Judah ha-Nasi] for judgement, if he accepted his verdict, well and good; if not, he would say to a member of his household, 'Show him the left side', and he would show him a chopping movement in that direction.[13]

The members of Rabbi Judah ha-Nasi's household mentioned in this source are presumably identical with the eunuchs mentioned elsewhere.[14] It is recorded that Rabbi Judah Nesiah, the grandson of Rabbi Judah ha-Nasi, had guards who are variously described as 'Goths'[15] or 'Germans'.[16] Both these peoples were well known for their military prowess, and it is possible that they acted as a kind of police guard already in the time of Rabbi Judah ha-Nasi.

Rabbi Abbahu also had Goths as guards,[17] for although he did not have the status of Patriarch, it is clear that he had special privileges as head of the rabbinic academy at Caesarea, and special relationships with the Roman provincial government there, as we shall see below.

Roman recognition of Jewish jurisdiction in the Land of Israel is also evident from those sources which show the involvement of the Roman authorities in the execution of the sentences of Jewish courts. For example, a bill of divorce given under compulsion is valid if ordered by a Jewish court, but invalid if ordered by a non-Jewish court. However, if the non-Jews beat a man and say to him, 'Do what the Jews bid you', it is valid.[18] It is unclear exactly to which time this ruling relates. However, it is found in the Mishnah, and since it fits in well with other evidence of Roman recognition of Jewish courts, we can probably assume that it relates to the time of Rabban Gamaliel of Yavneh and/or Rabbi Judah ha-Nasi. Parallel to this, we should mention another teaching, a *baraita* (a rabbinic tradition ascribed to the pre-third-century era, which in this case certainly comes from the time of Rabbi Judah ha-Nasi): 'Rabbi Hiyya taught: If non-Jews compel [a man] according to a decision

---

[13] Eccles. R. 10: 2.   [14] b. Ber. 16b.
[15] y. Hor. 3. 47a; cf. y. Sanh. 2. 19d.   [16] y. Shab. 6. 8c.
[17] y. Bez. 1. 60c. See Juster (1914), ii. 93–214; Rabello (1987), 71–87.
[18] m. Gitt. 9: 8.

[of a Jewish court], their action is valid.'[19] The possibility that the Roman authorities could be involved in the execution of decisions of the Jewish courts in matters of personal status is also found in the following ruling: 'A *halitzah* [requirement that a man should formally renounce his right and duty to marry the widow of his deceased brother] imposed on a man by a Jewish court is valid, in a non-Jewish court it is invalid [unless] the non-Jews beat him and said: "You do what Rabbi X told you".'[20] Lieberman has an extensive, reasoned discussion of this source in his commentary on the Tosefta ad loc., where he distinguishes between *halitzah* imposed by a non-Jewish court, which is invalid, and *halitzah* according to the ruling of a Jewish court, but imposed under compulsion by non-Jews, which is valid.

It is clear that it was permissible for the officers of the household of the Patriarch to use force, and that non-Jews could be used to compel the execution of a sentence laid down by a Jewish court. However, it is an open question whether, after the destruction of the Temple, the scriptural penalty of thirty-nine stripes continued to be imposed on someone who infringed various negative prescriptions. It is possible that all that remained was the punishment of *makkat mardut* (stripes for disobedience), which has rabbinical authority only and has no prescribed standard number of stripes. In the Mishnah there is a difference of opinion on the question of which sort of court had the authority to impose the penalty of stripes: 'Stripes [may be imposed] by a court of three judges. It is said in the name of Rabbi Ishmael that [it requires a court of] twenty-three.'[21] This division of opinion reflects the uncertainty with regard to the authority of different courts after the destruction of the Temple in 70 CE. In Rabbi Ishmael's opinion, only the 'small Sanhedrin' of twenty-three could rule on matters of corporal punishment, and there was no such body after the destruction of the Temple; the anonymous main authority cited, on the other hand, ruled that a court of three judges was sufficient to impose the penalty of stripes, and that there was therefore nothing to prevent the imposition of this penalty. We can assume that there was no objection from the Roman authorities against this penalty, for they did not restrict the right to judge and punish to civil cases alone, but also recognized

[19] y. Gitt. 9. 50d.
[20] t. Yeb. 12: 13 (ed. Lieberman), p. 44.
[21] m. Sanh. 1: 2.

the authority of the Jewish courts in criminal cases, in which the penalty of stripes must have been included without further differentiation.

Another text, albeit from a much later period, makes it clear that it was possible to appeal to the Roman authorities about a ruling of a Jewish court. A certain Tamar complained to the governor of Caesarea, apparently after she had been sentenced to stripes for prostitution by the sages of Tiberias, Rabbi Hiyya, Rabbi Yase, and Rabbi Ammi. These sages then turned to Rabbi Abbahu, who headed the rabbinic academy in Caesarea in the third century, and had access to the Roman governor. In this case Rabbi Abbahu replied that he had already sent presents to three legal rhetoricians, 'but Tamar *tamrurit be-tamrureha*—she bitterly persists, despite our attempts to sweeten her; so the silversmith has laboured in vain'.[22] We can also learn something of the dangers threatening Jewish judges as a result of a complaint to the Roman authorities from the incident in which Rabbi Bena'ah (who lived in the first half of the third century) ruled against some half-brothers in a case of inheritance of property. The losers then went and denounced him to the Roman authorities: 'There is a certain man among the Jews [they said] who separates people from their money, where there are no witnesses, no nothing.' [As a result] of this he was seized and put in prison.[23]

Another problematic area of criminal law is whether the Roman authorities condoned *dinei qenasot*—laws involving monetary punishment. The following source implies that these laws were cancelled:

Forty years before the destruction of the Temple the Sanhedrin was exiled [from its chamber] and held their meetings in the market. What can we understand from this? Rabbi Isaac b. Evdimi said: This is to say that they no longer judged cases involving monetary penalties.[24]

This tradition is reminiscent of the *baraita*: 'It is told: More than forty years before the Temple was destroyed, authority over *dinei nefashot*—capital cases—was taken away from Israel.'[25] Even though monetary penalties are said to have been cancelled some

---

[22] y. Meg. 3. 74a. According to Lieberman and others the term *litorin* is derived from *lictores*, who were members of the *officinium* of the Proconsul, cf. Lieberman (1939–44), 397 n. 12.

[23] b. B.B. 58a.   [24] b. A.Zar. 8b.

[25] y. Sanh. 7. 24b and parallels.

time before the destruction of the Temple, while capital cases are said to have been cancelled at an even earlier period before the destruction, the two pieces of evidence are very alike. At the same time the whole context of the cancellation of monetary penalties does not carry conviction as authentic. The tradition is quoted in the words of a Babylonian *amora*, and the Talmud itself questions it, noting that Rabbi Judah b. Bava handed on traditions including monetary penalties when he laid down his life in order to ordain his pupils at the height of the persecutions after the Bar Kokhba Revolt. An attempt to explain this is found quoted in the name of Rav Nahman b. Isaac: 'Monetary penalties did not cease, but they no longer judged capital cases.' (We should add here, too, that the whole account of Rabbi Judah b. Bava's death by martyrdom cannot be authentic.)[26] We must therefore conclude here, that while in the case of capital jurisdiction (apart from special concessions possibly given *de facto* by the Severans to Rabbi Judah ha-Nasi) there is support for the *baraita* which claims that this was taken out of Jewish hands, there is no real evidence for the removal of the right to judge cases involving monetary penalties.

The rabbinic legal sources do not only discuss cases of monetary penalties but also mention the actual imposition of such penalties, as in this text from the Mishnah:

If a man cuffed his fellow he must pay him a *sela*. Rabbi Judah says in the name of Rabbi Yose the Galilean: 100 *zuz*. If he slapped him he must pay him 200 *zuz*. If [he did it] with the back of his hand he must pay him 400 *zuz*. If he tore his ear, plucked out his hair, spat and his spittle touched him, or pulled his *tallit* off him, or if uncovered a woman's hair in the street, he must pay 400 *zuz*. This is the general rule: it is all in accordance with a person's self-respect. Rabbi Akiva said: 'Even the poorest in Israel are looked upon as free men who have lost their possessions, for they are the sons of Abraham, Isaac, and Jacob.' It once happened that a man uncovered a woman's hair in the street and she came before Rabbi Akiva, and he condemned him to pay her 400 *zuz*. He replied, 'Rabbi, give me time.' So he gave him time. He then saw her standing at the entry of her courtyard and he broke a jar in front of her that held an *as*'s worth of oil. She uncovered her hair and scooped up the oil with her hand and put her hand on her head. He had set up witnesses to her [act] and came before Rabbi Akiva and said to him, 'Rabbi, should I pay 400 *zuz* to such a woman [who is willing to disgrace herself for an *as*'s worth of oil]?' He answered,

---

[26] b. A.Zar. 8b; cf. b. Sanh. 13b–14a. On the authenticity of the account of R. Judah b. Bava's martyrdom see Oppenheimer (1991), 46–7.

'You have said nothing at all, for someone who harms himself, even if he is not allowed to, is not culpable; but if others have harmed him, they are culpable. If someone cuts down his own plants, even if he is not allowed to, he is not culpable; but if others cut them down, they are culpable.'[27]

It is clear from this that not only did Rabbi Akiva lay down rulings in cases of monetary penalties, but he also acted as judge in such cases himself. It is interesting that his attitude is intended not to differentiate between rich and poor in respect of the payments imposed for causing public shame. Beyond the legal rationale of this, there is a stress on the social aspects, which was an integral part of Rabbi Akiva's approach, as we can see in more than one text. To begin with, since he himself was originally an *am ha-Aretz*, he always disapproved of sages who made too much of themselves because of their knowledge of Torah. In addition, in his extremism towards the Romans and his attitude towards the Bar Kokhba Revolt, he perhaps saw as his first priority the inspiration of a feeling of equality which could help to unite the people.

Thus everything connected with the regulation of monetary transactions between Jews could stay within Jewish jurisdiction. The Roman authorities continued to recognize decisions of the Jewish courts in these matters, except on rare occasions, such as the time of persecution after the Bar Kokhba Revolt. During the Yavneh period after 70 CE we can identify an effort by the Jewish leadership to put monetary matters under the sole jurisdiction of officially ordained rabbis. The intention was not merely to improve the judicial system by making it more professional, but by doing this to give more power to the institutions of the leadership themselves, since they were responsible for rabbinical ordination. This also strengthened the connection of the leadership with Jewish towns and settlements through the ordained rabbis and judges who were sent to them. Ordination itself was first set up in the Yavneh period according to Rav Sherira Gaon: '[The title] "rabbi" began then, from Rabbi Zadoq and Rabbi Eliezer b. Jacob, and it spread from Rabban Yohanan b. Zakkai's disciples onwards.'[28]

The sages laid down various rulings which were intended to ascertain that rulings about monetary matters would be kept only in the hands of ordained rabbis. For example, they ruled that a judge

[27] m. B.K. 8: 6; cf. Avot de-Rabbi Nathan, version A, iii (ed. Schechter), p. 15.
[28] *Iggeret Shenit* (ed. Lewin), p. 125.

who made a mistake in his verdict would have to reimburse the injured party from his own money, unless he were an ordained rabbi, when he was free of this obligation.[29] Obviously rulings like this left the arena of civil law in the hands of sages who had undergone ordination. However, ordained rabbis were not the sole legal authority in the area. Side by side with the Jewish legal system, there was also a Roman civil legislature (and, of course, a Roman criminal legislature). It would seem that clients could choose for themselves whichever system they preferred. For only thus can we understand the words of Rabbi Tarfon: 'In all places where you can find *agoraiot*—non-Jewish courts in the market-place—even if they have the same laws as Jewish law, you are not permitted to use them.'[30] All this casts some degree of light on our opening case of Babatha and her family. The case of Rabbi Eliezer b. Hyrcanus is also connected with the existence of non-Jewish courts in the Land of Israel, for he was taken to court by the Roman authorities on suspicion of sympathizing with the *minim* (heretics). And similarly, an incident is related of Rabban Gamaliel and his sister who went to a judge suspected of Christian sympathies in order to expose him.[31]

Thus we can say that, side by side with the Jewish courts which existed under Roman supervision, the Roman government also had their own judicial system. However, it is clear that the dominant motive was the desire of the Roman governors where at all possible to support the Jewish legal system, and not to damage it. At times they even took steps to enable the Jewish courts to execute their decisions and impose the punishments they had ordered.

[29] See m. Bekh. 4: 4.
[30] b. Gitt. 88b.
[31] b. Shab. 116a–b.

PART IV

Differences?

13

Synagogue Leadership: The Case of the Archisynagogue

LEE LEVINE

INTRODUCTION

The cadre of synagogue leadership that determined synagogue policy and directed its affairs as well as the titles and types of offices involved are important issues in the study of the ancient synagogue, but have been only sporadically investigated over the last century. In recent decades, however, with the dramatic increase in the publication of epigraphical material, interest in this area has been revitalized.[1]

The study of synagogue leadership is fraught with uncertainties. Although the primary epigraphical and literary sources (the latter including both Jewish and non-Jewish sources) attesting to ancient synagogue leadership is far from negligible, the historical reality behind these sources is oft-times beclouded, resulting in strikingly diverse scholarly assessments. Moreover, the sources themselves often appear contradictory. This surfaces at every stage of investigation: when comparing literary and epigraphic data, rabbinic and Christian material, pagan and Roman legal sources, and, not least, when attempting to make sense of the rabbinic and epigraphic material from Jewish Palestine on the one hand and the Diaspora evidence—primarily epigraphic—on the other. It may well be that the seemingly contradictory sources in fact reflect a variety of historical settings throughout the Roman world, and this may be the best explanation for what often seems to be a bewildering range of titles and combinations.

[1] Based on the pioneering work of Frey (*CIJ*), the following publications focusing on the epigraphy in various regions have appeared in recent decades: Lifshitz (1967); Naveh (1978); Le Bohec (1981); Scheiber (1983); Kant (1987); Roth-Gerson (1987); Naveh (1989); Horbury and Noy (*JIGRE*); Noy (*JIWE*). See also van der Horst (1991); van Henten and van der Horst (1994).

Moreover, the relevant data regarding synagogue leadership are geographically diffuse, deriving from almost every corner of the Roman world and beyond—from Babylonia to Spain, from North Africa to eastern Europe and the Crimea. Its chronological range is likewise broad, with material stemming from as early as the Hellenistic period and continuing down to the end of late antiquity and beyond—a period of over one thousand years.

There were many titles for these synagogue leaders, some used more frequently than others. It has become clear with the passage of time and the accumulation of data that this material is spread unevenly throughout the Roman empire, varying from region to region. While some titles are prominent in certain geographical regions, they are negligible, if not almost entirely absent, in others. Moreover, it is unclear which titles relate directly to the synagogue and which to the Jewish community at large. To further complicate matters, some individuals bear more than one title, often leaving us to wonder what indeed were the areas of responsibility of each position.

Finally, these titles are recorded in the extant literary and epigraphic material with little or no explanation of their significance or meaning, offering little indication of their roles and functions. Even when we have an idea of the probable function of an official with a given title, it remains unclear to which communal framework this title refers. For example, if an archon was a lay individual with some sort of administrative or political responsibility, often of a supervisory nature, was he part of a community-wide board or did this title refer specifically to a synagogue context, possibly the governing body of that institution?

This last-mentioned consideration touches upon the fundamental question of how Jewish communities were organized, and how the synagogue, with its leadership and officialdom, fitted into the overall communal framework. The issues here are many and complex. Was there a difference, for example, between Diaspora and Palestinian communities? Was there a different administrative framework for communities of different sizes? For rural and urban settings? Did the communal structures in the latter settings, where Jews constituted the majority (e.g. in Tiberias or Sepphoris), operate differently from places where they were only a minority, especially in the Diaspora? Or was there a variety of possible models that could be drawn from the larger Graeco-Roman world from which each community might choose in order to suit its specific needs?

Over the course of the past century there has been a decided shift in scholarly opinion regarding the question of Jewish communal organization. At first there was a consensus that communal organizational patterns were largely the same for all Jewish communities throughout the empire. While some differences surfaced regarding nuances of definition and delineation *vis-à-vis* communal organization, the broader and more fundamental assumption of a common communal pattern was shared by virtually everyone.[2]

This consensus held that Jewish communities were governed by a *gerousia*, composed of archons and headed by a gerousiarch. All functions of the community were believed to have been controlled by this body, either directly or through appointed or elected officials charged with specific tasks. The situation in Alexandria and, to a much lesser extent, in Berenike played a significant role in forming this consensus. The situation in Rome, according to the catacomb inscriptions, was considered most unusual, as there appeared to have been an emphasis there on local synagogues and an apparent absence of any all-embracing communal organization.[3] Yet, even for Rome, some scholars still claimed that a similar kind of overarching communal apparatus existed.[4]

However, a significant conceptual change has taken place in this regard in the last decades. With the proliferation of studies relating to specific Jewish communities over the last half century,[5] there is an increasing awareness of the wide range of Jewish communal practices and organizational forms which existed throughout the Roman empire. Not only is it generally agreed that Rome and Alexandria present radically different organizational models, but we

---

[2] Schürer (1986), ii. 427–39; Juster (1914), i. 438–56; *CIJ* i. lxxxii–ci; Krauss (1966), 103–12; La Piana (1927); Elbogen (1993), 368–74; Applebaum (1974); Kasher (1985), 208–11, 289–309.

[3] Schürer (1879), 15–18; *CIJ* i. cii–cxi; Leon (1960), 170.

[4] Juster (1914), i. 418–24; Vogelstein (1940), 32; Krauss (1966), 137–9; La Piana (1927), 361–5; Baron (1942), i. 99–107; Schürer (1986), ii. 199.

[5] For the Diaspora, see the studies on the Jews in Rome: Vogelstein (1940); Leon (1960); Egypt: *CPJ*; Tcherikover (1961); Kasher (1985); Antioch: Meeks and Wilken (1978); Asia Minor: Trebilco (1991); and more general treatments: Smallwood (1976); Stern (1974), 117–83; Feldman (1993); and in Roman Palestine: Lydda: Schwartz (1991); Oppenheimer (1988), 115–36; Jericho: Schwartz (1988), 23–48; Sepphoris: Miller (1984); Caesarea: L. I. Levine (1975a and 1975b); Ringel (1975); Bet Shean: Fuks (1983); and Tiberias: Avissar (1973).

now know that this diversity is also evidenced in Berenike and Asia Minor, as well as in Palestine. As with many other aspects of the synagogue, so, too, the organizational structure of Jewish communities at large and the synagogue in particular were likely candidates to absorb and assimilate outside influences; this is evident from the very beginnings of Jewish history and until the present day.[6] The influence of a city, state, or region on a given Jewish community is marked, perhaps not as blatant in the unique and specifically Jewish religious and spiritual realms, but clearly evident in the social and political dimensions of the community's functioning.

THE ARCHISYNAGOGUE IN MODERN RESEARCH

Enquiry into the nature and definition of Jewish communal leadership, and especially synagogue leadership, has received increased scholarly attention over the last decade and a half. Several contributions are noteworthy. The first is the 1982 monograph by Brooten, who examined the evidence relating to women leaders in the ancient synagogue; in the course of this study she surveyed the sources which mention the various titles accorded synagogue officials generally. In the series, *New Documents Illustrating Early Christianity* (Horsley, 1981–94), the issue of synagogue leadership was addressed, especially in a long excursus in volume iv appearing in 1987. In 1992, Burtchaell published a monograph on synagogue and church leadership, espousing the thesis that Jewish community organization, and especially that of the synagogue, had a profound influence on the early church. In this context, Burtchaell accorded the former extensive treatment in order to account for the development of the latter. Finally, in 1993, Rajak and Noy examined the office of the archisynagogue in detail, arguing for a rather revolutionary understanding of the title (see below).

The archisynagogue is the official most commonly associated with the synagogue and its operation. Our discussion below will focus on this office not only because of its prominence, but also because most of the central issues regarding synagogue leadership generally revolve to a great extent around this position.

Scholarly opinions regarding the office of archisynagogue have varied over the last century. The dominant opinion to this day

[6] See Baron (1942), i. 10–21, 95–107, 283–347 (*inter alia*).

regards this position primarily, if not exclusively, as a spiritual and religious one (e.g., Schürer, Juster, Krauss, Frey, and La Piana).[7] Opinions differ, however, with regard to the type of religious status enjoyed by the archisynagogue, whether he was the primary religious and spiritual figure within the synagogue or merely in charge of worship details, a kind of glorified attendant (*shamash*).[8] The powerful influence of New Testament depictions, often supported by rabbinic passages, have helped the above perception gain ascendancy.

A second position, although in basic agreement with the first, also takes into consideration the epigraphic evidence, which focuses on the archisynagogue as a benefactor, one who contributed to the construction of the facility, or to its repair and restoration. The scholars holding this latter position have appended to the first view a statement which accounts for the financial contributions by the archisynagogue. Elbogen was the first to take note of this aspect, and he has since been joined by Leon, Schrage, and Linder.[9]

Only recently, however, the pendulum has come full swing in the above-noted article by Rajak and Noy which focuses on the epigraphic evidence and treats it as decisive for this issue.[10] The archisynagogue is viewed by Rajak and Noy primarily as a patron and benefactor whose title was honorary in nature, bestowed by Jewish communities on those individuals who helped maintain and enhance the physical and material dimension of the synagogue.

The basic difference between each of the above depictions revolves primarily around the sources upon which each relies. The first position is anchored in the New Testament evidence, which highlights the religious role of the archisynagogue, and this is also the thrust of the relevant rabbinic and patristic sources. Contrastingly, Rajak and Noy rely exclusively on epigraphical data, dismissing the literary material as tendentious and historically unreliable. The second school of thought noted above takes both the literary and epigraphical sources at face value and includes both

---

[7] Schürer (1879), 27–8; id. (1986), 434; Juster (1914), i. 450–3; Krauss (1966), 114–21; *CIJ* i. xcviii; La Piana (1929), 359–60. See also Trebilco (1991), 104–5; Vogelstein (1940), 30–1.

[8] See e.g. Marmorstein (1921), 24–5.

[9] Elbogen (1993), 368–9; Leon (1960), 171–2; Schrage (1971), 844–7; Linder (1987), 137 n. 10. See also Juster (1914), i. 452–3.

[10] Rajak and Noy (1993), 75–93.

the religious and financial components as part and parcel of its definition of the office of archisynagogue.

There is, however, a fourth position which recognizes the need to take all the primary sources into consideration, even those which at first glance seem polemical and historically problematic. This approach becomes more compelling in light of the fact that a number of these diverse sources indeed overlap, thus, in effect, reinforcing the depiction found in each. This would lead us to conclude that the archisynagogue often assumed not only a religious and financial role, but a political and administrative one as well. In short, the office involved responsibility for all facets of the institution, as, in fact, the title itself seems to convey. While several scholars have in the past attributed certain administrative and financial components to this office, for the most part these aspects have been alluded to only fleetingly. Leon, for example, mentions an additional administrative dimension en passant, when discussing the archisynagogue as representative of the synagogue to the larger community.[11] Brooten, following a remark by Juster,[12] speaks of the archisynagogue, together with the elders, as being responsible for transferring monies to the Patriarch.[13] All this, of course, comes in addition to the other functions clearly noted in literary and epigraphic sources, i.e. one in charge of worship and a financial patron. Stern has the following very succinct, yet unequivocal, remark to make on the subject: 'In the Roman period the *archisynagogus* had the most important function in the Jewish communities. The supervision of the synagogue was concentrated in his hands . . .'[14] Burtchaell, too, gives expression to this more encompassing view, although he qualifies it by proposing a reconstruction of Jewish communal organization which appears as cumbersome as it is artificial and speculative.[15]

---

[11] Leon (1960), 172. [12] Juster (1914), i. 452–3.
[13] Brooten (1982), 28. [14] *GLAJJ* ii. 630.
[15] Burtchaell (1992), 244: 'What emerges from the evidence is an enduring perception from within the Jewish people that this officer, the *archisynagôgos*, was not simply a master of religious ceremonies. He was the executive of the local community, acting under the formal oversight of the elders but the more active superintendance of the notables. He presided over the community, he convened it for its activities, he superintended its staff. It was a position of some permanency, and one in which fathers might hope to see their sons succeed them. The community chief was, if not the most prestigious member of his community socially, the one who worked, often professionally, as the man at the forefront of his people. As broad as were the interest and the programs and services of his community, so broadly

It is this last view of the archisynagogue which appears to me the most historically credible. In attempting to assess the nature and importance of the office, it is necessary to take into account all relevant sources, and not exclude any simply because they, at first glance, appear to be polemical, tendentious, late, or seemingly incoherent in nature. Incoherent sources may also reflect a historical reality in the details conveyed, especially if these details appear as *obiter dicta*. Polemical sources, too, must reflect some modicum of accuracy if they are to be believed, as the authors clearly intended. The fact remains that such sources exist and thus must be regarded as evidence; either they do, in fact, describe a historical reality as they purport to do, or they reflect a situation current in the author's day or one which he desired to project. Generally speaking, a source should be acknowledged to have some measure of historical value, unless a persuasive case can be made to disqualify it.

PRIMARY EVIDENCE

In turning to the evidence itself, a number of aspects of this office become eminently clear. First and foremost, is the extent to which it was to be found throughout the Jewish world of late antiquity: the office is attested in Palestine (Jerusalem, Caesarea, Sepphoris, Achziv, and the many Galilean settings mentioned in rabbinic sources); Phoenicia (Beirut, Tyre, and Sidon); Arabia (Bostra); Syria (Antioch and Apamea); Asia Minor (Phrygia, Lycia, Caria, Ephesus, Teos, Myndos, Acmonia, Smyrna, and Side); Crete, Cyprus, Greece (Corinth and Aegina); Lower Moesia (Oescus); Italy (Rome, Ostia, Brescia, Venosa, Capua); North Africa (Naro-Hammam Lif); Egypt (Alexandria); and Spain (Tarragona). In most of the above sources, the term *archisynagogos* appears just once. Rome and Venosa are unique; the title appears five times in the former and four in the latter. Thus, only a few fringe regions of the empire (the north-western, south-western, and north-eastern provinces) are bereft of any evidence for such an office, as they are for any other type of Jewish office.

Nevertheless, the term 'archisynagogue' seems to have been more popular in some areas than in others. It is almost totally absent from

reached the breadth of his responsibility. If he presided at worship, it was because he presided at all community functions.' See also Horsley (1981–94), iv. 218.

Egyptian (appearing only in one relatively late third-century CE inscription) and Cyrenaic material, but this may well be due to the fact that the term *synagoge* itself was not widely used in these regions, especially in Egypt, where the word *proseuche* was dominant. This is also true of the Black Sea region and the island of Delos.

The Hebrew equivalent of 'archisynagogue', *rosh knesset*, appears in rabbinic literature about a dozen times in nine independent passages, and specifically with regard to Achziv and Tiberias in Palestine, and Bostra in Provincia Arabia. The Church Fathers Justin and Epiphanius refer to the office, and the title also appears in a number of edicts of the Theodosian Code as well as in several books of the *Scriptores Historiae Augustae*.

Let us review the evidence preserved in the six types of sources at our disposal: the New Testament, the writings of the Church Fathers, rabbinic literature, pagan literature, imperial legislative documents, and inscriptions.[16]

New Testament. The term *archisynagogos* appears in three books—Mark, Luke, and Acts. The two gospels take note of an archisynagogue named Jairos whose daughter was healed by Jesus (Mark 5: 22, 35, 36, 38; Luke 8: 49). Of interest is Luke's use of another term, 'archon of the synagogue' in 8: 41, which is parallel to Mark 5: 22.[17] In Luke 13: 10–17, an archisynagogue is reportedly angry with Jesus when the latter heals a woman on the Sabbath: 'There are six days in which work ought to be done; so come during those days and be healed, but not on the Sabbath' (13: 14).

Of further import is the appearance of this official in Acts, where a religious component of the office is noted: the archisynagogues in Antioch of Pisidia invite Paul to speak immediately following the Torah and *haftarah* readings (Acts 13: 15). Moreover, Acts mentions two Corinthian archisynagogues by name—Crispus who became a believer in Jesus (18: 8), and Sosthenes who apparently led the opposition to Paul (18: 17). Both figures appear to have commanded respect within the community, for the former brought with him other converts to the new faith (18: 8), and the latter apparently organized a protest on behalf of the

---

[16] For a review of the evidence, see Juster (1914), i. 450–3; Brooten (1982), 15–27; Schrage (1971); Burtchaell (1992), 240–4; Roth-Gerson (1987), 168–80.

[17] In Matt. 9: 18, and 23, only the term 'archon' appears.

local Roman governor against Paul's perceived breach of the Law (18: 12–17).[18]

Finally, it is worth noting a textual variant to Acts 14: 2 found in Codex D. Instead of the usual reading: 'The Jews who did not believe . . .', this text reads: 'The archisynagogues of the Jews and the archons of the synagogue . . .' This is indeed a very unusual phraseology; whether it reflects an actual, though *sui generis*, use of these titles, rather than a confusion in the mind of the author/transmitter, is unclear.

In summary, the New Testament evidence attests to an office which was prestigious on the one hand and, on the other, functioned in a leadership role within the synagogue in the political and especially the religious realms.

Church Fathers. Several patristic sources mention the archisynagogue, albeit cryptically. Justin notes that, after prayer, the archisynagogues teach the people to mock Jesus.[19] Here, too, the holder of this office is cast as instructor in religious matters.

Epiphanius offers a somewhat more substantive picture. In describing the Ebionite sect,[20] he takes note of the presbyters and (or: who are) archisynagogues who function as leaders of this sect and have a hand in arranging matrimonial relationships within their 'synagogues'.[21] Given the fact that we are dealing with a Jewish-Christian group, the utilization of Jewish names and titles may reflect a desire to imitate Jewish usage. This would seem to apply not only to the title *archisynagogos* but also to the role assigned these officials.

Of greater import is a second passage which describes the officials in Diaspora synagogues, particularly those of Asia Minor.[22] In the context of the story of Joseph the Comes, who was sent to the region by the Patriarch to oversee synagogue affairs, presumably in the time of Constantine, Epiphanius names the following Jewish officials: archisynagogues, priests, presbyters, and *hazzanim* (the last of which he defines as *diakonoi* or *hyperetes*). There is really no compelling reason to dismiss this list as 'a curious

---

[18] Sosethenes here is probably the person of the same name in 2 Cor. 1: 1; see *International Critical Commentary*, loc. cit.; Haenchen (1971), 536–7.

[19] Justin, *Dialogue with Trypho* 137. 2.

[20] Epiphanius, *Panarion* 30. 18. 2.

[21] See Brooten (1982), 22; Horsley (1981–94), iv. 220.

[22] Epiphanius, *Panarion* 30. 11. 1.

and scarcely coherent collection of seemingly token titles'.[23] These are probably among the most prominent of synagogue officials whom Epiphanius chose to identify, and each had some sort of religious and/or administrative responsibilities.

The other patristic reference to the office which is of interest to us here was made by Palladius in the early fifth century.[24] Therein he notes a rumour ('it is said') that the Patriarch as well as the archisynagogues make annual appointments on the basis of bribes received. The obviously hostile and polemical tone of this report should not necessarily lead us to assume that it has no historical value. The fact that communal appointments were regularly made (whatever their nature and frequency) within the Jewish community by both Patriarchs and archisynagogues as part of their administrative responsibilities may certainly be an accurate reflection of current practice. It is difficult to imagine why Palladius or anyone else would invent such an accusation if there was absolutely no basis for such a practice. As noted above, even a distortion of reality may have a kernel of credibility. In fact, we have some indirect corroboration of Palladius' claim for regular appointments of certain synagogue officials in a late third-century Christian text which speaks of Jewish archons who were appointed prior to every Jewish New Year.[25]

Finally, we should mention the apocryphal *Martyrdom of Peter and Paul*, which claims that Jewish archisynagogues, along with pagan priests, were responsible for opposing the apostles Peter and Paul in Rome.[26]

Thus, the above patristic sources make it quite clear that archisynagogues not only had some sort of religious function, but held political and administrative responsibilities as well. Both Epiphanius and Palladius clearly refer to this dimension.

Rabbinic Literature. Interestingly and, perhaps, surprisingly, the archisynagogue is mentioned in rabbinic sources only on occasion. The context in which the title appears is most often a religious-liturgical one, which is quite understandable given the interests and agenda of the rabbis. None the less, even here there are hints of a much wider role for this official who, as noted, is referred to as *rosh*

---

[23] Rajak and Noy (1993), 79.
[24] Palladius, *Dialogue on the Life of John Chrysostom* 15.
[25] *JIWE* ii. 61; Talley (1986), 92–4.
[26] Lipsius (1972), 128. See also Juster (1914), i. 452 n. 3.

knesset. There has been some speculation as to which title, the Greek or the Hebrew, was the original and which was derivative.[27] As interesting and important as such a determination might be, it must remain a moot question for the present. While the Greek term is well attested from the first century CE, the Hebrew one appears only in the Mishnah around the turn of the third century; little can be said of its earlier history. If the mishnaic tradition regarding the *rosh knesset* in the Temple is authentic (see below), then, at the very least, a first-century CE date is called for; however, even such an assumption would hardly resolve the issue. To assume a correlation between the origin of a term and its first appearance in an extant source is patently unwarranted.

The earliest context in rabbinic literature associated with the *rosh knesset* relates to a Torah-reading ceremony in the Temple. Both a *hazzan* and a *rosh knesset* were part of the chain of officials who transferred the Torah to the High Priest or king for reading during the Yom Kippur and *haqhel* ceremonies.[28] Despite the apparent anachronism in associating synagogue-related officials with Temple proceedings, there is a possibility that this tradition is not entirely bereft of historical basis. When the functions of the city gate were transferred elsewhere in the course of the Persian or Hellenistic periods, the Temple precincts along with the Temple Mount area may well have incorporated some of the activities formerly associated with the Jerusalem city gate.[29] This would include elements of religious worship that had taken place at the gate during the First Temple period. As the *hazzan* and *rosh knesset* may already have functioned in some religious capacity in the city-gate area, the transference of the Torah-reading ceremony to the Temple, as to synagogues elsewhere, may have included the participation of persons bearing these titles. Thus, when the Torah was read in the Temple—albeit on rare occasions—a *hazzan* and a *rosh knesset*, either from one of the Jerusalem synagogues or directly associated with the Temple, participated. This line of reasoning is speculative, but it may not be a wholly unrealistic reconstruction.

Whatever the case, the Tosefta tradition of the *hazzan* and *rosh knesset* being in charge of the Torah-reading ceremony within the

---

[27] Horsley (1981–94), iv. 220.
[28] m. Yom. 7: 1; m. Sot. 7: 7–8.
[29] On the whole issue concerning the emergence of the synagogue in the Persian or Hellenistic period, see Levine (forthcoming).

synagogue clearly points to the religious dimension of this position: according to the Tosefta, on occasion, the *rosh knesset* also read from the Torah,[30] and this type of involvement dovetails rather neatly with the New Testament evidence.

A number of other second-century rabbinic sources also reflect the prominent status of the archisynagogue. One tradition regarding burial customs notes the addition of three cups of wine at a funeral meal in honour of the *hazzan knesset*, *rosh knesset*, and Rabban Gamaliel.[31] In a *baraita* (a rabbinic tradition ascribed to the tannaitic or pre-third-century era) listing those women who would be preferable wives, the following order is given: the highest pedigree is the daughter of a sage, followed by the daughter of one of 'the great men of the generation' (גדולי הדור, i.e. a wealthy communal leader), that of a *rosh knesset*, of a charity official, and, finally, of a school teacher.[32] Two second-century heads of synagogues are mentioned in connection with visiting sages. One Sagvion of Achziv, identified as a *rosh knesset*, addressed a question about a legal problem to Rabban Gamaliel II when the latter visited his town,[33] and the *rosh knesset* in Nisibis invited R. Judah ben Betera to dine with him on the eve of Yom Kippur.[34]

From the later third century, we have the account of a *rosh knesset* in Bostra who is described as arranging the seating in the synagogue (lit. dragging a bench) in the presence of R. Jeremiah.[35] In addition, some Galileans asked R. Helbo about the proper order in which to call people to the Torah following the Cohen and Levi. He responded:

> after them read sages who are appointed as *parnasim* in the community, after them sages who are qualified to be appointed *parnasim*, after them the sons of sages who function as *parnasim*, and after them the *rashei knesset*, and after them anyone else.[36]

In reviewing these nine different rabbinic traditions, which are divided between Palestinian and Babylonian sources (although referring, with but one exception, to Palestinian settings), it is clear that, for the rabbis, the *rosh knesset* was a significant enough personage so as to be accorded some recognition. Needless to say,

---

[30] T. Megillah 3: 21; and Lieberman (1962), ad loc.
[31] y. Ber. 3. 1. 6a; Tractate Semahot 14: 14. However, cf. b. Ket. 8b, which reads *parnas* instead of archisynagogue; see Ginzberg (1941), ii. 65–6.
[32] b. Pes. 49b. [33] t. Ter. 2: 13.
[34] Lev. R. 3: 17. [35] b. Shab. 29b. [36] b. Gitt. 60a.

his position was always considered inferior to that of the sage, but that is to be expected of almost any non-sage mentioned in rabbinic sources. What is of significance is that of all synagogue-related officials, the archisynagogue was accorded the highest honours.

Of particular interest are the functions actually depicted, alluded to or omitted in these reports. For example, nothing is said of the *rosh knesset* as a benefactor, unless being named right after 'the great men of the generation' and before the charity officers is of significance in this regard. Several traditions are quite explicit regarding his religious functions. Even if we were to disregard the mishnaic testimony relating to the Temple, the Tosefta tradition abut reading Scriptures and the legal query posed to Rabban Gamaliel in Achziv by the local *rosh knesset* are quite pointed in this respect. Of no lesser import are other indications that we have of his administrative responsibilities. The arranging of seats by the *rosh knesset* in the synagogue in Bostra and the ranking of the *rosh knesset* between the community's most powerful members and its charity officers may well point to other administrative and political aspects of the archisynagogue's duties.

Pagan Literature. There are two important pagan sources which relate to the archisynagogue, both found in the fourth-century collection of imperial biographies, the *Scriptores Historiae Augustae*. In a letter allegedly written by Hadrian, the following statement is made:

those who worship Serapis are, in fact, Christians, and those who call themselves bishops of Christ are, in fact, devotees of Serapis. There is no chief of the Jewish synagogue [i.e. archisynagogue], no Samaritan, no Christian presbyter who is not an astrologer, a soothsayer, or an anointer.[37]

As garbled as this text may appear, several details are nevertheless noteworthy. The first is the singling out of an archisynagogue from among all other Jewish officials; second is the implicit comparison of the archisynagogue with a Christian presbyter, perhaps even with a bishop (see also below).

Of more import, however, is the well-known reference in the *Life of Alexander Severus* to a mob scene in either Antioch or Alexandria (or both): 'On the occasion of a certain festival, the people of Antioch, of Egypt, and of Alexandria, had annoyed him with jibes

---

[37] *Life of Saturninus* 8, *GLAJJ* ii. 637–8. See also Rajak and Noy (1993), 81, who translate *aliptes* as 'wrestling master' instead of 'anointer'.

as was their custom, calling him a Syrian archisynagogue and a high priest.'[38] In contrast to the previous source, it is not impossible that such an incident, in one form or another, did, in fact, occur during the lifetime of Alexander Severus. As with other members of this dynasty, he was known for his sympathies towards Jews and Judaism, as well as for trying to conceal his Syrian origins. Such an accusation would thus have been especially poignant in both respects.[39] The selection of the title 'archisynagogue' for such an insult (whether it be an historical third-century account or a literary fourth-century one) would seem to reflect how well known—albeit in a pejorative way—this title was among the pagan masses.

Imperial Legislation. The Theodosian Code makes it quite clear that the archisynagogue was a pivotal communal official, and not only in the religious realm. As early as 330, Constantine issued several edicts which addressed the status of Jewish communal and religious officials:

> The same Augustus to the priests, the archisynagogues, fathers of synagogues, and the others who serve in the same place. We order that the priests, archisynagogues, fathers of synagogues, and the others who serve in synagogues shall be free from all corporal liturgy . . .[40]

Taken together with another version issued several days earlier,[41] the intention of the emperor becomes quite clear. Jewish 'clergy', i.e. those who take a leading role in synagogue affairs ('those who dedicated themselves with complete devotion to the synagogues of the Jews', ibid.), are to be exempt from certain liturgies, as were their pagan and Christian counterparts. A similar law exempting archisynagogues and others from liturgies was issued at the end of the century by the emperors Arcadius and Honorius:

> The Jews shall be bound to their rites; while we shall imitate the ancients in conserving their privileges, for it was established in their laws and confirmed by our divinity, that those who are subject to the rule of the Illustrious Patriarchs, that is the Archisynagogues, the patriarchs, the presbyters and the others who are occupied in the rite of that religion, shall persevere in keeping the same privileges that are reverently bestowed on the first clerics of the venerable Christian Law. For this was decreed in

---

[38] *Life of Alexander Severus* 28, *GLAJJ* ii. no. 521.
[39] Momigliano (1934), 151–3.
[40] *Cod. Theod.* 16. 8. 4, Linder (1987), 135.
[41] Ibid. 16. 8. 2, Linder (1987), 134.

divine order also by the divine Emperors Constantine and Constantius, Valentinian and Valens. Let them therefore be exempt even from the curial liturgies, and obey their laws.[42]

Finally, a third law notes a specific communal function ascribed to the archisynagogue:

It is a matter of shameful superstition that the Archisynagogues, the presbyters of the Jews, and those they call apostles, who are sent by the patriarch on a certain date to demand gold and silver, exact and receive a sum from each synagogue, and deliver it to him . . .[43]

Although there seems to be a lack of clarity regarding the precise role of archisynagogues and elders in this process of tax collection, i.e. they were not sent by the Patriarch to carry out this task as may have been the case with the apostles, there is little justification in dismissing this report in its entirety. These synagogue officials were apparently also involved in the collection of these monies from their communities, and thus the historical significance of this source for our purposes.

Epigraphic Evidence. The largest corpus of material regarding the archisynagogue is to be found in inscriptions. Horsley, followed by Rajak and Noy, have conveniently listed all known examples, which, by their count, toll more than thirty inscriptions containing names of about forty persons holding that title. Most of the inscriptions are funerary, and thus usually only take note of the fact that the person being honoured once held that position. Yet, even in this limited context some additional information regarding this office is recorded (see below).

Of especial importance are the dedicatory inscriptions from synagogues which relate to the functioning of the archisynagogue.[44]

---

[42] Ibid. 16. 8. 13, Linder (1987), no. 27.

[43] Ibid. 16. 8. 14, Linder (1987), no. 30. Moreover, there is every reason to believe that the term 'primates' in *Cod. Theod.* 16. 8. 8, the most important personage in the local Jewish community, may indeed refer to the archisynagogue: 'In the complaints of the Jews it was affirmed that some people are received in their sect on the authority of the judges, against the opposition of the Primates of their Law, who had cast them out by their judgement and will. We order that this injury should be utterly removed, and that a tenacious group in their superstition shall not earn aid from their undue readmission through the authority of judges or of ill-gotten rescript, against the will of their Primates, who are manifestly authorized to pass judgement concerning their religion, under the authority of the Most Renowned and the Illustrious patriarchs' (Linder (1987), 187–8).

[44] In addition to the above, see Lifshitz (1967); Burtchaell (1992), 243 n. 83; Brooten (1982), 23–33, 229–30 n. 93.

Eight such inscriptions exist—slightly more than for any other synagogue-related post.[45] In comparison, seven dedicatory inscriptions mention presbyters,[46] five (perhaps six) note an archon,[47] and five a *phrontistes*.[48] The archisynagogues mentioned as donors hailed from North Africa, Greece, Asia Minor, Syria, and Palestine. Some are noted as having built or founded the synagogue (Jerusalem, Teos, Aegina) or as having restored it (Acmonia), others as having contributed a chancel screen (Myndos), a mosaic pavement (Naro), the entrance to the building (Apamea) or a triclinium (Caesarea).

Clearly, these inscriptions indicate that an archisynagogue was not infrequently a major donor to the synagogue's physical appearance. However, it is a major—and unwarranted—leap to assume, on the basis of this evidence, that the donor dimension of this office was a *sine qua non* for becoming an archisynagogue[49] or that such an official only functioned in this capacity. What may have been common, and even in many cases expected, was not necessarily the sole or determinant factor in defining one's position. It is entirely conceivable that many archisynagogues did not contribute to the synagogue building; otherwise we might have expected many more such inscriptions, and not only eight! However, this last point is difficult to substantiate, as it rests on an *argumentum ex silentio*. Moreover, many other synagogue officials and non-officials also made substantial contributions toward synagogue-related projects, as did the community as a whole.[50] Thus, one need not have been an archisynagogue to contribute, nor did these people always do so. Indeed, the distinction made in rabbinic literature between 'the great men of the generation' (גדולי הדור) and the *rosh knesset* may, in fact, indicate that the latter was not always the primary benefactor, at least in Palestinian circles.

These inscriptions likewise confirm the overall prominence of this office, as evidenced in other sources as well. Not infrequently a

---

[45] Rajak lists nine, yet the Salamis inscription may be an epitaph. See also Lifshitz (1967), no. 85, and esp. p. 76.

[46] Ibid., nos. 14, 32, 37, 58, 82, 84, 101.

[47] Ibid., nos. 11, 33, 37, 100, 101, and possibly 9a.

[48] Ibid., nos. 1, 2, 36, 37, 66.

[49] Rajak and Noy (1993), 84–9.

[50] See, in general, Lifshitz (1967); for the Palestinian evidence in particular, see Roth-Gerson (1987), 147–52, 168–74. See also the inscription from Reggio di Calabria, *JIWE* i. no. 139.

lavish honorific title accompanies the mention of an archisynagogue: ἀξιολογώτατος—'the most respected' (Teos); τιμιώτατος—'the most honoured' (Apamea); and λαμπρότατος—'the most illustrious' (Sepphoris—twice). This evidence thus dovetails nicely with the report in the *Scriptores Historiae Augustae* of the pagan mob calling the emperor an archisynagogue, as well as the prominence of this office as reflected in the Theodosian Code.

It is also noteworthy that an archisynagogue may have held more than just one title. An archisynagogue might also have been an archon,[51] presbyter,[52] rabbi,[53] *didaskalos*,[54] *phrontistes*,[55] or priest.[56] Dual titles, however, were not unique to this office. A *phrontistes*, for example, could also have been a *pater synagoges*, archon, or presbyter.[57]

Moreover, the position of archisynagogue may have combined with another post, civilian or military, held in non-Jewish society. Both known instances of such a combination stem from the Danube region. An inscription from Moesia identifies one Joses as an archisynagogue and *principales*, a term which may refer to a military or civilian post.[58] From Intercisa, there is mention of an archisynagogue who was also head of a customs station.[59]

Furthermore, more than one person could have held the title of archisynagogue at any one time. At Apamea there were three archisynagogues honoured by Ilasios, himself an archisynagogue of Antioch,[60] and Acmonia had two archisynagogues and an archon who undertook the restoration of the building.[61] The office may have been hereditary in some instances, or at least customarily transmitted from one generation to another within a single family. Such was the case in the Theodotus inscription from Jerusalem, where leadership in the synagogue remained in the same family for at least three generations.[62] A similar situation (of two generations) is attested at Venosa.[63]

---

[51] Rome: *JIWE* ii. no. 322; Campania: ibid. i, no. 20.
[52] Crete: Lifshitz, 'Prolegomenon' to *CIJ* i. 88, no. 731c.
[53] Jerusalem: *CIJ* ii. no. 1414.
[54] Corinth: Horsley (1981–94), iv. no. 113.
[55] Aegina: Lifshitz (1967), no. 1; Caesarea: ibid. no. 66.
[56] Jerusalem: ibid., no. 79.
[57] See e.g. *JIWE* ii. nos. 164, 540; Lifshitz (1967), no. 37. See also ibid., no. 14.
[58] Moesia: Scheiber (1983), no. 10. See also Horsley (1981–94), iv. 215, no. 20.
[59] Scheiber (1983), no. 3.   [60] Lifshitz (1967), no. 38.
[61] Ibid., no. 33.   [62] Ibid., no. 79.
[63] *JIWE* i, no. 70.

Finally, the title may have been used in an honorary sense, as when it was bestowed on a child.[64] It is not clear if an 'archisynagogue for life' (διὰ βίου) was an honorary title or whether its holder actually continued to function in this capacity until death.[65]

While the material referring to non-Jewish *archisynagogoi*—perhaps because of its primarily epigraphical nature[66]—points clearly to a patron role for such an official, other functions of this office are also noted. Eusebius, for example, refers to a pagan by the name of Macrianus, describing him as 'a teacher and archisynagogue of Egyptian magicians';[67] Epiphanius relates that Ebionite leaders were called archisynagogues and presbyters, and that these officials served as teachers and also arranged marriages within the community.[68]

CONCLUSION

Our sources relate to the position of archisynagogue in ways that we might well have expected. Sources with primarily religious concerns, such as rabbinic material, the New Testament, and the Church Fathers, all emphasize the religious dimension of the office. Even imperial legislation, focusing, as it does, on the Jews as a religious community, addresses this aspect of Jewish life generally, and the archisynagogue in particular. Inscriptions, on the other hand, as might be expected, relate mostly to the benefactions of such individuals. But over and above each sources's specific concern, we have noted evidence time and again that this office included responsibilities other than religious or financial ones. An archisynagogue was looked upon by Jews and non-Jews alike as a leader and representative of his community. Our sources' proclivities should not prevent us from trying to recapture the full scope of this office's responsibilities among the many far-flung Jewish communities of late antiquity.

The office of Jewish archisynagogue is a fascinating example of

[64] Ibid., no. 53. On children given titles reserved for communal officials, see ibid. ii, nos. 288, 337.

[65] See e.g. Lifshitz (1967), no. 16 (Teos); ibid., no. 33 (Acmonia)—both in Asia Minor.

[66] See the non-Jewish incriptions cited by Horsley (1981–94), iv. 219–20; Rajak and Noy (1993), 92–3.

[67] Euseb. *Hist. Eccl.* 7. 10. 4.

[68] Epiphanius, *Panarion* 30. 18. 2.

adoption and adaptation. Jews clearly borrowed the term archisynagogue from their surroundings, whatever the origin or derivation of
the Hebrew title *rosh knesset* may have been.[69] On the basis of the
available evidence, pagans appear to have used this term largely in a
philanthropic sense, i.e. for one who was conspicuous in his
contributions to an association or organization. Nevertheless,
given the unique functions of the synagogue as a communal
organization and its all-encompassing role in the lives of the local
Jewish population, the responsibilities of the Jewish archisynagogue
were most probably broader and more comprehensive than those of
his pagan namesake. It is doubtful whether such a role was
influenced by previous Jewish communal history, since no comparable synagogue framework existed heretofore—either in Palestine or
the Diaspora. The office of archisynagogue is a phenomenon of the
Graeco-Roman world, but it was radically redefined when brought
into the Jewish context, thus attesting both to the responsiveness
and to the adaptability of these Jewish communities.

[69] Schrage (1971), 844–5.

14

The Structure of the Jewish Community in Rome

MARGARET WILLIAMS

Throughout the early Roman imperial period (i.e. the first three centuries CE), one of the largest concentrations of Jews to be found outside Judaea was at Rome itself. As early as the principate of Augustus they had come to number several thousands[1] and possess a multiplicity of synagogues.[2] And with the eclipse of Alexandrian Jewry after the Jewish revolt of 115–17 CE, they became the most important Diaspora community in the empire.[3] How did they manage their affairs? Standard opinion nowadays has it that, throughout its long history, ancient Roman Jewry was organized along traditional Roman lines and in consequence structured differently from the Alexandrian Jewish community. While the latter, from the late Augustan period at least, was always uni-fied—from 11/12 CE a supra-synagogal council (*gerousia*) comprised mainly of archons directed the community's affairs[4]—the Roman Jews 'had to be content' with far less.[5] No umbrella council was ever possible for them, basically because the collegiate nature of their synagogues (i.e. the fact that they were private, club-like, and, above all, autonomous institutions) precluded the emergence of a body of that kind. Such is the conventional view of the structure of Roman Jewry. Its history is long (Schürer first formulated it in 1879)[6] and its proponents numerous.[7] But is it right? Generally

---

[1] Joseph. *War* 2. 80 and *Ant.* 17. 300.
[2] Philo, *Leg. ad Gaium* 156–7.   [3] Hengel (1966), 181–2.
[4] For Augustus' instructions to the Prefect of Egypt concerning the establishment of this body, see Philo, *In Flacc.* 74; for its likely functions, see Applebaum (1974), 475.
[5] Schürer (1986), 96.   [6] Schürer (1879), 8–10.
[7] *Inter al.* note *CIJ* i. cii–cxi; Momigliano (1966), 523–33; Guterman (1951), 130–56 (synagogues in general, not specifically those of Rome); Leon (1960), 168–70; Smallwood (1976), 133–4; Wiefel (1991), 88, 91–2.

when this topic is discussed the focus is almost exclusively upon, first, a single sentence in Josephus (*Ant.* 14. 215) mentioning a ruling of Julius Caesar against religious associations (θίασοι) at Rome, and secondly the titular evidence from the Jewish catacombs there. Wider issues, such as Roman Jewry's general *modus operandi* and broad cultural orientation, the manner in which it was viewed and dealt with by the Roman authorities, and the way in which large, multicentred Jewish communities tended to be organized at that time, are not taken into account. Yet surely they ought to be. And once they are, it becomes apparent that, despite a few similarities between *collegium* and synagogue (e.g. each held regular meetings and possessed a common fund),[8] the collegiate model is seriously deficient as an explanation for the structure of the Roman Jewish community. I argue here that a better way of accounting for the totality of the evidence, Jewish, Roman, and Christian, is to conclude that Roman Jewry, no less than Alexandrian, did have a central council, and that the model for that council was Jewish. All that remains now is to present my case. First, I shall consider the evidence that leads people to assert the collegiate nature of the Roman synagogues. The arguments for positing, instead, a central structure will then be presented.

A COLLEGIATE STRUCTURE FOR ROMAN JEWRY?

That the structure of Roman Jewry was collegiate, is today regarded as received truth.[9] But there are problems with this view. References in Latin sources to *collegia* and anti-collegiate measures, such as the *SC* (senatorial decree) of 64 BCE and the *Lex Iulia de collegiis*, contain no mention at all of either the Jews or their associations. Disciplinary actions against the Jews, such as their expulsion from Rome in 19 CE, were not taken on the basis of any ruling against *collegia* (on that occasion, a decree of the Senate had to be enacted for the purpose).[10] The few superficial resemblances between synagogue and *collegium* are greatly outnumbered by some very fundamental differences, a comprehensive list of which was formulated by Juster.[11] That such difficulties exist is unsurprising,

---

[8] Smallwood (1976), 133.
[9] For detailed expositions of this view, see La Piana (1927), 348–51, and Smallwood (1976), 133–4.
[10] Tac. *Ann.* 2. 85.   [11] Juster (1914), i. 418–24.

given the flimsiness of the foundations on which the collegiate thesis has been erected. No ancient text, either Greek or Latin, specifically refers to synagogues either at Rome or elsewhere as *collegia/* κολλήγια. And in the one instance where *universitas*, a frequent synonym for *collegium*, is found in a Jewish context (a rescript of Caracalla to the Jews of Antioch),[12] it obviously does not bear the narrow, specialized meaning of 'college' or 'association'. What it designates is the entire, multi-synagogal community of that city.[13] As for the titulature of officials, in the synagogue that was much more civic in tone than ever was the case in the private associations of the Graeco-Roman world. 'Archon', the most commonly attested synagogal title of all, even at Rome,[14] was largely avoided by pagan religious societies.[15] Synagogues, conversely, even in the Latin-speaking West, used none of the common collegiate terms for offices.[16] So if no text actually refers specifically to synagogues as *collegia* and coincidences between synagogal and collegiate titulature are pretty minimal, on what basis does the collegiate hypothesis rest? It is an inference made possible only by conflating the sentence of Josephus alluded to above (*Ant.* 14. 215), in which Jews are mentioned but not, expressly, *collegia*, with two from Suetonius, which refer to *collegia* but not to Jews. Those passages must at once be quoted in full. Note that in my (very literal) translation of the Josephus passage, problematic parts of the text are underlined and the section of the document upon which discussion will be most sharply focused printed in bold. The text of Josephus (*Ant.* 14. 213–16) chosen for translation and discussion is that of Marcus in the Loeb Classical Library.

(213) Ἰούλιος Γάιος στρατηγὸς ὕπατος Ῥωμαίων Παριανῶν ἄρχουσι βουλῇ δήμῳ χαίρειν. ἐνέτυχόν μοι οἱ Ἰουδαῖοι ἐν Δήλῳ καί τινες τῶν παροίκων Ἰουδαίων, παρόντων καὶ τῶν ὑμετέρων πρέσβεων, καὶ ἐνεφάνισαν ὡς ὑμεῖς ψηφίσματι κωλύετε αὐτοὺς τοῖς πατρίοις ἔθεσι καὶ ἱεροῖς χρῆσθαι. (214) ἐμοὶ τοίνυν οὐκ ἀρέσκει κατὰ τῶν ἡμετέρων φίλων καὶ συμμάχων τοιαῦτα γίνεσθαι ψηφίσματα, καὶ κωλύεσθαι αὐτοὺς ζῆν κατὰ τὰ αὐτῶν ἔθη καὶ χρήματα εἰς σύνδειπνα καὶ τὰ ἱερὰ εἰσφέρειν, τοῦτο ποιεῖν αὐτῶν μηδ᾽ ἐν Ῥώμῃ κεκωλυμένων. (215) καὶ γὰρ Γάιος Καῖσαρ ὁ ἡμέτερος στρατηγὸς ὕπατος, ἐν τῷ διατάγματι

[12] *Cod. Just.* 1. 9. 1.
[13] For a recent discussion of this difficult text, see Linder (1987), 107–10.
[14] Applebaum (1974), 494–5; Schürer (1986), 98–9; van der Horst (1991), 89–90.
[15] Poland (1909), 361–2.
[16] Compare the lists in J.-P. Waltzing (1895–1900), iv. 323 ff. and *JIWE* i. 328–9; ii. 538–9.

κωλύων θιάσους (= *collegia*?) συνάγεσθαι κατὰ πόλιν, μόνους τούτους οὐκ ἐκώλυσεν οὔτε χρήματα συνεισφέρειν οὔτε σύνδειπνα ποιεῖν. (216) ὁμοίως δὲ κἀγὼ τοὺς ἄλλους θιάσους κωλύων, τούτοις μόνοις ἐπιτρέπω κατὰ τὰ πάτρια ἔθη καὶ νόμιμα συνάγεσθαί τε καὶ ἑστιᾶσθαι. καὶ ὑμᾶς οὖν καλῶς ἔχει, εἴ τι κατὰ τῶν ἡμετέρων φίλων καὶ συμμάχων ψήφισμα ἐποιήσατε, τοῦτο ἀκυρῶσαι διὰ τὴν περὶ ἡμᾶς αὐτῶν ἀρετὴν καὶ εὔνοιαν.

(213) Julius Gaius, Supreme Commander [i.e. Consul] of the Romans, to the magistrates, council, and people of Parium, greeting. The Jews in Delos and some of the neighbouring Jews, some of your envoys also being present, have appealed to me and made it plain that you are preventing them by decree from observing their national customs and sacred rites. (214) Now it does not please me that such decrees should be made against our friends and allies and that they should be prevented from living in accordance with their customs and contributing money to common meals and sacred rites, for this they are not prevented from doing even at Rome. (215) **For Gaius Caesar, our <u>Supreme Commander</u>, in his edict preventing religious societies from meeting in the city, these people alone did not prevent from either contributing money or holding common meals.** (216) **Likewise I, (while) forbidding other religious societies, these people alone permit to assemble and <u>feast</u> in accordance with their native customs and ordinances.** If you have passed any decree against our friends and allies, you therefore will do well to revoke it because of their worthy deeds on our behalf and their goodwill towards us.

Cuncta collegia praeter antiquitus constituta distraxit. (Suetonius, *Vita Iul.* 42. 3)
He [sc. Julius Caesar] disbanded all guilds, except those founded in ancient times.

Collegia praeter antiqua et legitima dissolvit. (Suetonius, *Vita Aug.* 32. 1)
He [sc. Augustus] dissolved [all] the guilds, except those that were ancient and legitimate.

As a preliminary to our discussion, two points need to be made in relation to the extract from Josephus. First, it is part of one of the most overtly apologetic sections of the *Antiquities*—the long catalogue of gentile documents at Book 14. 190–264, that are cited with the express purpose of showing how 'the kings of Asia and Europe have held us (sc. the Jews) in esteem and have admired our bravery and loyalty'.[17] Second, the genuineness of a number of those documents, in common with that of others cited elsewhere in his

---

[17] Joseph. *Ant.* 14. 186.

work, has long been viewed with suspicion.[18] To reject all as unsound is both extreme and unnecessary but caution is required. Even the advocates of their general authenticity (these days, the vast majority of scholars)[19] do not deny that on occasion words have been interpolated and modifications made to the text to bolster the Jews' civic position.[20] That being so, any passage in this archival material which advances claims about the juridical basis of a Diaspora community has to be subjected to the closest scrutiny before its use as evidence can be admitted.

If we turn now to the document quoted above by Josephus and purporting to be an official Roman communication from the mid-40s BCE, we are confronted by a host of problems. Some are relatively minor and of no consequence to the issue under discussion. It matters little, for instance, that the precise destination of the document can no longer be determined.[21] But some are so serious that they call into question the authenticity of, if not the whole document, at least the section that has been printed in bold. For what we there meet with is some extremely implausible Roman titulature, an extraordinary degree of ignorance on the part of the Roman official issuing the document[22] about the scope and nature of the enactment he was citing as a precedent, as well as a barely credible response by him to the problem with which he had been confronted. Take the title στρατηγὸς ὕπατος. Many scholars have commented on its peculiarity.[23] But it is not just peculiar; it is wholly anomalous in a document dating from the 40s BCE, as Holleaux pointed out in 1918.[24] For στρατηγὸς ὕπατος had become obsolete as a rendition of the Latin term consul at least fifty years before our document is supposed to have been written

---

[18] See Bickermann (1980), 24–7, for a résumé of the history of this scholarship.

[19] For an altogether more sceptical approach, see Moehring (1975).

[20] As in the Sardian decree at *Ant.* 14. 259 and Claudius' edict to the Alexandrians at *Ant.* 19. 283. For discussion of the former, see Trebilco (1991), 171. For the latter see *CPJ* i. 57 n. 22 and 70 n. 45, and Rajak (1984), 115.

[21] For the various conjectures on this and other uncertain parts of the text, see Marcus's critical notes in the Loeb edn. of *Antiquities* 14.

[22] The general sense of the document suggests that it is unlikely to have been Julius Caesar himself, as claimed by Marcus in his marginal note in the Loeb and Rajak (1984), 113. Would Caesar have referred to himself as Γάιος Καῖσαρ ὁ ἡμέτερος στρατηγὸς ὕπατος? Far better to assume with scholars such as Smallwood (1976), 135 n. 52, that it was some other Roman official, whose name has become 'hopelessly corrupt'.

[23] e.g. Marcus, Loeb edn. ad loc.; Smallwood (1976), 135; Yavetz (1983), 95.

[24] Holleaux (1918), 9 n. 1.

(plain ὕπατος had begun to replace στρατηγὸς ὕπατος in the last quarter of the second century BCE and by the beginning of the first it had become the universally accepted usage).²⁵ Then there is, as Yavetz pointed out,²⁶ the strikingly limited 'practical knowledge of the Roman law' demonstrated by the writer of this document. For Caesar did not ban *all* non-Jewish associations. A number of ancient foundations, by which minimally the eight venerable craft guilds that dated from the time of Numa are usually understood,²⁷ were exempted.²⁸ Nor would Caesar's banning order appear to have taken the form of an edict (διάταγμα), as our document uniquely claims. If, with De Robertis and his followers, we accept the implication of the word *legitima* at Suetonius *Vit. Aug.* 32. 1, the enactment was in the form of a *lex*—presumably the *Lex Iulia de collegiis*, which Augustus subsequently revised.²⁹ Finally there is the problem of the action taken by our curiously named official (as it stands, the name is impossible). Is it likely that he, or any Roman governor for that matter, would have attempted to suppress *all* religious societies (θίασοι) in his province, except for those of the Jews? The sheer number of them in the average Greek community, not to mention the critical contribution they made to the cohesiveness of Greek society, makes such an action unthinkable.³⁰

None of these difficulties has gone unnoticed in the past but the implications of so many of them cropping up in one short and easily detachable part of a document cited for apologetic purposes have gone unremarked. Yet surely they are obvious: a creative hand must have been at work. Whose it was, we have no means of knowing. It has recently been argued that the documents cited by Josephus are likely to have been copied and recopied several times before they reached him, sometimes even undergoing material alteration in the

---

²⁵ Holleaux (1918), 1–9; Mason (1974), 158. For the latest known example, see *AE* 1967, no. 532 (92 BCE). If στρατηγὸς ὕπατος 'Ρωμαίων in *Ant.* 14. 213 is accepted as authentic, a 2nd-cent. date for our document is likely. For other documents of that period carelessly included by Josephus in his dossier of alleged Caesarian material, note *Ant.* 14. 247–55 (a decree of Pergamum) with Rajak (1984) 111, and *Ant.* 14. 233 (rescript to Cos) with Holleaux (1918), 5 n. 1.

²⁶ Yavetz (1983), 95.

²⁷ For these, see Plut. *Num.* 17. 2.

²⁸ Others would extend the list to include 'all the others that were established before political agitation became one of their central activities'. See Yavetz (1983), 94.

²⁹ De Robertis (1938), 176–80; Linderski (1962), 322–8; Treggiari (1969), 177.

³⁰ On the impossibility of applying the *Lex Julia* to the provinces with their 'pullulating little associations', see Crook (1967), 266.

process.[31] If I am right in thinking that such may have been the fate of our rescript and the underlined section is a later addition,[32] then the consequences for our understanding of Roman Jewry are great. For it is *that passage alone* that provides the only 'hard' information there is for believing that the Romans formally classified the synagogues of the city as *collegia*. Neither of the Suetonian passages set out above mentions the Jews at all. Can the phrases *collegia antiquitus constituta* and *collegia antiqua* really be construed as veiled references to the synagogues of Rome? If the traditional date for the 'foundation' of Roman Jewish community is accepted (i.e. the late second to the early first century BCE),[33] none of the synagogues of Rome in Caesar's time will have been very old.

A CENTRALIZED STRUCTURE FOR ROMAN JEWRY?

But if the evidence for thinking that Roman Jewry was collegiate is so gravely inadequate, how was it structured? Did it ever function as a structural unity at all? If so, was that because it possessed an Alexandrian-style *gerousia*—i.e. a central council, comprised largely, if not exclusively, of men called archons, to which the individual synagogues of the city were somehow subordinated?[34] Of the advantages of such an institution there can be no doubt. If the Alexandrian evidence is anything to go by, the Romans would have found it a useful mechanism for controlling, albeit indirectly, a large segment of the city's population,[35] and to the Jews it would have offered a more effective means than the individual synagogal councils of lobbying the authorities and defending the interests of the wider group. But did it exist? To this question there are two conventional replies—the first, that the Romans would never have tolerated such an organization in their capital, and the second, that

---

[31] See Pucci Ben Zeev (1994), 46–59.

[32] Note that the only material difference between our document and the closely analogous, and usually presumed authentic, rescript to the Milesians cited at *Ant.* 14. 244–6 is the absence in the latter of the citation of any precedent.

[33] See Smallwood (1976), 131.

[34] On the composition and likely powers of the Alexandrian *gerousia*, see Applebaum (1974), 474–5.

[35] Applebaum (1974), 474, infers Roman interference in the composition of the Alexandrian *gerousia* from Philo *In Flacc.* 74. Roman influence upon Jewish community appointments at Antioch is specifically attested by Libanius. See *Epistulae* 1251 = *GLAJJ* ii. no. 504.

no good evidence exists for such a body.[36] These objections, while admittedly powerful, are not insuperable. Evidence for the structure of the early Christian church at Rome shows that Roman hostility to large, centralized organizations has been grossly exaggerated—long before Constantine and the Edict of Milan (and thus the official recognition of Christianity) the authority of the Roman bishop extended over a radius of 100 miles and his clerical and sub-clerical staff alone numbered 155.[37] As for the second objection, that can only be upheld on a very restricted view of the evidence—i.e. by making attestation of the term *gerousia* the sole criterion for determining whether there was a central Jewish council at Rome or not. That a *gerousia* of the kind found at Alexandria is not mentioned specifically *by name*, cannot be denied. But then hardly any of the institutions belonging to the Jews of ancient Rome are. With the exception of the distinguished but short-lived rabbinical court and seminary of Mattithiah ben Heresh (second century), mentioned in talmudic sources,[38] all are a matter of inference. But there are other kinds of evidence which may reasonably be taken into account here. Besides the titles of Roman Jewish officials and general Jewish organizational practice at that time, the language Josephus uses to describe the community is also relevant, as is the information that both he and Philo provide about the way the Jews were perceived and treated by the Roman authorities. Taken together, these four different kinds of evidence strongly imply that, for most of its history, ancient Roman Jewry was more than a congeries of independent mini-communities. Certainly from the latter part of the Augustan principate, it did function, on occasion at least, as a unity. The reason that it was able to do so must in all probability be because it already possessed some kind of supra-synagogal structure.

To establish my case, each of these four kinds of evidence must now be examined. The best starting point is Josephus and the language he uses when referring to the Jews of Rome. If we scrutinize the passages in his work in which Roman Jewry appears in action—viz. its large-scale attendance (there were around 8,000

[36] For these objections, see *inter al.* Penna (1982), 327; Solin (1983), 696–7; Schürer (1986), 95; Conzelmann (1987), 227; Lampe (1989), 368.

[37] Grant (1970), 189; Frend (1984), 401–5. For a precise breakdown of the 155, see Euseb. *HE* 6. 43. 11.

[38] e.g. b. Sanh. 32b. For discussion of these institutions, see Applebaum (1974), 461, 500.

present) at the public hearings conducted by Augustus into the fate of Herod's kingdom in 4 BCE[39] and its mass reception ('all Jewry' was present) of Herod's putative Hasmonaean son, Alexander, a few years later[40]—we find two types of expression routinely used to describe it. One centres on the word πᾶν (e.g. τὸ Ἰουδαϊκὸν ἅπαν as at *War* 2. 105), the other on τὸ πλῆθος, as, for instance, in τὸ Ἰουδαϊκὸν πλῆθος at *War* 2. 81 and τὸ πλῆθος τῶν αὐτόθι Ἰουδαίων at *Ant.* 17. 301. Of the implication of the first type of phrase there can be no doubt. But what of the second? Traditionally these expressions are translated 'the Jewish crowd' or, less flatteringly, 'the Jewish mob'.[41] But is that right? Although in both Classical and Koine Greek τὸ πλῆθος can have those meanings, equally it can be a precise, rather formal term for the community at large.[42] Acts uses the word several times in that sense, most notably in connection with the early Christian community in Jerusalem.[43] Can it be that Josephus' use of τὸ πλῆθος in connection with the Jews of Rome is comparable? General Judaeo-Greek usage is instructive here. If we examine the word in a number of such sources spanning half a millennium and more, we invariably find it used to denote the *entire* Jewish community. Thus, in 1 *Macc.* 8: 20 and 2 *Macc.* 11: 16, passages concerned with diplomatic interchanges between the Jews (of Judaea) and the Romans and Seleucids respectively, τὸ πλῆθος denotes the Jewish people as a whole. In the *Letter of Aristeas* 308, we find τὸ πλῆθος used to describe the totality of Alexandrian Jewry, formally assembled to celebrate the translation of the Septuagint.[44] In the so-called Helkias inscription from Egypt, a *psephisma* of uncertain date and origin, the enacting authority is the πλῆθος—a word interpreted by the latest editors of the document as the Jewish community.[45] And in a late fourth-century inscription (391 CE) from Apamea in northern Syria, the local Jewish community is referred to reverentially as πᾶν τὸ ἡγιασμένον ὑμῶν πλῆθος.[46] Since in Josephus the context never suggests that τὸ πλῆθος has to be

---

[39] Joseph. *War* 2. 80–1 and *Ant.* 17. 300–1.

[40] Joseph. *War* 2. 105 and *Ant.* 17. 330.

[41] For the latter, see e.g. Josephus (1981), 128.

[42] See under πλῆθος in Bauer (1952).

[43] Acts 6: 5, cf. 4: 32 and 6: 2. For discussion, Fitzmyer (1971), 290.

[44] The same term is used to describe the Jewish people in full assembly in Jerusalem in Aristeas' model for this passage—viz. 1 *Esdras* 38–41.

[45] See *JIGRE* no. 129 (comm. ad loc.).

[46] *CIJ* ii. no. 804 = Lifshitz (1967), no. 39. For a 3rd-cent. (?) example at Aphrodisias in Caria, see Reynolds and Tannenbaum (1987), 5, 38.

interpreted either vaguely as 'the crowd' or pejoratively as 'the mob', I can see no reason for not attributing to it its customary Judaeo-Greek meaning. If I am right in this, and Josephus' own use at *Ant.* 12. 107–8 of τὸ πλῆθος and τοὺς Ἰουδαίους ἅπαντας as synonymous expressions for Alexandrian Jewry in full and formal session suggests that I am, then we must conclude that Josephus never refers to the Jews of Rome except as a single community, acting in a united manner.

But it is not just Josephus' language that implies that Roman Jewry was an entity. The manner in which the Roman authorities dealt with the Jews of the capital strongly suggests that that was how they perceived them too. Augustus' famous concession to the Roman Jews over the collection of the corn dole (Philo informs us that they could collect it on another day if the distribution occurred on the Sabbath) was to *all* Jews in the capital regardless of the *proseuche* to which they were attached.[47] And when a few Jews were implicated in seriously criminal activity under Tiberius (they had defrauded a member of the high aristocracy), it was the whole community (πᾶν τὸ Ἰουδαϊκόν) that was held responsible and expelled from the city, not just the wrongdoers or the congregations to which they belonged.[48]

But if Roman Jewry was capable of functioning as a unity, how was it organized? Above I suggested that the Jews of Rome probably possessed some kind of supra-synagogal structure. What are the grounds for so thinking? First, there is the general likelihood that Roman Jewry was organized in the way common to large Jewish communities. The long-held but probably erroneous view that the Alexandrian-Jewish council was politeumatic,[49] and hence essentially *Greek*, has tended to obscure the fact that the central council, dealing mainly with broader issues of an administrative and legal nature, was and is a fairly regular feature of large, multicentred, *Jewish* communities. Examples, ancient, medieval, and modern, could be cited[50] but for my argument only those found in Judaea in the first centuries BCE and CE, the period when the Roman Jewish community was being built up mainly through

---

[47] Philo, *Leg. ad Gaium* 158.
[48] Joseph. *Ant.* 18. 83.
[49] Zuckermann (1985–8), 171–85; Lüderitz (1994), 208.
[50] For medieval Baghdad, see Krauss (1922), 139; for 16th-cent. Rome and 18th-cent. Piedmont, see Milano (1963), 466–7; for 19th-cent. British Jewry, see *Enc. Jud.*, s.v. 'Board of Deputies of British Jews'.

immigration from that area, need be mentioned here. Apart from the Sanhedrin itself, we might note the centralized organization of the sect known from the Qumran documents. General direction of the sectaries, interestingly sometimes referred to as רבים, a word closely analogous to τὸ πλῆθος,[51] lay with a small (possibly duodecimal) council.[52] Also of relevance is the structure attributed to the early, and therefore still predominantly Jewish, Christian church: from very early on the Jerusalem council under James and the Apostles is to be seen exercising authority over Christian groups not just throughout Judaea but even beyond.[53] Nor should we overlook Josephus' arrangements for the administration of Galilee during his short-lived control of the area in 66–7 CE. According to his account in *War* 2.571, a council of seventy old and wise men (τῶν γηραιῶν . . . τοὺς σωφρονεστάτους) was established to deal with capital cases and 'the larger issues'—τὰ μείζω πράγματα. Given that it was from Judaea that the greater part of the early Roman Jewish community was (unwillingly) drawn and that throughout its history it displayed a marked Palestinian orientation and was conspicuously conservative in its general outlook (on this, all our sources, pagan, Jewish, and Christian, agree), it seems reasonable to assume that in its organizational practices it would have been inclined towards traditionalism.

And that that was indeed the case is, I would argue, suggested by our one remaining type of evidence, Romano-Jewish titulature. Out of the dozens of (mainly third-century) Jewish epitaphs referring to community officials, a handful contain titles which have clear hierarchical connotations—ἀρχιγερουσιάρχης (archgerousiarch),[54] *archon alti ordinis* (archon of high rank),[55] and ἄρχων πάσης τιμῆς (archon of all honour).[56] Of these, the most interesting is archgerousiarch—a term not known until 1976 and hence unavailable to scholars such as Schürer and Frey. The most natural way of interpreting it, as its publisher and first editor perceived,[57] would

---

[51] Fitzmyer (1971), 290–1.
[52] Weinfeld (1986), 16–19.
[53] Grant (1970), 75–7.
[54] *JIWE* ii. no. 521.
[55] *CIJ* i. no. 470 = *JIWE* ii. no. 618. The arguments of Di Stefano Manzella against the Jewishness of this inscription (1989), 103–12, are not accepted here. Among the many difficulties posed by his thesis are the postulation of a name otherwise unknown in the Roman onomastikon (viz. Archon) and a title otherwise unattested, 'centurio alti ordinis'.
[56] *CIJ* i. nos. 85, 324, 337, and probably 216 = *JIWE* ii. nos. 259, 121, 164, and 265.
[57] Fasola (1976), 36–7.

be to assume that it points to an office higher than that of gerousiarch. Since the latter was the president of the synagogal board, it would follow that the archgerousiarch probably will have been the president of some supra-synagogal body. Customarily this interpretation is resisted, as, of course, it has to be if the collegiate status of the synagogues and hence the non-existence of a central council are to be maintained. Early commentators, in the main, chose to regard the title as a complete enigma.[58] Of late it has come increasingly to be taken as a synonym for gerousiarch—the prefix *arch* functioning, as it often does in the Koine, as a meaningless adjunct to the noun.[59] While that interpretation is possible, the fact remains that no Jewish examples of the usage have yet been attested and in Jewish sources generally *arch* always has a hierarchical function.[60] As for the other two officials, the archon of all honour and the archon of high rank, though the limitations of the evidence prevent us from determining what their role in Jewish Rome was, I can see no obstacle to viewing them as the members of a supra-synagogal council—the former representing one of the city's many Greek-speaking synagogues,[61] the latter perhaps a Latin-speaking congregation.

How big the council was, supposing that it existed, we have no means of knowing. One suspects, given the general history of the community, that its size will have been subject to frequent fluctuations. Immigration, a constant feature of our period,[62] will have led to the formation of new congregations.[63] Expulsions,[64] emigration,[65] and the high mortality rate among the poor of Rome[66] will have caused others to disappear. Whatever the size of the council,

[58] See e.g. Solin (1983), 696; Schürer (1986), 98.

[59] Horsley (1981–94), ii. 18–19; iii. 64; van der Horst (1991), 91.

[60] For the invariably hierarchical meaning of ἀρχιερεύς and ἀρχιερεῖς in a Jewish context, see Horsley (1981–94), ii. 18–19.

[61] That this official was of a higher status than the ordinary synagogal archon, is shown quite clearly by the sequence of offices in *CIJ* i. no. 337. Frey's view (*CIJ* i. lxxxix–xci) that he was a financial officer has been effectively disposed of by Leon (1960), 189–90.

[62] See e.g. Dio 57. 18. 5a (*c.*19 CE); the place-name index in *JIWE* ii, listing 3rd–4th-cent. data; and Vismara (1987), 119–21.

[63] Such, perhaps, as the synagogue of the Tripolitans. *CIJ* i. no. 390 = *JIWE* ii. no. 166.

[64] For a review of the evidence, see Smallwood (1976), 201–16.

[65] Acts 6: 9—synagogue of the Freedmen.

[66] On the transitory nature of plebeian associations at Rome, see Purcell (1994), 674.

there can be little doubt as to its general character. The aristocratic nature of the community[67] will have ensured that, like its Alexandrian counterpart, it was composed primarily of the great and good.

CONCLUSION

If we survey the evidence, literary and epigraphic, that relates to ancient Roman Jewry between the first century BCE and the third century CE, the overwhelming impression we get is of a community conservative in its values, wrapped up in its own affairs and, until 70 CE at least, focused on the Temple and Judaea. In Cicero[68] and Philo[69] we see it greatly concerned over the issue of the Temple tax, in Josephus, primarily exercised by the fate of Herod's kingdom and the arrival in Rome of a supposed Hasmonaean prince,[70] and in Suetonius we see it almost invariably treated as a *gens extera*, even though Jewish settlement at Rome by his time dated back over 150 years.[71] And Christian texts, such as the *Shepherd of Hermas* (early second century) bring out clearly just how very traditional in its outlook the strong Jewish element in the early Roman church could be.[72] The epigraphic evidence points in the same direction. If we did not know that it came from the heart of the imperial capital, it is unlikely that we would ever have guessed so. Only a minority of the texts is in Latin, values and iconography are overwhelmingly Jewish and overt signs of Roman cultural influence few and far between.[73] For a community whose origins go back over a quarter of a millennium, its 'isolation within the Roman environment' (the phrase is Momigliano's)[74] is very striking, and of crucial significance to anyone attempting to reconstruct its organization. Any

---

[67] On this, see Muñoz Valle (1972), 151–63.

[68] *Pro Flacc.* 66–7.

[69] *Leg. ad Gaium* 156–7.

[70] See above nn. 39–40.

[71] Note that the immediate context of the famous *impulsore Chresto* incident (*Vita Claud.* 25. 3–5) is Roman provincial problems. Cf. *Vita Iul.* 84. 5—Jews as part of the *exterarum gentium multitudo* at Caesar's obsequies.

[72] On Hermas, see Frend (1965), 194–5; on the implications to be drawn about traditional Jewish elements in the late 2nd-cent. Roman church from the quarrel over the dating of Easter, see Frend (1984), 340–2.

[73] *CIJ* i. no. 47 = *JIWE* ii. no. 486 for an allusion to the *ius trium liberorum*; *CIJ* i. no. 265 = *JIWE* ii. no. 322 for the phrase *honoribus omnibus functus*. Influence of clientela is probably to be seen in the titles Father (and Mother) of the Synagogue. See Williams (1994), 133–4.

[74] Momigliano (1962), 179–80.

valid hypothesis must take all this into account.[75] The one advanced
here, which deliberately stresses the Jewishness rather than the
Romanness of Roman Jewry, does that and it has the further
advantage over the collegiate hypothesis of also resting on a
whole raft of evidence. It is, of course, not entirely new. Juster
argued briefly for a centralized structure in 1914.[76] And in the 1920s
La Piana produced a whole series of studies, the purpose of which
was to demonstrate that monarchical episcopacy at Rome was
essentially Jewish in inspiration.[77] Unfortunately the evidence
adduced by those scholars was either inconclusive (e.g. the reference at Acts 28: 17 to τοὺς ὄντας τῶν Ἰουδαίων πρώτους)[78] or shown
to be invalid.[79] As a result, the whole 'centralist' case fell into
disrepute. Here I have attempted to re-establish it. The foundations
are now different. It is to be hoped that they may prove to be more
adequate.

[75] On the unromanized character of Roman Jewry, see now MacMullen (1993),
47–64.

[76] Juster (1914), i. 420–1 n. 3.

[77] For the complete list, see *CIJ* i. cii n. 1.

[78] Williams (1994), 130.

[79] The ἐξάρχων τῶν Ἑβρέων, first claimed by Juster (1914), i. 420–1 n. 3 as the
supreme head of Roman Jewry, was almost certainly simply a synagogal official. For
discussion, see *inter al.* Leon (1960), 189. And Mattithiah ben Heresh, whom Juster
cast in that role, was no more than the head of a rabbinical academy. So, correctly,
CIJ i. cvi.

15
The Gifts of God at Sardis

TESSA RAJAK

I. INTRODUCTION

The great late antique Sardis synagogue is often taken as a proof
and a symbol of the integration of a major, long-standing Jewish
community into its environment. A community of standing is
conjured up, allocated a former basilica in the heart of the city as
its synagogue, as early as the second century; a community, whose
worship in this edifice of marble and rich mosaic was, famously,
conducted hard up against the civic baths-gymnasium; a community which contributed to the city, producing, in the surviving
inscriptions alone, nine Sardian councillors among some thirty
donors.[1] Among its humbler members, this community could
number a maker of marble *menoroth* tellingly called Socrates.[2]
God-fearers, to be understood as sympathizers with Judaism or as
affiliates, emerge as an active part of the community, at least in their
operation as benefactors recorded on equal terms with others, just
as we find them in the comparable milieu of Aphrodisias.[3]

The terms acculturation, integration, and accommodation have
all been freely applied to this community.[4] There is much that we

This paper was reworked during a month spent as part of a research group at the
Institute for Advanced Studies, the Hebrew University, Jerusalem. For the excellent
environment, I must thank the director, David Shulman, as well as the organizers of
the group, Israel Shatzman and Uriel Rappaport. The latter, along with Daniel
Schwartz, discussed points of detail with me. I also owe thanks to Charlotte Roueché
for information and discussion and to Joyce Reynolds for her acute comments.

[1] For the figures, see Hanfmann (1972).
[2] See Kraabel's various papers in Overman and MacLennan (1992), esp. 'The
Impact of the Discovery of the Sardis Synagogue', 269–92 = Hanfmann 1983, 178–
90; Trebilco 1991: 37–54; Rajak 1992; Bonz 1990 and 1993.
[3] Reynolds and Tannenbaum (1987); note that *theosebeis* are not confined to the
list on face *b*: two are to be found among the Jews on face *a*.
[4] Though see now Barclay (1996), esp. 82–98, for some well-drawn distinctions
between the various concepts as applied to the Jewish Diaspora.

cannot know about the Sardian Jews and their world. Literary evidence is lacking, with the exception of the distorted picture which emerges from the writings of the anti-Jewish bishop Melito.[5] None the less, the situation at Sardis is better than many in that we are able to tie inscriptions up with fresh and thoroughly recorded (if not fully published) archaeology.

The excavations of 1958–75 produced a sizeable corpus of inscriptions naming over thirty donors of sections of the marble revetments, of the mosaic floor of the main hall and porch, and of individual items. All the texts are brief; those from the marble revetments had to be laboriously pieced together. Many of them lack names. They are only in part published. However, I have been able to see the texts and can discuss them here thanks to John H. Kroll.[6] These texts are usually ascribed to the third and fourth centuries, and understood by their first interpreters as emanating from at least three generations of Sardian donors. The phenomenon of the group donation, with many quite small donors, either in a list or, more often, inserting their names in a mosaic floor or decorated wall is readily paralleled, notably, from Berenice in Cyrenaica, from Apamea in Syria, and from sites in Palestine. This is by no means a specifically Jewish phenomenon, but Jewish communities seem to show a fondness for such equalizing modes of recording benefactions, which fit in with other detectable strategies to cut benefactors down to size.[7]

Kraabel has compellingly explored the apparent assimilation of Sardian Jewry. He has insisted that this is something quite different from syncretism, and he has seen the interaction as a two-way process, rightly mooting simultaneous Jewish influence on the pagan culture of Sardian society.[8] He locates this process in its late antique setting, seeing late antique paganism rather than Christianity as dictating the cultural tone of the city, and as allowing a particularly fruitful alliance between Jews and spiritually-minded pagans. This picture, though avowedly in part speculative, is an attractive one.

It may be possible to make a little further progress. The time has perhaps arrived to work towards a closer definition of the Sardian

[5] Kraabel in Overman and MacLennan (1992), 197–208.
[6] Kroll's numbering is used throughout for unpublished material.
[7] This phenomenon is explored in Rajak (1996).
[8] See esp. Kraabel (1978).

Jews' integration (to use a more neutral word for the phenomenon). Where were its limits? What, are we to imagine, kept the Jews as Jews? What distinguishing marks were attached to their public *personae*? At the same time, it is widely observable that, in many societies where Jews, as citizens, have been highly active in the wider society, there remain externally imposed limits on their participation—one thinks especially of post-enlightenment Germany and of Hapsburg Vienna. We shall never discover much of what these may have been in the case of late antique Sardis. But I would suggest that the inscriptions, together with their architectural context, expose traces of the mechanisms of self-differentiation, and thus produce a more nuanced picture. Here I look at a few points.

It is first worth pointing out, however, that some aspects of the established interpretation of the archaeological context remain open to question, and the general assessment has, indeed, recently been subjected to reinterpretation. The open-door character of the synagogue and the public character of the fountain are inferred from uncertain evidence: in the first case, a hypothetical archaeological reconstruction, in the second, the mere mention of the synagogue fountain in the city's list of fountains (*CIJ* 2. 751).

Again, there is the question of date: the synagogue's Severan origins have now been queried and, while its contiguity with the gymnasium is striking and visible for all to see, Boterman (1990) questions their coexistence, given that the third-century dating of the earliest inscriptions rests on the slender foundations of a single coin. A fuller reassessment is called for. She is at least correct in pointing out that the Aurelian names in the corpus can no longer be considered an adequate basis for this chronology. It does not seem possible, on the currently available publications, to judge the archaeological position, but Kroll's unpublished comments now support a lower chronology, and even a fourth-century start. The most extreme consequence of Boterman's proposed new framework could be to separate the synagogue from the period of functioning of the next-door gymnasium-baths altogether. Goodman (1994) goes the other way; his reading relies on identifying a variety of unique architectural and other features in the synagogue, and goes on to question whether we are dealing, until the very last phase, with Jews at all, rather than with a syncretizing group of monotheists, a meeting-place for some kind of sympathizers. However, there are no grounds for supposing that such people worshipped separately. Another weakness of this reading is that the limited knowledge of synagogue plans yielded by excavations suggests a very wide variety of type and perhaps even of function. None the less, this perhaps extreme reaction to the evidence serves well the purpose of drawing attention to the remaining uncertainties.

II. PRONOIA

The term *pronoia*, Providence, makes an unexpected appearance in eleven damaged Sardian texts, mostly from areas of marble wall facing, although one is from a wall mosaic and one from the base of a Menorah (ἑπταμύξιον).[9] Six of them are without names, while two individuals, Euphrosynos (Kroll 16 and 17) and Leontios (Kroll 22 and 23), each figure in a pair of texts. Leontios is described as a God-fearer, *theosebes* (Kroll 22). Some restoration is possible because these dedications clearly conform to a common pattern in spite of their variations. They incorporate a formula which appears to state that the donor is making his contribution out of the assets conferred on him by Divine Providence. Thus Leontios' first inscription, cast in the fullest form and apparently undamaged, reads: 'I Leontios, God-fearer, from the gifts of *pronoia*, in fulfil- ment of a vow, covered the bay (διαχώρον) with lozenges of marble (ἐσκούτλωτα).' Although *pronoia* stands alone, with the name of God left implicit, the interpretation is supported by a comparable inscription, the first to emerge from the excavations.[10] This inscrip- tion attracted the attention of Louis Robert, who published it promptly (1964: 48–9), followed by Lifshitz (1967: no. 20). Here a man whose name is missing, together with his wife Regina and his children, dedicates some area of facing (the text is damaged) along with painting, out of the gifts of Almighty God, ἐκ τῶν δωρεῶν τοῦ παντοκράτορος Θ(εο)ῦ.

The divine epithet Pantokrator, widespread both among Jews from the Septuagint on, but known in pagan cults, has been much discussed and requires no comment here. The gift ascription constitutes an established formula, and the sentiment was adopted into Christian epigraphic language, as we shall see. What is import- ant here is the appearance of a version in the Sardis synagogue

---

[9] Kroll nos. 12, 16–17, 19–24, 58, 66.
[10] Hanfmann (1972), 110.

whose structure matches the *pronoia* inscriptions so closely as to confirm that the gifts of God are referred to also there.

It should be stressed that the group of Sardian inscriptions which labels the ultimate source of wealth as *pronoia* is highly unusual in any wider context.[11] Kraabel (1996) has shown us that they, and the concept they incorporate, demand close attention, and he has offered a broad-ranging discussion in the context of the character of this cosmopolitan city. It should be stressed that my comments here rely on his work, even if they suggest a different emphasis. The connections drawn by Kraabel with late Greek thought are persuasive and illuminating: there is no doubt that *pronoia* was 'in the air'.[12] In particular, the possible role as cultural intermediary of the influential home-grown rhetor Eunapius, and of Chrysanthius, who lectured at Sardis, is not to be dismissed. But Kraabel goes considerably further than this, in two directions. First, he regards it as desirable to identify a single source of influence, thus arguing for the exclusivity of the pagan dimension. Second, *pronoia* is given considerable theological weight—a procedure which appears to gain justification when the keyword is printed with an initial capital *pi*. For, from these briefest of texts, the inference is drawn that *pronoia* was an independent cosmic force for the universally-minded Jews of Sardis; that this is not just an aspect of the Deity, but was capable of conveying in this milieu a complete conception of the supreme power. The difference is not a trivial one: the strong interpretation turns into key support for a Sardian Judaism intellectually and spiritually as well as socially indistinguishable from its pagan environment. However, a significantly different interpretation presents itself.

Pronoia has such an excellent Jewish-Greek pedigree that we discard it at our peril. Although the concept is virtually absent from the translated books of the Greek Bible and from the books of the New Testament (except as ascribed to Gallio the proconsul), it occupies a prominent position within other branches of the tradition. Kraabel himself provides ample documentation and even some enumeration, but is then at pains to marginalize the material on the very grounds of its scope and diversity. Yet that diversity in

---

[11] Paralleled it would seem only by recently discovered material from the synagogue at Philippopolis (Plovdiv), Bulgaria. See Kraabel (1996), 87.

[12] Cf. for some of the many late Greek philosophical and cultural ramifications of the concept, Sharples (1995).

no sense diminishes the significance of Philo's writing a dialogue on the subject. Of this dialogue only two fragments survive in Eusebius, one of them very short, but the rest exists in Armenian.[13] The work is in the form of a dialogue with one Alexander, perhaps Philo's brother or his better-known nephew Tiberius Julius, and it seems to have been among the most purely Greek of Philo's creations. Philo's arguments are Stoic in some of their technical detail, especially in his theory of attendant circumstances (ἐπακολουθημάτα, 43 ff.), and all the exempla are drawn from Greek literature and history, not from the Bible. They include familiar stories about Polycrates, Dionysius I the tyrant of Sicily, and the Sacred War of Philip of Macedon. Indeed, it has been observed that the mention of the author's pilgrimage is the only concrete Jewish element. None the less, Philo speaks consistently and unequivocally in terms of the one God—(ὁ) Θεός— and his purpose in writing is to show that His care for humankind is expressed in the ordering of Nature and the justice of the world, and that even the apparently detrimental or unjust has underlying beneficial consequences. In the same way, Philo in *De Opificio Mundi* (9) points to the beneficent *pronoia* presiding over creation as an inducement to faith. Thus Philonic Providence is comparable with the epigraphic agent that arranges for wealth to be allocated to those who will make good use of it.

In Josephus, the term is a common circumlocution for the name of God as beneficent planner and overseer, what we might call 'the management'. The form used is generally ἡ τοῦ Θεοῦ πρόνοια or ἡ Θεία πρόνοια. Occasionally, the adjective instead refers to the divine component. Thus, faced with conspiracy and revolt, Moses calls on God to demonstrate that all happens by His Providence, ὅτι πάντα σῇ προνοίᾳ διοικεῖται (*Ant.* 4. 47). The plot against Joseph by his brothers profaned, in Reuben's view, God's ubiquitous Providence μιανάντας αὐτοῦ τὴν πανταχοῦ παροῦσαν πρόνοιαν (*Ant.* 2. 24). That Josephus is also able to use *pronoia* in its regular Greek application to human action can scarcely be relevant to any consideration of the theological usage.[14]

Instances prior to Philo and Josephus, which show that the

---

[13] Philo, *De Providentia*, Loeb vol. 10. For the Armenian, we rely upon Aucher's 1822 edn. and Latin trans. I am grateful to Ian Rutherford for guiding me in this. For earlier doubts as to the authenticity of *De Prov.*, see Hadas-Lebel (1973), 23–46.

[14] *Contra* Kraabel 1996.

conception is well rooted in Jewish-Greek thought, have been noted by Trebilco (1991, 41–3 and nn.). These come from Daniel, the *Letter of Aristeas* 201, where Menedemus of Eritrea accepts the Jewish conception, and Second, Third and Fourth Maccabees, as well as the fifth Sibylline Oracle. Trebilco makes the sound observation that it was the term's double life, as both a powerful late Greek and an established Jewish conception, which made it a perfect fit for Sardis. His balanced assessment is worth quoting: 'the Jews recognized *pronoia* as a part of their tradition that was also understood by their contemporaries and which was thus a possible vehicle for communication.'

Yet the case for the Jewish-Greek heritage is not yet proven, for *pronoia tout court*, without mention of the name of God, as in the Sardis texts (with the Regina inscription speaking of Almighty God, but then not of *pronoia*) is arguably a different matter from the *pronoia* explicitly attached to the Deity, differentiating the epigraphy and the Jewish literary tradition. A closer look at the latter is necessary. In Josephus, the nearest to an absolute use occurs in the rendering of Balaam's oracle (*Ant.* 4. 114), where Providence is detached from God but this is still by the agency of God Himself: 'happy is this people to whom God grants possession of countless blessings and as ally and guide for all purposes his own Providence.' (Cf. *Ant.* 4. 185.)

Nearer to what we are looking for is one of the three appearances of *pronoia* in 4 Maccabees. Their presence is particularly significant for Sardis as closer in date, and not far off in milieu.[15] One of the martyred sons, as he dies, prays that 'the just Providence of our ancestors (πάτριος) will punish the tyrant' (9. 24). In the other instances (13. 19; 17. 22), divine *pronoia* instructs the new-born, in the one case, and redeems Israel, in the other. Jewish literature has therefore brought us within range of the inscriptions, but not right up to them. If we now direct our attention to their nature, the gap becomes perfectly intelligible. First, we should note that the name of God appears rarely in Jewish epigraphy: we might suspect a certain reluctance to deploy it. This preference would in itself constitute a reason to leave *pronoia* unqualified, quite apart from the sheer need for brevity (considering both the cost of the lettering and the limitations of the space).

[15] For the strong possibility of a 2nd-cent. date, and on the Antiochene provenance, see Rajak (1997).

Second, the context of benefaction may be seen as encouraging this particular term, since, the word itself figures prominently in donor epigraphy, as a designation for the care and concern of benefactors, and, again, sometimes as a description of the semi-formal responsibility of looking after a project.[16] The synagogue formula can be seen as consciously re-allocating the beneficence, giving current Greek terminology, which they must have known well, a deliberate and value-laden twist. If this is correct, the process is a very important one. Are there further examples?

III. THE GIFTS OF GOD

An equally notable aspect of our group of texts, and one which has not, to my knowledge, been discussed in a Jewish context, is the idea of donation as giving back to God what is His: the 'gifts of God' are returned to Him. This is a conception which is in keeping with what might be judged to be the general spirit of Jewish benefactions, with their tendency to indicate, by one means or another, a degree of reserve about munificence and to undercut the claims of donors (Rajak 1996); and it is one for which general, though not specific biblical models can be found in the many passages which stress that God is the ultimate source of wealth as of all other goods. The conception acquired a Christian currency, and was sometimes expressed in the neat form τὰ σὰ ἐκ τῶν σῶν.[17]

There does exist at least one uncertain case in the epigraphic record, where an ex-*primipilaris* from Aphrodisias, Flavius Euse-bius, offers a dedication containing our formula, with the same rare word δόμα as is found at Sardis, but prefaced by a phrase some-times considered pagan: Θε[.]ῷ ἐπηκόῳ; but the inscription is reckoned as possibly Jewish. Otherwise, this type of expression appears to belong in the Jewish and Christian spheres.[18] It

---

[16] Particularly common in the Hauran region. It is tempting to look to the secular sphere of *pronoia* in reading the Sardis material, giving a sense such as 'from the gifts he gave when in charge' which would refer to some kind of *summa honoraria*, or else perhaps 'from the funds he collected when in charge'. But Lifshitz 20 seems to preclude this, as does the lack of parallel.

[17] Discussed by Robert (1964). Cf. *SEG* 19 (old series; 1963), 719, a Christian monument from Lydia, probably 4th cent., and Robert, *Bulletin Épigraphique* 73 (1960), 196 and n. 364.

[18] Inscription in Rouéché (1989), 10; Reynolds and Tannenbaum (1987), appendix, no. 9; *SEG* 37 (1987), 851. On δόμα, see below. The religious affiliation

probably, therefore, originated in Jewish circles, though nowhere but at Sardis have we so far uncovered repeated appearances.

An important short text from Aegina concerning the building of a synagogue by a title-holder named Theodoros (*CIJ* 722 = Lifshitz 1), if correctly interpreted by Louis Robert,[19] reveals the extent to which the formula became a standard Jewish device (though not of course the only one) for speaking about a personal donation. For the inscription draws a contrast between the moneys contributed out of God's gifts, and those which had accrued from contributions, ἐκ τῶν Θεοῦ δωρέων and προσοδευ[θῆσαν]. It seems right to assimilate the 'gifts of God' formulae in the two cases. The alternative interpretation would make 'God's gifts' a designation for the synagogue treasury or for its accumulated offerings. But such an interpretation is scarcely possible in the cases, as at Sardis, where the formula is used in a personal construction.

At Sardis, there is another important Jewish marker, the unusual word δόμα or its plural δόματα for a gift or gifts, occurring in four of the texts (21, 22, 23, 58), where a more usual word such as δωρέα might have been expected. Epigraphic parallels are not numerous[20] and the literary appearances of δόμα and δόματα are Jewish, with two exceptions. There are three papyrological instances. In the Greek Bible, there is a special link both with the gifts made to God, as temple offerings, for example at Numbers 28.2, or else to his favours, as at Ecclesiastes 5. 18: καί γε πᾶς ἄνθρωπος, ᾧ ἔδωκεν αὐτῷ ὁ Θεὸς πλοῦτον καὶ ὑπάρχοντα . . . τοῦτο δόμα Θεοῦ ἐστιν. In the *Letter of Aristeas* (224), δόξα, the glory of kings, is the gift, δόμα, of God. We should not conclude that the epigraphic users of this somewhat specialized word were necessarily conscious of its precise origins. But what their practice reveals is its surviving connection with Judaism. Exactly what is meant in the inscriptions by 'God's gifts' is not self-evident. Is this just an allusion to the fulfilment of a vow? Yet in the case of Leontios a vow is specifically mentioned. Or again might some Diaspora tithing system lie behind the formula? The most likely is that the formula acknowledges God as the source

of the subject of *SEG* 41 (1991), 1593, from Arabia is unclear; a basilica is erected through his προνοίας καὶ σπουδῆς, and also ἐκ τῶν τοῦ θεοῦ.

[19] (1967), 49. However, Lifshitz disputes the interpretation. A related inscription, Lifshitz 723, is excessively restored. The Julia Severa inscription from Akmonia (*CIJ* 766; Lifshitz 33) yields the same combination in reverse: ἐκ τε τῶν ἰδίων καὶ τῶν συγκαταθεμένων.

[20] The word appears in the Aphrodisias text: see n. 21.

of wealth but that it is so wholly general and so conventional as to
not have any more specific applicability. Once again, however, what
stands out is the contrast with the expected. The usual run of Greek
donors, in any of the cities of the Roman empire, and even
including some few Jewish ones,[21] declare themselves proudly as
donating ἐκ τῶν ἰδίων and expect to be thanked for it. The gifts of
emperors or generals can also be referred to by such a formula. It
can only be a wholly deliberate departure when the Jews declare that
it is God who should be thanked.

IV. THE LABOURS OF THE EARLIER GENERATION

Sardis offers the opportunity to study a unified group of synagogue
inscriptions, albeit one consisting of less than a dozen items. At the
same time, we should remain alert to individual cases. A remarkable
fragmentary couplet (Kroll 58)[22] expands on the 'gifts of God' idea
in a strikingly free fashion: ἐκ τῶν τῆς προνοίας δομάτων | καὶ τῶν
γονικῶν ἡμῶν καμάτων. The gifts are represented as partnered by a
contribution from ancestral labours, mentioned second but equal, a
contribution curiously not seen as itself engendered by divine
beneficence. For a Jewish benefactor, there is apparently less
difficulty about praising these distant characters than praising
oneself. But who were they? It is difficult to say who is intended
by the term γονικῶν, whether ancestors who acquired merits and
transmitted them, according to something like the rabbinic principle
of *zechut avoth*; or those who had passed on a family inheritance,
direct ancestors or even parents. The Greek can mean all these
things. The former would be more logical, avoiding the criticism
voiced above; but inscriptions are not always logical. In any event,
the term is a resonant one; it and its cognates, especially γονεῖς and
προγονικός, are repeatedly applied to the patriarchs and the virtuous
individuals of yore in Israel, both in the Greek Bible, and in the
Maccabaean literature and Josephus.[23] Especially in the slightly
literary context of this small inscription, the word brings a particular
flavour with it. The obligation to the past is evoked, in the context
of a firm moral assertion that labour and not status truly empowers.

---

[21] Notably Polycharmos of Stobi, who uses the phrase ἐκ τῶν οἰκείων χρημάτων
(*CIJ* i. 694; Lifshitz 10).
[22] The lines have been thought to be intended as verse.
[23] See e.g. 3 Macc. 7: 7; 4 Macc. 2: 10; Joseph. *C. Apion.* 2. 217.

And we meet once more the familiar twist, for often enough Greek inscriptions expatiate upon the κάματα of those individuals who have benefited the city by their contributions and their organization, very often in the parallel phrase ἐκ τῶν ἰδίων καμάτων.[24]

V. CONCLUSION

The Sardian Jews could not have marked themselves off and asserted their own identity in small but significant ways in their benefaction formulae, if they had not been well acquainted with the world of Graeco-Roman euergetism. But they were capable also of deploying forms of expression characteristic of Greek-speaking Jewry at large and, it seems, of evolving new ones. That, in doing this, they evince certain local peculiarities is unsurprising. Regional patterns are as marked a characteristic of Jewish as of general epigraphy. It is another question how far ordinary pagan citizens of late-antique Sardis understood this subtle code, if indeed they did sometimes look into the great synagogue or drink at its fountain.

[24] See Le Bas-Waddington 2004.

16

Dissonance and Misunderstanding in Jewish–Roman Relations

SACHA STERN

It is to be expected that Jews and Romans will not always have understood each other, either because of their linguistic, cultural and religious differences, or because of the intrinsically different perspectives of ruler and of ruled. This paper is concerned, however, not with misunderstanding itself, but rather with its social and political consequences: i.e. to what extent did cultural difference (or 'dissonance') and misunderstanding between Jews and Romans[1] affect them or hinder them in their social and political relations?

The historical implications of such a question, which would also be applied to other areas of the Roman empire, should not be underrated. From a Roman perspective, mutual understanding must have been an essential condition for effective provincial government and administration. From a Jewish (or other provincial) perspective, mis/understanding of the Romans must have been an essential ingredient in political and cultural processes such as integration, syncretism, and 'Romanization'.

The best way to identify misunderstanding and its socio-political effects would be to capture at once the Roman and Jewish perspectives on the same events or mutual transactions. Unfortunately, and I should add, predictably, evidence to this effect is difficult to find. In the first section of this chapter I will examine a Roman imperial coin and a passage from the Mishnah which each present their own perspective on the same historical event; but cases such as

I am grateful in particular to Daniel Sperber, also to Martin Goodman, Benjamin Isaac, and Daniel Schwartz, for their constructive and challenging remarks.

[1] By 'Romans' I do not necessarily mean Romans from the city of Rome, but rather all the representatives of Roman imperial rule. As to 'Jews', for reasons of scope this paper will be restricted to the evidence of early rabbinic literature.

these are hard to come by. This paper, therefore, should be
regarded as experimental and illustrative rather than as comprehensive or conclusive. My aim, at present, is to raise questions
rather than to answer them.

THE PLOUGHING OF THE CITY

History text-books tell us that when the city of Aelia Capitolina was
founded by Hadrian on the site of Jerusalem, a plough was driven
through it as part of its foundation ritual.[2] A description of this
ritual is to be found in the works of Cato and Varro, and then later
in Servius' commentary on Virgil's *Aeneid*.[3] It consisted in driving a
plough, drawn by a cow and a bull, round the circuit of the new city;
the object of the ritual was to mark out the city walls and/or its
pomerium.

Evidence that this ritual was actually performed at the foundation of Aelia Capitolina is, however, slender. Servius (4. 212),
writing *c*.400 CE, refers to this custom as 'ancient' (*moris antiqui*),
but already Cato and Varro, writing in the second and first
centuries BCE respectively, describe it in the past tense. These
sources do not convince us, therefore, that this rite would still
have been practised by Roman rulers in the second century CE.
More informative, perhaps, is a series of coins that were minted in
Aelia and that commemorated its foundation. The first in this
series was minted under Hadrian, and shows on the reverse a
figure ploughing with two bulls (or possibly, as in Cato's account,
with a cow and a bull), and the legend: COL(onia) AEL(ia)
KAPIT(olina) COND(ita).[4] Still, this does not tell us that the site
of Jerusalem was *actually* ploughed at the foundation of Aelia: the
ploughing image on this coin may be no more than a *symbolic*
motif.

Rabbinic sources, on the other hand, record the ploughing of
Jerusalem as an event that actually took place. In the Mishnah
(redacted less than a century later), it is counted as one of the five
national disasters which occurred on the date of the 9th of Av:

---

[2] Schürer (1973), 550–1 and nn. 163–4; Smallwood (1976), 459 and nn. 121–2.
Whether this took place before or after the Bar Kokhba Revolt is irrelevant to this
paper.
[3] Varro, *Lingua Latina* 5. 143; Servius *ad Verg. Aen.* 4. 212 and, citing Cato, 5. 755.
[4] Kadman (1956), 53–4.

Five things happened to our fathers . . . on the 9th of Av . . .:
1. it was decreed against our fathers that they would not enter the land [of Israel];
2–3. the Temple was destroyed, the first and the second time;
4. Betar was captured;
5. the City was ploughed (m. Taanit 4: 6).

The 'City' in question is likely to be Jerusalem, as it is referred to in this way elsewhere in the Mishnah.[5] Indeed, according to a tradition quoted in the Talmuds, it was specifically the site of the Temple that was ploughed, by the infamous Turnus Rufus (alias Tineius Rufus, who was contemporary with the Bar Kokhba Revolt—y. Taan. 4: 7, 69b, b. Taan. 29a; the same account is found in Jerome, *In Zach.* 8. 18–19, who cites the rabbinic tradition virtually word for word). This alternative tradition not only confirms the identification of the 'City' in the Mishnah with Jerusalem, but also the timing of this event around the Bar Kokhba Revolt (as already implicit in the Mishnah itself, with the juxtaposition of this event with the capture of Betar). Thus the Mishnah's 'ploughing of the city' corresponds, most probably, to the Hadrianic ploughing of Jerusalem depicted on the Aelia coin.

It is tempting to believe that rabbinic sources would have seen the ploughing of Jerusalem as the fulfilment of Micah's prophecy that 'Zion will be ploughed like a field' (Micah 3: 12; also cited in Jer. 26: 18). This rather obvious association, indeed, is made by Pseudo-Rashi (ad b. Taan. ib.) (12th century?) and again, quite independently from him, by Maimonides (late twelfth century) in his code (*Laws of Fast Days* 5. 3). One wonders why it was not made in earlier rabbinic sources.[6]

The point I wish to make, however, is that the Mishnah interprets the ploughing of Jerusalem as a *destructive* act: it is listed, indeed, alongside the destruction of the Temples and of Betar. In the Aelia coin, by contrast, ploughing is interpreted as a *constructive* act; indeed, its legend associates it with the *foundation* of the new city.[7]

---

[5] See m. Shek. 4: 2; m. Sanh. 1: 5; m. Zeb. 5: 6–8; and above all, this same mishna (m. Taan. 4: 6), earlier in the text (not cited above). It is less likely that the 'City' refers here to the city of Betar.

[6] It is found in one MS version of the Babylonian Talmud, fragmentary MS Göttingen (approx. 13th cent.): see Malter (1930), 137. But as Malter comments, this is obviously a scribal interpolation.

[7] As pointed out by Kadman (1956), ibid.—notwithstanding that according to Servius (4. 212) the same ritual of ploughing *could* have been used for both symbolic

This contrast illustrates how a traditional Roman ritual could be invested, by Jewish onlookers, with almost its opposite interpretation. Obviously, this largely reflected their conflicting *political* standpoints: the Roman foundation of Aelia would naturally have been equated, by the Jews, with the destruction of Jerusalem. But the Mishnah's reinterpretation of a specific aspect of the Roman ritual—the act of ploughing—also reflects something of its own, distinctive cultural milieu. The practice of founding cities, indeed, is alien to rabbinic culture and tradition; moreover, to my knowledge, foundations of Hellenistic and Roman cities, including of Aelia itself, are almost totally ignored in rabbinic literature.[8] In the Babylonian Talmud, for instance, the Romans are praised (or praise themselves) for having built markets, bridges, and baths,[9] but not for having founded cities[10]—by contrast with Graeco-Roman literature where the foundation of cities is presented as a major source of imperial *kudos* and fame.[11] The context of rabbinic culture dictated, therefore, that the ploughing of an already existing city would not be interpreted as a symbol of its new foundation. It was more natural, for the Mishnah, to interpret it as a symbol of its eradication. Thus the contrast between the Aelia coin and the mishnaic passage distinctly reflects, I would argue, *cultural* discordance or 'dissonance' between the Roman and the Jewish rabbinic perspectives.[12]

Yet in political terms, the significance of this cultural dissonance was probably minimal. Whether the act of ploughing was inter-

purposes; cf. Schürer (1973). The motif of ploughing as a destructive act is found elsewhere in rabbinic sources; see b. Yoma 69a on the destruction of Mount Gerizim.

[8] Samuel Krauss can find only one reference to Hellenistic and Roman foundations of cities (but not including that of Aelia), in a relatively late source: Midrash Tehilim, 9: 7, in both recensions (Krauss (1948), 10–14). The biblical account of the foundation of cities by the tribes of Gad, Reuven, and Menashe (Num. 32: 34–42) receives virtually no treatment in early rabbinic sources. This silence is in my view significant. See also b. A.Zar. 10a, on the grant of colonial status to the city of Tiberias.

[9] b. Shab. 33b; b. A.Zar. 2b. Curiously, I have not found any parallels to these pasages in Palestinian sources.

[10] As Daniel Sperber points out to me, the building of roads is also, curiously, omitted.

[11] See e.g. Aelius Aristides' *Oration to Rome*, 93–101, in Oliver (1953).

[12] There is no evidence that the authors of the Mishnah actually *misunderstood* the Roman ritual, in the sense that they did not know that it really signified, to the Romans, an act of ritual foundation. But whether they knew this or not, the Roman perspective appears to have been to them of no importance.

preted as the destruction of Jerusalem or as the foundation of Aelia did not really affect, in substance, the political message which the Roman authorities were attempting to convey: namely, that Jerusalem was now irreversibly in Roman hands. We may thus conclude that communication between ruler and ruled effectively prevailed, in this case, over their minor cultural differences.

One further point. In comparison with the other items listed in the same mishnaic passage, i.e. the destruction of the first and second Temples and the quashing of the Bar Kokhba Revolt in Betar, the ploughing of the city—a merely symbolic ritual—strikes one as remarkably insignificant. The inordinate importance given to this event in this passage may be related, I would tentatively suggest, to the Aelian coin itself. Between the Bar Kokhba Revolt (in the 130s CE) and the middle of the third century, the 'ploughing of Aelia' coin type was minted again on a number of occasions;[13] it was thus sufficiently common to have been known to the Jews and rabbis of Palestine, and to have played a significant part, I would suggest, in the making of the mishnaic tradition. Firstly, this coin may have conveyed to the rabbis the very notion that Jerusalem had been ploughed (whether actually or only in a figurative sense).[14] Secondly, the frequent circulation of this coin type may have had the effect of magnifying the *perceived* historical importance of the ploughing of Jerusalem, to the extent that it came to be listed in the Mishnah alongside some other, major historical events. Which leads us to an additional observation of some importance to Roman historians: that the Roman imperial practice of using coinage as a medium for political propaganda may have been, in this case, effective.[15]

[13] According to Kadman (1956), 81, seventeen specimens of the above-mentioned Hadrian coin are known. The same type was minted again in the reigns of Marcus Aurelius, Macrinus, Elagabalus, and Hostilianus (the latter in 250–1 CE) (Kadman (1956), 80–119, nos. 1, 43, 97, 111, 112, 194).

[14] Whether or not Jerusalem was ever actually ploughed is a secondary question which I shall not attempt to answer. The extent to which Palestinian rabbis would have understood the Latin legends of the Aelia coins, particularly the reference to the notion of *foundation* ('CONDita') in Hadrian's Aelia coin (see Kadman 1956), is debatable. But this is irrelevant to our question, inasmuch as the legend would have prevented the Mishnah from *reinterpreting* the act of ploughing in its own way, as I have outlined above. (Post-Hadrianic issues bear the legend: COL AEL KAPIT COMM(odiana); see again Kadman.)

[15] On the use of coin types for imperial propaganda, see Sutherland (1959), 46–55; Levick (1982), 104 (*n.v.*); Sutherland (1986), 85–93. Sutherland (1959), 53; (1986), 93 argues that coin types and legends were deliberately selected so as to be

THE GIFT

In the case I will now present, by contrast, cultural misunderstanding between Jew and Roman was detrimental to the effectiveness of their transaction. This episode, recounted in both Talmuds, is set in the mid or late third century and probably in Tiberias; it does not relate to historical events on a national scale, but rather to mundane transactions between individual rabbis and Roman rulers.[16]

The text in the Palestinian Talmud translates as follows: 'A *ducenar[ius]* honoured Rabbi Yudan the Patriarch with a plate full of dinars. He took one of them and returned the rest. He asked Rabbi Shimon ben Lakish, who said to him: cast it [lit., its benefit] into the Dead Sea' (y. A.Zar. 1, 1, 39b). The office of *ducenarius* was relatively high-ranking in the provincial administration of the Roman empire;[17] we must bear in mind, however, that rabbinic sources are not always accurate in their usage of such titles.[18] There is no reason to assume that this *ducenarius* was offering an official gift as the representative of Rome,[19] rather than acting simply on his own behalf.

R. Shimon b. Lakish instructed that the coin, or any benefit deriving from it, should be 'cast into the Dead Sea'—i.e. be destroyed. His reasons are not given in the story, but the talmudic redactor implies, from the context within which this story appears, that the occasion of this gift was a pagan festival.[20] The Mishnah

understood by their various recipients throughout the Roman empire; but as to whether they would have been trusted and believed—in other words, whether this propaganda medium was actually effective—Sutherland finds himself unable to answer (1959), 54.

[16] On this episode see Blidstein (1972), 150–2.

[17] From the 3rd cent. onwards, it also denotes an honorary title which could be granted to lower-ranking officials: see for instance *Cod. Theod.* 8. 4. 3, 10. 7. 1, 10. 20. 1, 12. 1. 5; Pflaum (1960), 948–52. See also Vegetius, *Milit.* 2. 8 (late 4th cent.), where the title denotes a relatively low-ranking military commander. I am grateful to Benjamin Isaac for his remarks.

[18] As pointed out to me by Daniel Sperber.

[19] As according to Blidstein (1972), 152.

[20] Blidstein (1972) (cf. also Mireille Hadas-Lebel (1979), 429) suggests that the *ducenarius* was offering R. Yudan the traditional *strenae* at the *kalendae* of January. However, other possibilities should also be considered. Gifts of this kind were common at Saturnalia and on birthdays (Saller (1982), 55, 123), which are also considered pagan festivals in m. A.Zar. 1: 2. The Talmud's failure to state explicitly that the occasion of this gift was a pagan festival is probably not significant, for as Blidstein rightly points out (1972), 151 n. 10, a similar phenomenon occurs at the end of y. Betza.

forbids commercial transactions with pagans on their festivals, for the reason that this might increase their idolatrous rejoicing.[21] Borrowing from non-Jews on their festivals is also forbidden by the Mishnah, because, the Palestinian Talmud explains, if a non-Jew lends he earns a good reputation,[22] and this may again increase his idolatrous festivities. In our story, it appears that R. Shimon b. Lakish extended the prohibition to *receiving gifts* from non-Jews on their festivals. R. Yudan should not have accepted, therefore, the *ducenarius'* coin.[23]

The fact that R. Yudan consulted with R. Shimon b. Lakish after the event suggests that he was aware himself that he might not have acted correctly. The Talmud goes on to object, however, that R. Yudan should have been allowed to accept this gift, because the ducenarius knew him personally, and in this case it was obvious that they were only flattering each other,[24] i.e. acting without sincerity and in self-interest; hence, acceptance of such a gift would not have enhanced the non-Jew's festivities. These conflicting considerations may explain why R. Yudan had hesitated at the time, and why he had cautiously accepted one coin.

The Babylonian Talmud presents the same characters[25] in a similar dilemma, but in a different order of events:

A certain gentile (*min*) sent an imperial[26] *dinar* (*denarius*) to Rabbi Yehuda the Patriarch on his festival day. Resh Lakish was seated before him. He

---

[21] m. A.Zar. 1: 1. This reason is also implicit in t. A.Zar. 1: 3, and at the end of y. A.Zar. 1: 1, 39b (l. 8 from bottom).

[22] y. A.Zar. 1: 1, 39b (l. 32 from bottom): מפני שהוא כמשיאו שם.

[23] This explanation may be implicit in the story itself, inasmuch as the phrase 'cast into the Dead Sea' which R. Shimon ben Lakish is said to have used derives from a *baraita* y. A.Zar. 1: 4, 39c; also in t. A.Zar. 3: 19, etc.) which refers, similarly, to objects purchased at pagan fairs (see also m. A.Zar. 3: 3 and 3: 9).

[24] As according to a *baraita* quoted by the Talmud just before the story, which uses the phrase [להן] כמחניף (להן is unsound and should be deleted, as it clearly originates from a textual omission in MS Leiden having been re-inserted in a marginal note in the wrong place; for the correct text see Tosafot ad b. A.Zar. 2a s.v. *assur*, R. Asher (*Rosh*) ad loc., etc.). This phrase ostensibly refers to the Jew flattering the non-Jew, but I would assume that in a situation where it is a non-Jew who does a favour to a Jew (and thereby earns a good reputation), his reputation is tarnished if *he* appears to be only flattering the Jew. The ambiguity of the text allows for this 'open' interpretation.

[25] 'R. Yehuda' and 'Resh Lakish' are the Babylonian equivalent to 'R. Yudan' and 'R. Shimon b. Lakish'. The substitution of *min* for *ducenar* is typical of the Babylonian Talmud, and reflects its lack of interest in Roman technical terms: see Kimelman (1981), 230–1.

[26] My suggestion for קיסרנאה. See Blidstein (1972), 150 n. 3.

said: 'What shall I do? If I accept it, he will go and thank [his god]; if I do not accept it, it will cause resentment.'
Resh Lakish answered: 'Take it and throw it before him in a pit.'
He said: 'This will cause him all the more resentment!'
'I mean, do it with the back of your hand' [i.e. as though by accident]   (b. A.Zar. 6b).

Here, it is explicit that the occasion of the gift was a pagan festival; the gentile is said to have sent only one coin. More importantly, R. Yehuda is said to have acted from the outset on the advice of Resh Lakish:[27] the question was, how to refuse the coin without causing the Roman officer's resentment (איבה). It was taken for granted, however, that accepting this gift would be forbidden, because this would cause the gentile to 'go and thank' his god (אזיל ומודה).[28]

Assuming that this story, in one of its variant versions, did actually happen—what would have been the perspective of the Roman official? In the absence of evidence, we can only advance a reasonable hypothesis. The practice of gift-giving, widespread in the Roman empire, could serve a number of socio-political functions: depending on the relative status of donor and recipient, it could be a way of seeking either patronage, or friendship, or—as an act of munificence or largess—the loyalty and dependence of the recipient. This ducenarius may have been a high-ranking official, but in third-century Jewish Palestine, the Patriarch was also a relatively high-ranking figure in his own right.[29] Thus it is possible that the *ducenarius* intended, by sending this gift, to seek the political friendship of R. Yudan. As was customary among pagans, he may have chosen to send this gift on the occasion of a birthday or of some other festival,[30] which would have been regarded by him either as propitious, or merely as a socially

[27] This seems rather like white-washing. In general terms, halachic concepts are given more emphasis in this version; this version shows more signs of literary recasting than the version of the Palestinian Talmud.

[28] R. Menahem ha Meiri (in *Beit ha Behira*) comments on this passage that since R. Yehuda was an important person, his acceptance of the gift would have been a source of pleasure to the gentile (cf. b. Kidd. 7a). 'Lest he goes and thanks his god' is also the reason given in b. A.Zar. 6b (attributed to Rava) for the Mishnaic prohibition of borrowing from non-Jews on non-Jewish festivals.

[29] See Levine (1979); also Levine (1989), 186–91.

[30] See Saller (1982). On gifts by imperial officials of dishes and coins in the later empire (4th–7th cents.), see Kazhdan (1991), s.v. 'largess' and 'largitio dishes', pp. 1178–80.

acceptable pretext for sending gifts. Either way, the religious significance of this occasion may actually have been quite limited.

Successful interaction between the Patriarch and the Roman official was frustrated, however, by mutual misunderstanding. The *ducenarius* apparently did not realize that if he had sent the gift on another day, R. Yudan would have gladly accepted it. And R. Yudan's concern that accepting a gentile's gift would enhance his festive, idolatrous rejoicing or cause him to 'go and thank his god'—which led to his semi-refusal of the gift—*may* have had limited relevance to the reality of pagan religious behaviour.[31]

The *ducenarius* could not have been happy to hear that R. Yudan had only accepted one coin (as in the Palestinian version).[32] Nor could he have been happy to hear (as in the Babylonian version) that R. Yudan had dropped the coin into a pit. If this gift had been intended to earn his friendship, then by sending it back or throwing it away, R. Yudan may have wasted an attractive political opportunity. Cultural misunderstanding led this transaction, therefore, to an abortive outcome.

CONCLUSION

Whilst it is impossible to generalize from the two, very different cases I have examined, we may look at them as suggestive illustrations of the difficulties which Jews and Romans would have encountered in their socio-political relations. It so happens that in the case of the ploughing of Jerusalem, the Jewish reinterpretation of the foundation ritual of Aelia did not detract, in real terms, from the political message which the Roman government was attempting to

[31] R. Yudan appears to have been unaware of this possibility, and likewise his colleague. It is clear, at least in the Babylonian version, that R. Yudan's course of action was not dictated by rigid and 'ready-made' rules, but rather by a sincere concern that if he accepted the gift, the ducenarius would actually 'go and thank his god'. His refusal of the gift may well have resulted, therefore, from a *misunderstanding* of the *ducenarius*' intentions. By contrast, some Babylonian rabbis are reported in the same talmudic tractate to have acted leniently because they knew that the non-Jew would not worship *avoda zara* (R. Yehuda and Rava, in b. A.Zar. 64b–65a). Nevertheless, on the rabbinic tendency to regulate their relations with non-Jews on the sole basis of internalized, pre-conceived halakhic categories, see my discussion in Stern (1994), 194–8.

[32] In the absence of evidence to the contrary, it is plausible that gifts of this kind were meant to be accepted in their entirety. Blidstein (1972), 152, surmises that taking only one coin must have been the accepted practice, but he provides no evidence to this effect.

convey. On the contrary, I have suggested that imperial propaganda may have been successfully conveyed, in this case, through the medium of imperial coinage.

The episode of the gift is more representative, perhaps, of ordinary Jewish–Roman interactions. Considering that gift-giving was an important method, for Roman imperial officials, to secure the friendship and loyalty of local, provincial magnates, this episode reveals a relative failure to implement it in the case of the Jewish Patriarchs. It epitomizes the difficulties which the Romans would have generally experienced in the administration of the Jewish province.[33]

I would not dismiss the possibility that similar problems existed among other peoples in other Roman provinces, certainly in the early, formative stages of the empire. But the persistence of such misunderstandings as late as the third century was more specific to Palestinian Jews, and resulted from their deliberate resistance to Romanization and to political integration into the Roman empire. By refusing the Roman's gift, R. Yudan may well have been wasting a political opportunity—but then again, he would not have been too upset about it.

---

[33] It would be interesting to know how the Patriarchs reacted when the Roman authorities awarded them senatorial and high imperial honorary titles at the end of the 4th and in the early 5th cents., as mentioned in imperial legislation dating from 392 to 415 (see *Cod. Theod.* 16. 8. 8, 11, 13, 15, 22; Linder (1987), 188–9 n. 7, 221–2 n. 3, 271 n. 7). They certainly could not have ignored these awards, since they were sent *codicilli* (documents) as tangible confirmation of their titles (*Cod. Theod.* 16. 8. 22). Unfortunately rabbinic sources have nothing to tell us on this, just as, in fact, they have nothing to tell us about the Patriarchs of the period (R. Yehuda IV and R. Gamliel VI: see Bacher (1914), 206 n. 12). Incidentally, this silence of rabbinic sources is not necessarily due to a change, in the 4th cent., in the sages' attitude towards the Patriarch and a loss of interest towards him, as often argued (see most recently Levine (1996), esp. n. 17), but may be due to the simple reason that all the classical early rabbinic works were redacted before the 390s (i.e. the Mishnah, Tosefta, halachic *Midrashim*, and even the Palestinian Talmud according to Sussman (1990), 132–3) or not much later (i.e. Genesis Rabba, Leviticus Rabba, Lamentations Rabba, Pesikta de R. Kahana: see Strack and Stemberger (1991)); they are likely, therefore, to have predated this historical event. Later Palestinian rabbinic works, which were redacted in subsequent centuries, were mainly literary adaptations of older sources; as a result, they would not normally refer to historical events post-dating the mid-4th century.

Works Cited

1. Jews, Greeks, and Romans

Bowersock, G. W. (1980), 'A Roman Perspective on the Bar Kochba War', in W. S. Green (ed.), *Approaches to Ancient Judaism* (Chico, Calif.), ii. 131–41.

Chadwick, H. (1952), *Origen: Contra Celsum* (Cambridge).

Cohen, S. J. D. (1981–2), 'Epigraphical Rabbis', *JQR* 72: 1–17.

——(1987a), *From the Maccabees to the Mishnah* (Philadelphia).

——(1987b), 'Pagan and Christian Evidence on the Ancient Synagogue', in L. I. Levine (ed.), *The Synagogue in Late Antiquity* (Philadelphia), 159–81.

——(1993), ' "Those who say they are Jews and are not." How do you know a Jew in Antiquity when you see one?', in S. J. D. Cohen and E. S. Frerichs (eds.), *Diasporas in Antiquity* (Atlanta, Ga.), 1–45.

Cotton, H. M., Cockle, W. E. H., and Millar, F. G. B. (1995), 'The Papyrology of the Roman Near East', *JRS* 85: 214–35.

Foerster, G. (1976), 'Art and architecture in Palestine', in S. Safrai and M. Stern (eds.), *The Jewish People in the First Century* (Assen), ii. 971–1006.

Gager, J. G. (1972), *Moses in Graeco-Roman Paganism* (Abingdon).

Goodenough, E. R. (1953–68), *Jewish Symbols in the Graeco-Roman Period*, 13 vols. (New York).

Goodman, M. D. (1983), *State and Society in Roman Galilee, A.D. 132–212* (Totowa).

——(1987), *The Ruling Class of Judaea: The Origins of the Jewish Revolt against Rome, A.D. 66–70* (Cambridge).

——(1990), 'Sacred Scripture and "Defiling the Hands" ', *JTS* 41: 99–107.

——(1997), *The Roman World, 44 BC–AD 180* (London).

Hengel, M. (1974), *Judaism and Hellenism: Studies in their Encounter in Palestine during the Early Hellenistic Period*, trans. J. Bowden, 2 vols. (London).

Kadman, L. (1960), *The Coins of the Jewish War of 66–73 CE* (Tel Aviv).

Kloner, A. (1996), *Mareshah* (in Hebrew; Jerusalem).

Kraabel, A. T. (1982), 'The Roman Diaspora: Six Questionable Assumptions', *JJS* 33: 445–64.

——(1996), 'Pronoia at Sardis', in B. Isaac and A. Oppenheimer (eds.), *Studies on the Jewish Diaspora in the Hellenistic and Roman Periods* (*Te'uda*, xii) (Tel Aviv), 75–83.

KRAELING, C. H. (1956), *The Excavations at Dura Europus: Final Report:* viii, pt. 1, *The Synagogue* (New Haven).

LEWIS, N. (1989), *The Documents from the Bar Kokhba Period in the Cave of Letters: Greek Papyri* (Jerusalem).

LIEU, J., NORTH, J., and RAJAK, T. (1992) (eds.), *The Jews among Pagans and Christians in the Roman Empire* (London).

LINDER, A. (1987) (ed.), *The Jews in Roman Imperial Legislation* (Detroit, Mich., and Jerusalem).

LÜDERITZ, G. (1983), *Corpus Jüdische Zeugnisse aus der Cyrenaika* (Wiesbaden).

MESHORER, Y. (1982), *Ancient Jewish Coinage*, 2 vols. (New York).

MILLAR, F. (1993), *The Roman Near East, 31 BC–AD 337* (Cambridge, Mass., and London).

NAVEH, J. (1992), '*Al heres ve-gome: ketuvot Aramiyot ve-'Ivriyot mi-yeme Bayit sheni, ha-Mishnah veha-Talmud* (Jerusalem).

NETZER, E., and WEISS, Z. (1994), *Zippori* (Jerusalem).

NEUSNER, J., FRERICHS, E. S., and GREEN, W. S. (1987), *Judaisms and their Messiahs at the Turn of the Christian Era* (Cambridge).

RUTGERS, L. V. (1995), *The Jews in Late Ancient Rome: Evidence of Cultural Interaction in the Roman Diaspora* (Leiden).

SANDERS, E. P. (1992), *Judaism: Practice and Belief, 63 BCE–66 CE* (London and Philadelphia).

SCHÄFER, P. (1981), *Der Bar Kokhba Aufstand: Studien zum zweiten Jüdischen Krieg gegen Rom* (Tübingen).

SCHIFFMAN, L. H. (1991), *From Text to Tradition: A History of Second Temple and Rabbinic Judaism* (Hoboken, NJ).

SCHÜRER, E. (1973–87), *The History of the Jewish People in the Age of Jesus Christ*, rev. and ed. G. Vermes *et al.*, 3 vols. (Edinburgh).

STERN, E. (1993) (ed.), *New Encyclopaedia of Archaeological Excavations in the Holy Land*, 4 vols. (Jerusalem).

VERMES, G. (1977), *The Dead Sea Scrolls: Qumran in Perspective* (London).

——(1997), *The Complete Dead Sea Scrolls in English* (Harmondsworth).

WACHOLDER, B. Z. (1974), *Eupolemus: A Study of Judaeo-Greek Literature* (Cincinnati).

2. JEWS, GREEKS, AND ROMANS IN THE THIRD SIBYLLINE ORACLE

ALEXANDRE, C. (1841–56), *Oracula Sibyllina*, 2 vols. (Paris).

——(1856), *Excursus ad Sibyllina* (Paris).

BOUSSET, W. (1902), 'Die Beziehungen der ältesten jüdischen Sibylle zur chaldäischen Sibylle', *Zeitschrift für die Neutestamentliche Wissenschaft*, 3: 23–49.

—— (1906), 'Sibyllen und Sibyllinische Bücher', in *Real-Encyclopädie für protestantische Theologie und Kirche*, 18: 265–80.

CAMPONOVO, O. (1984), *Königherrschaft und Reich Gottes in den frühjüdischen Schriften* (Freiburg).

CHARLES, R. H. (1913), *The Apocrypha and Pseudepigrapha of the Old Testament*, ii (Oxford).

CHARLESWORTH, J. H. (1983), *The Old Testament Pseudepigrapha*, i (Garden City, NY).

COLLINS, J. J. (1974a), *The Sibylline Oracles of Egyptian Judaism* (Missoula).

—— (1974b), 'The Provenance and Date of the Third Sibyl', *Bulletin of the Institute of Jewish Studies*, 2: 1–18.

—— (1983), *Between Athens and Jerusalem* (New York).

—— (1987), 'The Development of the Sibylline Tradition', *ANRW* II. 20. 1: 421–59.

DAVIES, W. D., and FINKELSTEIN, L. (1989), *The Cambridge History of Judaism*, ii (Cambridge).

EDDY, S. K. (1961), *The King is Dead* (Lincoln).

FELDMAN, L. H. (1993), *Jew and Gentile in the Ancient World* (Princeton).

FRASER, P. M. (1972), *Ptolemaic Alexandria*, 2 vols. (Oxford).

GAGER, J. G. (1972), 'Some attempts to label the *Oracula Sibyllina*, Book 7', *HTR* 65: 91–7.

GEFFCKEN, J. (1902a), *Die Oracula Sibyllina* (Leipzig).

—— (1902b), *Komposition und Entsthungszeit der Oracula Sibyllina* (Leipzig).

GRAFTON, A. (1991), *Defenders of the Text* (Cambridge, Mass.).

GRUEN, E. S. (1984), *The Hellenistic World and the Coming of Rome* (Berkeley).

GRUEN, E. S. (1998), *Heritage and Hellenism: The Reinvention of Jewish Tradition* (Berkeley).

HELLHOLM, D. (1983), *Apocalypticism in the Mediterranean World and the Near East* (Tübingen).

JEANMAIRE, H. (1939), *La Sibylle et le retour de l'âge d'Or* (Paris).

KOCSIS, E. (1962), 'Ost–West Gegensatz in den jüdischen Sibyllinen', *Novum Testamentum*, 5: 105–10.

KOENEN, L. (1968), 'Die Prophezeiungen des "Töpfers"', *ZPE* 2: 178–209.

KURFESS, A. (1951), *Sibyllinische Weissagungen* (Berlin).

MOMIGLIANO, A. (1980), *Sesto contributo alla storia studi classici*, ii (Rome).

NEWSOME, J. D. (1992), *Greeks, Romans, Jews* (Philadelphia).

NIKIPROWETZKY, V. (1970), *La Troisème Sibylle* (Paris).

—— (1987), 'La Sibylle juive depuis Charles Alexandre', *ANRW* II. 20. 1: 460–542.

NOLLAND, J. (1979), 'Sib. Or. III. 265–94, An Early Maccabean Messianic Oracle', *JTS* 30: 158–66.

PARKE, H. W. (1988), *Sibyls and Sibylline Prophecy in Classical Antiquity* (London).

PERETTI, A. (1943), *La Sibilla babilonese nella propaganda ellenistica* (Florence).

POTTER, D. (1994), *Prophets and Emperors* (Cambridge, Mass.).

ROWLEY, H. H. (1926), 'The Interpretation and Date of Sibylline Oracles III 388–400', *Zeitschrift für die Alttestamentliche Wissenschaft*, 44: 324–7.

RZACH, A. (1923), 'Sibyllinischer Orakel', *PWRE* II. A. 2: 2103–83.

SCHÜRER, E. (1886), *Geschichte des jüdischen Volkes im Zeitalter Jesu Christi*, ii (Leipzig).

——(1986), *The History of the Jewish People in the Age of Jesus Christ*, iii. 1. rev. G. Vermes, *et al.* (Edinburgh).

STONE, M. E. (1984), *Jewish Writings of the Second Temple Period* (Philadelphia).

TARN, W. W. (1932), 'Alexander Helios and the Golden Age', *JRS* 22: 135–60.

3. THE HELLENIZATION OF JERUSALEM AND SHECHEM

ATTRIDGE, H. and ODEN, R. (1981), *Philo of Byblos: The Phoenician History* (*Catholic Biblical Quarterly* monograph series, ix; Washington, DC).

BICKERMAN, E. J. (1979), *The God of the Maccabees* (Leiden).

BROWN, P. (1995), *Authority and the Sacred: Aspects of Christianisation of the Roman World* (Cambridge).

COHEN, S. (1990), 'Religion, Ethnicity and "Hellenism" in the Emergence of Jewish Identity in the Maccabean Period', in P. Bilde *et al.* (eds.), *Religion and Religious Practice in the Seleucid Kingdom* (Studies in Hellenistic Civilization, i; Aarhus), 204–23.

DONNER, H., and RÖLLIG, W. (1962–4), *Kanaanäische und aramäische Inschriften*, i–ii (Wiesbaden).

GOLDSTEIN, J. (1984), *II Maccabees* (Anchor Bible, 41a; Garden City, NY).

HABICHT, C. (1976), *2. Makkabäerbuch: historische und legendarische Erzählungen* (Jüdische Schiften aus hellenistisch-römischer Zeit, 1.3; Gütersloh).

JONES, A. H. M. (1964), *The Later Roman Empire* (Oxford).

KENNEDY, H. (1985), 'The Last Century of Byzantine Syria: A Reinterpretation', *Byzantinische Forschungen*, 10: 141–83.

KLONER, A. (1991), 'Maresha', *Qadmoniot*, 95–6: 70–85 (in Hebrew).

LeRIDER, G. (1965), *Suse sous les Séleucides et les Parthes: les trouvailles monétaires et l'histoire de la ville* (Mémoires de la mission archéologique en Iran, 38; Paris).

MILLAR, F. (1978), 'The Background to the Maccabean Revolution', *JJS* 29: 1–21.

—— (1983), 'The Phoenician Cities: A Case Study in Hellenisation', *PCPS* 209: 55–71.

OREN, E., and RAPPAPORT, U. (1984), 'The Necropolis of Maresha-Beth Govrin', *IEJ* 34: 114–53.

RAPPAPORT, U. (1990), 'The Samaritan Sect in the Hellenistic Period', *Zion*, 55: 373–96.

SCHWARTZ, S. (1993), 'John Hyrcanus I's Destruction of the Gerizim Temple and Judaean-Samaritan Relations', *Jewish History*, 7: 9–25.

—— (1995), 'Language, Power and Identity in Ancient Palestine', *Past & Present*, 148: 3–47.

SHERWIN-WHITE, S., and KUHRT, A. (1993), *From Samarkhand to Sardis: A New Approach to the Seleucid Empire* (London).

TCHERIKOVER, V. (1958), *Hellenistic Civilization and the Jews* (Philadelphia).

WHITTOW, M. (1990), 'Ruling the Late Roman and Early Byzantine City: A Continuous History', *Past & Present*, 129: 3–29.

WILL, E. (1988), 'Poleis hellénistiques: deux notes', *Échos du monde classique/Classical Views*, 15: 329–51.

4. JOSEPHUS' TOBIADS

ASTIN, A. E. *et al.* (1989), *Cambridge Ancient History*, vol. 8, 2nd edn. (Cambridge).

BARAG, D. (1992/3), 'New Evidence on the Foreign Policy of John Hyrcanus I', *Israel Numismatic Journal*, 12: 1–12.

BENGTSON, H. (1944), *Die Strategie in der hellenistischen Zeit*, ii (Munich).

—— (1997), *Griechische Geschichte*, 5th edn. (Munich).

BERGMANN, J. (1938), 'Die runden und hyperbolischen Zahlen in der Agada', *Monatsschrift für Geschichte und Wissenschaft des Judentums*, 82: 361–76.

BIKERMAN, E. (1938), *Institutions des Séleucides* (Paris).

CUQ, E. (1927), 'La Condition juridique de la Coelé-Syrie au temps de Ptolémée V Épiphane', *Syria*, 8: 143–62.

DERFLER, S. L. (1990), *The Hasmonean Revolt: Rebellion or Revolution* (Lewiston, NY).

DROYSEN, J. G. (1894), *De Lagidarum regno Ptolemaeo VI Philometore rege*, in id., *Kleine Schriften zur alten Geschichte* (Leipzig), ii. 351–443. (Orig. pub. 1831.)

GERA, D. (1990), 'On the Credibility of the History of the Tobiads', in A. Kasher, U. Rappaport, and G. Fuks (eds.), *Greece and Rome in Eretz Israel* (Jerusalem), 21–38.

GOLDSTEIN, J. A. (1975), 'Tales of the Tobiads', *Christianity, Judaism and*

Other Greco-Roman Cults: Studies for Morton Smith at Sixty, iii (ed. J. Neusner; Leiden), 85–123.

GRESSMANN, H. (1921), 'Die ammonitischen Tobiaden', *Sitzungsberichte der preussischen Akademie der Wissenschaften*, 663–71.

GRUEN, E. S. (1984), *The Hellenistic World and the Coming of Rome*, 2 vols. (Berkeley).

HEINEN, H. (1984), 'The Syrian-Egyptian Wars and the New Kingdoms of Asia Minor', in *Cambridge Ancient History*, 2nd edn., vii. 1, ed. F. W. Walbank *et al.* (Cambridge), 412–45.

HOFFMANN, J. F. (1873), *Antiochus IV. Epiphanes: König von Syrien* (Diss.; Leipzig).

HOFMANN, J. C. C. (1835), *De bellis ab Antiocho Epiphanae adversus Ptolemaeos gestis* (Diss.; Erlangen).

HOLLEAUX, M. (1942), 'La chronologie de la cinquième guerre de Syrie', in idem, *Études d'épigraphie et d'histoire grecques* (Paris), iii. 317–35. (Orig. pub. *Klio* 8 (1908).)

ISAAC, B. (1991), 'A Seleucid Inscription from Jamnia-on-the-Sea: Antiochus V Eupator and the Sidonians', *IEJ* 41: 132–44.

JAHN, J. (1800), *Biblische Archäologie*, ii.1 (Vienna).

JOUGUET, P. (1937), 'Les débuts du règne de Ptolémée Philométor et la sixième guerre syrienne', *Revue de Philologie*, 3rd ser., 11: 193–238.

KENNARD, J. S. (1945/6), 'Judas of Galilee and his clan', *JQR* 36: 281–6.

LE RIDER, G. (1993), 'Les Ressources financières de Séleucos IV (187–175) et le paiement de l'indemnité aux Romains', in M. Price, A. Burnett, and R. Bland (eds.), *Essay in Honour of Robert Carson and Kenneth Jenkins* (London), 49–67.

MAGO, U. (1907), *Antioco IV. Epifan, Re di Siria* (Sassari).

MAZAR, B. (1957), 'The Tobiads', *Israel Exploration Journal* 7: 137–45, 229–38.

MØRKHOLM, O. (1966), *Antiochus IV of Syria* (Copenhagen).

MOMIGLIANO, A. (1975), 'I Tobiadi nella preistoria del moto maccabaico', in id., *Quinto contributo alla storia degli studi classici e del mondo antico* (Rome), i. 597–628. (Orig. pub. 1931/2.)

ORRIEUX, C. (1986), 'Flavius Josèphe est-il credible?', *Kentron*, 2: 8–11.

——(1988), 'Flavius Josèphe est-il credible? (II)', *Kentron*, 4/5: 133–41.

OTTO, W. (1914), 'Hyrkanos', in *PWRE* i. 17: 527–34.

——(1934), *Zur Geschichte der Zeit des 6. Ptolemäers* (Munich).

PRIDEAUX, H. (1808), *The Old and New Testaments Connected in the History of the Jews and Neighbouring Nations*, 16th edn., iii (London).

SAMUEL, A. E. (1962), *Ptolemaic Chronology* (Munich).

SCHWARTZ, D. R. (1990), 'On Some Papyri and Josephus' Sources and Chronology for the Persian Period', *JSJ*, 21: 175–99.

——(1992), *Studies in the Jewish Background of Christianity* (Tübingen).

SEIBERT, J. (1967), *Historische Beiträge zu den dynastischen Verbindungen in hellenistischer Zeit* (Wiesbaden).

STARK, K. B. (1852), *Gaza und die philistäische Kuste* (Jena).

STERN, M. (1962/3), 'Notes on the Story of Joseph the Tobiad', *Tarbiz*, 32: 35–47 (= id., *Studies in Jewish History* (Jerusalem, 1991), 22–34). (In Hebrew.)

——(1982/3), 'Jewish Hellenistic Literature', in id. (ed.), *The Diaspora in the Hellenistic-Roman World* (Jerusalem), 208–37 (in Hebrew).

TAYLOR, J. E. (1979), 'Seleucid Rule in Palestine' (unpub. PhD. diss., Duke University).

TCHERIKOVER, V. A. (1959), *Hellenistic Civilization and the Jews* (Philadelphia).

VINCENT, L. H. (1920), 'La Palestine dans les papyrus ptolémaïques de Gerza', *Revue biblique*, 29: 161–202.

WALBANK, F. W. (1979*a*), *A Historical Commentary on Polybius*, iii (Oxford).

——(1979*b*), 'Egypt in Polybius', in J. Ruffle, G. A. Gaballa, and K. A. Kitchen (eds.), *Orbis Aegyptiorum Speculum—Glimpses of Ancient Egypt: Studies in Honour of H. W. Fairman* (Warminster), 180–9.

WELLES, C. B. (1962), 'Hellenistic Tarsus', *Mélanges de l'Universite Saint Joseph* 38: 43–75.

WELWEI, K.-W. (1963), *Könige und Königtum im Urteil des Polybius* (Diss.; Cologne).

WILCKEN, U. (1894), 'Antiochos III. der Grosse', *PWRE* I.2, col. 2466.

WILL, E. (1982), *Histoire politique du monde hellénistique*, 2nd edn., ii (Nancy).

WILLIAMSON, H. G. M. (1977), 'The Historical Value of Josephus' Jewish *Antiquities XI*. 297–301', *JTS*, NS 28: 49–66.

YARSHATAR, E. (1983), *The Cambridge History of Iran*, iii.1 (Cambridge).

5. JEWS, CHRISTIANS, AND OTHERS IN PALESTINE:
THE EVIDENCE FROM EUSEBIUS

ABEL, F.-M. (1967), *Geographie de la Palestine*, ii (Paris).

ALON, G. (1980–4), *The Jews in their Land in the Talmudic Age*, 2 vols. (Jerusalem).

AVI-YONAH, M. (1962), *Geschichte der Juden im Zeitalter des Talmud* (Berlin).

——(1976), *Gazeteer of Roman Palestine* (Jerusalem).

——(1977), *The Holy Land: From the Persian to the Arab Conquest. A Historical Geography*, 2nd edn. (Grand Rapids, Mich.).

BARNES, T. D. (1975), 'The composition of Eusebius' *Onomasticon*', *JTS* NS 26: 412–15.

FISCHER, M., ISAAC, B., and ROLL, I. (1996), *Roman Roads in Judaea*, ii, *The Jaffa–Jerusalem Roads* (BAR International Series; Oxford).

HÜTTENMEISTER, F., and REEG, G. (1977), *Die antiken Scynagogen in Israel*, 2 vols. (Wiesbaden).

HUMPHREY, J. (1995) (ed.), *The Roman and Byzantine Near East: Some Recent Archaeological Research* (Ann Arbor, Mich.).

ISAAC, B., and ROLL, I. (1982), *Roman Roads in Judaea*, i, *The Scythopolis-Legio Road* (BAR International Series; Oxford).

KENNEDY, D. (1996), *The Roman Army in the East* (Ann Arbor, Mich.).

KLOSTERMANN, E. (1904) (ed.), *Eusebius, Das Onomastikon der biblischen Ortsnamen* (Leipzig).

KUBITSCHEK, W. (1905), 'Ein Strassennetz in Eusebius' Onomasticon', *Jahrbuch des Österreichischen Archäologischen Instituts*, 8: 119–27.

LEWIS, N. (1989) (ed.), *The Documents from the Bar Kokhba Period in the Cave of Letters. Greek Papyri*, ed. N. Lewis, with Y. Yadin and J. C. Greenfield (eds.), *Aramaic and Nabatean Signatures and Subscriptions* (Jerusalem).

MAYERSON, P. (1984), 'Antiochus Monachus' Homily on Dreams: an Historical Note', *JJS* 35: 51–6.

—— (1994), *Monks, Martyrs, Soldiers and Saracens* (New York and Jerusalem).

MEYERS, E. M., NETZER, E., and MEYERS, C. L. (1986), 'Sepphoris, "Ornament of all Galilee"', *Biblical Archaeologist*, 49: 4–19.

MILLAR, F. (1993), *The Roman Near East* (Cambridge, Mass.).

MILLER, S. S. (1984), *Studies in the History and Traditions of Sepphoris* (Leiden).

NETZER, E., and WEISS, Z. (1994), *Zippori* (Jerusalem) (in Hebrew).

NOTH, M. (1943), 'Die topographischen Angeben im Onomasticon des Eusebius', *ZDPV* 66: 32–63.

OPPENHEIMER, A. (1988), 'Jewish Lydda in the Roman Era', *HUCA* 59: 115–36.

REEG, G. (1989), *Die Ortsnamen Israels nach der rabbinischen Literatur* (Wiesbaden).

SARTRE, M. (1991), *L'Orient romain* (Paris).

—— (1993) (ed.), *Inscriptions Grecques et Latines de la Syrie*, xxi, *Inscriptions de la Jordaine*, iv.

SCHMITT, G. (1995), *Siedlungen Palästinas in griechische-römischer Zeit* (Wiesbaden).

SCHWARTZ, J. (1986), *Jewish Settlement in Judaea after the Bar-Kochba War until the Arab Conquest* (Jerusalem) (in Hebrew).

—— (1991), *Lod (Lydda), Israel* (BAR International Series; Oxford).

TAYLOR, J. E. (1994), *Christians and the Holy Places: The Myth of Jewish-Christian Origins* (Oxford).

VANN R. L. (1992) (ed.), *Caesarea Papers* (Ann Arbor, Mich.).

6. WHERE WERE THE JEWS OF THE DIASPORA BURIED?

ASHBY, T. (1907), 'The Classical Topography of the Roman Campagna, Part III', *PBSR* 4: 1–159.

AUDIN, A. (1960), 'Inhumation et incinération', *Latomus*, 19: 312–22, 518–32.

BODEL, J. (1994), *Graveyards and Groves: A Study of the Lex Lucerina* (Cambridge, Mass.).

CANNON, A. (1989), 'The Historical Dimension in Mortuary Expressions of Status and Sentiment', *Current Anthropology*, 30: 437–58.

CONDE GUERRI, E. (1979), *Los 'fossores' de Roma paleocristiana (estudio iconografico, epigrafico y social)* (Studi di Antichità Cristiana xxxiii; Vatican City).

DAVIES, G. (1977), 'Burial in Italy up to Augustus', in R. Reece (ed.), *Burial in the Roman World* (CBA Research Report no. 22; London), 13–19.

DEGRASSI, A. (1962), 'Nerva funeraticum plebi urbanae instituit', in *Scritti vari di antichità* (Rome), i. 697–702.

FASOLA, U. M. (1976), 'Le due catacombe ebraiche di Villa Torlonia', *RivAC* 52: 7–62.

FASOLA, U. M., and FIOCCHI NICOLAI, V. (1989), 'Le necropoli durante la formazione delle città cristiana', in *Actes du XIe congrès international d'archéologie chrétienne (21–28.IX.1986)* (Vatican City and Rome), ii. 1153–205.

FERRUA, A. (1991), *The Unknown Catacomb*, tr. I. Inglis (New Lanark).

FINEGAN, J. (1946), *Light from the Ancient Past* (Princeton).

——(1992), *The Archaeology of the New Testament* (rev. edn.; Princeton).

FUKS, A. (1985), 'Where Have All the Freedmen Gone?', *JJS* 36: 25–32.

GAFNI, I. (1981), 'Reinterment in the Land of Israel: Notes on the Origin and Development of the Custom', *Jerusalem Cathedra*, 1: 96–104.

GUYON, J. (1974), 'La Vente des tombes à travers l'épigraphie de la Rome chrétienne (IIIe–VIE siècles)', *MEFRA* 86: 546–96.

HACHLILI, R. (1988), *Ancient Jewish Art and Archaeology in the Land of Israel* (Leiden).

HOPKINS, K. (1983), *Death and Renewal* (London).

——(1987), 'Graveyards for Historians', in F. Hinard (ed.), *La Mort, les morts et l'au-delà dans le monde romain* (Caen), 113–26.

KAIMIO, J. (1979), *The Romans and the Greek Language* (Commentationes Humanarum Litterarum 64; Helsinki).

KAJANTO, I. (1963a), *Onomastic Studies in the Early Christian Inscriptions of Rome and Carthage* (Acta Instituti Romani Finlandiae II.1; Helsinki).

——(1963b), *A Study of the Greek Epitaphs of Rome* (Acta Instituti Romani Finlandiae II.3; Helsinki).

LANCIANI, R. (1888), *Ancient Rome in the Light of Recent Discoveries* (London).

LEON, H. J. (1960), *The Jews of Ancient Rome* (Philadelphia).

MACMULLEN, R. (1983), 'The Epigraphic Habit in the Roman Empire', *AJPh* 103: 233–46.

MARTIN, D. B. (1993), 'Slavery and the Ancient Jewish Family', in S. J. D. Cohen (ed.), *The Jewish Family in Antiquity* (Brown Judaic Studies 289; Providence, RI), 113–29.

MEYER, E. A. (1990), 'Explaining the Epigraphic Habit in the Roman Empire: The Evidence of Epitaphs', *JRS* 80: 74–96.

MORRIS, I. (1992), *Death-ritual and Social Structure in Classical Antiquity* (Cambridge).

NOCK, A. D. (1932), 'Cremation and Burial in the Roman Empire', *HTR* 25: 321–59, repr. in *Essays on Religion and the Ancient World* (2 vols.; Oxford, 1972).

NOY, D. (1997), 'Writing in tongues: the use of Greek, Latin and Hebrew in Jewish inscriptions from Roman Italy', *JJS* 48: 300–11.

PATTERSON, J. R. (1992), 'Patronage, *Collegia* and Burial in Imperial Rome', in S. Bassett (ed.), *Death in Towns* (Leicester), 15–27.

PERGOLA, PH. (1986), 'Le Catacombe romane: miti e realtà (a proposito del cimitero di Domitilla)', in *Società romana e impero tardantico* (Bari), ii. 333–48.

PRICE, J. (1994), 'The Jewish Diaspora of the Graeco-Roman Period', *SCI* 13: 169–86.

RAJAK, T. (1994), 'Reading the Jewish Catacombs of Rome', in J. W. van Henten and P. W. van der Horst (eds.), *Studies in Early Jewish Epigraphy* (Leiden), 226–41.

REYNOLDS, J. M., and TANNENBAUM, R. (1987), *Jews and Godfearers at Aphrodisias* (Cambridge).

RUTGERS, L. V. (1990), 'Überlegungen zu den jüdischen Katakomben Roms', *JAC* 33: 140–57.

—— (1992), 'The Interaction of Jews and Non-Jews in Late Antiquity', *AJA* 96: 101–18.

—— (1995), *The Jews in Late Ancient Rome* (Leiden).

SAFRAI, S. (1976), 'Home and Family', in S. Safrai and M. Stern (eds.), *The Jewish People in the First Century* (Assen), ii. 728–92.

SOLIN, H. (1983), 'Juden und Syrer in der römischen Welt', *ANRW* II.29.2: 590–789, 1222–49.

STEVENSON, J. (1978), *The Catacombs: Rediscovered Monuments of Early Christianity* (London).

STRANGE, J. F. (1975), 'Late Hellenistic and Herodian Ossuary Tombs at French Hill, Jerusalem', *BASOR* 219: 39–68.

STRUBBE, J. H. M. (1994), 'Curses against Violation of the Grave in Jewish Epitaphs of Asia Minor', in J. W. van Henten and P. W. van der Horst (eds.), *Studies in Early Jewish Epigraphy* (Leiden), 70–128.

TAYLOR, L. R. (1961), 'Freedmen and Freeborn in the Epitaphs of Imperial Rome', *AJPh* 82: 113–33.

TESTINI, P. (1966), *Le catacombe e gli antichi cimiteri cristiani in Roma* (Bologna).

TOYNBEE, J. M. C. (1971), *Death and Burial in the Roman World* (London).

TOYNBEE, J. M. C., AND WARD PERKINS, J. (1952), *The Shrine of St Peter and the Vatican Excavations* (London).

TREBILCO, P. M. (1991), *Jewish Communities in Asia Minor* (Cambridge).

TURCAN, R. (1958), 'Origines et sens de l'inhumation à l'époque impériale', *Revue des Études Anciennes* 60: 323–47.

VISMARA, C. (1986), 'I cimiteri ebraici di Roma', in *Società romana e impero tardantico* (Bari), ii. 351–503.

VON HESBERG, H. (1992), *Römische Grabbauten* (Darmstadt).

WILLIAMS, M. H. (1994), 'The Organisation of Jewish Burials in Ancient Rome', *ZPE* 101: 165–82.

WILSON, R. J. A. (1990), *Sicily under the Roman Empire* (Warminster).

7. GRAECO-ROMAN VOLUNTARY ASSOCIATIONS AND ANCIENT JEWISH SECTS

ANDERSON, B. (1991), *Imagined Communities: Reflections on the Origin and Spread of Nationalism*, 2nd edn. (London).

ARJOMAND, S. (1988), *The Turban for the Crown—The Islamic Revolution in Iran* (New York and Oxford).

BAILEY, C. (1926), *Epicurus—The Extant Remains* (Oxford).

BAUMGARTEN, A. I. (1981), 'R. Judah I and His Opponents', *JSJ* 12: 135–72.

——(1983*a*), 'Miracles and Halakah in Rabbinic Judaism', *JQR* 73: 238–53.

——(1983*b*), 'The Name of the Pharisees', *JBL* 102: 411–28.

——(1994*a*), 'Josephus on Essene Sacrifice', *JJS* 35: 169–83.

——(1994*b*), 'The Rule of the Martian as Applied to Qumran', *Israel Oriental Studies*, 14: 121–42.

——(1995), 'Rabbinic Literature as a Source for the History of Jewish Sectarianism in the Second Temple Period', *Dead Sea Discoveries*, 2: 14–57.

——(1996*a*), 'The Temple Scroll, Toilet Practices, and the Essenes', *Jewish History*, 10: 9–20.

——(1996*b*), 'City Lights—Urbanization and Sectarianism in Hasmonean Jerusalem', in M. Porthuis (ed.), *The Centrality of Jerusalem: Historical Perspectives*, 50–64.

——(1996*c*), '*Hatta't* Sacrifices', *Revue Biblique*, 337–42.

——(1997), *The Flourishing of Jewish Sects in the Maccabean Era: An Interpretation* (Leiden).

BLOCH, M. (1967), 'A Contribution Towards a Comparative History of European Societies', *Land and Work in Medieval Europe, Selected Papers by Marc Bloch* (London), 44–81.

BRUHL, A. (1953), *Liber Pater* (Paris).

BUECHLER, A. (1956), 'The Patriarch R. Judah I and the Graeco-Roman Cities of Palestine', *Studies in Jewish History* (London), 179–245.

BURKERT, W. (1982), 'Craft Versus Sect: The Problem of Orphics and Pythagoreans', in B. F. Meyer and E. P. Sanders (eds.), *Jewish and Christian Self-Definition*, iii, *Self-Definition in the Greco-Roman World* (London), 1–22, 183–9.

CANCIK-LINDEMAIER, H. (1996), 'Der Diskurs Religion im Senatsbeschluss über die Bacchanalia von 186 v. Chr. und bei Livius (B. xxxlx)', in H. Cancik, H. Lichtenberger, and P. Schäfer (eds.), *Geschichte—Tradition—Reflexion: Festschrift für Martin Hengel zum 70 Geburtstag* (Tübingen), ii. 77–96.

CANTARELLA, E. (1987), *Pandora's Daughters: The Role & Status of Women in Greek & Roman Antiquity* (Baltimore).

COHEN, S. (1980), 'A Virgin Defiled: Some Rabbinic and Christian Views of the Origins of Heresy', *USQR* 36: 1–11.

——(1984), 'The Significance of Yavneh: Pharisees, Rabbis and the End of Jewish Sectarianism', *HUCA* 55: 27–53.

COSER, L. (1974), *Greedy Institutions: Patterns of Undivided Commitment* (New York and London).

COVA, P. (1974), 'Livio e la repressione dei baccanali', *Athenaeum*, 52: 82–109.

DE LACEY, P. (1948), 'Lucretius and the History of Epicureanism', *TAPA* 79: 12–23.

DE WITT, N. (1936), 'Organization and Procedure in Epicurean Groups', *CP* 31: 205–11.

DOUGLAS, M. (1984), *Purity and Danger* (London).

——(1987), *Constructive Drinking* (Cambridge and Paris).

DUMONT, L. (1979), *Homo Hierarchicus—The Caste System and its Implications*, 2nd edn. (Chicago and London).

ESHEL, E. (1994), '4Q477: The Rebukes by the Overseer', *JJS* 45: 117–54.

FESTUGIÈRE, A. J. (1954), 'Ce que Tite-Live nous apprend sur les mystères de Dionysos', *Mélanges d'archéologie et d'histoire, École Française de Rome*, 66: 79–99.

FEVRIER, J. G. (1931), *La Religion des Palmyriens* (Paris).

FISHER, N. (1988a), 'Greek Associations, Symposia and Clubs', in M. Grant and R. Kitzinger (eds.), *Civilizations of the Ancient Mediterranean* (New York), ii. 1167–97.

——(1988b), 'Roman Associations, Dinner Parties and Clubs', in M. Grant and R. Kitzinger (eds.), *Civilizations of the Ancient Mediterranean* (New York), ii. 1199–225.

FITZMYER, J. (1985), *The Gospel According to Luke (X–XXIV)* (New York and London).

FORBES, C. A. (1933), *Neoi—A Contribution to the Study of Greek Associations* (Middletown, Conn.).

FRANK, T. (1927), 'The Bacchanalian Cult of 186 BC', *CQ* 21: 128–32.

GOODMAN, M. (1995), 'A Note on the Qumran Sectarians, the Essenes and Josephus', *JJS* 46: 161–6.

GOODY, J. (1982), *Cooking, Cuisine and Class—A Study in Comparative Sociology* (Cambridge).

——(1987), *The Interface between the Written and the Oral* (Cambridge).

GREENFIELD, J. (1974), 'The Marzeah as a Social Institution', *Acta Antiqua*, 22: 451–5.

GUELICH, R. (1989), *Word Bible Commentary Mark 1: 8–26* (Dallas, Tex.).

HARRINGTON, H. (1995), 'Did the Pharisees Eat Ordinary Food in a State of Ritual Purity?', *JSJ* 26: 42–54.

HENGEL, M., and DEINES, R. (1995), 'E. P. Sanders' "Common Judaism", Jesus and the Pharisees. A Review Article', *JTS* 46: 1–70.

HERRMANN, P. *et al.* (1978), 'Genossenschaft', *RAC* x, cols. 83–155.

HILL, C. (1975), *The World Turned Upside Down* (Harmondsworth).

KIDD, I. G. (1988), *Posidonius, II. The Commentary: (i) Testimonia and Fragments 1–149* (Cambridge).

KLOPPENBORG, J., and WILSON, S. (1996) (eds.), *Voluntary Associations in the Graeco-Roman World* (London and New York).

KRAEMER, R. (1992), *Her Share of the Blessings: Women's Religions Among Pagans, Jews and Christians in the Greco-Roman World* (New York and Oxford).

KUPFERSCHMIDT, U. (1987), 'Reformist and Militant Islam in Urban and Rural Egypt', *Middle Eastern Studies*, 23: 403–18.

LIEBERMAN, S. (1939), *Tosefeth Rishonim*, iii (Jerusalem).

MCDONALD, A. H. (1944), 'Rome and the Italian Confederation (200–186 B.C.)', *JRS* 34: 11–33.

MALHERBE, A. (1982), 'Self Definition Among Epicureans and Cynics', in B. F. Meyer and E. P. Sanders (eds.), *Jewish and Christian Self-Definition*, iii, *Self-Definition in the Greco-Roman World* (London), 46–59, 192–7.

MASON, S. (1992), 'Greco-Roman, Jewish and Christian Philosophies', in J. Neusner (ed.), *Approaches to Ancient Judaism, New Series, Volume Four*, 1–28 (Atlanta, Ga.).

MEENS, R. (1995), 'Pollution in the Early Middle Ages: The Case of the Food Regulations in Penitentials', *Early Medieval Europe*, 4: 3–19.

MENDELS, D. (1979), 'Hellenistic Utopia and the Essenes', *HTR* 72: 205–22.

NEUSNER, J. (1971), *Rabbinic Traditions About the Pharisees before 70* (Leiden).

Nock, A. D. (1924), 'On the Historical Importance of Cult Associations', *CR* 38: 105–9.

—— (1972), 'The Gild of Zeus Hypsistos', *Essays on Religion and the Ancient World* (Oxford), i. 414–42.

Pallier, J. M. (1982), 'La Spirale de l'interpretation: les bacchanales', *Annales*, 37: 929–52.

Rist, J. (1972), *Epicurus: An Introduction* (Cambridge).

Rostovtzeff, M. (1941), *Social and Economic History of the Hellenistic World* (Oxford).

Safrai, S. (1965/6; 1966/7), 'Practical Implementation of the Sabbatical Year after the Destruction of the Temple', *Tarbiz*, 35: 304–28; *Tarbiz*, 36: 1–21 (in Hebrew).

Saldarini, A. J. (1988), *Pharisees, Scribes and Sadducees in Palestinian Society: A Sociological Approach* (Wilmington, Del.).

Sanders, E. P. (1977), *Paul and Palestinian Judaism* (Philadelphia).

—— (1990), *Jewish Law from Jesus to the Mishnah* (London and Philadelphia).

Sewell, W., Jr. (1967), 'Marc Bloch and the Logic of Comparative History', *History and Theory. Studies in the Philosophy of History*, 6: 208–18.

Stark, R., and Bainbridge, W. S. (1985), *The Future of Religion* (Berkeley).

Sussmann, Y. (1973/4), 'The Halakic Inscription from Bet Shean', *Tarbiz*, 43: 88–158 (in Hebrew).

Tapper, R., and N. (1987), '"Thank God We're Secular"', Aspects of Fundamentalism in a Turkish Town', in L. Caplan (ed.), *Studies in Religious Fundamentalism* (London), 51–78.

Teixidor, J. (1981), 'Le Thiase de Belastor et de Béelshamen d'après une inscription récemment découverte à Palmyre', *Comptes Rendus de l'Academie des Inscriptions et Belles Lettres*, 306–14.

Thomas, K. (1971), *Religion and the Decline of Magic* (Harmondsworth).

von Staden, H. (1982), 'Hairesis and Heresy: The Case of the *haireseis iatrikai*', in B. F. Meyer and E. P. Sanders (eds.), *Jewish and Christian Self-Definition*, iii, *Self-Definition in the Greco-Roman World* (London), 76–100, 199–206.

Weinfeld, M. (1973), 'The Origin of the Apodictic Law', *VT* 23: 63–75.

—— (1986), *The Organizational Pattern and the Penal Code of the Qumran Sect—A Comparison with Guilds and Religious Associations of the Hellenistic-Roman Period* (Fribourg and Göttingen).

Wilson, B. (1973), *Magic and the Millennium* (London).

8. Antichrist among Jews and Gentiles

Allegro, J. M. (1968), *Qumrân Cave 4* (DJD V) (Oxford).

Barthélemy, D., and Milik, J. T. (1955), *Qumrân Cave 1* (*DJD* i; Oxford).

BOUSSET, W. (1896), *The Antichrist Legend: A Chapter in Christian and Jewish Folklore* (London).

——(1908), 'Antichrist', *ERE* 1: 578–81.

CHADWICK, H. (1965), *Origen: Contra Celsum*, corrected reprint of 1953 edn. (Cambridge).

CHARLESWORTH, J. H. (1983) (ed.), *The Old Testament Pseudepigrapha*, i (London).

COLLINS, J. J. (1995), *The Scepter and the Star* (New York).

DOWNING, F. G. (1995), 'Common Strands in Pagan, Jewish, and Christian Eschatologies in the First Century', *TZ* 51: 196–211.

FRAENKEL, E. (1957), *Horace* (Oxford).

FRIEDLÄNDER, M. (1899), 'L'Anti-Messie', *REJ* 38: 14–37.

GARCIA MARTINEZ, F. (1994), *The Dead Sea Scrolls Translated*, ET by W. G. E. Watson (Leiden).

GINZBERG, L. (1901), 'Antichrist', *Jewish Encyclopedia*, i: 625–7.

HART, J. H. A. (1909), *Ecclesiasticus: The Greek Text of Codex 248* (Cambridge).

HAYWARD, C. T. R. (1990), 'Jacob's Second Visit to Bethel in Targum Pseudo-Jonathan', in P. R. Davies and R. T. White (eds.), *A Tribute to Geza Vermes* (Sheffield), 175–92.

HEID, S. (1993), *Chiliasmus und Antichrist-Mythos. Eine frühchristliche Kontroverse um das Heilige Land* (Bonn).

HENGEL, M. (1989), *The Johannine Question*, ET by John Bowden (London and Philadelphia).

HILL, C. E. (1995), 'Antichrist from the Tribe of Dan', *JTS* NS 46: 99–117.

HORBURY, W. (1981), 'Suffering and Messianism in Yose ben Yose', in W. Horbury and B. McNeil (eds.), *Suffering and Martyrdom in the New Testament* (Cambridge), 143–82.

JELLINEK, Ad. (1967), *Bet ha-Midrasch*, ii (orig. pub. Leipzig, 1853, repr. 1967; Jerusalem).

JENKS, G. C. (1991), *The Origins and Early Development of the Antichrist Myth* (BZNW 59; Berlin and New York).

LAMPE, G. W. H. (1973), '"Grievous Wolves" (Acts 20: 29)', in B. Lindars and S. S. Smalley (eds.), *Christ and Spirit in the New Testament* (Cambridge), 253–68.

LÉVI, I. (1922), 'Le Ravissement du Messie à sa naissance', *REJ* 74: 113–26.

LIETAERT PEERBOLTE, L. J. (1996), *The Antecedents of Antichrist: A Traditio-Historical Study of the Earliest Christian Views on Eschatological Opponents* (Leiden).

LOESCH, S. (1933), *Deitas Jesu und antike Apothese* (Rottenburg a.N.).

MACLEOD, C. W. (1983), 'Horace and the Sibyl', in Colin Macleod, *Collected Essays* (Oxford), 218–19.

MIRSKY, A. (1977), *Yosse ben Yosse: Poems* (Jerusalem).

O'NEILL, J. C. (1966), *The Puzzle of I John* (London).

PARKE, H. W. (1988), *Sibyls and Sibylline Prophecy in Classical Antiquity*, ed. B. C. McGing (London).

PÉREZ FERNÁNDEZ, M. (1981), *Tradiciones mesiánicas en el Targum palestiñense* (Valencia and Jerusalem).

RAINBOW, P. A. (1997), 'Melchizedek as a Messiah at Qumran', *Bulletin for Biblical Research*, 7: 179–94.

SHARF, A. (1971), *Byzantine Jewry* (London).

VAN HENTEN, J. W. (1993), 'Antiochus IV as a Typhonic Figure in Daniel 7', in A. S. van der Woude (ed.), *The Book of Daniel* (Leuven), 223–43.

VERMES, G. (1992), 'Qumran Forum Miscellanea i', *JJS* 43: 299–305.

——, *et al.* (1992), 'The Oxford Forum for Qumran Research: Seminar on the Rule of War from Cave 4 (4Q 285)', *JJS* 43: 85–94.

9. RHETORIC AND ASSUMPTIONS: ROMANS AND RABBIS ON SEX

COHEN, B. (1966), *Jewish and Roman Law*, 2 vols. (New York).

CORRINGTON, G. P. (1992), 'The Defense of the Body and the Discourse of Appetite: Continence and Control in the Greco-Roman World', *Semeia*, 57: 65–74.

DOVER, K. J. (1974), *Greek Popular Morality in the Time of Plato and Aristotle* (Berkeley).

GILMORE, D. D. (1987) (ed.), *Honor and Shame and the Unity of the Mediterranean* (Washington, DC).

HALPERIN, D. (1990), 'One Hundred Years of Homosexuality', in D. Halperin (ed.), *One Hundred Years of Homosexuality* (New York and London), 15–40.

LEVINE, L. I. (1987) (ed.), *The Synagogue in Late Antiquity* (Philadelphia).

——(1989), *The Rabbinic Class of Roman Palestine in Late Antiquity* (New York).

LIEBERMAN, S. (1942), *Greek in Jewish Palestine* (New York).

——(1950), *Hellenism in Jewish Palestine* (New York).

MILLAR, F. (1993), *The Roman Near East 31 BC–AD 337* (Cambridge, Mass.).

NEUSNER, J. (1969–70), *A History of the Jews in Babylonia*, 5 vols. (Leiden).

OLYAN, S. (1994), '"And With a Male You Shall Not Lie the Lying Down of a Woman": On the Meaning and Significance of Leviticus 18: 22 and 20: 13', *Journal of the History of Sexuality*, 5: 179–206.

RICHLIN, A. (1992), *The Garden of Priapus: Sexuality & Aggression in Roman Humor*, rev. edn. (New York).

——(1993), 'Not Before Homosexuality: The Materiality of the *Cinaedus* and the Roman Law Against Love Between Men', *Journal of the History of Sexuality*, 3: 523–73.

SATLOW, M. L. (1994*a*), '"They Abused Him Like A Woman": Homoeroticism, Gender Blurring, and the Rabbis in Late Antiquity', *Journal of the History of Sexuality*, 5: 1–25.

——(1994*b*), '"Wasted Seed", The History of a Rabbinic Idea', *HUCA* 65: 137–75.

——(1995), *Tasting the Dish: Rabbinic Rhetorics of Sexuality* (Atlanta).

——(1996), '"Try to Be a Man": The Rabbinic Construction of Masculinity', *HTR* 89: 19–40.

SMITH, J. Z. (1985), 'What a Difference a Difference Makes', in J. Neusner and E. S. Frerichs (eds.), *'To See Ourselves as Others See Us': Christians, Jews, 'Others' in Late Antiquity* (Chico, Calif.), 3–48.

10. GAMBLING IN ANCIENT JEWISH SOCIETY AND IN THE GRAECO-ROMAN WORLD

AHARONI, Y. (1961), 'The Expedition to the Judaean Desert: Expedition B', *IEJ* 11: 11–24.

ALFOELDI-ROSENBAUM, E. (1971), 'The Finger Calculus in antiquity and in the Middle Ages: Studies on Roman Game Counters 1', *Fruehmittelalterische Studien*, 5: 1–9.

AUSTIN, R. G. (1934), 'Roman Board-Games. I', *Greece & Rome*, 10: 24–34.

——(1935), 'Roman Board-Games. II', *Greece & Rome*, 11: 76–82.

——(1940), 'Greek Board Games', *Antiquity*, 14: 257–71.

AVIGAD, N. (1980), *Discovering Jerusalem* (Jerusalem).

BAZAK, Y. (1968), 'Mishakei-Kubiya ke-Ba'ayat Beri'ut ha-Nefesh be-Halachah', *Sinai*, 48: 111–22.

BELL, R. C. (1979), *Board-Games from many Civilizations* (New York).

BIEBER, M. (1961), *The History of Greek and Roman Theatre*, 2nd edn. (Princeton).

BRUCE, A. C., and JOHNSON, J. E. V. (1992), 'Toward an Explanation of Betting as a Leisure Pursuit', *Leisure Studies*, 12: 210–28.

CORBO, V., et al. (1970), *La Sinagoga di Cafarnao dopo gli scavi del 1969* (Jerusalem).

DANBY, H. (1933), *The Mishnah* (Oxford).

DAVID, F. N. (1962), *Games, Gods and Gambling: The Origin and History of Probability and Statistical Ideas from the Earliest Time to the Newtonian Era* (London).

DE SION, M. A. (1955), *La Fortresse Antonia à Jerusalem et la Question du Pretoire*, diss. (Paris).

DOWNES, D. M., et al. (1976) (eds.), *Gambling, Work and Leisure: A Study Across Three Areas* (London).

ELON, M. (1988), *Ha-Mishpat ha Ivri: Toldotav, Meqorotav, Egronotav*, 3rd edn. (Jerusalem).

GARLAND, R. (1990), *The Greek Way of Life from Conception to Old Age* (Ithaca, NY).

GOLDBERG, A. (1976), *Perush le-Mishnah Masekhet Shabbat* (Jerusalem).

HAMBURGER, A. (1986), 'Surface Finds from Caesarea Maritima-Tesserae', in L. I. Levine and E. Netzer, *Excavations at Caesarea Maritima: 1975, 1976, 1979—Final Report*, Qedem, 21 (Jerusalem).

HEINEVETTER, F. (1912), *Wuerful-und-Buchstabenorakel in Griechenland und Kleinasien, Inaugural Dissertation* (Breslau).

HERR, M. D. (1971), 'Edom in the aggadah', *Enc. Jud.* 6: 378–9 (Jerusalem).

HUEBNER, U. (1992), *Spiele und Spielzeug im antiken Palaestina* (Göttingen).

JONES, J. P. (1973), *Gambling Yesterday and Today: A Complete History* (Newton Abbot).

KRAUSS, S. (1910–12), *Talmudische Archäologie*, 3 vols. (Leipzig).

LAMER, H. (1927), 'Lusoria Tabula', in *PWRE* 13. 2: 1933–61.

LANCIANI, R. (1892), 'Gambling and Cheating in Ancient Rome', *North American Review*, 155: 97–105.

LANDMAN, L. (1966/7; 1967/8), 'Jewish Attitudes Toward Gambling: The Professional and Compulsive Gambler', *JQR* 57: 298–318; 58: 34–62.

LIEBERMAN, S. (1991), *Mehkarim be-Torat Eretz-Israel* (Jerusalem).

LIFSHITZ, B. (1988), *Asmakhta: Hiyuv ve-Kinyan be-Mishpat ha-Ivri* (Jerusalem).

MACALISTER, R. A. S. (1912), *The Excavations of Gezer 1902–1905 and 1907–1909*, ii (London).

MURRAY, H. J. R. (1952), *A History of Board-Games Other than Chess* (Oxford).

PENNICK, N. (1988), *Games of the Gods* (London).

PURCELL, N. (1995), 'Literate Games: Roman Urban Society and the Game of Alea', *Past and Present*, 147: 3–37.

RABINOVITCH, N. L. (1973), *Probability and Statistical Inference in Ancient and Medieval Jewish Literature* (Toronto).

RAHMANI, L. Y. (1967), 'Jason's Tomb', *IEJ* 17: 61–100.

SAWICKI, M. (1997), 'Spatial Management of Gender and Labor in Greco-Roman Galilee', in D. R. Edwards and T. McCollough (eds.), *Archaeology and the Galilee: Texts and Contexts in the Graeco-Roman and Byzantine Periods* (Atlanta, Ga.).

SCHMIDT, R. (1977), *Die Darstellung von Kinderspielzeug und Kinderspiel in der griechischen Kunst* (Vienna).

SELLERS, O. R. (1933), *The Citadel of Beth Zur* (Philadelphia).

TUSHINGHAM, A. D. (1985), *Excavations in Jerusalem 1961–1967*, i (Toronto).

VAETERLEIN, J. (1976), *Roma Ludens: Kinder und Erwachsene beim Spiel im antiken Rom* (Amsterdam).

WARHAFTIG, S. (1972), 'Hozeh, Hagralah ve-Himur lefi ha-Halachah', *Sinai*, 71: 229–40.

YADIN, Y. (1966), *Masada: Herod's Fortress and the Zealots' Last Stand* (London).

11. THE RABBIS AND THE DOCUMENTS

ALON, G. 1984), *The Jews in their Land in the Talmudic Age (70–640 C.E.)*, ii (Jerusalem).

ARCHER, L. J. (1990), *Her Price is Beyond Rubies: The Jewish Woman in Graeco-Roman Palestine* (Sheffield).

BAGNALL, R. S., and FRIER, B. W. (1994), *The Demography of Roman Egypt* (Cambridge).

BICKERMAN, E. (1976), 'Two Legal Interpretations of the Septuagint', *Studies in Jewish and Christian History*, 1: 201–24.

BURKHALTER, F. (1990), 'Archives locales et archives centrales en Egypte romaine', *Chiron*, 20: 191–216.

COCKLE, W. E. H. (1984), 'State Archives in Graeco-Roman Egypt from 30 BC to the Reign of Septimius Severus', *JEA* 70: 106–22.

COTTON, H. M. (1993*a*), 'Another Fragment of the Declaration of Landed Property from the Province of Arabia', *ZPE* 99: 115–21.

——(1993*b*), 'The Guardianship of Jesus son of Babatha: Roman and Local Law in the Province of Arabia', *JRS* 83: 94–113.

——(1994), 'A Cancelled Marriage Contract from the Judaean Desert (XHev/Se Gr. 2)', *JRS* 84: 64–86.

——(1995*a*), 'The Archive of Salome Komaïse Daughter of Levi: Another Archive from the "Cave of Letters"', *ZPE* 105: 171–208.

——(1995*b*), 'Subscriptions and Signatures in the Papyri from the Judaean Desert: the χειροχρηϲτήϲ', *JJP* 25: 29–40.

——(1997), 'Deeds of Gift and the Law of Succession in Archives from the Judaean Desert', *Akten des 21. Internationalen Papyrologenkongress Berlin*, *13–19. August 1995*, I, *Archiv für Papyrusforschung Beiheft*: 3: 179–88.

——(1998), 'The Law of Succession in the Documents from the Judaean Desert Again', *SCI* 17: 115–23.

COTTON, H. M., and GREENFIELD, J. C. (1994), 'Babatha's Property and the Law of Succession in the Babatha Archive', *ZPE* 104: 211–24.

COTTON, H. M., and YARDENI, A. (1997), *Aramaic, Hebrew and Greek Texts from Nahal Hever and Other Sites with an Appendix Containing Alleged Qumran Texts (The Seiyâl Collection II)*. Discoveries in the Judaean Desert xxvii (Oxford).

CRISCI, E. (1996), *Scrivere Greco fuori d'Egitto*, Papyrologia Florentina xxvii (Florence).

FALK, Z. (1952), 'The Inheritance of the Daughter and the Widow in the Bible and the Talmud', *Tarbiz*, 23: 9–15 (in Hebrew).

FRIEDMAN, M. A. (1986), *Jewish Marriage in Palestine: A Cairo Geniza Study*, i (Tel-Aviv).

GELLER, M. J. (1978), 'New Sources for the Origin of the Rabbinic Ketubah', *HUCA* 49: 227–45.

GULAK, A. (1929), *Towards a Study of the History of Jewish Law in the Talmudic Period*, i (Jerusalem) (in Hebrew).

HOMBERT, M. and PRÉAUX, CL. (1952), *Recherches sur le recensement dans l'Égypte Romaine* (Leiden).

ILAN, T. (1993), 'Premarital Cohabitation in Ancient Judaea: The Evidence of the Babatha Archive and the Mishnah (*Ketubbot* 1: 4)', *HTR* 86: 247–64.

KATZOFF, R. (1991), 'Papyrus Yadin 18 again: A Rejoinder', *JQR* 82: 171–6.

LAPIN, H. (1995), 'Early Rabbinic Civil Law and the Literature of the Second Temple Period', *Jewish Studies Quarterly*, 2: 1–36.

LEVINE, B. (1979), 'Comparative Perspectives on Jewish and Christian History', *JAOS* 99: 81–6.

LEWIS, N. (1989), *The Documents from the Bar Kokhba Period in the Cave of Letters* (Jerusalem).

LEWIS, N., KATZOFF, R., and GREENFIELD, J. (1987), 'Papyrus Yadin 19', *IEJ* 37: 229–50.

LIEBERMAN, S. (1984), *Greek and Hellenism in Jewish Palestine* (Jerusalem) (in Hebrew).

——(1988), *Tosefta Ki-feshutah, Part X: Order Nezikin* (New York) (in Hebrew).

SAFRAI, Z. (1995), *The Jewish Community in the Talmudic Period* (Jerusalem) (in Hebrew).

SATLOW, M. (1993), 'Reconsidering the Rabbinic ketubah Payment', in S. J. D. Cohen (ed.), *The Jewish Family in Antiquity* (Atlanta), 133–51.

SCHÜRER, E., VERMES, G., and MILLAR, F. (1979), *The History of the Jewish People in the Age of Jesus Christ (175 B.C.–A.D. 135)*, ii (Edinburgh).

SIRAT, C., CAUDERLIER, P., DUKAN, M., and FRIEDMAN, M. A. (1986), *La Ketouba de Cologne: Un contrat de mariage juif à Antinoopolis, Papyrologica Coloniensia 12* (Cologne).

WASSERSTEIN, A. (1989), 'A Marriage Contract from the Province of Arabia Nova: Notes on Papyrus Yadin 18', *JQR* 80: 105–30.

——(1995), 'Non-Hellenized Jews in the Semi-Hellenized East', *SCI* 14: 111–37.

WOLFF, H. J. (1939), *Written and Unwritten Marriages in Hellenistic and Post Classical Roman Law* (Boston, Mass.).

YADIN, Y., GREENFIELD, J. C., and YARDENI, A. (1994), 'Babatha's Ketubba', *IEJ* 44: 75–101.

——(1996), 'A Deed of Gift in Aramaic found in Naḥal Ḥever: *Papyrus Yadin 7*', *Eretz-Israel* 25: 383–405 (in Hebrew).

12. JEWISH PENAL AUTHORITY IN ROMAN JUDAEA

ALON, G. (1984), *The Jews in their Land in the Talmudic Age*, ii (Jerusalem).
COLIN, J. (1965), *Les Villes libres de l'Orient greco-romain* (Brussels).
HABAS-RUBIN, E. (1991), *The Patriarch in the Roman-Byzantine Era—the Making of a Dynasty*, Ph.D. diss. (Tel-Aviv) (in Hebrew).
ISAAC, B. (1992), 'The Babatha Archive: a Review Article', *IEJ* 42: 62–75.
JUSTER, J. (1914), *Les Juifs dans l'empire romain*, 2 vols. (Paris).
KATZ, S. (1936), *Die Strafe im Talmudischen Recht* (Berlin).
LEWIS, N. (1989) (ed.), *The Documents from the Bar-Kokhba Period in the Cave of Letters. Greek Papyri* (Jerusalem).
LIEBERMAN, S. (1939–44), 'The Martyrs of Caesarea', *Annuaire de l'Institut de Philologie et d'Histoire Orientales et Slaves*, 7: 395–446.
LIPSIUS, J. H. (1905), *Das Attische Recht und Rechtsverfahren* (Leipzig).
OPPENHEIMER, A. (1988), 'Rabban Gamaliel of Yavneh and his Tours of Inspection in the Land of Israel', in W. Z. Rubinsohn and H. Roisman (eds.), *Sefer Perlman* (Tel-Aviv), 8–18 (in Hebrew).
——(1991), *Galilee in the Mishnaic Period* (Jerusalem) (in Hebrew).
RABELLO, A. M. (1987), *The Legal Condition of the Jews in the Roman Empire (Based on J. Juster)* (Jerusalem) (in Hebrew).
SAFRAI, S. (1962), 'The Status of Provincia Judaea after the Destruction of the Second Temple', *Zion*, 27: 216–22 (repr. in S. Safrai, *In the Time of the Second Temple and in Mishmaic Times* (Jerusalem, 1993), ii. 287–93) (in Hebrew).
STERN, M. (1981), 'The Roman Administration in Provincia Judaea from the Destruction of the Second Temple to the Bar-Kokhva Revolt', in Z. Baras *et al.* (eds.), *Eretz Israel from the Destruction of the Second Temple to the Muslim Conquest* (Jerusalem), i. 1–39 (in Hebrew).
URBACH, E. E. (1972), 'The Sanhedrin of 23 and Capital Punishment', *Proceedings of the Fifth World Congress of Jewish Studies* (Jerusalem), ii. 37–48 (in Hebrew). (Repr. in E. E. Urbach, *The World of the Sages* (Jerusalem, 1988), 294–305.)
——(1973), 'From Judaea to Galilee', in S. Pines (ed.), *Jacob Friedman Memorial Volume* (Jerusalem), 66–9 (in Hebrew). (Repr. in E. E. Urbach, *The World of the Sages* (Jerusalem, 1988), 337–40.)

13. SYNAGOGUE LEADERSHIP:
THE CASE OF THE ARCHISYNAGOGUE

APPLEBAUM, S. (1974), 'The Organization of the Jewish Communities in the Diaspora', in S. Safrai and M. Stern (eds.), *The Jewish People in the*

First Century: Historical Geography, Political History, Social, Cultural and Religious Life and Institutions (Assen), i. 464–503.

AVISSAR, O. (1973) (ed.), *Sepher Tiberias* (Jerusalem) (in Hebrew).

BARON, S. W. (1942), *The Jewish Community*, 3 vols. (Philadelphia).

BROOTEN, B. J. (1982), *Women Leaders in the Ancient Synagogue* (Brown Judaic Studies, 36; Chico, Calif.).

BURTCHAELL, J. T. (1992), *From Synagogue to Church: Public Services and Offices in the Earliest Christian Communities* (Cambridge).

ELBOGEN, I. (1993), *Jewish Liturgy: A Comprehensive History*, trans. R. P. Scheindlin (New York and Jerusalem).

FELDMAN, L. H. (1993), *Jew and Gentile in the Ancient World: Attitudes and Interactions from Alexander to Justinian* (Princeton).

FUKS, G. (1983), *Scythopolis—A Greek City in Eretz-Israel* (Jerusalem) (in Hebrew).

GINZBERG, L. (1941), *A Commentary on the Palestinian Talmud*, 3 vols. (New York) (in Hebrew).

HAENCHEN, E. (1971), *The Acts of the Apostles* (Oxford and Philadelphia).

HORSLEY, G. H. R. (1981–94), *New Documents Illustrating Early Christianity*, 7 vols. (MacQuarrie).

JUSTER, J. (1914), *Les Juifs dans l'empire romain: leure condition juridique, économique et sociale*, 2 vols. (Paris).

KANT, L. H. (1987), 'Jewish Inscriptions in Greek and Latin', *ANRW* II. 20.2: 671–713.

KASHER, A. (1985), *The Jews in Hellenistic and Roman Egypt: The Struggle for Equal Rights* (Tübingen).

KRAUSS, S. (1966), *Synagogale Altertümer* (Hildesheim).

LA PIANA, G. (1927), 'Foreign Groups during the First Centuries of the Empire', *HTR* 20: 361–5.

LE BOHEC, Y. (1981), 'Inscriptions juives et judaïsantes de l'Afrique Romaine', *Antiquités Africaines* 17: 165–207.

LEON, H. J. (1960), *The Jews of Ancient Rome* (Philadelphia).

LEVINE, L. I. (1975*a*), *Caesarea under Roman Rule* (Leiden).

——(1975*b*), *Roman Caesarea: An Archaeological-Topographical Study* (Qedem, 2; Jerusalem).

——(1996), 'The Nature and Origin of the Palestinian Synagogue Reconsidered', *JBL* 115: 425–48.

——(forthcoming), *The Ancient Synagogue: The First Thousand Years* (New Haven).

LIEBERMAN, S. (1962), *Tosefta Ki-fshutah*, 5: *Mo'ed* (New York) (in Hebrew).

LIFSHITZ, B. (1967), *Donateurs et fondateurs dans les synagogues juives* (Paris).

LINDER, A. (1987), *The Jews in Roman Imperial Legislation* (Detroit and Jerusalem).

LIPSIUS, R. A. (1972) (ed.), *Acta apostolorum apocrypha* (Hildesheim).

MARMORSTEIN, A. (1921), 'The Inscription of Theodotus', *PEFQSt* 23–8.

MEEKS, W. A., and WILKEN, R. L. (1978), *Jews and Christians in Antioch in the First Four Centuries of the Common Era* (SBL Sources for Biblical Study, 13; Missoula).

MILLER, S. S. (1984), *Studies in the History and Tradition of Sepphoris* (Studies in Judaism in Late Antiquity, 37; Leiden).

MOMIGLIANO, A. (1934), 'Severo Alessandro Archisynagogus', *Athenaeum*, NS 12: 151–3.

NAVEH, J. (1978), *On Stone and Mosaic: The Aramaic and Hebrew Inscriptions from Ancient Synagogues* (Tel-Aviv) (in Hebrew).

——(1989), 'The Aramaic and Hebrew Inscriptions from Ancient Synagogues', *Eretz Israel*, 20: 302–10 (in Hebrew).

OPPENHEIMER, A. (1988), 'Jewish Lydda in the Roman Era', *HUCA* 59: 115–36.

RAJAK, T., and NOY, D. (1993), 'Archisynagogoi: Office, Title and Social Status in the Graeco-Jewish Synagogue', *JRS* 83: 75–93.

RINGEL, J. (1975), *Césarée de Palestine: Étude historique et archéologique* (Paris).

ROTH-GERSON, L. (1987), *The Greek Inscriptions from the Synagogues in Eretz-Israel* (Jerusalem) (in Hebrew).

SCHEIBER, A. (1983), *Jewish Inscriptions in Hungary: From the Third century to 1686* (Budapest and Leiden).

SCHRAGE, W. (1971), "ἀρχισυναγωγος", *TDNT* 7: 844–7.

SCHÜRER, E. (1879), *Die Gemeindeverfassung der Juden in Rom in der Kaiserzeit* (Leipzig).

——(1986), *The History of the Jewish People in the Age of Jesus Christ*, rev. and ed. G. Vermes *et al.*, iii.1 (Edinburgh).

SCHWARTZ, J. J. (1988), 'On Priests and Jericho in the Second Temple Period', *JQR* 79: 23–48.

——(1991), *Lod (Lydda), Israel: From its origins through the Byzantine Period, 5600 B.C.E.–640 C.E.* (BAR International Series, 571; Oxford).

SMALLWOOD, E. M. (1976), *The Jews under Roman Rule* (Studies in Judaism in Late Antiquity, 20; Leiden).

STERN, M. (1974), 'The Jewish Diaspora', in S. Safrai and M. Stern (eds.), *The Jewish People in the First Century* (Assen) i. 117–83.

TALLEY, T. J. (1986), *The Origins of the Liturgical Year* (New York).

TCHERIKOVER, V. (1961), *Hellenistic Civilisation and the Jews*, trans. S. Applebaum (Philadephia).

TREBILCO, P. (1991), *Jewish Communities in Asia Minor* (Society for New Testament Studies Monograph Series, 69; Cambridge).

VAN DER HORST, P. W. (1991), *Ancient Jewish Epitaphs: An Introductory Survey of a Millennium of Jewish Funerary Epigraphy (300 BCE–700 CE)* (Kampen).

VAN HENTEN, J. W., and VAN DER HORST, P. W. (1994) (eds.), *Studies in Early Jewish Epigraphy* (Arbeiten zur Geschichte des Antiken Judentums und Urchristentums, 21; Leiden, New York, and Cologne).

VOGELSTEIN, H. (1940), *History of the Jews in Rome*, trans. M. Hadas (Philadelphia).

14. THE STRUCTURE OF THE JEWISH COMMUNITY IN ROME

APPLEBAUM, S. (1974), 'The Organization of Jewish Communities in the Diaspora', in S. Safrai and M. Stern (eds.), *The Jewish People in the First Century* (Assen), 464–503.

BAUER, W. (1952), *A Greek-English Lexicon of the New Testament and Other Early Christian Literature*, rev. W. F. Arndt and F. W. Gingrich (Chicago).

BICKERMANN, E. (1980), 'Une Question d'authenticité: les privilèges juifs', in *Studies in Jewish and Christian History* (Leiden), ii. 24–43.

CONZELMANN, H. (1987), *Acts of the Apostles*, trans. J. Limburg, A. T. Kraabel, and D. H. Juel (Philadelphia).

CROOK, J. A. (1967), *Law and Life of Rome* (London).

DE ROBERTIS, F. M. (1938), *Il Diritto Associativo Romano dai collegi della reppublica alle corporazioni del basso impero* (Bari).

DI STEFANO MANZELLA, I. (1989), 'L. Maecius Archon, centurio alti ordinis. Nota critica su *CIL*, VI, 39084 = *CII*, I, 470', *ZPE* 77: 103–12.

FASOLA, U. (1976), 'Le due Catacombe Ebraiche di Villa Torlonia', *RAC* 52: 7–62.

FITZMYER, J. A. (1971), *Essays on the Semitic Background of the New Testament* (London).

FREND, W. H. C. (1965), *Martyrdom and Persecution in the Early Church* (Oxford).

——(1984), *The Rise of Christianity* (London).

GRANT, R. (1970), *Augustus to Constantine: The Thrust of the Christian Movement into the Roman World* (New York).

GUTERMAN, S. L. (1951), *Religious Toleration and Persecution in Ancient Rome* (London).

HENGEL, M. (1966), 'Die Synagogeninschrift von Stobi', *ZNTW* 57: 145–83.

HOLLEAUX, M. (1918), Στρατηγὸς ὕπατος. *Étude sur la traduction en Grec du titre consulaire* (Paris).

HORSLEY, G. H. R. (1981–94), *New Documents Illustrating Early Christianity*, 7 vols. (MacQuarrie).

VAN DER HORST, P. W. (1991), *Ancient Jewish Epitaphs* (Kampen).

JOSEPHUS (1981), *The Jewish War*, trans. G. A. Williamson, rev. E. M. Smallwood (Harmondsworth).

JUSTER, J. (1914), *Les Juifs dans l'empire romain*, 2 vols. (Paris).

KRAUSS, S. (1922), *Synagogale Altertümer* (Berlin).

LAMPE, P. (1989), *Die stadtrömischen Christen in den ersten beiden Jahrhunderten*, 2nd edn. (Tübingen).

LA PIANA, G. (1927), 'Foreign Groups in Rome during the First Centuries of the Empire', *HTR* 20: 183–403.

LEON, H. J. (1960), *The Jews of Ancient Rome* (Philadelphia).

LIFSHITZ, B. (1967), *Donateurs et Fondateurs dans les synagogues juives* (Paris).

LINDER, A. (1987), *The Jews in Roman Imperial Legislation* (Mich.).

LINDERSKI, J. (1962), 'Suetons Bericht über die Vereinsgesetzgebung unter Caesar und Augustus', *Zeitschrift der Savigny-Stiftung für Rechsgeschichte, romanistische Abteilung*, 79: 322–8.

LÜDERITZ, G. (1994), 'What is the Politeuma?', in J. W. Van Henten and P. W. Van der Horst (eds.), *Studies in Early Jewish Epigraphy* (Leiden), 183–225.

MACMULLEN, R. (1993), 'The Unromanized in Rome', in S. J. D. Cohen and E. S. Frerichs (eds.), *Diasporas in Antiquity* (Atlanta, Ga.), 47–64.

MASON, H. J. (1974), *Greek Terms for Roman Institutions* (Toronto).

MILANO, A. (1963), *Storia degli ebrei in Italia* (Turin).

MOEHRING, H. (1975), 'The *Acta pro Judaeis* in the *Antiquities* of Flavius Josephus: A Study in Hellenistic and Modern Apologetic Historiography', in J. Neusner (ed.), *Christianity, Judaism and Other Greco-Roman Cults, Studies for Morton Smith at Sixty* (Leiden), 124–58.

MOMIGLIANO, A. (1962), Review of H. J. Leon, *The Jews of Ancient Rome*, *Gnomon*, 34: 179–80.

——(1966), 'I nomi delle prime "sinagoghe" romane e la condizione giuridica della communità in Roma sotto Augusto', in *Terzo Contributo alla Storia degli Studi Classici e del Mondo Antico* (Rome), 523–33.

MUÑOZ VALLE, I. (1972), 'El testimonio de las inscripciones sobre el régimen de las comunidades judías en la Roma imperial', *Cuadernos de Filología Clásica*, 4: 151–63.

PENNA, R. (1982), 'Les Juifs à Rome au temps de l'apôtre Paul', *NTS* 28: 321–47.

POLAND, F. (1909), *Geschichte des griechischen Vereinswesens* (Leipzig).

PUCCI BEN ZEEV, M. (1994), 'Greek and Roman Documents from Republican Times in the *Antiquities*: What was Josephus' Source?', *SCI* 13: 46–59.

PURCELL, N. (1994), 'The City of Rome and the *plebs urbana* in the Late Republic', in the *Cambridge Ancient History*, 2nd edn. (Cambridge), ix. 644–88.

RAJAK, T. (1984), 'Was there a Roman charter for the Jews?', *JRS* 74: 107–23.

REYNOLDS, J., and TANNENBAUM, R. (1987), *Jews and Godfearers at Aphrodisias* (Cambridge).

SCHÜRER, E. (1879), *Die Gemeindeverfassung der Juden in Rom in der Kaiserzeit nach den Inschriften dargestellt* (Leipzig).

——(1986), *The History of the Jewish People in the Age of Jesus Christ*, iii, rev. G. Vermes, F. Millar, and M. Goodman (Edinburgh).

SMALLWOOD, E. M. (1976), *The Jews under Roman Rule from Pompey to Diocletian* (Leiden).

SOLIN, H. (1983), 'Juden und Syrer im westichen Teil der römischen Welt. Eine ethnisch-demographische Studie mit besonderer Berücksichtigung der sprachlichen Zustände', *ANRW* II.29.2: 587–789, 1222–49.

TREBILCO, P. (1991), *Jewish Communities in Asia Minor* (Cambridge).

TREGGIARI, S. (1969), *Roman Freedmen during the Late Republic* (Oxford).

VISMARA, C. (1987), 'Orientali a Roma: Nota sull'origine geografica degli Ebrei nelle testimonianze età imperiale', *Dialoghi di Archeologica*, NS 5: 119–21.

WALTZING, J-P. (1895–1900), *Étude historique sur les corporations professionelles chez les romains*, 4 vols. (Louvain).

WEINFELD, M. (1986), *The Organizational Pattern and the Penal Code of the Qumran Sect* (Fribourg).

WIEFEL, W. (1991), 'The Jewish Community in Ancient Rome and the Origins of Roman Christianity', in K. P. Dronfield (ed.), *The Romans Debate*, 2nd edn. (Edinburgh).

WILLIAMS, M. H. (1994), 'The Structure of Roman Jewry Reconsidered—were the Synagogues of Rome Entirely Homogeneous?', *ZPE* 104: 129–41.

YAVETZ, Z. (1983), *Julius Caesar and his Public Image* (London).

ZUCKERMANN, C. (1985–8), 'Hellenistic Politeumata and the Jews: A reconsideration', *SCI* 8–9: 171–85.

15. THE GIFTS OF GOD AT SARDIS

BARCLAY, J. M. G. (1966), *Jews in the Mediterranean Diaspora: From Alexander to Trajan (323 BCE–117 CE)* (Edinburgh).

BONZ, M. P. (1990), 'The Jewish Community of Ancient Sardis: A Reassessment of its Rise to Prominence', *HSCP* 93: 343–59.

——(1993), 'Differing Approaches to Religious Benefaction: The Late Third-Century Acquisition of the Sardis Synagogue', *HTR* 86. 2: 139–54.

BOTERMAN, H. (1990), 'Die Synagoge von Sardes: Eine Synagoge aus dem 4. Jahrhundert?', *ZNW* 81: 103–21.

GOODMAN, M. (1994), 'Jews and Judaism in the Mediterranean Diaspora in the Late-Roman Period: the Limitations of Evidence', *Journal of Mediterranean Studies*, 4. 2: 208–24.

HADAS-LEBEL, M. (1973) (ed.), *De Providentia I and II. Introduction, Traduction et Notes* (Les Oeuvres de Philon d'Alexandrie, 25; Paris).

HANFMANN, G. M. A. (1972), *Letters from Sardis* (Cambridge, Mass.).

——(1983), *Sardis from Prehistoric to Roman Times: Results of the Archae-ological Expedition of Sardis 1958–75* (Cambridge, Mass., and London).

HANFMANN, G. M. A., and BLOOM, J. B. (1987), 'Samoe, Priest and Teacher of Wisdom', *IEJ* 19: 10–14.

KRAABEL, A. T. (1978), 'Paganism and Judaism: the Sardis Evidence', in *Paganisme, Judaïsme, Christianisme: Influences et affrontements dans le monde antique. Mélanges Offerts à Marcel Simon* (Paris), 13–33. (Repr. in Overman and MacLennan (1992), 237–55.)

——(1996), 'Pronoia at Sardis', in B. Isaac and A. Oppenheimer (eds.), *Studies on the Jewish Diaspora in the Hellenistic and Roman Periods. Te'uda* 12 (Tel-Aviv), 75–96.

LE BAS, P. and WADDINGTON, W. H. (1853–70), *Voyage Archéologique en Grèce et en Asie Mineure* (Paris).

LIFSHITZ, B. (1967), *Donateurs et fondateurs dans les synagogues juives* (Paris).

OVERMAN, J. A., and MACLENNAN, R. S. (1992), *Diaspora Jews and Judaism: Essays in Honor of and in Dialogue with A. Thomas Kraabel* (South Florida Studies in the History of Judaism, 41; Atlanta, Ga.).

RAJAK, T. (1992), 'The Jewish Community and Its Boundaries', in J. Lieu, J. North, and T. Rajak (eds.), *The Jews among Pagans and Christians in the Roman Empire* (London).

——(1996), 'Benefactors in the Greco-Jewish Diaspora', in P. Schäfer (ed.), *Geschichte-Tradition-Reflexion. Festschrift für Martin Hengel zum 70 Geburtstag*, Band I. Judentum (Tübingen), 305–23.

——(1997), 'Dying for the Law: the Martyr's Portrait in Jewish-Greek Literature', in M. J. Edwards and S. Swain (eds.), *Portraits: biographical representation in the Greek and Latin literature of the Roman Empire* (Oxford).

REYNOLDS, J., and TANNENBAUM, R. (1987), *Jews and Godfearers at Aphrodisias* (Cambridge Philological Society, Supplementary vol. 12; Cambridge).

ROBERT, L. (1964), *Nouvelles Inscriptions de Sardes* (Paris).

ROUECHÉ, C. (1989), *Aphrodisias in Late Antiquity* (Roman Society Monographs; London).

SHARPLES, R. W. (1995), *World under Management? Details, Delegation and Divine Providence, 400 B.C.–A.D. 1200* (Inaugural Lecture given at University College, London).

TREBILCO, P. (1991), *Jewish Communities in Asia Minor* (Cambridge).

16. DISSONANCE AND MISUNDERSTANDING IN JEWISH–ROMAN RELATIONS

BACHER, W. (1914), *Tradition und Tradenten in den Schulen Palästinas und Babyloniens* (Leipzig).

BLIDSTEIN, G. J. (1972), 'A Roman Gift of Strenae to the Patriarch Judah II', *IEJ* 22: 150–2.

HADAS-LEBEL, M. (1979), 'Le Paganisme à travers les sources rabbiniques des IIe et IIIe siècles. Contributions à l'étude du syncrétisme dans l'empire romain', *ANRW* II.19.2: 397–485.

KADMAN, L. (1956), *The Coins of Aelia Capitolina. Corpus Nummorum Palaestinensium*, i (Jerusalem).

KAZHDAN, A. P. (1991) (ed.), *Oxford Dictionary of Byzantium*, 3 vols. (New York and Oxford).

KIMELMAN, R. (1981), '*Birkat Ha-Minim* and the lack of evidence for an anti-Christian Jewish prayer', in E. P. Sanders *et al.*, *Jewish and Christian Self-Definition* (Philadelphia and London), ii. 226–44.

KRAUSS, S. (1948), *Paras ve-Romi ba Talmud u-vaMidrashim* (Jerusalem).

LEVICK, B. (1982), 'Propaganda and the Imperial Coinage', *Antichthon*, 16: 104–16.

LEVINE, L. I. (1979), 'The Jewish Patriarch (Nasi) in 3rd Century Palestine', *ANRW* II.19.2: 649–88.

——(1989), *The Rabbinic Class of Roman Palestine in Late Antiquity* (New York and Jerusalem).

——(1996), 'The Status of the Patriarch in the Third and Fourth Centuries: Sources and Methodology', *JJS* 47: 1–32.

LINDER, A. (1987), *The Jews in Roman Imperial Legislation* (Detroit and Jerusalem).

MALTER, H. (1930), *The Treatise Ta'anit of the Babylonian Talmud* (New York).

OLIVER, J. H. (1953), *The Ruling Power* (Philadelphia).

PFLAUM, H. G. (1960), *Les Carrières procuratoriennes équestres sous le haut-empire romain* (Paris).

SALLER, R. (1982), *Personal Patronage under the Early Empire* (Cambridge).

SCHÜRER, E. (1973), *The History of the Jewish People in the Age of Jesus Christ*, rev. and ed. G. Vermes *et al.*, i (Edinburgh).

SMALLWOOD, E. M. (1976), *The Jews under Roman Rule* (Leiden).

STERN, S. (1994), *Jewish Identity in Early Rabbinic Writings* (Leiden).

STRACK, H. L., and STEMBERGER, G. (1991), *Introduction to the Talmud and Midrash* (Edinburgh).

SUSSMAN, Y. (1990), 'Ve-shuv li-Yerushalmi Nezikin', in Y. Sussman and D. Rosenthal, *Mehqerei Talmud* (Jerusalem), i. 55–133.

SUTHERLAND, C. H. V. (1959), 'The Intelligibility of Roman Imperial Coin Types', *JRS* 49: 46–55.

——(1986), 'Compliment or Complement? Dr. Levick on Imperial Coin Types', *Numismatic Chronicle*, 146: 85–93.

Index